Computing Security & Cryptography Handbook

Computing Security & Cryptography Handbook

Edited by **Stephen Mason**

CLANRYE
INTERNATIONAL

New Jersey

Published by Clanrye International,
55 Van Reypen Street,
Jersey City, NJ 07306, USA
www.clanryeinternational.com

Computing Security & Cryptography Handbook
Edited by Stephen Mason

© 2015 Clanrye International

International Standard Book Number: 978-1-63240-113-7 (Hardback)

Printed in the United States of America.

Contents

Preface

This book presents some critical security challenges that are faced in today's computing world. It discusses, in detail, the defense mechanisms against these kinds of attacks with the help of classical and modern approaches of cryptography and other defense mechanisms. The book not only deals with theoretical and fundamental aspects of cryptography, but also talks in length about different applications of cryptographic protocols and techniques in designing computing and network security solutions. This book will prove itself to be beneficial for researchers, engineers, graduate and doctoral students who are working in the same and related field.

The information contained in this book is the result of intensive hard work done by researchers in this field. All due efforts have been made to make this book serve as a complete guiding source for students and researchers. The topics in this book have been comprehensively explained to help readers understand the growing trends in the field.

I would like to thank the entire group of writers who made sincere efforts in this book and my family who supported me in my efforts of working on this book. I take this opportunity to thank all those who have been a guiding force throughout my life.

Editor

Part 1

Cryptography and Security in Computing

Provably Secure Cryptographic Constructions

Sergey I. Nikolenko

Steklov Mathematical Institute, St. Petersburg

Russia

1. Introduction

1.1 Cryptography: treading uncertain paths

Modern cryptography has virtually no provably secure constructions. Starting from the first Diffie–Hellman key agreement protocol (Diffie & Hellman, 1976) and the first public key cryptosystem RSA (Rivest et al., 1978), not a single public key cryptographic protocol has been proven secure. Note, however, that there exist secure secret key protocols, e.g., the one-time pad scheme (Shannon, 1949; Vernam, 1926); they can even achieve information–theoretic security, but only if the secret key carries at least as much information as the message.

An *unconditional* proof of security for a public key protocol would be indeed hard to find, since it would necessarily imply that $P \neq NP$. Consider, for instance, a one-way function, i.e., a function such that it is easy to compute but hard to invert. One-way functions are basic cryptographic primitives; if there are no one-way functions, there is no public key cryptography. The usual cryptographic definition requires that a one-way function can be computed in polynomial time. Therefore, if we are given a preimage $y \in f^{-1}(x)$, we can, by definition, verify in polynomial time that $f(y) = x$, so the inversion problem is actually in NP. This means that in order to prove that a function is one-way, we have to prove that $P \neq NP$, a rather daring feat to accomplish. A similar argument can be made for cryptosystems and other cryptographic primitives; for example, the definition of a trapdoor function (Goldreich, 2001) explicitly requires an inversion witness to exist.

But the situation is worse: there are also no *conditional* proofs that might establish a connection between natural structural assumptions (like $P \neq NP$ or $BPP \neq NP$) and cryptographic security. Recent developments in lattice-based cryptosystems relate cryptographic security to worst-case complexity, but they deal with problems unlikely to be NP-complete (Ajtai & Dwork, 1997; Dwork, 1997; Regev, 2005; 2006).

An excellent summary of the state of our knowledge regarding these matters was given by Impagliazzo (1995); although this paper is now more than 15 years old, we have not advanced much in these basic questions. Impagliazzo describes five possible worlds – we live in exactly one of them but do not know which one. He shows, in particular, that it may happen that NP problems are hard even on average, but cryptography does not exist (*Pessiland*) or that one-way functions exist but not public key cryptosystems (*Minicrypt*). [1]

---

[1] To learn the current state of affairs, we recommend to watch Impagliazzo's lecture at the 2009 workshop "Complexity and Cryptography: Status of Impagliazzo's Worlds"; video is available on the web.

Another angle that might yield an approach to cryptography relates to *complete* cryptographic primitives. In regular complexity theory, much can be learned about complexity classes by studying their complete representatives; for instance, one can study any of the numerous well-defined combinatorial NP-complete problems, and any insight such as a fast algorithm for solving any of them is likely to be easily transferrable to all other problems from the class NP. In cryptography, however, the situation is worse. There exist known complete cryptographic constructions, both one-way functions (Kojevnikov & Nikolenko, 2008; 2009; Levin, 1986) and public key cryptosystems (Grigoriev et al., 2009; Harnik et al., 2005). However, they are still mostly useless in that they are not really combinatorial (their hardness relies on enumerating Turing machines) and they do not let us relate cryptographic security to key assumptions of classical complexity theory. In short, it seems that modern cryptography still has a very long way to go to *provably* secure constructions.

1.2 Asymptotics and hard bounds

Moreover, the asymptotic nature of cryptographic definitions (and definitions of complexity theory in general) does not let us say anything about how hard it is to break a given cryptographic protocol for keys of a certain fixed length. And this is exactly what cryptography means in practice. For real life, it makes little sense to say that something is asymptotically hard. Such a result may (and does) provide some intuition towards the fact that an adversary will not be able to solve the problem, but no real guarantees are made: why is RSA secure for 2048-bit numbers? Why cannot someone come up with a device that breaks into all credit cards that use the same protocol with keys of the same length? There are no theoretical obstacles here. In essence, asymptotic complexity is not something one really wants to get out of cryptographic constructions. Ultimately, I do not care whether my credit card's protocol can or cannot be broken in the limit; I would be very happy if breaking my specific issue of credit cards required constant time, but this constant was larger than the size of the known Universe.

The proper computational model to prove this kind of properties is *general circuit complexity* (see Section 2). This is the only computational model that can deal with specific bounds for specific key lengths; for instance, different implementations of Turing machines may differ by as much as a quadratic factor. Basic results in classical circuit complexity came in the 1980s and earlier, many of them provided by Soviet mathematicians (Blum, 1984; Khrapchenko, 1971; Lupanov, 1965; Markov, 1964; Nechiporuk, 1966; Paul, 1977; Razborov, 1985; 1990; Sholomov, 1969; Stockmeyer, 1977; 1987; Subbotovskaya, 1961; 1963; Yablonskii, 1957). Over the last two decades, efforts in circuit complexity have been relocated mostly towards results related to circuits with bounded depth and/or restricted set of functions computed in a node (Ajtai, 1983; Cai, 1989; Furst et al., 1984; Håstad, 1987; Immerman, 1987; Razborov, 1987; 1995; Smolensky, 1987; Yao, 1985; 1990). However, we need classical results for cryptographic purposes because the bounds we want to prove in cryptography should hold in the most general $\mathbb{B}_{2,1}$ basis. It would be a very bold move to advertise a credit card as "secure against adversaries who cannot use circuits of depth more than 3".

1.3 Feebly secure cryptographic primitives

We cannot, at present, hope to prove security either in the "hard" sense of circuit complexity or in the sense of classical cryptographic definitions (Goldreich, 2001; 2004; Goldwasser & Bellare, 2001). However, if we are unable to prove a superpolynomial gap between the complexities of honest parties and adversaries, maybe we can prove at least *some* gap? Alain Hiltgen (1992) managed to present a function that is *twice* $(2 - o(1)$ times) harder to invert than to compute. His example is a linear function over $GF(2)$ with a matrix that has few non-zero entries while the inverse matrix has many non-zero entries; the complexity gap follows by a simple argument of Lamagna and Savage (Lamagna & Savage, 1973; Savage, 1976): every bit of the output depends non-idly on many variables and all these bits correspond to different functions, hence a lower bound on the complexity of computing them all together (see Section 3.2). The model of computation here is the most general one: the number of gates in a Boolean circuit that uses arbitrary binary Boolean gates. We have already noted that little more could be expected for this model at present. For example, the best known lower bound for general circuit complexity of a specific Boolean function is $3n - o(n)$ (Blum, 1984) even though a simple counting argument proves that there exist plenty of Boolean functions with circuit complexity $\geq \frac{1}{n} 2^n$ (Wegener, 1987).

In this chapter, we briefly recount feebly one-way functions but primarily deal with another feebly secure cryptographic primitive: namely, we present constructions of *feebly trapdoor functions*. Of course, in order to obtain the result, we have to prove a lower bound on the circuit complexity of a certain function. To do so, we use the *gate elimination* technique which dates back to the 1970s and which has been used in proving virtually every single known bound in general circuit complexity (Blum, 1984; Paul, 1977; Stockmeyer, 1977). New methods would be of great interest; alas, there has been little progress in general circuit complexity since Blum's result of $3n - o(n)$. A much simpler proof has been recently presented by Demenkov & Kulikov (2011), but no improvement has been found yet.

We begin with linear constructions; in the linear case, we can actually nail gate elimination down to several well-defined techniques that we present in Section 3.3. These techniques let us present linear feebly trapdoor functions; the linear part of this chapter is based mostly on (Davydow & Nikolenko, 2011; Hirsch & Nikolenko, 2008; 2009). For the nonlinear case, we make use of a specific nonlinear feebly one-way function presented in (Hirsch et al., 2011; Melanich, 2009).

2. Basic definitions

2.1 Boolean circuits

Boolean circuits (see, e.g., (Wegener, 1987)) represent one of the few computational models that allow for proving *specific* rather than asymptotic lower bounds on the complexity. In this model, a function's complexity is defined as the minimal size of a circuit computing this function. Circuits consist of *gates*, and gates can implement various Boolean functions.

We denote by $\mathbb{B}_{n,m}$ the set of all 2^{m2^n} functions $f : \mathbb{B}^n \to \mathbb{B}^m$, where $\mathbb{B} = \{0,1\}$ is the field with two elements.

Definition 1. *Let Ω be a set of Boolean functions $f : \mathbb{B}^m \to \mathbb{B}$ (m may differ for different f). Then an Ω-circuit is a directed acyclic labeled graph with vertices of two kinds:*

- *vertices of indegree 0 (vertices that no edges enter) labeled by one of the variables $x_1, \ldots, x_n$,*
- *and vertices labeled by a function $f \in \Omega$ with indegree equal to the arity of f.*

Vertices of the first kind are called inputs *or* input variables; *vertices of the second kind,* gates. *The size of a circuit is the number of gates in it.*

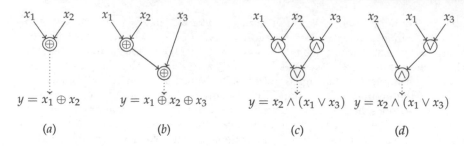

Fig. 1. Simple circuits: (a) $y = x_1 \oplus x_2$; (b) $y = x_1 \oplus x_2 \oplus x_3$; (c) a suboptimal circuit for $y = x_2 \wedge (x_1 \vee x_3)$; (d) an optimal one.

We usually speak of *outputs* of a circuit and draw them on pictures, but in theory, every gate of an Ω-circuit computes some Boolean function and can be considered as an output of the circuit. The circuit complexity of a function $f : \mathbb{B}^n \to \mathbb{B}^m$ in the basis Ω is denoted by $C_\Omega(f)$ and is defined as the minimal size of an Ω-circuit that computes f (that has m gates which compute the result of applying function f to input bits).

In order to get rid of unary gates, we will assume that a gate computes both its corresponding function and its negation (the same applies to the inputs, too). Our model of computation is given by Boolean circuits with arbitrary binary gates (this is known as *general circuit complexity*); in other words, each gate of a circuit is labeled by one of 16 Boolean functions from $\mathbb{B}_{2,1}$. Several simple examples of such circuits are shown on Fig. 1.

In what follows, we denote by $C(f)$ the circuit complexity of f in the $\mathbb{B}_{2,1}$ basis that consists of all binary Boolean functions. We assume that each gate in this circuit depends of both inputs, i.e., there are no gates marked by constants and unary functions Id and $\neg$. This can be done without loss of generality because such gates are easy to exclude from a nontrivial circuit without any increase in its size.

2.2 Feebly secure one-way functions

We want the size of circuits breaking our family of trapdoor functions to be larger than the size of circuits that perform encoding. Following Hiltgen (1992; 1994; 1998), for every injective function of n variables $f_n \in \mathbb{B}_{n,m}$ we can define its *measure of one-wayness* as

$$M_F(f_n) = \frac{C(f_n^{-1})}{C(f_n)}. \tag{1}$$

The problem now becomes to find sequences of functions $f = \{f_n\}_{n=1}^\infty$ with a large asymptotic constant $\liminf_{n\to\infty} M_F(f_n)$, which Hiltgen calls f's *order of one-wayness*.

Hiltgen (1992; 1994; 1998) presented several constructions of feebly secure one-way functions. To give a flavour of his results, we recall a sample one-way function. Consider a function $f : \mathbb{B}^n \to \mathbb{B}^n$ given by the following matrix:

$$f(x_1,\ldots,x_n) = \begin{pmatrix} 1 & 1 & 0 & \cdots & 0 & \cdots & 0 & 0 \\ 0 & 1 & 1 & \cdots & 0 & \cdots & 0 & 0 \\ \vdots & \vdots & \vdots & & \vdots & & \vdots & \vdots \\ 1 & 0 & 0 & \cdots & 0 & \cdots & 1 & 1 \\ 1 & 0 & 0 & \cdots & 1 & \cdots & 0 & 1 \end{pmatrix} \begin{pmatrix} x_1 \\ x_2 \\ \vdots \\ x_{n-1} \\ x_n \end{pmatrix}, \tag{2}$$

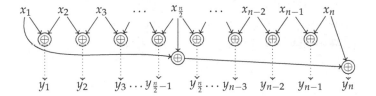

Fig. 2. Hiltgen's feebly one-way function of order $\frac{3}{2}$: a circuit for f.

that is (we assume for simplicity that n is even),

$$f_j(x_1,\ldots,x_n) = \begin{cases} x_j \oplus x_{j+1}, & j=1,\ldots,n-1, \\ x_1 \oplus x_{\frac{n}{2}} \oplus x_n, & j=n. \end{cases} \tag{3}$$

Straighforward computations show that f is invertible, and its inverse is given by

$$f^{-1}(y_1,\ldots,y_n) = \begin{pmatrix} 0\,0\,\ldots\,0\,1\,1\,\ldots\,1\,1 \\ 1\,0\,\ldots\,0\,1\,1\,\ldots\,1\,1 \\ 1\,1\,\ldots\,0\,1\,1\,\ldots\,1\,1 \\ \vdots\quad\vdots\quad\vdots \\ 1\,1\,\ldots\,0\,1\,1\,\ldots\,1\,1 \\ 1\,1\,\ldots\,1\,1\,1\,\ldots\,1\,1 \\ 1\,1\,\ldots\,1\,0\,1\,\ldots\,1\,1 \\ \vdots\quad\vdots\quad\vdots \\ 1\,1\,\ldots\,1\,0\,0\,\ldots\,0\,1 \end{pmatrix} \begin{pmatrix} y_1 \\ y_2 \\ y_3 \\ \vdots \\ y_{\lfloor\frac{n}{2}\rfloor} \\ y_{\frac{n}{2}+1} \\ y_{\frac{n}{2}+2} \\ \vdots \\ y_n \end{pmatrix}, \tag{4}$$

that is,

$$f_j^{-1}(y_1,\ldots,y_n) = \begin{cases} \left(y_1 \oplus \ldots \oplus y_{j-1}\right) \oplus \left(y_{\frac{n}{2}+1} \oplus \ldots \oplus y_n\right), & j=1,\ldots,\frac{n}{2}, \\ \left(y_1 \oplus \ldots \oplus y_{\frac{n}{2}}\right) \oplus \left(y_{j-1} \oplus \ldots \oplus y_n\right), & j=\frac{n}{2}+1,\ldots,n. \end{cases} \tag{5}$$

It remains to invoke Proposition 6 (see below) to show that f^{-1} requires at least $\lfloor\frac{3n}{2}\rfloor - 1$ gates to compute, while f can be obviously computed in $n+1$ gates. Fig. 2 shows a circuit that computes f in $n+1$ gates; Fig. 3, one of the optimal circuits for f^{-1}. Therefore, f is a feebly one-way function with order of security $\frac{3}{2}$. For this particular function, inversion becomes strictly harder than evaluation at $n=7$ (eight gates to compute, nine to invert).

2.3 Feebly trapdoor candidates

In the context of feebly secure primitives, we have to give a more detailed definition of a trapdoor function than the regular cryptographic definition (Goldreich, 2001): since we are interested in constants here, we must pay attention to all the details. The following definition does not say anything about the complexity and hardness of inversion, but merely sets up the dimensions.

Definition 2. *For given functions* pi, ti, $m, c : \mathbb{N} \to \mathbb{N}$, *a feebly trapdoor candidate is a sequence of triples of circuits*

$$\mathcal{C} = \{(\text{Seed}_n, \text{Eval}_n, \text{Inv}_n)\}_{n=1}^{\infty}, \text{ where:} \tag{6}$$

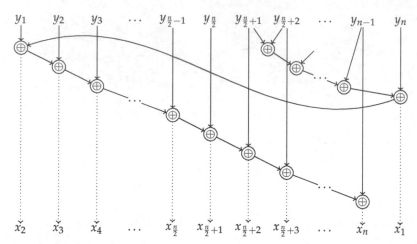

Fig. 3. Hiltgen's feebly one-way function of order $\frac{3}{2}$: a circuit for f^{-1}.

- $\{\text{Seed}_n\}_{n=1}^{\infty}$ *is a family of sampling circuits* $\text{Seed}_n : \mathbb{B}^n \to \mathbb{B}^{\text{pi}(n)} \times \mathbb{B}^{\text{ti}(n)}$,
- $\{\text{Eval}_n\}_{n=1}^{\infty}$ *is a family of evaluation circuits* $\text{Eval}_n : \mathbb{B}^{\text{pi}(n)} \times \mathbb{B}^{m(n)} \to \mathbb{B}^{c(n)}$, *and*
- $\{\text{Inv}_n\}_{n=1}^{\infty}$ *is a family of inversion circuits* $\text{Inv}_n : \mathbb{B}^{\text{ti}(n)} \times \mathbb{B}^{c(n)} \to \mathbb{B}^{m(n)}$

such that for every security parameter n, every seed $s \in \mathbb{B}^n$, *and every input* $m \in \mathbb{B}^{m(n)}$,

$$\text{Inv}_n(\text{Seed}_{n,2}(s), \text{Eval}_n(\text{Seed}_{n,1}(s), m)) = m, \tag{7}$$

where $\text{Seed}_{n,1}(s)$ *and* $\text{Seed}_{n,2}(s)$ *are the first* $\text{pi}(n)$ *bits ("public information") and the last* $\text{ti}(n)$ *bits ("trapdoor information") of* $\text{Seed}_n(s)$, *respectively.*

Informally speaking, n is the security parameter (the length of the random seed), $m(n)$ is the length of the input to the function, $c(n)$ is the length of the function's output, and $\text{pi}(n)$ and $\text{ti}(n)$ are lengths of the public and trapdoor information, respectively. We call these functions "candidates" because Definition 2 does not imply any security, it merely sets up the dimensions and provides correct inversion. In our constructions, $m(n) = c(n)$ and $\text{pi}(n) = \text{ti}(n)$.

To find how secure a function is, one needs to know the size of the minimal circuit that could invert the function without knowing the trapdoor information. In addition to the worst-case complexity $C(f)$, we introduce a stronger notion that we will use in this case.

Definition 3. *We denote by* $C_\alpha(f)$ *the minimal size of a circuit that correctly computes a function* $f \in \mathcal{B}_{n,m}$ *on more than* α *fraction of its inputs (of length n). Obviously,* $C_\alpha(f) \leq C(f)$ *for all f and* $0 \leq \alpha \leq 1$.

Definition 4. *A circuit N breaks a feebly trapdoor candidate* $\mathcal{C} = \{\text{Seed}_n, \text{Eval}_n, \text{Inv}_n\}$ *on seed length n with probability* α *if, for uniformly chosen seeds* $s \in \mathcal{B}^n$ *and inputs* $m \in \mathcal{B}^{m(n)}$,

$$\Pr_{(s,m) \in U} \left[N(\text{Seed}_{n,1}(s), \text{Eval}_n(\text{Seed}_{n,1}(s), m)) = m \right] > \alpha. \tag{8}$$

A size s circuit that breaks a feebly trapdoor candidate $C = \{\text{Seed}_n, \text{Eval}_n, \text{Inv}_n\}$ on seed length n in the sense of Definition 4 provides a counterexample for the statement $C_\alpha(Inv_n) > s$.

In fact, in what follows we prove a stronger result: we prove that no circuit (of a certain size) can break our candidate *for any random seed s*, that is, for every seed s, every adversary fails. For a trapdoor function to be secure, circuits that break the function should be larger than the circuits computing it. In fact, in our results we can require that every such adversary fails with probability at least $\frac{1}{4}$.

Definition 5. *We say that a feebly trapdoor candidate $C = \{(\text{Seed}_n, \text{Eval}_n, \text{Inv}_n)\}_{n=1}^{\infty}$ has order of security k with probability α if*

$$\lim_{n \to \infty} \inf \min \left\{ \frac{C_\alpha(f_{\text{pi}(n)+c(n)})}{C(\text{Seed}_n)}, \frac{C_\alpha(f_{\text{pi}(n)+c(n)})}{C(\text{Eval}_n)}, \frac{C_\alpha(f_{\text{pi}(n)+c(n)})}{C(\text{Inv}_n)} \right\} \geq k, \qquad (9)$$

where the function $f_{\text{pi}(n)+c(n)} \in \mathbb{B}_{\text{pi}(n)+c(n),m(n)}$ maps

$$(\text{Seed}_{n,1}(s), \text{Eval}_n(\text{Seed}_{n,1}(s), m)) \mapsto m. \qquad (10)$$

We say that a feebly trapdoor candidate has order of security k *if it has order of security k with probability $\alpha = \frac{3}{4}$.*

Let us first give a few simple examples. If there is no secret key at all, that is, $\text{pi}(n) = 0$, then each feebly trapdoor candidate $\{(\text{Seed}_n, \text{Eval}_n, \text{Inv}_n)\}_{n=1}^{\infty}$ has order of security 1, since the sequence of circuits $\{\text{Inv}_n\}_{n=1}^{\infty}$ successfully inverts it. If $\{(\text{Seed}_n, \text{Eval}_n, \text{Inv}_n)\}_{n=1}^{\infty}$ implement a trapdoor function in the usual cryptographic sense then $k = \infty$. Moreover, $k = \infty$ even if the bounds on the size of adversary are merely superlinear, e.g., if every adversary requires $\Omega(n \log n)$ gates. Our definitions are not designed to distinguish between these (very different) cases, because, unfortunately, any nonlinear lower bound on general circuit complexity of a specific function appears very far away from the current state of knowledge.

One could also consider key generation as a separate process and omit its complexity from the definition of the order of security. However, we prove our results for the definition stated above as it makes them stronger.

In closing, let us note explicitly that we are talking about *one-time* security. An adversary can amortize his circuit complexity on inverting a feebly trapdoor candidate for the second time for the same seed, for example, by computing the trapdoor information and successfully reusing it. Thus, in our setting one has to pick a new seed for every input.

3. Gate elimination techniques

3.1 Classical gate elimination

In this section, we first briefly cover classical gate elimination and then introduce a few new ideas related to gate elimination that have recently been presented by Davydow & Nikolenko (2011). Gate elimination is the primary (and, to be honest, virtually the only) technique we have to prove lower bounds in general circuit complexity; so far, it has been used for every single lower bound (Blum, 1984; Paul, 1977; Stockmeyer, 1977; Wegener, 1987). The basic idea of this method lies in the following inductive argument. Consider a function f and a circuit of minimal size C that computes it. Now substitute some value c for some variable x thus obtaining a circuit for the function $f\mid_{x=c}$. The original circuit C can now be simplified, because the gates that had this variable as inputs become either unary (recall that negation can be embedded into subsequent gates) or constant (in this case we can even proceed to eliminating subsequent gates). After figuring out how many gates one can eliminate on every step, one proceeds by induction as long as it is possible to find a suitable variable that eliminates enough gates. Evidently, the number of eliminated gates is a lower bound on the complexity of f.

Usually, the important case here is when a gate is nonlinear, such as an AND or an OR gate. In that case, it is always possible to choose a value for an input of such a gate so that this gate becomes a constant and, therefore, its immediate descendants can also be eliminated. However, for linear functions this kind of reasoning also works, and in Section 3.3 we distill it to two relatively simple ideas.

To give the reader a flavour of classical gate elimination, we briefly recall the proof of the $2n - 3$ lower bound for the functions of the form $f_{3,c}^{(n)} : \mathbb{B}^n \to \mathbb{B}$ defined by

$$f_{3,c}^{(n)}(x_1, \ldots, x_n) = ((x_1 + \ldots + x_n + c) \mod 3) \mod 2). \tag{11}$$

This proof can be found in many sources, including (Wegener, 1987). Note that every function $f_{3,c}^{(n)}$ has the following property: for every pair of variables x_j and x_k, $f_{3,c}^{(n)}$ has at least three different restrictions out of four possible assignments of values to x_j and x_k; this is easy to see since different assignments of x_j and x_k give three different values of $x_j + x_k$, resulting in functions with three different constants: $f_{3,0}^{(n-2)}$, $f_{3,1}^{(n-2)}$, and $f_{3,2}^{(n-2)}$. Now consider the topmost gate in some topological order on the optimal circuit computing $f_{3,c}^{(n)}$. Since it is topmost, there are two variables, say x_j and x_k, that come to this gate as inputs. At least one of these variables enters at least one other gate because otherwise, $f_{3,c}^{(n)}$ would depend only on $x_j \oplus x_k$ and not on x_j and x_k separately, giving rise to only two possible subfunctions among four restrictions. Therefore, there exists a variable that enters at least two gates; therefore, by setting this variable to a constant we eliminate at least two gates from the circuit. It remains to note that setting a variable to a constant transforms $f_{3,c}^{(n)}$ into $f_{3,c'}^{(n-1)}$, and we can invoke the induction hypothesis.

3.2 Gate elimination for feebly secure one-way functions

The following very simple argument is due to Lamagna and Savage; this argument actually suffices for all Hiltgen's linear examples.

Proposition 6 ((Lamagna & Savage, 1973; Savage, 1976); (Hiltgen, 1992, Theorems 3 and 4)).

1. *Suppose that $f : \mathbb{B}^n \to \mathbb{B}$ depends non-idly on each of its n variables, that is, for every i there exist values $a_1, \ldots, a_{i-1}, a_{i+1}, \ldots, a_n \in \mathbb{B}$ such that*

$$f(a_1, \ldots, a_{i-1}, 0, a_{i+1}, \ldots, a_n) \neq f(a_1, \ldots, a_{i-1}, 1, a_{i+1}, \ldots, a_n). \tag{12}$$

Then $C(f) \geq n - 1$.

2. *Let $f = (f^{(1)}, \ldots, f^{(m)}) : \mathbb{B}^n \to \mathbb{B}^m$, where $f^{(k)}$ is the kth component of f. If the m component functions $f^{(i)}$ are pairwise different and each of them satisfies $C(f^{(i)}) \geq c \geq 1$ then $C(f) \geq c + m - 1$.*

Proof. 1. Consider the minimal circuit of size s computing f. Since f depends (here and in what follows we say "depends" meaning "depends nontrivially") on all n of its variables, each input gate must have at least one outgoing edge. Since the circuit is minimal, each of the other gates, except possibly the output, also must have at least one outgoing edge. Therefore, the circuit has at least $s + n - 1$ edges. On the other hand, a circuit with s binary gates cannot have more than $2s$ edges. Therefore, $2s \geq s + n - 1$.

2. Consider a circuit computing f. Note that it has at least $c - 1$ gates that do not compute any function of circuit complexity c or more (they are the first $c - 1$ gates in some topological order). However, to compute any component function $f^{(i)}$ we have to add at least one more gate, and we have to add at least one gate for each component, since every new gate adds only one new function. Thus, we get the necessary bound of $c + m - 1$ gates.

$\square$

Hiltgen counted the minimal complexity of computing one bit of the input (e.g., since each row of A^{-1} has at least $\frac{n}{2}$ nonzero entries, the minimal complexity of each component of $A^{-1}\vec{y}$ is $\frac{n}{2}$) and thus produced lower bounds on the complexity of inverting the function (e.g. the complexity of computing $A^{-1}\vec{y}$ is $\frac{n}{2} + n - 2 = \frac{3n}{2} - 2$).

Besides, in cryptography it is generally desirable to prove not only worst-case bounds, but also that an adversary is unable to invert the function on a substantial fraction of inputs. In Hiltgen's works, this fact followed from a very simple observation (which was not even explicitly stated).

Lemma 7. *Consider a function $f = \bigoplus_{i=1}^{n} x_i$. For any g that depends on only $m < n$ of these variables,*

$$\Pr_{x_1,\dots,x_n} \left[f(x_1,\dots,x_n) = g(x_{i_1},\dots,x_{i_m}) \right] = \frac{1}{2}. \tag{13}$$

Proof. Since $m < n$, there exists an index $j \in 1..n$ such that g does not depend on x_j. This means that for every set of values of the other variables, whatever the value of g is, for one of the values of x_j f coincides with g, and on the other value f differs from g. This means that f differs from g on precisely $\frac{1}{2}$ of the inputs. $\square$

This argument suffices for Hiltgen's feebly one-wayness result for the square matrix A^{-1}: first we apply the first part of Proposition 6 and see that every output has complexity at least $\frac{n}{2} - 1$, and then the second part of Proposition 6 yields the necessary bound of $\frac{3n}{2} - 1$. Moreover, if a circuit has less than the necessary number of gates, one of its outputs inevitably depends on less than the necessary number of input variables, which, by Lemma 7, gives the necessary $\frac{1}{2}$ error rate.

3.3 Gate elimination for linear functions

In this section, we deal with gate elimination for *linear* functions. We do not know how to prove that one cannot, in general, produce a smaller circuit for a linear function with nonlinear gates, but it is evident that we cannot assume any gates to be nonlinear in this setting. Thus, gate elimination distills to two very simple ideas. Idea 1 is trivial and has been noted many times before, while Idea 2 will allow us to devise feebly secure constructions in Section 4.

Since we are dealing with linear functions, we will, for convenience, state our results in terms of matrices over $\mathbb{F}_2$; the circuit complexity of a matrix $C_\alpha(A)$ is the circuit complexity of the corresponding linear function. By A_{-i} we denote the matrix A without its ith column; note that if A corresponds to f then A_{-i} corresponds to $f\mid_{x_i=0}$. If a matrix A has a zero column A_i, it means that the corresponding function does not depend on the input x_i; in what follows, we will always assume that functions depend nontrivially on all their inputs and thus the matrices do not have zero columns; we call such matrices *nontrivial*. Note that if A is a submatrix of B then $C_\alpha(A) \leq C_\alpha(B)$ for all $\alpha \in [0,1]$.

Idea 1. Suppose that for n steps, there is at least one gate to eliminate. Then $C(f) \geq n$.

Theorem 8. *Fix a real number $\alpha \in [0,1]$. Suppose that $\mathcal{P} = \{P_n\}_{n=1}^\infty$ is a series of predicates defined on matrices over $\mathbb{F}_2$ with the following properties:*

- *if $P_1(A)$ holds then $C_\alpha(A) \geq 1$;*
- *if $P_n(A)$ holds then $P_m(A)$ holds for every $1 \leq m \leq n$;*
- *if $P_n(A)$ holds then, for every index i, $P_{n-1}(A_{-i})$ holds.*

Then, for every matrix A with $\geq n+1$ columns, if $P_n(A)$ holds then $C_\alpha(A) \geq n$.

Proof. The proof goes by straightforward induction on the index of P_i; the first property of $\mathcal{P}$ provides the base, and other properties takes care of the induction step. For the induction step, consider the first gate of an optimal circuit C implementing A. By the monotonicity property of $\mathcal{P}$ and the induction base, the circuit is nontrivial, so there is a first gate. Consider a variable x_i entering that gate. Note that if C computes f on fraction α of its inputs then for some c, $C\mid_{x_i=c}$ computes $f\mid_{x_i=c}$ on fraction α of its inputs. If we substitute this value into this variable, we get a circuit $C\mid_{x_i=c}$ that has at most $(\text{size}(C) - 1)$ gates and implements A_{-i} on at least α fraction of inputs. □

Note that the first statement of Proposition 6 is a special case of Theorem 8 for $P_n(A) = $ "A has a row with $n+1$ ones". We also derive another corollary.

Corollary 9. *If A is a matrix of rank n, and each column of A has at least two ones, then $C(A) \geq n-2$.*

Proof. Take $P_n(A) = $"rank$(A) \geq n+2$ and each column of A has at least 2 ones". □

Idea 2. Suppose that for n steps, there exists an input in the circuit with two outgoing edges, and, moreover, in m of these cases both of these edges go to a gate (rather than a gate and an output). Then $C(f) \geq n+m$.

Theorem 10. *We call a nonzero entry* unique *if it is the only nonzero entry in its row. Fix a real number $\alpha \in [0,1]$. Suppose that $\mathcal{P} = \{P_n\}_{n=1}^\infty$ is a series of predicates defined on matrices over $\mathbb{F}_2$ with the following properties:*

- *if $P_1(A)$ holds then $C(A) \geq 1$;*
- *if $P_n(A)$ holds then $P_m(A)$ holds for every $1 \leq m \leq n$;*
- *if $P_n(A)$ holds then, for every index i, if the ith column has no unique entries then $P_{n-2}(A_{-i})$ holds, otherwise $P_{n-1}(A_{-i})$ holds.*

Then, for every matrix A with $\geq n+1$ different columns, if $P_n(A)$ holds for some n then $C(A) \geq n$ and, moreover, $C_{\frac{3}{4}}(A) \geq n$.

Proof. We argue by induction on n; for $n = 1$ the statement is obvious.

Consider the first gate g in the optimal circuit implementing A. Since g is first, its incoming edges come from the inputs of the circuit; we denote them by x_i and x_j. There are three possible cases.

1. One of the input variables of g, say x_i, goes directly to an output y_k. Then by setting x_i to a constant we can eliminate one gate. however, in this case y_k corresponds to a row with only one nonzero element, so ith colum has a unique element, so $P_{n-1}(A_{-i})$ hold. Therefore, we invoke the induction hypothesis as $C(A_{-i}) \geq n-1$ and get the necessary bound.

2. One of the input variables of g, say x_i, goes to another gate. Then by setting x_i to a constant we can eliminate two gates, and by properties of P_n $P_{n-2}(A_{-i})$ holds, so we invoke the induction hypothesis as $C(A_{-i}) \geq n-2$.

3. Neither x_i nor x_j enters any other gate or output. In this case, A is a function of neither x_i nor x_j but only $g(x_i, x_j)$; we show that this cannot be the case for a function computing A on more than $\frac{3}{4}$ of the inputs. A itself depends on x_i and x_j separately because all of its columns are different; in particular, for one of these variables, say x_i, there exists an output y_k that depends only on x_i: $y_k = x_i \oplus \bigoplus_{x \in X} x$, where $x_j \notin X$. On the other hand, since every gate in an optimal circuit nontrivially depends on both inputs, there exist values a and b such that $g(0, a) = g(1, b)$. Thus, for every assignment of the remaining variables, either on input strings with $(x_i = 0, x_j = a)$ or on input strings with $(x_i = 1, x_j = b)$ the circuit makes a mistake, which makes it wrong on at least $\frac{1}{4}$ of all inputs. $\square$

Note that Theorem 10 directly generalizes and strengthens Theorem 8.

Corollary 11. *Fix a real number $\alpha \in [0,1]$. Suppose that $\mathcal{R} = \{R_n\}_{n=1}^{\infty}$ and $\mathcal{Q} = \{Q_m\}_{m=1}^{\infty}$ are two series of predicates defined on matrices over $\mathbb{F}_2$ with the following properties:*

- *if $R_1(A)$ holds then $C(A) \geq 1$;*
- *if $R_n(A)$ holds then $R_k(A)$ holds for every $1 \leq k \leq n$;*
- *if $R_n(A)$ holds then, for every i, $R_{n-1}(A_{-i})$ holds;*
- *if $Q_1(A)$ holds then $C(A) \geq 1$;*
- *if $Q_m(A)$ holds then $Q_k(A)$ holds for every $1 \leq k \leq n$;*
- *if $Q_m(A)$ holds then, for every i, $Q_{m-1}(A_{-i})$ holds;*
- *if $Q_m(A)$ holds and A_{-i} has more zero rows than A (i.e., removing the ith column has removed the last nonzero element from at least one row) then $Q_m(A_{-i})$ holds.*

Then, for every matrix A with $\geq n+1$ columns all of which are different, if $R_n(A)$ and $Q_m(A)$ hold for some $n \geq m$ then $C(A) \geq n+m$ and, moreover, $C_{\frac{3}{4}}(A) \geq n+m$.

Proof. Immediately follows from Theorem 10 for $P_n(A) = \exists k R_k(A) \wedge Q_{n-k}(A)$. $\square$

Theorem 10 and Corollary 11 generalize several results that have been proven independently. For example, here is the "master lemma" of the original paper on feebly trapdoor functions.

Corollary 12 ((Hirsch & Nikolenko, 2009, Lemma 5))**.** *Let* $t, u \geq 1$. *Assume that* χ *is a linear function with matrix* A *over* $\mathbb{F}_2$. *Assume also that all columns of* A *are different, every row of* A *has at least* u *nonzero entries, and after removing any* t *columns of* A, *the matrix still has at least one row containing at least two nonzero entries. Then* $C(\chi) \geq u + t$ *and, moreover,* $C_{3/4}(\chi) \geq u + t$.

Proof. Take $P_n(A)$ ="After removing any n columns of A, it still has at least one nonzero row", $Q_0(A)$ ="true", and $Q_m(A)$ ="Every row of A has at least $m + 1$ ones" for $m > 0$. Then $P_{t+1}(A)$ and $Q_{u-1}(A)$ hold, and $\mathcal{P}$ and $\mathcal{Q}$ satisfy the conditions of Corollary 11, which gives the desired bound. Note that in this case, Q_m for $m > 0$ cannot hold for a matrix where a row has only a single one, so in the gate elimination proof, for the first $u - 1$ steps two gates will be eliminated, and then for $t - u + 2$ steps, one gate will be eliminated. □

We also derive another, even stronger corollary that will be important for new feebly secure constructions.

Corollary 13. *Let* $t \geq u \geq 2$. *Assume that* A *is a* $u \times t$ *matrix with different columns, and each column of* A *has at least two nonzero elements (ones). Then* $C(A) \geq 2t - u$ *and, moreover,* $C_{\frac{3}{4}}(A) \geq 2t - u$.

Proof. Take $P_n(A)$ ="twice the number of nonzero columns in A less the number of nonzero rows in A is at least n". Then $P_{2t-u}(A)$ holds, and $\mathcal{P}_n$ satisfy the conditions of Theorem 10. □

Naturally, we could prove Corollaries 9 and 13 directly. We have chosen the path of generalization for two reasons: one, to make Theorem 14 more precise and more general, and two, to show the limits of gate elimination for linear functions. As we have already mentioned, for linear functions we cannot count on nonlinear gates that could eliminate their descendants. In Theorems 8 and 10, we have considered two basic cases: when there is only one edge outgoing from a variable and when there are two edges (going either to two gates or to a gate and an output). It appears that we can hardly expect anything more from classical gate elimination in the linear case.

3.4 Extension to block diagonal matrices

We finish this section with an extension of these results to block diagonal matrices. In general, we cannot prove that the direct sum of several functions has circuit complexity equal to the sum of the circuit complexities of these functions; counterexamples are known as "mass production" (Wegener, 1987). However, for linear functions and gate elimination in the flavours of Theorems 8 and 10, we can. The following theorem generalizes Lemma 6 of (Hirsch & Nikolenko, 2009).

Theorem 14. *Suppose that a linear function* χ *is given by a block diagonal matrix*

$$
\begin{pmatrix}
A_1 & 0 & \cdots & 0 \\
0 & A_2 & \cdots & 0 \\
\vdots & \vdots & & \vdots \\
0 & 0 & \cdots & A_k
\end{pmatrix},
\tag{14}
$$

every A_j satisfies the conditions of Theorem 10 with predicates $\mathcal{P}^j = \{P_n^j\}_{n=1}^{\infty}$, and $P_{n_j}^j(A_j)$ hold for every j. Then $C(\chi) \geq \sum\limits_{j=1}^{k} n_j$.

Proof. We invoke Theorem 10 with the predicate composed of original predicates:

$$P_n = \bigvee_{i_1+\ldots+i_k=n} P_{i_1}^1 \wedge P_{i_2}^2 \wedge \ldots \wedge P_{i_k}^k. \tag{15}$$

It is now straightforward to check that $\mathcal{P} = \{P_n\}_{n=1}^{\infty}$ satisfies the conditions of Theorem 10 (since every deleted column affects only one block), and the block diagonal matrix satisfies $P_{n_1+\ldots+n_k}$.   □

4. Feebly secure trapdoor functions

4.1 Idea of the construction

Over this section, we will present two constructions of feebly secure trapdoor functions, a linear construction and a nonlinear one. Both of them have the same rather peculiar structure. It turns out that when we directly construct a feebly secure candidate trapdoor function such that an adversary has to spend more time inverting it than honest participants, we will not be able to make encoding (i.e., function evaluation) faster than inversion. In fact, evaluation will take *more* time than even an adversary requires to invert our candidates.

To achieve a feebly secure trapdoor function, we will add another block as a direct sum to that candidate. This block will represent a feebly secure one-way function, one of the constructions presented by Hiltgen (1992; 1994; 1998). In this construction, honest inversion and break are exactly the same since there is no secret key at all; nevertheless, both of them are harder than evaluating the function. Thus, in the resulting block diagonal construction break remains harder than honest inversion but they both gain in complexity over function evaluation. This idea was first presented by Hirsch & Nikolenko (2009) and has been used since in every feebly secure trapdoor function.

4.2 Linear feebly secure trapdoor functions

This section is based on (Davydow & Nikolenko, 2011). Let us first introduce some notation. By U_n we denote an upper triangular matrix of size $n \times n$ which is inverse to a bidiagonal matrix:

$$U_n = \begin{pmatrix} 1 & 1 & \cdots & 1 \\ 0 & 1 & \cdots & 1 \\ \vdots & \vdots & & \vdots \\ 0 & 0 & \cdots & 1 \end{pmatrix}, \qquad U_n^{-1} = \begin{pmatrix} 1 & 1 & 0 & \cdots & 0 \\ 0 & 1 & 1 & \cdots & 0 \\ \vdots & \vdots & \vdots & & \vdots \\ 0 & 0 & 0 & \cdots & 1 \end{pmatrix};$$

note that U_n^2 is an upper triangular matrix with zeros and ones chequered above the main diagonal. We will often use matrices composed of smaller matrices as blocks; for instance, $(U_n\ U_n)$ is a matrix of size $n \times 2n$ composed of two upper triangular blocks.

Lemma 15. *1. $C_{\frac{3}{4}}(U_n) = n - 1$.*

2. $C_{\frac{3}{4}}(U_n^2) = n - 2$.

3. $C_{\frac{3}{4}}(U_n^{-1}) = n - 1$.

4. $C_{\frac{3}{4}}((u_n\, u_n)) = 2n - 1.$

5. $3n - 6 \leq C_{\frac{3}{4}}((u_n^2\, u_n)) \leq C((u_n^2\, u_n)) \leq 3n - 3.$

6. $3n - 4 \leq C_{\frac{3}{4}}((u_n\, u_n^{-1})) \leq C((u_n\, u_n^{-1})) \leq 3n - 2.$

Proof. Lower bounds in items 1–3 are obvious: the matrices have no identical rows, and not a single input except one (two for item 2) is linked directly to an output. The lower bound in item 4 follows by simple counting: the first row of the matrix contains $2n$ nonzero elements, so at least $2n - 1$ gates are needed to compute it. The lower bound from item 5 (respectively, 6) follows from Corollary 13: the matrix $(u_n^2\, u_n)$ (respectively, $(u_n\, u_n^{-1})$) satisfies the assumptions of Corollary 13 for all except three (respectively, two) columns, and we can use Corollary 13 for $t = 2n - 3$ (respectively, $t = 2n - 2$) and $u = n$.

To prove upper bounds, we give direct constructions. To compute the matrix from item 1, note that each row differs from the previous one in only one position, so we can compute the outputs as $\text{out}_i = \text{out}_{i+1} \oplus \text{in}_i$. Moreover, $\text{out}_n = \text{in}_n$, so we do not need more gates to compute it. The same idea works for item 2, but in this case, out_n and out_{n-1} are computed immediately, and $\text{out}_i = \text{out}_{i-2} \oplus \text{in}_i$. To compute the matrix from item 3, we compute each row directly. To compute item 4, we note that $(u_n\, u_n) \cdot \left(\begin{smallmatrix} a \\ b \end{smallmatrix} \right) = U_n \cdot a \oplus U_n \cdot b = U_n \cdot (a \oplus b)$. Thus, we can use n gates to compute $a \oplus b$ and then get the result with $n - 1$ more gates. To compute 5 and 6 note that $(A\, B) \cdot \left(\begin{smallmatrix} a \\ b \end{smallmatrix} \right) = A \cdot a \oplus B \cdot b$. Thus, we have divided the computation in two parts that can be done independently with previously shown circuits, and then we can use n gates to XOR the results of these subcircuits. $\qquad\square$

We use the general idea outlined in Section 4.1. In the first construction, we assume that the lengths of the public key pi, secret key ti, message m, and ciphertext c are the same and equal n. Let $ti = U_n \cdot pi$, $c = (u_n^{-1}\, u_n) \cdot \left(\begin{smallmatrix} m \\ pi \end{smallmatrix} \right)$. In this case, an adversary will have to compute the matrix $(u_n\, u_n) \cdot \left(\begin{smallmatrix} c \\ ti \end{smallmatrix} \right) = (u_n\, u_n^2) \cdot \left(\begin{smallmatrix} c \\ pi \end{smallmatrix} \right)$. Thus, breaking this trapdoor function is harder than honest inversion, but the evaluation complexity is approximately equal to the complexity of the break, so we cannot yet call this function a feebly secure trapdoor function.

To augment this construction, consider a weakly one-way linear function A and use it in the following protocol (by I_n we denote the unit matrix of size n):

$$\text{Seed}_n = \begin{pmatrix} U_n & 0 \\ 0 & I_n \end{pmatrix} \cdot (s\ s) = \begin{pmatrix} ti \\ pi \end{pmatrix},$$

$$\text{Eval}_n = \begin{pmatrix} U_n^{-1}\ U_n & 0 \\ 0 & 0 & A \end{pmatrix} \cdot \begin{pmatrix} m_1 \\ pi \\ m_2 \end{pmatrix} = \begin{pmatrix} c_1 \\ c_2 \end{pmatrix},$$

$$\text{Inv}_n = \begin{pmatrix} U_n\ U_n & 0 \\ 0 & 0 & A^{-1} \end{pmatrix} \cdot \begin{pmatrix} c_1 \\ ti \\ c_2 \end{pmatrix} = \begin{pmatrix} m_1 \\ m_2 \end{pmatrix}.$$

An adversary is now supposed to compute

$$\text{Adv}_n = \begin{pmatrix} U_n\ U_n^2 & 0 \\ 0 & 0 & A^{-1} \end{pmatrix} \cdot \begin{pmatrix} c_1 \\ pi \\ c_2 \end{pmatrix} = \begin{pmatrix} m_1 \\ m_2 \end{pmatrix}.$$

As a feebly one-way function A we take one of Hiltgen's functions with order of security $2 - \epsilon$ that have been constructed for every $\epsilon > 0$ Hiltgen (1992); we take the matrix of this function to have order λn, where λ will be chosen below. For such a matrix, $C_{\frac{3}{4}}(A) = \lambda n + o(n)$, and

$C_{\frac{3}{4}}(A^{-1}) = (2 - \epsilon)\lambda n + o(n)$. Now Lemma 15 and Theorem 14 yield the following complexity bounds:

$$C_{\frac{3}{4}}(\text{Seed}_n) = n - 1,$$
$$C_{\frac{3}{4}}(\text{Eval}_n) = 3n + \lambda n + o(n) \qquad = (3 + \lambda)n + o(n),$$
$$C_{\frac{3}{4}}(\text{Inv}_n) = 2n + (2 - \epsilon)\lambda n + o(n) = (2 + (2 - \epsilon)\lambda)n + o(n),$$
$$C_{\frac{3}{4}}(\text{Adv}_n) = 3n + (2 - \epsilon)\lambda n + o(n) = (3 + (2 - \epsilon)\lambda)n + o(n).$$

The order of security for this protocol is

$$\lim_{n \to \infty} \left(\min \left(\frac{C_{3/4}(\text{Adv}_n)}{C(\text{Eval}_n)}, \frac{C_{3/4}(\text{Adv}_n)}{C(\text{Inv}_n)}, \frac{C_{3/4}(\text{Adv}_n)}{C(\text{Seed}_n)} \right) \right) =$$
$$= \min \left(\frac{3 + (2 - \epsilon)\lambda}{3 + \lambda}, \frac{3 + (2 - \epsilon)\lambda}{2 + (2 - \epsilon)\lambda} \right).$$

This expression reaches maximum for $\lambda = \frac{1}{1-\epsilon}$, and this maximum equals $\frac{5-4\epsilon}{4-\epsilon}$, which tends to $\frac{5}{4}$ as $\epsilon \to 0$. Thus, we have proven the following theorem.

Theorem 16. *For every $\epsilon > 0$, there exists a linear feebly secure trapdoor function with seed length* $pi(n) = ti(n) = n$, *input and output length* $c(n) = m(n) = 2n$, *and order of security* $\frac{5}{4} - \epsilon$.

4.3 Nonlinear feebly secure trapdoor functions

Over the previous two sections, we have discussed *linear* feebly secure one-way functions. However, a *nonlinear* approach can yield better constants. This section is based on (Hirsch et al., 2011; Melanich, 2009).

Our nonlinear feebly trapdoor constructions are based on a feebly one-way function resulting from uniting Hiltgen's linear feebly one-way function with the first computationally asymmetric function of four variables (Massey, 1996). Consider a sequence of functions $\{f_n\}_{n=1}^{\infty}$ given by the following relations (we denote $y_j = f_j(x_1, \ldots, x_n)$):

$$y_1 = (x_1 \oplus x_2)x_n \oplus x_{n-1},$$
$$y_2 = (x_1 \oplus x_2)x_n \oplus x_2,$$
$$y_3 = x_1 \oplus x_3,$$
$$y_4 = x_3 \oplus x_4, \tag{16}$$
$$\ldots$$
$$y_{n-1} = x_{n-2} \oplus x_{n-1},$$
$$y_n = x_n.$$

In order to get f_n^{-1}, we sum up all rows except the last one:

$$y_1 \oplus \ldots \oplus y_{n-1} = x_1 \oplus x_2. \tag{17}$$

Further, substituting y_n instead of x_n, we find x_2 and x_{n-1}. The other x_k can be expressed via x_{n-1} in turn, so the inverse function is given by

$$
\begin{aligned}
x_n &= y_n, \\
x_2 &= (y_1 \oplus \ldots \oplus y_{n-1})y_n \oplus y_2, \\
x_{n-1} &= (y_1 \oplus \ldots \oplus y_{n-1})y_n \oplus y_1, \\
x_{n-2} &= (y_1 \oplus \ldots \oplus y_{n-1})y_n \oplus y_1 \oplus y_{n-1}, \\
x_{n-3} &= (y_1 \oplus \ldots \oplus y_{n-1})y_n \oplus y_1 \oplus y_{n-1} \oplus y_{n-2}, \\
&\ \ \ldots \\
x_3 &= (y_1 \oplus \ldots \oplus y_{n-1})y_n \oplus y_1 \oplus y_{n-1} \oplus \ldots \oplus y_4, \\
x_1 &= (y_1 \oplus \ldots \oplus y_{n-1})y_n \oplus y_1 \oplus y_{n-1} \oplus \ldots \oplus y_3.
\end{aligned}
\tag{18}
$$

Lemma 17. *The family of functions $\{f_n\}_{n=1}^{\infty}$ is feebly one-way of order 2.*

Proof. It is easy to see that f_n can be computed in $n+1$ gates. Each component function of f_n^{-1}, except for the last one, depends non-trivially of all n variables, and all component functions are different. Therefore, to compute f_n^{-1} we need at least $(n-1) + (n-2) = 2n-3$ gates (since f_n is invertible, Proposition 6 is applicable to f_n and f_n^{-1}). Therefore,

$$
M_F(f_n) \geq \frac{2n-3}{n+1}.
\tag{19}
$$

On the other hand, f_n cannot be computed faster than in $n-1$ gates because all component functions f_n are different, and only one of them is trivial (depends on only one variable). At the same time, f_n^{-1} can be computed in $2n-2$ gates: one computes $(y_1 \oplus \ldots \oplus y_{n-1})y_n$ in $n-1$ gates and spends one gate to compute each component function except the last one. We get

$$
\frac{2n-3}{n+1} \leq M_F(f_n) \leq \frac{2n-2}{n-1},
\tag{20}
$$

which is exactly what we need. $\qquad\square$

For the proof of the following theorem, we refer to (Hirsch et al., 2011; Melanich, 2009).

Theorem 18. $C_{3/4}(f_n^{-1}) \geq 2n - 4.$

We can now apply the same direct sum idea to this nonlinear feebly one-way function. The direct sum consists of two blocks. First, for f as above, we have:

$$
\begin{aligned}
\mathrm{Key}_n(s) &= (f_n(s), s), \\
\mathrm{Eval}_n(pi, m) &= f_n^{-1}(pi) \oplus m, \\
\mathrm{Inv}_n(ti, c) &= f_n^{-1}(pi) \oplus c = ti \oplus c, \\
\mathrm{Adv}_n(pi, c) &= f_n^{-1}(pi) \oplus c.
\end{aligned}
\tag{21}
$$

In this construction, evaluation is no easier than inversion without trapdoor.

For the second block we have

$$
\begin{aligned}
\mathrm{Eval}_n(m) &= f(m), \\
\mathrm{Inv}_n(c) &= f^{-1}(c), \\
\mathrm{Adv}_n(c) &= f^{-1}(c).
\end{aligned}
\tag{22}
$$

Again, as above, it is not a trapdoor function at all because inversion is implemented with no regard for the trapdoor. For a message m of length $|m| = n$ the evaluation circuit has $n + 1$ gates, while inversion, by Theorem 18, can be performed only by circuits with at least $2n - 4$ gates. Thus, in this construction evaluation is easy and inversion is hard, both for an honest participant of the protocol and for an adversary.

We can now unite these two trapdoor candidates and get the following construction:

$$
\begin{aligned}
\text{Key}_n(s) &= (f_n(s), s), \\
\text{Eval}_n(pi, m_1, m_2) &= (f_n^{-1}(pi) \oplus m_1, f_{\alpha n}(m_2)), \\
\text{Inv}_n(ti, c_1, c_2) &= (f_n^{-1}(pi) \oplus c_1, f_{\alpha n}^{-1}(c_2)) = (ti \oplus c_1, f_{\alpha n}^{-1}(c_2)), \\
\text{Adv}_n(pi, c_1, c_2) &= (f_n^{-1}(pi) \oplus c_1, f_{\alpha n}^{-1}(c_2)),
\end{aligned}
\tag{23}
$$

The proofs of lower bounds on these constructions are rather involved; we refer to (Hirsch et al., 2011; Melanich, 2009) for detailed proofs and simply give the results here.

Lemma 19. *The following upper and lower bounds hold for the components of our nonlinear trapdoor construction:*

$$
\begin{aligned}
C(\text{Key}_n) &\leq n + 1, \\
C(\text{Eval}_n) &\leq 2n - 2 + n + \alpha n + 1 = 3n + \alpha n - 1, \\
C(\text{Inv}_n) &\leq n + 2\alpha n - 2, \\
C_{3/4}(\text{Adv}_n) &\geq 3n + 2\alpha n - 8.
\end{aligned}
\tag{24}
$$

To maximize the order of security of this trapdoor function (Definition 5), we have to find α that maximizes

$$
\begin{aligned}
\liminf_{i \to \infty} \min \left\{ \frac{C_{3/4}(Adv_n)}{C(Key_n)}, \frac{C_{3/4}(Adv_n)}{C(Eval_n)}, \frac{C_{3/4}(Adv_n)}{C(Inv_n)} \right\} &= \\
= \min \left\{ \frac{3 + 2\alpha}{1}, \frac{3 + 2\alpha}{3 + \alpha}, \frac{3 + 2\alpha}{1 + 2\alpha} \right\} &= \min \left\{ \frac{3 + 2\alpha}{3 + \alpha}, \frac{3 + 2\alpha}{1 + 2\alpha} \right\}.
\end{aligned}
\tag{25}
$$

It is easy to see that this expression is maximized for $\alpha = 2$, and the optimal value of the order of security is $\frac{7}{5}$. We summarize this in the following theorem.

Theorem 20. *There exists a nonlinear feebly trapdoor function with seed length* $pi(n) = ti(n) = n$, *input and output length* $c(n) = m(n) = 3n$, *and order of security* $\frac{7}{5}$.

5. Conclusion

In this chapter, we have discussed recent developments in the field of feebly secure cryptographic primitives. While these primitives can hardly be put to any practical use at present, they are still important from the theoretical point of view. As sad as it sounds, this is actually the·frontier of provable, mathematically sound results on security; we do not know how to prove anything stronger.

Further work in this direction is twofold. One can further develop the notions of feebly secure primitives. Constants in the orders of security can probably be improved; perhaps, other primitives (key agreement protocols, zero knowledge proofs etc.) can find their feebly secure counterparts. This work can widen the scope of feebly secure methods, but the real breakthrough can only come from one place.

It becomes clear that cryptographic needs call for further advances in general circuit complexity. General circuit complexity has not had a breakthrough since the 1980s; nonconstructive lower bounds are easy to prove by counting, but constructive lower bounds remain elusive. The best bound we know is Blum's lower bound of $3n - o(n)$ proven in 1984. At present, we do not know how to rise to this challenge; none of the known methods seem to work, so a general breakthrough is required for nonlinear lower bounds on circuit complexity. The importance of such a breakthrough can hardly be overstated; in this chapter, we have seen only one possible use of circuit lower bounds.

6. Acknowledgements

This work has been partially supported by the Russian Fund for Basic Research, grants no. 11-01-00760-a and 11-01-12135-ofi-m-2011, the Russian Presidential Grant Programme for Leading Scientific Schools, grant no. NSh-3229.2012.1, and the Russian Presidential Grant Programme for Young Ph.D.Ss, grant no. MK-6628.2012.1.

7. References

Ajtai, M. (1983). σ_1^1-formulae on finite structures, *Annals of Pure and Applied Logic* 24: 1–48.
Ajtai, M. & Dwork, C. (1997). A public-key cryptosystem with worst-case/average-case equivalence, *Proceedings of the 29th Annual ACM Symposium on Theory of Computing*, pp. 284–293.
Blum, N. (1984). A boolean function requiring $3n$ network size, *Theoretical Computer Science* 28: 337–345.
Cai, J. (1989). With probability 1, a random oracle separates PSPACE from the polynomial-time hierarchy, *Journal of Computer and System Sciences* 38: 68–85.
Davydow, A. & Nikolenko, S. I. (2011). Gate elimination for linear functions and new feebly secure constructions, *Proceedings of the 6th Computer Science Symposium in Russia, Lecture Notes in Computer Science*, Vol. 6651, pp. 148–161.
Demenkov, E. & Kulikov, A. (2011). An elementary proof of a 3n-o(n) lower bound on the circuit complexity of affine dispersers, *Proceedings of the 36th International Symposium on Mathematical Foundations of Computer Science, Lecture Notes in Computer Science*, Vol. 6907, pp. 256–265.
Diffie, W. & Hellman, M. (1976). New directions in cryptography, *IEEE Transactions on Information Theory* IT-22: 644–654.
Dwork, C. (1997). Positive applications of lattices to cryptography, *Proceedings of the 22nd International Symposium on Mathematical Foundations of Computer Science, Lecture Notes in Computer Science*, Vol. 1295, pp. 44–51.
Furst, M., Saxe, J. & Sipser, M. (1984). Parity, circuits, and the polynomial-time hierarchy, *Mathematical Systems Theory* 17: 13–27.
Goldreich, O. (2001). *Foundations of Cryptography. Basic Tools*, Cambridge University Press.
Goldreich, O. (2004). *Foundations of Cryptography II. Basic Applications*, Cambridge University Press.
Goldwasser, S. & Bellare, M. (2001). *Lecture Notes on Cryptography*, Summer course on cryptography at MIT.
Grigoriev, D., Hirsch, E. A. & Pervyshev, K. (2009). A complete public-key cryptosystem, *Groups, Complexity, and Cryptology* 1: 1–12.

Harnik, D., Kilian, J., Naor, M., Reingold, O. & Rosen, A. (2005). On robust combiners for oblivious transfers and other primitives, *Proceedings of EuroCrypt âĂŹ05, Lecture Notes in Computer Science*, Vol. 3494, pp. 96–113.

Håstad, J. (1987). *Computational Limitations for Small Depth Circuits*, MIT Press, Cambridge, MA.

Hiltgen, A. P. (1992). Constructions of feebly-one-way families of permutations, *Proc. of AsiaCrypt '92*, pp. 422–434.

Hiltgen, A. P. (1994). Cryptographically relevant contributions to combinatorial complexity theory, *in* J. L. Massey (ed.), *ETH Series in Information Processing*, Vol. 3, Konstanz: Hartung-Gorre.

Hiltgen, A. P. (1998). Towards a better understanding of one-wayness: Facing linear permutations, *Proceedings of EuroCrypt '98, Lecture Notes in Computer Science*, Vol. 1233, pp. 319–333.

Hirsch, E. A., Melanich, O. & Nikolenko, S. I. (2011). Feebly secure cryptographic primitives.

Hirsch, E. A. & Nikolenko, S. I. (2008). A feebly secure trapdoor function, PDMI preprint 16/2008.

Hirsch, E. A. & Nikolenko, S. I. (2009). A feebly secure trapdoor function, *Proceedings of the 4th Computer Science Symposium in Russia, Lecture Notes in Computer Science*, Vol. 5675, pp. 129–142.

Immerman, M. (1987). Languages which capture complexity classes, *SIAM Journal of Computing* 4: 760–778.

Impagliazzo, R. (1995). A personal view of average-case complexity, *Proceedings of the 10th Annual Structure in Complexity Theory Conference (SCT'95)*, IEEE Computer Society, Washington, DC, USA, p. 134.

Khrapchenko, V. M. (1971). Complexity of the realization of a linear function in the class of π-circuits, *Mat. Zametki* 9(1): 36–40.

Kojevnikov, A. A. & Nikolenko, S. I. (2008). New combinatorial complete one-way functions, *Proceedings of the 25th Symposium on Theoretical Aspects of Computer Science*, Bordeaux, France, pp. 457–466.

Kojevnikov, A. A. & Nikolenko, S. I. (2009). On complete one-way functions, *Problems of Information Transmission* 45(2): 108–189.

Lamagna, E. A. & Savage, J. E. (1973). On the logical complexity of symmetric switching functions in monotone and complete bases, *Technical report*, Brown University, Rhode Island.

Levin, L. A. (1986). Average case complete problems, *SIAM Journal of Computing* 15(1): 285–286.

Lupanov, O. B. (1965). On a certain approach to the synthesis of control systems – the principle of local coding, *Problemy Kibernet.* 14: 31–110.

Markov, A. A. (1964). Minimal relay-diode bipoles for monotonic symmetric functions, *Problems of Cybernetics* 8: 205–212.

Massey, J. (1996). The difficulty with difficulty: A guide to the transparencies from the EUROCRYPT'96 IACR distinguished lecture.

Melanich, O. (2009). Nonlinear feebly secure cryptographic primitives, PDMI preprint 12/2009.

Nechiporuk, E. I. (1966). A Boolean function, *Soviet Mathematics. Doklady* 7: 999–1000.

Paul, W. J. (1977). A 2.5n lower bound on the combinational complexity of boolean functions, *SIAM Journal of Computing* 6: 427–443.

Razborov, A. A. (1985). Lower bounds on monotone complexity of the logical permanent, *Mat. Zametki* 37(6): 887–900.

Razborov, A. A. (1987). Lower bounds on the size of bounded depth circuits over a complete basis with logical addition, *Mat. Zametki* 41(4): 598–608.

Razborov, A. A. (1990). Lower bounds of the complexity of symmetric boolean functions of contact-rectifier circuit, *Mat. Zametki* 48(6): 79–90.

Razborov, A. A. (1995). Bounded arithmetic and lower bounds, *in* P. Clote & J. Remmel (eds), *Feasible Mathematics II*, Vol. 13 of *Progress in Computer Science and Applied Logic*, Birkhäuser, pp. 344–386.

Regev, O. (2005). On lattices, learning with errors, random linear codes, and cryptography, *Proceedings of the 37th Annual ACM Symposium on Theory of Computing*, pp. 84–93.

Regev, O. (2006). Lattice-based cryptography, *Proceedings of the 26th Annual International Cryptology Conference (CRYPTO'06), Lecture Notes in Computer Science*, Vol. 4117, pp. 131–141.

Rivest, R. L., Shamir, A. & Adleman, L. (1978). A method for obtaining digital signatures and public-key cryptosystems, *Communications of the ACM* 21(2): 120–126.

Savage, J. E. (1976). *The Complexity of Computing*, Wiley, New York.

Shannon, C. E. (1949). Communication theory of secrecy systems, *Bell System Technical Journal* 28(4): 656–717.

Sholomov, L. A. (1969). On the realization of incompletely-defined boolean functions by circuits of functional elements, *Trans: System Theory Research* 21: 211–223.

Smolensky, R. (1987). Algebraic methods in the theory of lower bounds for boolean circuit complexity, *Proceedings of the 19th Annual ACM Symposium on Theory of Computing*, pp. 77–82.

Stockmeyer, L. (1977). On the combinational complexity of certain symmetric boolean functions, *Mathematical Systems Theory* 10: 323–326.

Stockmeyer, L. (1987). Classifying the computational complexity of problems, *Journal of Symbolic Logic* 52: 1–43.

Subbotovskaya, B. A. (1961). Realizations of linear functions by formulas using $\lor$, &, $\neg$, *Soviet Mathematics. Doklady* 2: 110–112.

Subbotovskaya, B. A. (1963). On comparison of bases in the case of realization of functions of algebra of logic by formulas, *Soviet Mathematics. Doklady* 149(4): 784–787.

Vernam, G. S. (1926). Cipher printing telegraph systems for secret wire and radio telegraphic communications, *Journal of the IEEE* 55: 109–115.

Wegener, I. (1987). *The Complexity of Boolean Functions*, B. G. Teubner, and John Wiley & Sons.

Yablonskii, S. V. (1957). On the classes of functions of logic algebra with simple circuit realizations, *Soviet Math. Uspekhi* 12(6): 189–196.

Yao, A. C.-C. (1985). Separating the polynomial-time hierarchy by oracles, *Proceedings of the 26th Annual IEEE Symposium on the Foundations of Computer Science*, pp. 1–10.

Yao, A. C.-C. (1990). On ACC and threshold circuits, *Proceedings of the 31st Annual IEEE Symposium on the Foundations of Computer Science*, pp. 619–627.

Cryptographic Criteria on Vector Boolean Functions

José Antonio Álvarez-Cubero and Pedro J. Zufiria
Universidad Politécnica de Madrid (UPM)
Spain

1. Introduction

Most modern block and stream ciphers can be expressed as certain arrangement of Vector Boolean Functions. Thus, in the context of block and stream ciphers' design (mainly in S-boxes and combining functions respectively), it is essential to define criteria which measure the cryptographic strength of Boolean Functions and Vector Boolean Functions. Ideally, some of the following requirements must be fulfilled by this criteria:

1. The principles of confusion and diffusion must be enforced by the criterion Shannon (1949). *Confusion* obscures the relationship between the plaintext and the ciphertext Schneier (1995). *Difussion* dissipates the redundancy of the plaintext by spreading it over the ciphertext. Both techniques make more difficult for a cryptanalyst to find out redundancy and statistical patterns in the ciphertext.

2. The criterion must be expressed in terms of a distance to an appropriate set S of cryptographically weak functions Meier & Staffelbach (1990). Functions that exhibit properties common to cryptographically weak functions are also considered to be cryptographically weak.

3. The criterion should remain invariant under a certain group of transformations Meier & Staffelbach (1990). This symmetry group should contain the group of affine transformations.

A function is considered to be cryptographically weak if it is easily breakable or it can be turned into a weak function by means of simple (e.g. linear or affine) transformations. This definition is congruent with the notion of similar secrecy introduced by Shannon in Shannon (1949), so that two functions R and S are said to be "similar" if there exists a fixed transformation A, with an inverse A^{-1}, such that $R = AS$. Hereunder are described the best known cryptographically weak functions.

- *Linear and affine functions.* These functions are easily breakable because the simultaneous complementation of a subset of the input variables causes the value of a linear or an affine function to always change (from the original value before complementation) or to never change.

- *Functions with non-zero linear structures.* The cryptanalytic value of linear structures lies in their potential to map a nonlinear function to a degenerate function via a linear transformation, which may reduce the size of the keyspace.

- *Functions not balanced.* The output of these kind of functions are not uniformly distributed, avoiding statistical dependence between the input and the output (which can be used in attacks).

- *Functions with low algebraic degree* can be approximated by low complex functions easing their attack.

- *m-th order correlation-immune functions* are those whose output distribution probability are unaltered when any m (or, equivalently, at most m) of the inputs are kept constant.

- *Functions with low degree of Propagation Criterion* has little diffusion property and their output distribution probability are altered when some coordinates of the input are complemented.

The main objective of this chapter is to characterize the more relevant cryptographic criteria (nonlinearity, linear distance, balancedness, algebraic degree, correlation immunity, resiliency and propagation criterion) for constructions of Vector Boolean Functions such as composition, addition of coordinate functions, direct sum and bricklayering, from the knowledge of their components. The study of these functions are relevant in cryptology due to the strong connection between cryptographic attacks on the one hand and cryptographic properties of these building blocks on the other hand. In most cases, the security against a particular class of attack can be expressed by the existence of a certain property of the Vector Boolean function, which results in a measure of security against that class of attacks:

- *Linear cryptanalysis* is based on the idea of finding high probable linear or affine relations between the inputs and outputs of S-boxes present in the cipher, that is, finding S-boxes with low nonlinearity Matsui (1994).

- *Differential cryptanalysis* is a chosen-plaintext attack based on the idea of finding high probable differentials pairs between the inputs and outputs of S-boxes present in the cipher, that is, finding S-boxes with low linearity distance. Differential cryptanalysis Biham & Shamir (1991) can be seen as an extension of the ideas of attacks based on the presence of linear structures Nyberg (1991).

- *Distinguishing attacks* are able to distinguish the pseudorandom sequence from a random sequence by observing that the distribution of the sequences is not uniform for not balanced functions.

- Jakobsen and Knudsen identified *interpolation attacks* on block ciphers with S-boxes having small algebraic degree Jakobsen & Knudsen (1997). Later Canteaut and Videau provided *Higher order differential attacks* which exploit the fact that the algebraic degree of the S-box is low. In the case of combining functions, the sequence produced by n combined LSFRs can be obtained by a single LSFR.

- For the pseudo-random generators, the best known cryptanalytic technique is the *correlation attack*, which is based on the idea of finding correlation between the outputs and the inputs, that is, finding S-boxes with low resiliency.

- Propagation Characteristic (PC) is an important cryptographic property for S-boxes to resist differential cryptanalysis. To get uniform output distribution, S-boxes in block ciphers should have $PC(l)$ of higher order for $l \geq 1$.

2. Preliminaries

2.1 Definitions

Let $< GF(2), +, \cdot >$ be the finite field of order 2, where $GF(2) = Z_2 = \{0, 1\}$, '+' the 'integer addition modulo 2' and '$\cdot$' the 'integer multiplication modulo 2'. V_n is the vector space of n-tuples of elements from $GF(2)$. The *direct sum* of $x \in V_{n_1}$ and $y \in V_{n_2}$ is defined as $x \oplus y = (x_1, \ldots, x_{n_1}, y_1, \ldots, y_{n_2}) \in V_{n_1+n_2}$. The *inner product* of $x, y \in V_n$ is denoted by $x \cdot y$, and of real vectors $x, y \in \mathbb{R}^n$ is denoted by $\langle x, y \rangle$. Let $x, y \in \mathbb{R}^n$, the pointwise product is defined as $x \cdot y = (x_1 \cdot y_1, \ldots, x_n \cdot y_n)$.

$f : V_n \rightarrow GF(2)$ is called a *Boolean function* and $\mathcal{F}_n$ is the set of all Boolean functions on V_n. $\mathcal{L}_n$ is the set of all linear Boolean functions on V_n: $\mathcal{L}_n = \{l_u \; \forall u \in V_n \mid l_u(x) = u \cdot x\}$ and $\mathcal{A}_n$ is the set of all affine Boolean functions on V_n. The *directional derivative* of $f \in \mathcal{F}_n$ in the direction of $u \in V_n$ is defined by $\Delta_u f(x) = f(x + u) + f(x)$, $x \in V_n$. If the following equality is satisfied: $\Delta_u f(x) = c$, $c \in GF(2) \; \forall x \in V_n$ then $u \in V_n$ is called a linear structure of f.

The real-valued mapping $\chi_u(x) = (-1)^{\sum_{i=1}^{i=n} u_i x_i} = (-1)^{u \cdot x}$ for $x, u \in V_n$ is called a *character*. The character form of $f \in \mathcal{F}_n$ is defined as $\chi_f(x) = (-1)^{f(x)}$. The truth table of χ_f is called as the $(1, -1)$-*sequence vector* or *sequence vector* of f and is denoted by $\xi_f \in \mathbb{R}^{2^n}$. In other words: $\xi_f = T_{\varnothing_f} = ((-1)^{f(\alpha_0)}, (-1)^{f(\alpha_1)}, \ldots, (-1)^{f(\alpha_{2^n-1})})$.

Let two real functions $\varphi, \psi : V_n \rightarrow \mathbb{R}$, the *circular convolution* or *cross-correlation* $(\varphi * \psi)$: $V_n \rightarrow \mathbb{R}$ is defined by: $(\varphi * \psi)(x) = \sum_{u \in V_n} \varphi(u)\psi(x + u)$.

$F : V_n \rightarrow V_m$, $F(x) = (f_1(x), \ldots, f_m(x))$ is called a *Vector Boolean function* and $\mathcal{F}_{n,m}$ is the set of all Vector Boolean functions $F : V_n \rightarrow V_m$. Each $f_i : V_n \rightarrow GF(2) \; \forall i \in \{1, \ldots, m\}$ is a coordinate function of F. The *indicator function* of $F \in \mathcal{F}_{n,m}$, denoted by $\theta_F : V_n \times V_m \rightarrow \mathbb{R}$, is defined in Chabaud & Vaudenay (1994) as $\theta_F(x, y) = 1$ if $y = F(x)$ and $\theta_F(x, y) = 0$ if $y \neq F(x)$. The character form of $(u, v) \in V_n \times V_m$ can be defined as follows: $\chi_{(u,v)}(x, y) = (-1)^{u \cdot x + v \cdot y}$.

Let $F \in \mathcal{F}_{n,m}$ and $u \in V_n$, then the *difference Vector Boolean function* of F in the direction of $u \in V_n$, denoted by $\Delta_u F \in \mathcal{F}_{n,m}$ is defined as follows: $\Delta_u F(x) = F(x + u) + F(x)$, $x \in V_n$. If the following equality is satisfied: $\Delta_u F(x) = c$, $c \in V_n \; \forall x \in V_n$ then $u \in V_n$ is called a linear structure of F.

We define the simplifying notation for the maximum of the absolute values of a set of real numbers $\{a_{uv}\}_{u,v}$, characterized by vectors u and v, as: $\max (a_{uv}) = \max_{(u,v)} \{|a_{uv}|\}$.

Using the same simplifying notation, we define the $\overset{*}{\max} (\cdot)$ operator on a set of real numbers $\{a_{uv}\}_{u,v}$, as: $\overset{*}{\max} (a_{uv}) = \max_{(u,v) \neq (0,0)} \{|a_{uv}|\}$.

2.2 Constructions of Vector Boolean Functions

In this chapter, some secondary contructions are studied, which build (n, m) variable Vector Boolean Functions from (n', m') variable ones (with $n' \leq n, m' \leq m$). The direct sum construction has been used to construct resilient and bent Boolean functions Carlet (2004), Maitra & Pasalic (2002), Pasalic et al. (2001), Sarkar & Maitra (2000a), Sarkar & Maitra (2000b). Adding coordinate functions and bricklayering are operations used to build modern ciphers such as CAST Adams & Tavares (1993), DES Des (1977) and AES Daemen & Rijmen (2002).

2.2.1 Direct sum

Definition 1. *Let* $n = n_1 + n_2, n_1, n_2 \geq 1, m \geq 1, F_1 \in \mathcal{F}_{n_1,m}$ *and* $F_2 \in \mathcal{F}_{n_2,m}$. *The direct sum of* F_1 *and* F_2 *is the function:*

$$(F_1 \oplus F_2) : V_{n_1} \times V_{n_2} \to V_m$$
$$(\mathbf{x}, \mathbf{y}) \to (F_1 \oplus F_2)(\mathbf{x}, \mathbf{y}) = F_1(\mathbf{x}) + F_2(\mathbf{y}) \tag{1}$$

This is a generalization for Vector Boolean functions of the construction of Boolean functions first introduced in Rothaus (1976).

2.2.2 Adding coordinate functions

Definition 2. *Let* $n \geq 1, m = m_1 + m_2, m_1, m_2 \geq 1$ *and* $F \in \mathcal{F}_{n,m_1}$ *and* $G \in \mathcal{F}_{n,m_2}$. *The result of adding coordinate functions of F and G is the function:*

$$(F, G) : V_n \to V_{m_1} \times V_{m_2}$$
$$\mathbf{x} \to (F, G)(\mathbf{x}) = (f_1(\mathbf{x}), \dots, f_{m_1}(\mathbf{x}), g_1(\mathbf{x}), \dots, g_{m_2}(\mathbf{x})) \tag{2}$$

This is a generalization for Vector Boolean functions of the method used in the CAST algorithm and studied in Nyberg (1995) by adding more than one coordinate function at the same time.

2.2.3 Bricklayer

Definition 3. *Let* $n = n_1 + n_2, n_1, n_2 \geq 1, m = m_1 + m_2, m_1, m_2 \geq 1, F \in \mathcal{F}_{n_1,m_1}$ *and* $G \in \mathcal{F}_{n_2,m_2}$. *The Bricklayer of F and G is the function* $F|G \in \mathcal{F}_{n,m}$:

$$F|G : V_{n_1} \times V_{n_2} \to V_{m_1} \times V_{m_2}$$
$$(\mathbf{x}, \mathbf{y}) \to F|G(\mathbf{x}, \mathbf{y}) = (f_1(\mathbf{x}), \dots, f_{m_1}(\mathbf{x}), g_1(\mathbf{y}), \dots, g_{m_2}(\mathbf{y})) \tag{3}$$

This construction corresponds to the bricklayer function Daemen & Rijmen (2002) as a parallel application of a number of Vector Boolean functions operating on smaller inputs.

Another interesting operation is the restriction o projection of a Vector Boolean Function, which can be found in ciphers such as MacGuffin Blaze & Schneier (1995).

2.2.4 Projection

Definition 4. *Let* $F \in \mathcal{F}_{n,m}$ *and ordered set* $A = \{i_1, \dots, i_p\} \subseteq \{1, \dots, m\}$. *The result of projecting F onto A is the function:*

$$F|_A : V_n \to V_p$$
$$\mathbf{x} \to F|_A(\mathbf{x}) = (f_{i_1}(\mathbf{x}), \dots, f_{i_p}(\mathbf{x})) \tag{4}$$

2.3 Walsh spectrum, autocorrelation spectrum and differential profile

The Walsh and Autocorrelation Spectrum together with the Differential Profile of the Vector Boolean Functions conforming a cipher play an important role. The cryptograhic criteria nonlinearity, resiliency, balancedness, linearity distance and propagation criteria can be obtained from these three matrices.

Definition 5. *Let a Boolean function* $f \in \mathcal{F}_n$, *the Walsh Transform of* f *at* $\mathbf{u} \in V_n$ *is the n-dimensional Discrete Fourier Transform and can be calculated as follows:*

$$\mathcal{W}_f(\mathbf{u}) = \hat{\chi}_f(\mathbf{u}) = \left\langle \xi_f, \xi_{l_{\mathbf{u}}} \right\rangle = \sum_{\mathbf{x} \in V_n} \chi_f(\mathbf{x}) \chi_{\mathbf{u}}(\mathbf{x}) = \sum_{\mathbf{x} \in V_n} (-1)^{f(\mathbf{x})+\mathbf{u}\mathbf{x}} \tag{5}$$

The *Walsh Spectrum* of f can be represented by a matrix whose rows are characteristiced by $\mathbf{u} \in V_n$ in lexicographic order, denoted by $WS(f) \in M_{2^n \times 1}(\mathbb{R})$ and defined as $WS(f) = \left(\hat{\chi}_f(\mathbf{ff_0}) \cdots \hat{\chi}_f(\mathbf{u}) \cdots \hat{\chi}_f(\mathbf{ff_{2^n-1}}) \right)^T$ where $\hat{\chi}_f(\mathbf{u}) = WS(f)(\mathbf{u})$ and satisfying that $-2^n \leq \hat{\chi}_f(\mathbf{u}) \leq 2^n$.

The following fundamental result can be seen as an extension of the usual Fourier Transform properties:

Theorem 1. $\forall f, g \in \mathcal{F}_n$ *it holds that:*

$$\xi_f \cdot \xi_g \overset{W}{\longleftrightarrow} \frac{1}{2^n} WS(f) * WS(g) \tag{6}$$

Proof.

$$\mathcal{W}\{\xi_f \cdot \xi_g\}(\mathbf{u}) = \sum_{\mathbf{x} \in V_n} (\xi_f \cdot \xi_g)(\mathbf{x})\chi_{\mathbf{u}}(\mathbf{x}) = \sum_{\mathbf{x} \in V_n} \chi_f(\mathbf{x})\chi_g(\mathbf{x})\chi_{\mathbf{u}}(\mathbf{x})$$
$$= \sum_{\mathbf{x} \in V_n} \left(\frac{1}{2^n} \sum_{\mathbf{v} \in V_n} \hat{\chi}_f(\mathbf{v})\chi_{\mathbf{v}}(\mathbf{x}) \right) \chi_g(\mathbf{x})\chi_{\mathbf{u}}(\mathbf{x})$$
$$= \frac{1}{2^n} \sum_{\mathbf{v} \in V_n} \hat{\chi}_f(\mathbf{v}) \sum_{\mathbf{x} \in V_n} \chi_{\mathbf{v}}(\mathbf{x})\chi_g(\mathbf{x})\chi_{\mathbf{u}}(\mathbf{x})$$
$$= \frac{1}{2^n} \sum_{\mathbf{v} \in V_n} \hat{\chi}_f(\mathbf{v}) \sum_{\mathbf{x} \in V_n} \chi_g(\mathbf{x})\chi_{\mathbf{u}+\mathbf{v}}(\mathbf{x})$$
$$= \frac{1}{2^n} \sum_{\mathbf{v} \in V_n} \hat{\chi}_f(\mathbf{v})\hat{\chi}_g(\mathbf{u}+\mathbf{v}) = \frac{1}{2^n}(WS(f) * WS(g))(\mathbf{u})$$

$\square$

Theorem 2. *Let* $\mathbf{u} \in V_n, \mathbf{u_1} \in V_{n_1}, \mathbf{u_2} \in V_{n_2}, n = n_1 + n_2$ *so that* $\mathbf{u} = \mathbf{u_1} \oplus \mathbf{u_2}$. *Let* $f_1 \in \mathcal{F}_{n_1}$ *and* $f_2 \in \mathcal{F}_{n_2}$, *their direct sum* $f_1 \oplus f_2 \in \mathcal{F}_n$, *and it satisfies:* $\hat{\chi}_{f_1 \oplus f_2}(\mathbf{u}) = \hat{\chi}_{f_1}(\mathbf{u_1}) \cdot \hat{\chi}_{f_2}(\mathbf{u_2})$ *Sarkar & Maitra (2000a).*

Definition 6. *Let the Vector Boolean function* $F \in \mathcal{F}_{n,m}$, *its Walsh Transform is the two-dimensional Walsh Transform defined by:*

$$\mathcal{W}_F(\mathbf{u}, \mathbf{v}) = \hat{\theta}_F(\mathbf{u}, \mathbf{v}) = \sum_{\mathbf{x} \in V_n} \sum_{\mathbf{y} \in V_m} \theta_F(\mathbf{x}, \mathbf{y})\chi_{(\mathbf{u},\mathbf{v})}(\mathbf{x}, \mathbf{y}) = \sum_{\mathbf{x} \in V_n} (-1)^{\mathbf{u}\mathbf{x}+\mathbf{v}F(\mathbf{x})} \tag{7}$$

Corollary 1. *The value of the Walsh transform of Vector Boolean function* $F \in \mathcal{F}_{n,m}$ *at* $(\mathbf{u}, \mathbf{v})$ *coincides with the value of the Walsh transform of the Boolean function* $\mathbf{v} \cdot F$ *at* $\mathbf{u}$: $\hat{\theta}_F(\mathbf{u}, \mathbf{v}) = \hat{\chi}_{\mathbf{v}\cdot F}(\mathbf{u}) \; \forall (\mathbf{u}, \mathbf{v}) \in V_n \times V_m$.

The *Walsh Spectrum* of F can be represented by a matrix whose rows are characteristiced by $\mathbf{u} \in V_n$ and whose columns are characteristiced by $\mathbf{v} \in V_m$ in lexicographic order, denoted by $WS(F) \in M_{2^n \times 2^m}(\mathbb{R})$. It holds that $\hat{\theta}_F(\mathbf{u}, \mathbf{v}) = WS(F)(\mathbf{u}, \mathbf{v})$, $WS(F)_{\mathbf{u}}$ is the row of the Walsh Spectrum characteristiced by $\mathbf{u}$ and $WS(F)^{\mathbf{v}}$ is the column of the Walsh Sprectrum characteristiced by $\mathbf{v}$.

Theorem 3. *Let $L_{A,b} \in \mathcal{F}_{n,m}$ an affine Vector Boolean function where $L_{A,b}(x) = Ax + b$ with $A \in M_{n \times m}(GF(2))$ and $b \in V_m$, its spectrum holds that Pommerening (2005):*

$$\hat{\theta}_{L_{A,b}}(u, v) = \begin{cases} 2^n & \text{if } v^T A = u^T, \ v^T b = 0 \\ -2^n & \text{if } v^T A = u^T, \ v^T b = 1 \\ 0 & \text{if } v^T A \neq u^T \end{cases}$$

Theorem 4. *If $F \in \mathcal{F}_{n,n}$ is bijective then it holds that: $\hat{\theta}_F(u, v) = \hat{\theta}_{F^{-1}}(v, u)$.*

Definition 7. *The autocorrelation of $f \in \mathcal{F}_n$ with respect to the shift $u \in V_n$ is the cross-correlation of f with itself, denoted by $r_f(u) : V_n \to \mathbb{R}$ and defined by:*

$$r_f(u) = \frac{1}{2^n} \sum_{x \in V_n} \chi_f(x) \chi_f(x + u) = \frac{1}{2^n} \sum_{x \in V_n} (-1)^{f(x) + f(u+x)} \tag{8}$$

Definition 8. *The autocorrelation of $F \in \mathcal{F}_{n,m}$ with respect to the shift $(u, v) \in V_n \times V_m$ is the cross-correlation of F with itself, denoted by $r_F(u, v) : V_n \times V_m \to R$, so that Nyberg (1995):*

$$r_F(u, v) = \frac{1}{2^n} \sum_{x \in V_n} \chi_{vF}(x + u) \chi_{vF}(x) = \frac{1}{2^n} \sum_{x \in V_n} (-1)^{vF(x+u) + vF(x)} \tag{9}$$

Let $F \in \mathcal{F}_{n,m}$, if we denote by $D_F(u, v)$ the set of vectors where the difference Vector Boolean function of F in the direction of $u \in V_n$ coincides with $v \in V_m$ by: $D_F(u, v) = \{x \in V_n \mid \Delta_u F(x) = v\}$.

Let $F \in \mathcal{F}_{n,m}$ where $n \geq m$. The matrix containing all posible values of $\#D_F(u, v)$ is referred to as its *XOR* or *Differential Distribution Table*. Let $DU(F)$ be the largest value in differential distribution table of F (not counting the first element in the first row), namely,

$$DU(F) = \max_{(u,v) \neq (0,0)} \#D_F(u, v) = \max_{(u,v) \neq (0,0)} \#\{x \in V_n \mid \Delta_u F(x) = v\} \tag{10}$$

Then F is said to be differentially $DU(F)$-uniform, and accordingly, $DU(F)$ is called the *differential uniformity* of F J. Seberry & Zheng (1994). By normalizing the elements of the differential distribution table we obtain the Differential profile:

Definition 9. *Let the function $\delta_F : V_n \times V_m \to Q$ $\delta_F(u, v) = \frac{1}{2^n} \#D_F(u, v)$, then the Differential Profile of F can be represented by a matrix whose rows are characterized by $u \in V_n$ and whose columns are characterized by $v \in V_m$ in lexicographic order, denoted by $DP(F) \in M_{2^n \times 2^m}(\mathbb{R})$ where $\delta_F(ff_i, ff_j)$ with $i \in \{1, \ldots, 2^n - 1\}$ and $j \in \{1, \ldots, 2^m - 1\}$.*

Definition 10. *The maximum value of $\delta_F(u, v)$ is called the differential potential of F: $dp(F) = \max\{\delta_F(u, v) \mid \forall u \in V_n, v \in V_m, (u, v) \neq (0, 0)\}$.*

Let $F \in \mathcal{F}_{n,m}$ then $\frac{1}{2^m} \leq dp(F) \leq 1$ and the lower bound holds if and only if F is bent and the upper bound is reached when F is linear or affine. The differential uniformity of $F \in \mathcal{F}_{n,m}$ and its differential potential are related as follows: $dp(F) = \frac{1}{2^n} DU(F)$. The differential profile at (u, v) is related with the autocorrelation in the same point in the following way Nyberg (1995): $\delta_F(u, v) = \frac{1}{2^{n+m}} \sum_{w \in V_m} r_F(u, w) \chi_v(w)$.

3. Characteristics

The resistance of the cryptosystems to the known attacks can be quantified through some fundamental characteristics of the Vector Boolean functions used in them. In this chapter, we consider the characteristics most commonly employed for the design of cryptographic functions present in modern block and stream ciphers.

3.1 Nonlinearity

Definition 11. *The nonlinearity of the Boolean function $f \in \mathcal{F}_n$ is a characteristic defined as the distance to the nearest affine function as follows: $\mathcal{NL}(f) = \min_{a_u \in \mathcal{A}_n} d(f, a_u) = 2^{n-1} - \frac{1}{2}\max_{u \in V_n} |\hat{\chi}_f(u)|$ Meier & Staffelbach (1990).*

Definition 12. *The nonlinearity of a Vector Boolean function $F \in \mathcal{F}_{n,m}$ is defined as the minimum among the nonlinearities of all nonzero linear combinations of the coordinate functions of F Nyberg (1993):*

$$\mathcal{NL}(F) = \min_{\mathbf{v} \neq 0 \in V_m} \mathcal{NL}(\mathbf{v} \cdot F) = 2^{n-1} - \frac{1}{2} \overset{*}{\max}\left(\mathsf{WS}(F)(\mathbf{u}, \mathbf{v})\right) \tag{11}$$

Alternatively, and also associated with the cardinality of the sets of values for which $F \in \mathcal{F}_{n,m}$ satisfies any given linear relation parametrized by $(\mathbf{u}, \mathbf{v})$ we can define the *linear potential* of $F \in \mathcal{F}_{n,m}$ as $lp(F) = \frac{1}{2^{2n}} \cdot \overset{*}{\max}\left(\mathsf{WS}(F)(\mathbf{u}, \mathbf{v})^2\right)$ which is also exploited as a measure of linearity in linear cryptanalysis, and satisfies Chabaud & Vaudenay (1994) $\frac{1}{2^n} \leq lp(F) \leq 1$ so that the lower bound holds if and only if F has maximum nonlinearity (F is bent) and the upper bound is reached when F is linear or affine.

3.2 Linearity distance

Definition 13. *The linearity distance of the Vector Boolean function $F \in \mathcal{F}_{n,m}$ is defined as the minimum among the linearity distances of all nonzero linear combinations of the coordinate functions of F:*

$$\mathcal{LD}(F) = \min_{\mathbf{v} \neq 0 \in V_m} \mathcal{LD}(\mathbf{v} \cdot F) = 2^{n-1} \cdot \min_{\mathbf{u} \neq 0 \in V_n, \mathbf{v} \neq 0 \in V_m} \{\delta_F(\mathbf{u}, \mathbf{v})\} \tag{12}$$

Definition 14. *The linearity distance can be expressed in terms of the differential potential as follows:*
$\mathcal{LD}(F) = 2^{n-1} \cdot (1 - dp(F)) = 2^{n-1} \cdot \left(1 - \overset{*}{\max}\left(\mathsf{DP}(F)\right)\right)$ *Pommerening (2005).*

3.3 Balancedness

Definition 15. *$f \in \mathcal{F}_n$ is balanced if its output is uniformly distributed over $\mathrm{GF}(2)$ satisfying $\hat{\chi}_f(0) = 0$.*

Definition 16. *$F \in \mathcal{F}_{n,m}$ is balanced (or to have balanced output) if each possible output m-tuple occurs with equal probability $\frac{1}{2^m}$, that is, its output is uniformly distributed in V_m. This is equivalent to say that for every $\mathbf{y} \in V_m$:*

$$\#\{\mathbf{x} \in V_n \mid F(\mathbf{x}) = \mathbf{y}\} = 2^{n-m} \longleftrightarrow \hat{\theta}_F(\mathbf{0}, \mathbf{v}) = 0, \, \forall \mathbf{v} \neq \mathbf{0} \in V_m \tag{13}$$

3.4 Correlation immunity

Definition 17. $f \in \mathcal{F}_n$ *is called correlation-immune of order* t *(t-CI) if for every subset* $\{i_1, i_2, \ldots, i_t\} \subseteq \{1, 2, \ldots, n\}$, f *is statistically independent of* $(x_{i_1}, x_{i_2}, \ldots, x_{i_t})$, *satisfying Xiao & Massey (1988):* $\hat{\chi}_f(\mathbf{u}) = 0$, $\forall \mathbf{u} \in V_n$, $1 \leq wt(\mathbf{u}) \leq t$. f *can also be denoted as* $(n, 1, t)$*-CI function.*

Definition 18. $F \in \mathcal{F}_{n,m}$ *is an* (n, m, t)*-CI function if and only if every nonzero linear combination* $f(\mathbf{x}) = \sum_{i=1}^{m} v_i f_i(\mathbf{x})$ *of coordinate functions of* F *is an* $(n, 1, t)$*-CI function, where* $\mathbf{x} \in V_n$, $v_i \in GF(2)$ $i = 1, \ldots, m$ *and not all zeroes. This is equivalent to say Chen et al. (2004):*

$$\hat{\theta}_F(\mathbf{u}, \mathbf{v}) = 0, \ \forall \mathbf{u} \in V_n, \ 1 \leq wt(\mathbf{u}) \leq t, \ \forall \mathbf{v} \neq \mathbf{0} \in V_m \tag{14}$$

3.5 Resiliency

Definition 19. $f \in \mathcal{F}_n$ *is a t-resilient function if if it is balanced and t-CI, satisfying:* $\hat{\chi}_f(\mathbf{u}) = 0$, $\forall \mathbf{u} \in V_n$, $0 \leq wt(\mathbf{u}) \leq t$. *A balanced Boolean function* f *can be considered as a 0-resilient function.*

Definition 20. $F \in \mathcal{F}_{n,m}$ *is said to be t-resilient if it is balanced and t-CI, satisfying:*

$$\hat{\theta}_F(\mathbf{u}, \mathbf{v}) = 0, \ \forall \mathbf{u} \in V_n, \ 0 \leq wt(\mathbf{u}) \leq t, \ \forall \mathbf{v} \neq \mathbf{0} \in V_m \tag{15}$$

F *can also be denoted as an* (n, m, t)*-resilient. A balanced Vector Boolean function* F *can be considered as a 0-resilient function.*

3.6 Propagation

Definition 21. *Let* $f \in \mathcal{F}_n$, *then* f *satisfies the propagation criterion of degree* l, $PC(l)(1 \leq l \leq n)$, *if* $f(\mathbf{x})$ *changes with a probability of* $1/2$ *whenever* $i(1 \leq i \leq t)$ *bits of* $\mathbf{x}$ *are complemented Preneel et al. (2006).*

Definition 22. $F \in \mathcal{F}_{n,m}$ *satisfies the* $PC(l)$ *if any nonzero linear combination of the component boolean functions satisfies the* $PC(l)$:

$$r_F(\mathbf{u}, \mathbf{v}) = 0, \ \forall \mathbf{u} \in V_n, \ 1 \leq wt(\mathbf{u}) \leq l, \ \forall \mathbf{v} \neq \mathbf{0} \in V_m \tag{16}$$

4. Criteria for constructions with Vector Boolean functions

In this Section, we address the behavior of Walsh Spectra, Differential Profiles, Autocorrelation Spectra and the cited characteristics under several operations of Vector Boolean functions. We present the known properties without a proof and the new to the best of our knowledge results appear with their respective proofs.

4.1 Composition of Vector Boolean functions

Let $F \in \mathcal{F}_{n,p}$, $G \in \mathcal{F}_{p,m}$ and the composition function $G \circ F \in \mathcal{F}_{n,m}$.

Theorem 5. *The Walsh Spectrum for the composition of two Vector Boolean function can be calculated from the product of their respective Walsh Spectra in the following way Pommerening (2005):*

$$WS(G \circ F) = \frac{1}{2^p} WS(F) \cdot WS(G) \tag{17}$$

Theorem 6. *Let $F \in \mathcal{F}_{n,m}$ and let $L_{A,b} \in \mathcal{F}_{n,n}$ an affine bijection. The Differential Profile for their composition can be calculated from the product of their respective Differential Profiles in the following way:*

$$DP(F \circ L_{A,b}) = \frac{1}{2^n} DP(L_{A,b}) \cdot DP(F) \tag{18}$$

Proof. Taking into account the equality $r_{F \circ L_{A,b}}(\mathbf{u}, \mathbf{v}) = r_F(A\mathbf{u}, \mathbf{v})$ described in Millan (1998), it holds that:

$$\delta_{F \circ L_{A,b}}(\mathbf{u}, \mathbf{w}) = \frac{1}{2^{n+m}} \sum_{\mathbf{w} \in V_m} r_{F \circ L_{A,b}}(\mathbf{u}, \mathbf{w}) \chi_{\mathbf{v}}(\mathbf{w})$$
$$= \frac{1}{2^{n+m}} \sum_{\mathbf{w} \in V_m} r_F(A\mathbf{u}, \mathbf{w}) \chi_{\mathbf{v}}(\mathbf{w}) = \delta_F(A\mathbf{u}, \mathbf{w})$$

$\square$

Theorem 7. *If F is a t-resilient function and G is balanced, then $G \circ F$ is also a t-resilient function.*

Corollary 2. *If F is a balanced function, then $G \circ F$ is also a balanced function.*

4.2 Affine bijections of Vector Boolean functions

Let $F \in \mathcal{F}_{n,m}$ and let $L_{A,b} \in \mathcal{F}_{m,m}$ and $L_{C,d} \in \mathcal{F}_{n,n}$ be linear (or affine) bijections.

Lemma 1. *From Theorem 5 and Theorem 3 we can conclude that the effect of applying an invertible linear function before (or after) a function is only a permutation of its columns (or rows). In case it is an affine bijection, the sign of all the elements of some of its columns (or rows) are changed.*

Corollary 3. *As a corollary of Lemma 1, we get the following:*

$$\overset{*}{\max} \left(WS(L_{A,b} \circ F \circ L_{C,d}) \right) = \overset{*}{\max} \left(WS(F) \right)$$
$$\overset{*}{\max} \left(DP(L_{A,b} \circ F \circ L_{C,d}) \right) = \overset{*}{\max} \left(DP(F) \right)$$

Corollary 4. *The nonlinearity and the linearity distance are invariant under linear (or affine) bijections of the input space and of the output space, so that Nyberg (1995):*

$$\mathcal{NL}(L_{A,b} \circ F \circ L_{C,d}) = \mathcal{NL}(F) \quad \mathcal{LD}(L_{A,b} \circ F \circ L_{C,d}) = \mathcal{LD}(F)$$

Here we give alternative proofs as those given by Nyberg in Nyberg (1995) by using corollary 3:

Proof.

$$\mathcal{NL}(L_{A,b} \circ F \circ L_{C,d}) = 2^{n-1} - \frac{1}{2} \overset{*}{\max} \left(WS(L_{A,b} \circ F \circ L_{C,d}) \right)$$
$$= 2^{n-1} - \frac{1}{2} \overset{*}{\max} \left(WS(F) \right) = \mathcal{NL}(F)$$

$$\mathcal{LD}(L_{A,b} \circ F \circ L_{C,d}) = 2^{n-1} \cdot \left(1 - \overset{*}{\max} \left(DP(L_{A,b} \circ F \circ L_{C,d}) \right) \right)$$
$$= 2^{n-1} \cdot \left(1 - \overset{*}{\max} \left(DP(F) \right) \right) = \mathcal{LD}(F)$$

$\square$

Theorem 8. *Let $F \in \mathcal{F}_{n,m}$ and let $L_{A,b} \in \mathcal{F}_{n,n}$ an affine bijection, then $F \circ L_{A,b}$ satisfies the $PC(l)$ if and only if F satisfies the $PC(l)$.*

Proof. If we use the equality $r_{F \circ L_{A,b}}(\mathbf{u}, \mathbf{v}) = r_F(A\mathbf{u}, \mathbf{v})$ described in Millan (1998), we can obtain the following:

$$F \circ L_{A,b} \text{ satisfies the } PC(l)$$
$$\longleftrightarrow r_{F \circ L_{A,b}} = 0, \, \forall \mathbf{u} \in V_n, \, 1 \le wt(\mathbf{u}) \le l, \, \forall \mathbf{v} \in V_m$$
$$\longleftrightarrow r_F(A\mathbf{u}, \mathbf{v}) = 0, \, \forall \mathbf{u} \in V_n, \, 1 \le wt(\mathbf{u}) \le l, \, \forall \mathbf{v} \in V_m$$
$$\longleftrightarrow r_F(\mathbf{u}, \mathbf{v}) = 0, \, \forall \mathbf{u} \in V_n, \, 1 \le wt(\mathbf{u}) \le l, \, \forall \mathbf{v} \in V_m$$

$\square$

4.3 Adding coordinate functions

Let $F = (f_1, \ldots, f_{m_1}) \in \mathcal{F}_{n,m_1}$, $G = (g_1, \ldots, g_{m_2}) \in \mathcal{F}_{n,m_2}$ and the function conformed by adding the coordinate functions $(F, G) = (f_1, \ldots, f_{m_1}, g_1, \ldots, g_{m_2}) \in \mathcal{F}_{n,m_1+m_2}$. Let $\mathbf{v} \in V_{m_1+m_2}, \mathbf{v_F} \in V_{m_1}$ and $\mathbf{v_G} \in V_{m_2}$ so that $\mathbf{v} = \mathbf{v_F} \oplus \mathbf{v_G}$.

Theorem 9. *The columns of the Walsh Spectrum of the Vector Boolean function constructed by adding the coordinate functions of two Vector Boolean functions are calculated by the correlation of their respective columns in the following way:*

$$\mathsf{WS}((F,G))^{\mathbf{v}} = \frac{1}{2^n} \mathsf{WS}(F)^{\mathbf{v_F}} * \mathsf{WS}(G)^{\mathbf{v_G}}$$

where $\mathsf{WS}((F,G))^{\mathbf{v}}$ is the column of the Walsh Spectrum characteristiced by $\mathbf{v}$.

Proof.

$$\hat{\theta}_{(F,G)}(\mathbf{u}, \mathbf{v}) = \hat{\chi}_{\mathbf{v_F} \oplus \mathbf{v_G} \cdot (F,G)}(\mathbf{u}) = \mathcal{W}\{\xi_{\mathbf{v_F} \cdot F} \cdot \tilde{\xi}_{\mathbf{v_G} \cdot G}\}(\mathbf{u})$$
$$= \tfrac{1}{2^n} \textstyle\sum_{\mathbf{x} \in V_n} \hat{\chi}_{\mathbf{v_F} \cdot F}(\mathbf{u} + \mathbf{x}) \hat{\chi}_{\mathbf{v_G} \cdot G}(\mathbf{x})$$

$\square$

Corollary 5. *The exact value of the nonlinearity of (F, G) cannot be easily obtained from the knowledge of the nonlinearities of F and G.*

Corollary 6. *The columns of both $\mathsf{WS}(F)$ and $\mathsf{WS}(G)$ are contained in the matrix $\mathsf{WS}((F,G))$.*

Corollary 7. *From corollary 6 it can be deduced that:*

$$\mathcal{NL}((F,G)) \le \min\{\mathcal{NL}(F), \mathcal{NL}(G)\} \tag{19}$$

The corollary 7 is a generalization of the Theorem 16 in Nyberg (1995). It can be useful, for instance, to find upper bounds of nonlinearity in S-boxes whose number of output bits is high by calculating the nonlinearities of shorter S-boxes (see Example 2).

Example 1. *The F-function of the MacGuffin block cipher algorithm consists of the 8 S-boxes of the DES, but the two middle output bits of each S-box are neglected so that $S_i(MacG) \in \mathcal{F}_{6,2}$. Let define the 4-th S-box of DES as $S_4(DES) - (f_1, f_2, f_3, f_4)$, then it holds that $S_4(MacG) = (f_1, f_4)$. If we denote MacDES the S-box which uses the second and third component functions of DES, then $S_4(MacDES) = (f_2, f_3)$. The S-box $S_4(DES)$ can be obtained by adding the coordinate functions which constitute MacDES and aplying a permutation to reorder the coordinate functions. If we want to obtain the last column of the Walsh Spectrum of $S_4(DES)$ from the last columns of the Walsh Spectra of $S_4(MacG)$ and $S_4(MacDES)$, then the effect of the permutation can be omitted and the results are the following:*

$$\mathsf{WS}\left(S_4(DES)\right)^{(1111)} = \tfrac{1}{2^6}\mathsf{WS}\left(S_4(MacG)\right)^{(11)} * \mathsf{WS}\left(S_4(MacDES)\right)^{(11)} \tag{20}$$

Example 2. *The first substitution function of the CAST algorithm Adams & Tavares (1993) , Adams (1994) denoted by $S_1 \in \mathcal{F}_{8,32}$ has a nonlinearity of 74 Youssef et al. (1997). If we decompose this Vector Boolean function into two, taking the first 16 output bits ($S_{1a} \in \mathcal{F}_{8,16}$) and the second 16 output bits ($S_{1b} \in \mathcal{F}_{8,16}$) respectively, we can see that the corollary 7 is satisfied:*

$$74 = \mathcal{NL}(S_1) \leq \min\{\mathcal{NL}(S_{1a}), \mathcal{NL}(S_{1b})\} = \min\{86, 82\} \tag{21}$$

Theorem 10. *If $F, G \in \mathcal{F}_{n,n}$ are bijective, F^{-1} is a t_1-resilient function and G^{-1} is a t_2-resilient function, then the inverse of the Vector Boolean function obtained by adding the coordinates functions of F and G, denoted by $(F, G)^{-1} \in \mathcal{F}_{2n,n}$ is a $2 \cdot \min\{t_1, t_2\}$-resilient function.*

Proof.

$$F^{-1} \text{ is a } t_1\text{-resilient function} \wedge G^{-1} \text{ is a } t_2\text{-resilient function}$$
$$\leftrightarrow \hat{\theta}_F(\mathbf{v}, \mathbf{u_F}) = 0, \ \forall \mathbf{v} \neq \mathbf{0} \in V_n, \ \forall \mathbf{u_F} \in V_n, \ 0 \leq wt(\mathbf{u_F}) \leq t_1$$
$$\wedge \hat{\theta}_G(\mathbf{v}, \mathbf{u_G}) = 0, \ \forall \mathbf{v} \neq \mathbf{0} \in V_n, \ \forall \mathbf{u_G} \in V_n, \ 0 \leq wt(\mathbf{u_G}) \leq t_2$$
$$\leftrightarrow \hat{\theta}_{(F,G)^{-1}}(\mathbf{u}, \mathbf{v}) = 0 \ \forall \mathbf{u} \in V_{2n}, \ 0 \leq wt(\mathbf{u}) \leq 2 \cdot \min\{t_1, t_2\}, \ \forall \mathbf{v} \neq \mathbf{0} \in V_n$$

where $\mathbf{u} = \mathbf{u_F} \oplus \mathbf{u_G}$ □

Corollary 8. *If $F, G \in \mathcal{F}_{n,n}$ are bijective, F^{-1} is a balanced Vector Boolean function and G^{-1} is a balanced Vector Boolean function, then the inverse of the Vector Boolean function resulting of adding the coordinates functions of F and G, denoted by $(F, G)^{-1}$ is a balanced Vector Boolean function.*

Theorem 11. *The autocorrelation of the Vector Boolean function resulting by adding the coordinate functions of two Vector Boolean functions can be expressed in terms of their respective directional derivatives as follows:*

$$r_{(F,G)}(\mathbf{u}, \mathbf{v}) = \tfrac{1}{2^n} \sum_{\mathbf{x} \in V_n} (-1)^{\Delta_\mathbf{u} \mathbf{v_F} F(\mathbf{x})} \cdot (-1)^{\Delta_\mathbf{u} \mathbf{v_G} G(\mathbf{x})}$$

Proof.

$$r_{(F,G)}(\mathbf{u}, \mathbf{v}) = \tfrac{1}{2^n} \sum_{\mathbf{x} \in V_n} (-1)^{\mathbf{v_F} \oplus \mathbf{v_G}(F,G)(\mathbf{x}+\mathbf{u}) + \mathbf{v_F} \oplus \mathbf{v_G}(F,G)(\mathbf{x})}$$
$$= \tfrac{1}{2^n} \sum_{\mathbf{x} \in V_n} (-1)^{\mathbf{v_F} F(\mathbf{x}+\mathbf{u}) \oplus \mathbf{v_G} G(\mathbf{x}+\mathbf{u}) + \mathbf{v_F} F(\mathbf{x}) \oplus \mathbf{v_G} G(\mathbf{x})}$$
$$= \tfrac{1}{2^n} \sum_{\mathbf{x} \in V_n} (-1)^{\mathbf{v_F} F(\mathbf{x}+\mathbf{u}) + \mathbf{v_F} F(\mathbf{x})} \cdot (-1)^{\mathbf{v_G} G(\mathbf{x}+\mathbf{u}) + \mathbf{v_G} G(\mathbf{x})}$$

□

Corollary 9. *If* **u** *is a linear structure of G, then the autocorrelation of* (F, G) *is proportional to the autocorrelation of F:*

$$r_{(F,G)}(\mathbf{u}, \mathbf{v}) = (-1)^{c_{\mathbf{v}_G}G} \cdot r_F(\mathbf{u}, \mathbf{v_F})$$

where $\Delta_{\mathbf{u}}\mathbf{v}_G G(\mathbf{x}) = c_{\mathbf{v}_G G} \ \forall \mathbf{x} \in V_n, \forall \mathbf{v_G} \in V_{m_2}$.

Corollary 10. *Let* $F \in \mathcal{F}_{n,m_1}$ *satisfy the* $PC(l)$ *and let all the vectors in* V_n *with weight at most* l *be linear structures of* $G \in \mathcal{F}_{n,m_2}$, *then* $(F, G) \in \mathcal{F}_{n,m_1+m_2}$ *satisfies* $PC(l)$.

Proof. By applying corollary 10:

$$r_F(\mathbf{u}, \mathbf{v_F}) = 0, \ \forall \mathbf{u} \in V_n, \ 1 \le wt(\mathbf{u}) \le l, \ \forall \mathbf{v_F} \neq \mathbf{0} \in V_{m_1}$$

$$r_{(F,G)}(\mathbf{u}, \mathbf{v}) = 0, \ \forall \mathbf{u} \in V_n, \ 1 \le wt(\mathbf{u}) \le l, \ \forall \mathbf{v} \neq \mathbf{0} \in V_m$$

$\square$

Corollary 11. *If we add coordinates of a Vector Boolean function which satisfies the* $PC(l)$ *and a Linear (or Affine) Vector Boolean function then the resulting Vector Boolean function satisfies the* $PC(l)$.

Corollary 12. *If* **u** *is a linear structure of G, then the coefficients of the Differential Profile of* (F, G) *is proportional to the coefficients of the Differential Profile of F:*

$$\delta_{(F,G)}(\mathbf{u}, \mathbf{v}) = (-1)^{c_{\mathbf{v}_G}G} \cdot \delta_F(\mathbf{u}, \mathbf{v_F})$$

Proof.

$$\delta_{(F,G)}(\mathbf{u}, \mathbf{v}) = \frac{1}{2^{n+m}} \sum_{\mathbf{w} \in V_m} r_{(F,G)}(\mathbf{u}, \mathbf{w}) \chi_{\mathbf{v}}(\mathbf{w})$$

$$= \frac{1}{2^{n+m_1+m_2}} \sum_{\mathbf{w_F} \in V_{m_1}} \sum_{\mathbf{w_G} \in V_{m_2}} (-1)^{c_{\mathbf{v}_G}G} r_F(\mathbf{u}, \mathbf{w_F}) \chi_{\mathbf{v_F}}(\mathbf{w_F}) \chi_{\mathbf{v_G}}(\mathbf{w_G})$$

$$= \frac{(-1)^{c_{\mathbf{v}_G}G}}{2^{n+m_1+m_2}} \sum_{\mathbf{w_G} \in V_{m_2}} \chi_{\mathbf{v_G}}(\mathbf{w_G}) \sum_{\mathbf{w_F} \in V_{m_1}} r_F(\mathbf{u}, \mathbf{w_F}) \chi_{\mathbf{v_F}}(\mathbf{w_F})$$

$$= \frac{(-1)^{c_{\mathbf{v}_G}G}}{2^{n+m_1}} \sum_{\mathbf{w_F} \in V_{m_1}} r_F(\mathbf{u}, \mathbf{w_F}) \chi_{\mathbf{v_F}}(\mathbf{w_F})$$

$\square$

4.4 Projection of a Vector Boolean function

Let $F = (f_1, \ldots, f_m) \in \mathcal{F}_{n,m}$, $A = \{i_1, \ldots, i_{m_1}\} \subseteq \{1, \ldots, m\}$, $B = \{j_1, \ldots, j_{m_2}\} \subseteq \{1, \ldots, m\}$, $A \cap B = \varnothing$ so that $m = m_1 + m_2$ then $F|_A = (f_{i_1}, \ldots, f_{i_{m_1}}) \in \mathcal{F}_{n,m_1}$ and $F|_B = (f_{j_1}, \ldots, f_{j_{m_2}}) \in \mathcal{F}_{n,m_2}$.

Corollary 13. *By Theorem 9, it can be demonstrated that the Walsh spectrum of the projection* $F|_A$ *is obtained by extracting the columns of* $WS(F)$ *characteristiced by* $\mathbf{v} = (v_1, \ldots, v_m)$ *so that if* $i \in A$ *then* $v_i = 1$ *and if* $i \notin A$ *then* $v_i = 0$.

Theorem 12. *The set of vectors where the difference Vector Boolean function of F in the direction of* $\mathbf{u} \in V_n$ *coincides with* $\mathbf{v} \in V_m$ *is a subset of the respective set of vectors of* $F|_A$.

Proof. Let $\mathbf{v} = \mathbf{v}|_A \oplus \mathbf{v}|_B$:

$$D_F(\mathbf{u}, \mathbf{v}) = \{\mathbf{x} \in V_n \mid F(\mathbf{x} + \mathbf{u}) + F(\mathbf{x}) = \mathbf{v}\} = \{\mathbf{x} \in V_n \mid F|_A(\mathbf{x} + \mathbf{u}) + F|_A(\mathbf{x}) = \mathbf{v}|_A\}$$
$$\cap \{\mathbf{x} \in V_n \mid F|_B(\mathbf{x} + \mathbf{u}) + F|_B(\mathbf{x}) = \mathbf{v}|_B\} \subseteq D_{F|_A}(\mathbf{u}, \mathbf{v})$$

$\square$

Corollary 14. $\overset{*}{\max}(\text{WS}(F|_A)) \leq \overset{*}{\max}(\text{WS}(F))$, $\overset{*}{\max}(\text{DP}(F|_A)) \geq \overset{*}{\max}(\text{DP}(F))$.

Corollary 15. $\mathcal{NL}(F|_A) \geq \mathcal{NL}(F)$, $\mathcal{LD}(F|_A) \leq \mathcal{LD}(F)$.

Example 3. *The F-function of the DES block cipher algorithm consists of 8 S-boxes $S_i(DES) \in \mathcal{F}_{6,4}$ whose respective nonlinearities and linearity distances are the following:*

i	1	2	3	4	5	6	7	8
$\mathcal{NL}(S_i(DES))$	14	16	16	16	16	18	14	16
$\overset{*}{\max}(\text{WS}(S_i(DES)))$	36	32	32	32	32	28	36	32

$$\mathcal{LD}(S_i(DES)) = 24, dp(S_i(DES)) = \tfrac{1}{4} \, \forall i = 1, \ldots, 8$$

MacGuffin's S-boxes result from restriction of DES S-Boxes, and its characteristics satisfy Corollary 15:

i	1	2	3	4	5	6	7	8
$\mathcal{NL}(S_i(MG))$	18	18	18	16	20	20	18	20
$\overset{*}{\max}(\text{WS}(S_i(MG)))$	28	28	28	32	24	24	28	24

and

$$\mathcal{LD}(S_1(MG)) = 15, \quad dp(S_1(MG)) = 0.53125$$
$$\mathcal{LD}(S_2(MG)) = 14, \quad dp(S_2(MG)) = 0.5625$$
$$\mathcal{LD}(S_3(MG)) = 15, \quad dp(S_3(MC)) = 0.53125$$
$$\mathcal{LD}(S_4(MG)) = 16, \quad dp(S_4(MG)) = 0.5$$
$$\mathcal{LD}(S_5(MG)) = 16, \quad dp(S_5(MG)) = 0.5$$
$$\mathcal{LD}(S_6(MG)) = 18, \quad dp(S_6(MG)) = 0.4375$$
$$\mathcal{LD}(S_7(MG)) = 15, \quad dp(S_7(MG)) = 0.53125$$
$$\mathcal{LD}(S_8(MG)) = 16, \quad dp(S_8(MG)) = 0.5$$

Corollary 16. *By Theorem 9, it can be demonstrated that if F is t-resilient, then $F|_A$ is at least t-resilient.*

4.5 Direct sum of Vector Boolean functions

Let $n_1, n_2 \geq 1$, $F_1 \in \mathcal{F}_{n_1,m}$, $F_2 \in \mathcal{F}_{n_2,m}$ and their direct sum $F_1 \oplus F_2 \in \mathcal{F}_{n_1+n_2,m}$. Let $\mathbf{u_1} \in V_{n_1}$, $\mathbf{u_2} \in V_{n_2}$, $\mathbf{v} \in V_m$ and $\mathbf{u} = \mathbf{u_1} \oplus \mathbf{u_2}$.

Theorem 13. *The elements which conform a row in the Walsh Spectrum of the direct sum of two Vector Boolean functions are equal to the product of the respective components of the rows in both Walsh Spectra. The rows of the Differential Profile of the direct sum of two Vector Boolean functions are obtained by the correlation of the rows of the Differential Profiles of each Vector Boolean function.*

$$\hat{\theta}_{F_1 \oplus F_2}(\mathbf{u}, \mathbf{v}) = \hat{\theta}_{F_1}(\mathbf{u_1}, \mathbf{v}) \cdot \hat{\theta}_{F_2}(\mathbf{u_2}, \mathbf{v})$$
$$\text{DP}(F_1 \oplus F_2)_{\mathbf{u}} = \frac{1}{2^m} \text{DP}(F_1)_{\mathbf{u_1}} * \text{DP}(F_2)_{\mathbf{u_2}}$$

The first result was already known for Boolean functions Sarkar & Maitra (2000a), here we give a proof for Vector Boolean functions.

Proof.

$$\hat{\theta}_{F_1 \oplus F_2}(\mathbf{u}, \mathbf{v}) = \hat{\chi}_{\mathbf{v}\cdot(F_1 \oplus F_2)}(\mathbf{u}_1 \oplus \mathbf{u}_2) = \hat{\chi}_{\mathbf{v}\cdot F_1 \oplus \mathbf{v}\cdot F_2}(\mathbf{u}_1 \oplus \mathbf{u}_2) = \hat{\chi}_{\mathbf{v}\cdot F_1}(\mathbf{u}_1) \cdot \hat{\chi}_{\mathbf{v}\cdot F_2}(\mathbf{u}_2)$$

□

The second result is new and the proof is given below:

Proof.

$$(DP(F_1)_{\mathbf{u}_1} * DP(F_2)_{\mathbf{u}_2})(\mathbf{v}) = \sum_{\mathbf{w}\in V_m} \delta_{F_1}(\mathbf{u}_1, \mathbf{w}+\mathbf{v}) \cdot \delta_{F_2}(\mathbf{u}_2, \mathbf{w})$$

$$= \sum_{\mathbf{w}\in V_m} \frac{1}{2^{n_1+m}} \sum_{\mathbf{s}\in V_m} r_{F_1}(\mathbf{u}_1, \mathbf{s}) \chi_{\mathbf{w}+\mathbf{v}}(\mathbf{s}) \frac{1}{2^{n_2+m}} \sum_{\mathbf{t}\in V_m} r_{F_2}(\mathbf{u}_2, \mathbf{t}) \chi_{\mathbf{w}}(\mathbf{t})$$

$$= \frac{1}{2^{n_1+n_2+2m}} \sum_{\mathbf{z}\in V_m} r_{F_1}(\mathbf{u}_1, \mathbf{z}) r_{F_2}(\mathbf{u}_2, \mathbf{z}) \chi_{\mathbf{v}}(\mathbf{z})$$

$$= \frac{1}{2^{n+2m}} \sum_{\mathbf{z}\in V_m} r_{F_1 \oplus F_2}(\mathbf{u}, \mathbf{z}) \chi_{\mathbf{v}}(\mathbf{z}) = \frac{1}{2^m} DP(F_1 \oplus F_2)_{\mathbf{u}}(\mathbf{v})$$

□

Corollary 17.

$$\overset{*}{\max}(WS(F_1 \oplus F_2)) = \max_{\mathbf{v}\in V_m}\{\overset{*}{\max}(WS(\mathbf{v}\cdot F_1))\cdot \overset{*}{\max}(WS(\mathbf{v}\cdot F_2))\} \qquad (22)$$

Corollary 18.

$$\mathcal{NL}(F_1 \oplus F_2) = 2^{n_1+n_2-1} - \tfrac{1}{2}\max_{\mathbf{v}\in V_m}\{(2^{n_1} - 2\mathcal{NL}(\mathbf{v}\cdot F_1))(2^{n_2} - 2\mathcal{NL}(\mathbf{v}\cdot F_2))\}$$

Proof.

$$\mathcal{NL}(F_1 \oplus F_2) = 2^{n-1} - \tfrac{1}{2}\overset{*}{\max}(\hat{\theta}_{F_1 \oplus F_2}(\mathbf{u}, \mathbf{v}))$$

$$= 2^{n-1} - \tfrac{1}{2}\max_{\mathbf{v}\in V_m}\{\overset{*}{\max}(\hat{\theta}_{F_1}(\mathbf{u}_1, \mathbf{v}))\cdot \overset{*}{\max}(\hat{\theta}_{F_2}(\mathbf{u}_2, \mathbf{v}))\}$$

$$= 2^{n_1+n_2-1} - \tfrac{1}{2}\max_{\mathbf{v}\in V_m}\{(2^{n_1} - 2\mathcal{NL}(\mathbf{v}\cdot F_1))(2^{n_2} - 2\mathcal{NL}(\mathbf{v}\cdot F_2))\}$$

□

This result is a generalization of what is obtained for Boolean functions. Let $f \in \mathcal{F}_{n_1}, g \in \mathcal{F}_{n_2}$ then $f \oplus g \in \mathcal{F}_{n_1+n_2}$ holds that:

$$\mathcal{NL}(f \oplus g) = 2^{n_1+n_2-1} - \tfrac{1}{2}(2^{n_1} - 2\mathcal{NL}(f))(2^{n_2} - 2\mathcal{NL}(g))$$

Corollary 19. *Let* $F_1 \oplus \cdots \oplus F_i \in \mathcal{F}_{n_i,m}$

$$\mathcal{NL}(F_1 \oplus \cdots \oplus F_i) =$$
$$= 2^{n-1} - \tfrac{1}{2}\max_{\mathbf{v}\in V_m}\{\overset{*}{\max}(WS(\mathbf{v}\cdot F_1))\cdots \overset{*}{\max}(WS(\mathbf{v}\cdot F_i))\} \qquad (23)$$

Example 4. *The full substitution function of the CAST algorithm* $S(CAST) \in \mathcal{F}_{32,32}$ *is constructed by forming the direct sum of* 4 *S-boxes* $S_i(CAST) \in \mathcal{F}_{8,32}$ *satisfying:*

$$\max_{\mathbf{v} \in V_{32}} \{ \overset{*}{\max} \, (\text{WS} \, (\mathbf{v} \cdot S_1(CAST))) \cdot \overset{*}{\max} \, (\text{WS} \, (\mathbf{v} \cdot S_2(CAST))) \cdot \\ \overset{*}{\max} \, (\text{WS} \, (\mathbf{v} \cdot S_3(CAST))) \cdot \overset{*}{\max} \, (\text{WS} \, (\mathbf{v} \cdot S_4(CAST))) \} = 29417472 \tag{24}$$

For the exact calculation of the $S(CAST)$ *nonlinearity we need to find out the maximum value from all the elements of a* $2^{32} \times 2^{32}$ *matrix representing its Walsh Spectrum, or alternatively, to determine the Walsh Spectra of the* 2^{32} *linear combinations of its coordinate functions which are* $2^{32} \times 1$ *matrices. Nevertheless, by 19, the nonlinearity is obtained by calculating the maximum value of the product of the maxima values of four Walsh Spectra (* $2^8 \times 1$ *matrices) for each of the* 2^{32} *linear combinations of its coordinate functions.*

$$\mathcal{NL} \, (S(CAST)) = 2^{32-1} - \tfrac{1}{2} 29417472 = 2132774912$$
$$lp \, (S(CAST)) = 4.69127 \cdot 10^{-5}$$

This result coincides with the estimation of nonlinearity done in Youssef et al. (1997).

Theorem 14. *Let* Γ_1 *be an* (n_1, m, t_1) *resilient function and* F_2 *be an* (n_2, m, t_2)-*resilient function, then* $F_1 \oplus F_2$ *is an* $(n_1 + n_2, m, t_1 + t_2 + 1)$-*resilient function.*

Here we give alternative proof as those given in Zhang & Zheng (1997):

Proof. For all $\mathbf{u} \in V_{n_1 + n_2}$ satisfying $wt(\mathbf{u}) = t_1 + t_2 + 1$, exists either $\mathbf{u_1} \in V_{n_1}$ with $wt(\mathbf{u_1}) = t_1 + 1$ and $\mathbf{u_2} \in V_{n_2}$ with $wt(\mathbf{u_2}) = t_2$ so that $\mathbf{u} = \mathbf{u_1} \oplus \mathbf{u_2}$ or $\mathbf{u_1} \in V_{n_1}$ with $wt(\mathbf{u_1}) = t_1$ and $\mathbf{u_2} \in V_{n_2}$ with $wt(\mathbf{u_2}) = t_2 + 1$ so that $\mathbf{u} = \mathbf{u_1} \oplus \mathbf{u_2}$. In both scenarios, it holds that:

$$\hat{\theta}_{F_1}(\mathbf{u_1}, \mathbf{v}) \ \hat{\theta}_{F_2}(\mathbf{u_2}, \mathbf{v}) = 0, \ \forall \, \mathbf{u} \subset V_{n_1 + n_2}, \ 0 \leq wt(\mathbf{u}) \leq t_1 + t_2 + 1, \ \forall \, \mathbf{v} \neq \mathbf{0} \subset V_m$$
$$\longrightarrow \hat{\theta}_{F_1 \oplus F_2}(\mathbf{u}, \mathbf{v}) = 0, \ \forall \, \mathbf{u} \in V_{n_1 + n_2}, \ 0 \leq wt(\mathbf{u}) \leq t_1 + t_2 + 1, \ \forall \, \mathbf{v} \neq \mathbf{0} \in V_m$$

$\square$

Corollary 20. *Let* F_1 *anf* F_2 *balanced functions, then* $F_1 \oplus F_2$ *is an* $(n_1 + n_2, m, 1)$-*resilient function. This result is an extension of what was obtained in Seberry & Zhang (1993) for Boolean functions.*

Theorem 15. *The elements which conform a row in the Autocorrelation Spectrum of the direct sum of two Boolean functions are obtained by the product of the respective components of the rows in both Autocorrelation Spectra. Let* $f_1 \in \mathcal{F}_{n_1}, f_2 \in \mathcal{F}_{n_2}$, *then:*

$$r_{f_1 \oplus f_2}(\mathbf{u}) = r_{f_1}(\mathbf{u_1}) \cdot r_{f_2}(\mathbf{u_2})$$

Proof.

$$r_{f_1 \oplus f_2}(\mathbf{u}) = \tfrac{1}{2^n} \sum_{\mathbf{x} \in V_n} \chi_{f_1 \oplus f_2}(\mathbf{x} + \mathbf{u}) \chi_{f_1 \oplus f_2}(\mathbf{x})$$
$$= \tfrac{1}{2^{n_1 + n_2}} \sum_{\mathbf{x_1} \in V_{n_1}} \sum_{\mathbf{x_2} \in V_{n_2}} \chi_{f_1}(\mathbf{x_1}) \chi_{f_2}(\mathbf{x_2}) \chi_{f_1}(\mathbf{x_1} + \mathbf{u_1}) \chi_{f_2}(\mathbf{x_2} + \mathbf{u_2})$$
$$= \left(\tfrac{1}{2^{n_1}} \sum_{\mathbf{x_1} \in V_{n_1}} \chi_{f_1}(\mathbf{x_1} + \mathbf{u_1}) \chi_{f_1}(\mathbf{x_1}) \right) \left(\tfrac{1}{2^{n_2}} \sum_{\mathbf{x_2} \in V_{n_2}} \chi_{f_2}(\mathbf{x_2} + \mathbf{u_2}) \chi_{f_2}(\mathbf{x_2}) \right)$$
$$= r_{f_1}(\mathbf{u_1}) \cdot r_{f_2}(\mathbf{u_2})$$

$\square$

Theorem 16. *Let f_1 satisfies the $PC(l_1)$ and f_2 satisfies the $PC(l_2)$, then $f_1 \oplus f_2$ satisfies the $PC(l)$ with $l = \min\{l_1, l_2\}$. Moreover, it holds that $r_{f_1 \oplus f_2}(\mathbf{u}) = 0$ for all $\mathbf{u} = \mathbf{u_1} \oplus \mathbf{u_2}$ with $wt(\mathbf{u}) = l_1 + l_2 + 1$ except those which satisfies $\mathbf{u_1} = \mathbf{0}$ or $\mathbf{u_2} = \mathbf{0}$.*

Proof. By Theorem 15 we can show:

$$f_1 \text{ satisfies the } PC(l_1) \text{ and } f_2 \text{ satisfies the } PC(l_2)$$
$$r_{f_1}(\mathbf{u_1}) = 0, \ \forall \mathbf{u_1} \in V_{n_1}, \ 1 \leq wt(\mathbf{u_1}) \leq l_1 \text{ and}$$
$$r_{f_2}(\mathbf{u_2}) = 0, \ \forall \mathbf{u_2} \in V_{n_2}, \ 1 \leq wt(\mathbf{u_2}) \leq l_2$$
$$r_{f_1}(\mathbf{u_1}) \cdot r_{f_2}(\mathbf{u_2}) = 0, \ \forall \mathbf{u} = \mathbf{u_1} \oplus \mathbf{u_2} \in V_{n_1 + n_2}, \ 1 \leq wt(\mathbf{u}) \leq \min\{l_1, l_2\}$$
$$\longrightarrow r_{f_1 \oplus f_2}(\mathbf{u}) = 0, \ \forall \mathbf{u} \in V_{n_1 + n_2}, \ 1 \leq wt(\mathbf{u}) \leq \min\{l_1, l_2\}$$

Besides, for all $\mathbf{u} \in V_{n_1 + n_2}$ satisfying $wt(\mathbf{u}) = l_1 + l_2 + 1$, exists either $\mathbf{u_1} \in V_{n_1}$ with $wt(\mathbf{u_1}) = l_1 + 1$ and $\mathbf{u_2} \in V_{n_2}$ with $wt(\mathbf{u_2}) = l_2$ so that $\mathbf{u} = \mathbf{u_1} \oplus \mathbf{u_2}$ or $\mathbf{u_1} \in V_{n_1}$ with $wt(\mathbf{u_1}) = l_1$ and $\mathbf{u_2} \in V_{n_2}$ with $wt(\mathbf{u_2}) = l_2 + 1$ so that $\mathbf{u} = \mathbf{u_1} \oplus \mathbf{u_2}$. In both scenarios, it holds that:

$$r_{f_1}(\mathbf{u_1}) \cdot r_{f_2}(\mathbf{u_2}) = 0, \ \forall \mathbf{u} = \mathbf{u_1} \oplus \mathbf{u_2} \in V_{n_1 + n_2}, \ 1 \leq wt(\mathbf{u}) \leq l_1 + l_2 + 1$$

except those where $\mathbf{u_1} = \mathbf{0}$ because $r_{f_1}(\mathbf{0}) = 1$ and $r_{f_2}(\mathbf{u_2})$ could be non-zero or where $\mathbf{u_2} = \mathbf{0}$ because $r_{f_2}(\mathbf{0}) = 1$ and $r_{f_1}(\mathbf{u_1})$ could be non-zero. $\square$

Example 5. *Let $f_1, f_2 \in \mathcal{F}_5$ which both satisfy $PC(2)$ where $f_1(\mathbf{x}) = x_1 x_2 x_3 x_4 + x_1 x_2 x_3 x_5 + x_1 x_2 x_4 x_5 + x_1 x_3 x_4 x_5 + x_2 x_3 x_4 x_5 + x_1 x_4 + x_1 x_5 + x_2 x_3 + x_2 x_5 + x_3 x_4$ and $f_2(\mathbf{x}) = x_1 x_2 x_3 x_4 + x_1 x_2 x_3 x_5 + x_1 x_2 x_4 x_5 + x_1 x_3 x_4 x_5 + x_2 x_3 x_4 x_5 + x_1 x_4 + x_1 x_5 + x_2 x_3 + x_2 x_5 + x_3 x_4 + x_1 + x_2 + x_3 + x_4 + x_5$. By Theorem 16 then $f_1 \oplus f_2$ satisfies $PC(2)$.*

4.6 Bricklayer of Vector Boolean functions

Let $n_1, n_2, m_1, m_2 \geq 1$ and $F_1 \in \mathcal{F}_{n_1, m_1}$, $F_2 \in \mathcal{F}_{n_2, m_2}$ and the Bricklayer function $F_1 | F_2 \in \mathcal{F}_{n_1 + n_2, m_1 + m_2}$. Let $\mathbf{u_1} \in V_{n_1}, \mathbf{u_2} \in V_{n_2}$ and $\mathbf{u} = \mathbf{u_1} \oplus \mathbf{u_2}, \mathbf{v_1} \in V_{m_1}, \mathbf{v_2} \in V_{m_2}$ and $\mathbf{v} = \mathbf{v_1} \oplus \mathbf{v_2}$.

Theorem 17. *The elements which conform the Walsh Spectrum (respect. Differential Profile) of the Bricklayer of two Vector Boolean functions are obtained by the product of the respective components in both Walsh Spectra (respect. Differential Profiles).*

$$\hat{\theta}_{F_1 | F_2}(\mathbf{u}, \mathbf{v}) = \hat{\theta}_{F_1}(\mathbf{u_1}, \mathbf{v_1}) \cdot \hat{\theta}_{F_2}(\mathbf{u_2}, \mathbf{v_2})$$
$$\delta_{F_1 | F_2}(\mathbf{u}, \mathbf{v}) = \delta_{F_1}(\mathbf{u_1}, \mathbf{v_1}) \cdot \delta_{F_2}(\mathbf{u_2}, \mathbf{v_2})$$

Proof.

$$\hat{\theta}_{F_1 | F_2}(\mathbf{u}, \mathbf{v}) = \hat{\chi}_{(\mathbf{v_1}, \mathbf{v_2}) \cdot (F_1 | F_2)}((\mathbf{u_1}, \mathbf{u_2})) = \hat{\chi}_{\mathbf{v_1} \cdot F_1}(\mathbf{u_1}) \cdot \hat{\chi}_{\mathbf{v_2} \cdot F_2}(\mathbf{u_2})$$

$\square$

Proof.

$$\delta_{F_1 | F_2}(\mathbf{u}, \mathbf{v}) = \frac{1}{2^{n+m}} \sum_{\mathbf{w} \in V_m} r_{F_1 | F_2}(\mathbf{u}, \mathbf{w}) \chi_{\mathbf{v}}(\mathbf{w})$$
$$= \frac{1}{2^{n+m}} \sum_{\mathbf{w} \in V_m} r_{F_1 | F_2}(\mathbf{u_1}, \mathbf{w}) r_{F_1 | F_2}(\mathbf{u_2}, \mathbf{w}) \chi_{\mathbf{v_1}}(\mathbf{w}) \chi_{\mathbf{v_2}}(\mathbf{w})$$
$$= \left(\frac{1}{2^{n_1 + m_1}} \sum_{\mathbf{w} \in V_m} r_{F_1 | F_2}(\mathbf{u_1}, \mathbf{w}) \chi_{\mathbf{v_1}}(\mathbf{w}) \right) \left(\frac{1}{2^{n_2 + m_2}} \sum_{\mathbf{w} \in V_m} r_{F_1 | F_2}(\mathbf{u_2}, \mathbf{w}) \chi_{\mathbf{v_2}}(\mathbf{w}) \right)$$
$$= \delta_{F_1}(\mathbf{u_1}, \mathbf{v_1}) \cdot \delta_{F_2}(\mathbf{u_2}, \mathbf{v_2})$$

$\square$

Corollary 21. *The Walsh Spectrum (respectively Differential Profile) of the Bricklayer of i Vector Boolean functions $F_1| \cdots |F_i$ is equal to the Kronecker products of their Walsh Spectra (respectively Differential Profiles):*

$$WS(F_1| \cdots |F_i) = WS(F_1) \otimes \cdots \otimes WS(F_i)$$
$$DP(F_1| \cdots |F_i) = DP(F_1) \otimes \cdots \otimes DP(F_i)$$

(25)

Corollary 22.

$$\mathcal{NL}(F_1|F_2) = 2^{n_1+n_2-1} - \tfrac{1}{2} \max\{2^{n_1}(2^{n_2} - 2\mathcal{NL}(F_2)), 2^{n_2}(2^{n_1} - 2\mathcal{NL}(F_1))\}$$
$$\mathcal{LD}(F_1|F_2) = 2^{n_1+n_2-1} \cdot (1 - \max\{1 - \tfrac{\mathcal{LD}(F_1)}{2^{n_1-1}}, 1 - \tfrac{\mathcal{LD}(F_2)}{2^{n_2-1}}\})$$

Proof. On one hand

$$\mathcal{NL}(F_1|F_2) = 2^{n-1} - \tfrac{1}{2} \overset{*}{\max} (\hat{\theta}_{F_1|F_2}(\mathbf{u}, \mathbf{v}))$$
$$= 2^{n-1} - \tfrac{1}{2} \max\{\hat{\theta}_{F_1}(\mathbf{u_1}, \mathbf{v_1}) \cdot \max(\hat{\theta}_{F_2}(\mathbf{u_2}, \mathbf{v_2}))\} \text{ where } ((\mathbf{u_1}, \mathbf{u_2}) \neq 0) \wedge ((\mathbf{v_1}, \mathbf{v_2}) \neq 0)$$
$$= 2^{n-1} - \tfrac{1}{2} \max\{2^{n_1} \cdot \overset{*}{\max} (\hat{\theta}_{F_2}(\mathbf{u_2}, \mathbf{v_2})), 2^{n_2} \cdot \overset{*}{\max} (\hat{\theta}_{F_1}(\mathbf{u_1}, \mathbf{v_1}))\}$$
$$= 2^{n_1+n_2-1} - \tfrac{1}{2} \max\{2^{n_1} \cdot (2^{n_2} - 2\mathcal{NL}(F_2)), 2^{n_2} \cdot (2^{n_1} - 2\mathcal{NL}(F_1))\}$$

On the other hand

$$\mathcal{LD}(F_1|F_2) = 2^{n-1} \cdot \left(1 - \overset{*}{\max} (\delta_{F_1|F_2}(\mathbf{u}, \mathbf{v}))\right)$$
$$= 2^{n-1} \cdot (1 - \max\{\delta_{F_1}(\mathbf{u_1}, \mathbf{v_1}) \cdot \delta_{F_2}(\mathbf{u_2}, \mathbf{v_2})\}) \text{ where } ((\mathbf{u_1}, \mathbf{u_2}) \neq 0) \wedge ((\mathbf{v_1}, \mathbf{v_2}) \neq 0)$$
$$= 2^{n-1} \cdot (1 - \max\{\overset{*}{\max} (\delta_{F_1}(\mathbf{u_1}, \mathbf{v_1})), \overset{*}{\max} (\delta_{F_2}(\mathbf{u_2}, \mathbf{v_2}))\})$$
$$= 2^{n_1+n_2-1} \cdot \left(1 - \max\left\{1 - \tfrac{\mathcal{LD}(F_1)}{2^{n_1-1}}, 1 - \tfrac{\mathcal{LD}(F_2)}{2^{n_2-1}}\right\}\right)$$

□

Corollary 23. *Let $F_1| \cdots |F_i \in \mathcal{F}_{n,m}$*

$$dp(F_1| \cdots |F_i) = \max\{dp(F_1), \ldots, dp(F_i)\}$$

(26)

The following theorem and corollary are presented without proofs as they are very similar to the analogous in the previous subsection.

Theorem 18. *Let F_1 be an (n_1, m_1, t_1)-resilient function and F_2 be an (n_2, m_2, t_2)-resilient function, then $F_1|F_2$ is an $(n_1 + n_2, m_1 + m_2, t_1 + t_2)$-resilient function.*

Corollary 24. *$F_1|F_2$ is an $(n_1 + n_2, m, 1)$-resilient function if and only if F_1 or F_2 are balanced functions.*

Example 6. *Let denote S the result of bricklayering all DES S-boxes $S_i \in \mathcal{F}_{6,4} \, \forall i = 1, \ldots, 8$, so that $S = S_1| \cdots |S_8$. Thanks to the corollary 22, it is possible to calculate the nonlinearity and linearity distance of S by calculating the maximum values of the Walsh Spectra and Differential Profiles of the 8 S-boxes. This algorithm deals with eight $2^6 \times 2^4$ matrices instead of one $2^{48} \times 2^{32}$ matrix.*

$$\mathcal{NL}(S) = 2^{48-1} - \tfrac{1}{2} 36 \cdot 2^{42} = 61572651155456$$
$$lp(S) = 0.31640625 \; dp(S) = \tfrac{1}{4}$$
$$\mathcal{LD}(S) = 2^{48-1} \cdot \left(1 - \tfrac{1}{4}\right) = 3 \cdot 2^{45}$$

As all $S_i \in \mathcal{F}_{6,4} \, \forall i = 1, \ldots, 8$ are balanced S-boxes, then by Theorem 18 it holds that S is an $(48, 32, 7)$-resilient function.

5. Conclusions

In this chapter, several characteristics have been obtained for Vector Boolean Functions which are constructed using simpler functions combined in different ways. Precisely, the Walsh Spectrum of the overall function is obtained from the spectra of the functions when they are combined via composition, addition of coordinate functions, direct sum or bricklayer construction. In addition, when affine bijections or projection are employed, the maximum value of the overall Walsh Spectrum is obtained from the maximum values of the involved elements spectra. These results allow for the computation of nonlinearity, balancedness and resiliency of the mentioned constructions.

Alternatively, the Differential Profile of the system resulting from the composition with an affine function, direct sum, or bricklayer is also derived from the Differential Profiles of the involved elements. Moreover, when affine bijections or projections are employed, bounds on the maximum value of the Differential Profile for the resulting Function are also obtained. Therefore, the linearity distance for the cited constructions is computed.

Finally, the Autocorrelation Spectrum of a Vector Boolean Function constructed via affine bijections of Vector Boolean Functions and direct sum of Boolean functions is provided from the knowledge of the respective elements Autocorrelation Spectra. Moreover, the autocorrelation coefficients resulting from adding coordinate functions with linear structures are obtained. As a consequence, the propagation criterion resulting from the cited constructions is also provided.

5.1 Acknowledgements

This work has been partially supported by project MTM2010-15102 of Ministerio de Ciencia e Innovación, Spain, and by projects Q09 0930-182 and Q10 0930-144 of the Universidad Politécnica de Madrid (UPM), Spain.

6. References

Adams, C. (1994). Simple and effective key scheduling for symmetric ciphers, *Workshop on Selected Areas in Cryptography*, pp. 129–133.

Adams, C. M. & Tavares, S. E. (1993). Designing s-boxes for ciphers resistant to differential cryptanalysis (extended abstract), *Proceedings of the 3rd Symposium on State and Progress of Research in Cryptography*, pp. 181–190.

Biham, E. & Shamir, A. (1991). Differential cryptanalysis of des-like cryptosystems, *Proceedings of the 10th Annual International Cryptology Conference on Advances in Cryptology*, CRYPTO '90, Springer-Verlag, London, UK, UK, pp. 2–21.

Blaze, M. & Schneier, B. (1995). The macguffin block cipher algorithm, *Fast Software Encryption, volume 1008 of Lecture*, Springer-Verlag, pp. 97–110.

Carlet, C. (2004). On the secondary constructions of resilient and bent functions, *Progress in Computer Science and Applied Logic* 23: 3–28.

Chabaud, F. & Vaudenay, S. (1994). Links between differential and linear cryptanalysis, *Advances in Cryptology- Eurorypt 1994*, pp. 356–365.

Chen, L., Fu, F.-W. & Wei, V. K.-W. (2004). On the constructions and nonlinearity of binary vector-output correlation-immune functions, *J. Complex.* 20: 266–283.

Daemen, J. & Rijmen, V. (2002). *The Design of Rijndael*, Springer-Verlag New York, Inc., Secaucus, NJ, USA.

Des (1977). Data encryption standard, *In FIPS PUB 46, Federal Information Processing Standards Publication*, pp. 46–2.

J. Seberry, X. Z. & Zheng, Y. (1994). Nonlinearity characteristics of quadratic substitution boxes, *Proceedings of the Workshop on SAC'94*.

Jakobsen, T. & Knudsen, L. R. (1997). The interpolation attack on block ciphers, *Proceedings of the 4th International Workshop on Fast Software Encryption*, FSE '97, Springer-Verlag, London, UK, pp. 28–40.

Maitra, S. & Pasalic, E. (2002). Further constructions of resilient boolean functions with very high nonlinearity, *IEEE Transactions on Information Theory* 48(7): 1825 –1834.

Matsui, M. (1994). Linear cryptanalysis method for des cipher, *Workshop on the theory and application of cryptographic techniques on Advances in cryptology*, EUROCRYPT '93, Springer-Verlag New York, Inc., Secaucus, NJ, USA, pp. 386–397.

Meier, W. & Staffelbach, O. (1990). Nonlinearity criteria for cryptographic functions, *Proceedings of the workshop on the theory and application of cryptographic techniques on Advances in cryptology*, Springer-Verlag New York, Inc., New York, NY, USA, pp. 549–562.

Millan, W. L. (1998). *Analysis and Design of Boolean. Functions for Cryptographic Applications*, PhD thesis, Queensland University of Technology, Faculty of Information Technology.

Nyberg, K. (1991). Perfect nonlinear s-boxes, *Proceedings of the 10th annual international conference on Theory and application of cryptographic techniques*, EUROCRYPT'91, Springer-Verlag, Berlin, Heidelberg, pp. 378–386.

Nyberg, K. (1993). On the construction of highly nonlinear permutations, *Proceedings of the 11th annual international conference on Theory and application of cryptographic techniques*, EUROCRYPT'92, Springer-Verlag, Berlin, Heidelberg, pp. 92–98.

Nyberg, K. (1995). S-boxes and round functions with controllable linearity and differential uniformity, *in* B. Preneel (ed.), *Fast Software Encryption*, Vol. 1008 of *Lecture Notes in Computer Science*, Springer Berlin / Heidelberg, pp. 111–130.

Pasalic, E., Maitra, S., Johansson, T. & Sarkar, P. (2001). New constructions of resilient and correlation immune boolean functions achieving upper bound on nonlinearity, *Electronic Notes in Discrete Mathematics* 6(0): 158 – 167. WCC2001, International Workshop on Coding and Cryptography.

Pommerening, K. (2005). LinearitatsmaSSe fur boolesche abbildungen, *Technical report*, Fachbereich Mathematik der Johannes-Gutenberg-Universitaet.

Preneel, B., Van Leekwijck, W., Van Linden, L., Govaerts, R. & Vandewalle, J. (2006). Propagation characteristics of boolean functions, *in* I. DamgÃěrd (ed.), *Advances in Cryptology EUROCRYPT'90*, Vol. 473 of *Lecture Notes in Computer Science*, Springer Berlin / Heidelberg, pp. 161–173.

Rothaus, O. S. (1976). On "bent" functions., *J. Comb. Theory, Ser. A* 20(3): 300–305.

Sarkar, P. & Maitra, S. (2000a). Construction of nonlinear boolean functions with important cryptographic properties, *Proceedings of the 19th international conference on Theory and application of cryptographic techniques*, EUROCRYPT'00, Springer-Verlag, Berlin, Heidelberg, pp. 485–506.

Sarkar, P. & Maitra, S. (2000b). Nonlinearity bounds and constructions of resilient boolean functions, *Proceedings of the 20th Annual International Cryptology Conference on Advances in Cryptology*, CRYPTO '00, Springer-Verlag, London, UK, pp. 515–532.

Schneier, B. (1995). *Applied cryptography (2nd ed.): protocols, algorithms, and source code in C*, John Wiley & Sons, Inc., New York, NY, USA.

Seberry, J. & Zhang, X.-M. (1993). Highly nonlinear 0-1 balanced boolean functions satisfying strict avalanche criterion, *Proceedings of the Workshop on the Theory and Application of Cryptographic Techniques: Advances in Cryptology*, ASIACRYPT '92, Springer-Verlag, London, UK, pp. 145–155.

Shannon, C. E. (1949). Communication theory of secrecy systems, *Bell System Technical Journal* 28(4): 657–715.

Xiao, G.-Z. & Massey, J. (1988). A spectral characterization of correlation-immune combining functions, *IEEE Transactions on Information Theory* 34(3): 569 –571.

Youssef, A., Chen, Z. & Tavares, S. (1997). Construction of highly nonlinear injective s-boxes with application to cast-like encryption algorithms, *IEEE 1997 Canadian Conference on Electrical and Computer Engineering, 1997*, Vol. 1, pp. 330 –333 vol.1.

Zhang, X.-M. & Zheng, Y. (1997). Cryptographically resilient functions, *IEEE Transactions on Information Theory* 43(5): 1740 –1747.

Construction of Orthogonal Arrays of Index Unity Using Logarithm Tables for Galois Fields

Jose Torres-Jimenez[1], Himer Avila-George[2],
Nelson Rangel-Valdez[3] and Loreto Gonzalez-Hernandez[1]
[1]CINVESTAV-Tamaulipas, Information Technology Laboratory
[2]Instituto de Instrumentación para Imagen Molecular (I3M). Centro mixto CSIC -
Universitat Politécnica de Valéncia - CIEMAT, Valencia
[3]Universidad Politécnica de Victoria
[1,3]México
[2]Spain

1. Introduction

A wide variety of problems found in computer science deals with combinatorial objects. Combinatorics is the branch of mathematics that deals with finite countable objects called combinatorial structures. These structures find many applications in different areas such as hardware and software testing, cryptography, pattern recognition, computer vision, among others.

Of particular interest in this chapter are the combinatorial objects called Orthogonal Arrays (OAs). These objects have been studied given of their wide range of applications in the industry, Gopalakrishnan & Stinson (2008) present their applications in computer science; among them are in the generation of error correcting codes presented by (Hedayat et al., 1999; Stinson, 2004), or in the design of experiments for software testing as shown by Taguchi (1994).

To motivate the study of the OAs, it is pointed out their importance in the development of algorithms for the cryptography area. There, OAs have been used for the generation of authentication codes, error correcting codes, and in the construction of universal hash functions (Gopalakrishnan & Stinson, 2008).

This chapter proposes an efficient implementation for the Bush's construction (Bush, 1952) of OAs of index unity, based on the use of logarithm tables for Galois Fields. This is an application of the algorithm of Torres-Jimenez et al. (2011). The motivation of this research work born from the applications of OAs in cryptography as shown by Hedayat et al. (1999). Also, it is discussed an alternative use of the logarithm table algorithm for the construction of cyclotomic matrices to construct CAs (Colbourn, 2010).

The remaining of the chapter is organized as follows. Section 2 presents a formal definition of OAs and the basic notation to be used through this chapter. Section 3 shows the relevance of OAs for cryptography by showing three of their applications, one in the authentication without secrecy, other in the generation of universal hash functions, and a last one in the construction of difference schemes. Section 4 shows the construction methods, reported in the literature, for the construction of OAs. Section 5 presents the algorithm described in Torres-Jimenez et al. (2011) for the construction of the logarithm table of a Galois Field, this algorithm served as basis for a more efficient construction of OAs using the Bush's construction. Section 6 contains the efficient implementation, proposed in this chapter, for the Bush's construction of OAs, based on discrete logarithms. Section 7 presents an extension of the use of the algorithm presented by Torres-Jimenez et al. (2011), in the construction of cyclotomic matrices for CAs. Section 8 shows as results from the proposed approach, a set of bounds obtained for CAs using the constructions of cyclotomic matrices aided by the algorithm described in this chapter. Finally, Section 9 presents the main conclusions derived from the research proposed in this chapter.

2. Orthogonal arrays

The Orthogonal Arrays (OAs) were introduced by Rao (1946; 1947) under the name of *hypercubes* and for use in factorial designs. Figure 1 shows an example of an Orthogonal Array $OA_3(12; 2, 11, 2)$. The definition of an OA involves that any pair of columns of this

$$\begin{pmatrix} 0 & 0 & 0 & 0 & 0 & 0 & 0 & 0 & 0 & 0 & 0 \\ 1 & 1 & 1 & 0 & 1 & 1 & 0 & 1 & 0 & 0 & 0 \\ 0 & 1 & 1 & 1 & 0 & 1 & 1 & 0 & 1 & 0 & 0 \\ 0 & 0 & 1 & 1 & 1 & 0 & 1 & 1 & 0 & 1 & 0 \\ 0 & 0 & 0 & 1 & 1 & 1 & 0 & 1 & 1 & 0 & 1 \\ 1 & 0 & 0 & 0 & 1 & 1 & 1 & 0 & 1 & 1 & 0 \\ 0 & 1 & 0 & 0 & 0 & 1 & 1 & 1 & 0 & 1 & 1 \\ 1 & 0 & 1 & 0 & 0 & 0 & 1 & 1 & 1 & 0 & 1 \\ 1 & 1 & 0 & 1 & 0 & 0 & 0 & 1 & 1 & 1 & 0 \\ 0 & 1 & 1 & 0 & 1 & 0 & 0 & 0 & 1 & 1 & 1 \\ 1 & 0 & 1 & 1 & 0 & 1 & 0 & 0 & 0 & 1 & 1 \\ 1 & 1 & 0 & 1 & 1 & 0 & 1 & 0 & 0 & 0 & 1 \end{pmatrix}$$

Fig. 1. Example of an $OA_3(12; 2, 11, 2)$. The interaction, or strength, is 2; also, it has 11 parameters and 12 runs (or test cases) and the combinations $\{(0,0), (0,1), (1,0), (1,1)\}$ in each pair of columns extracted from it.

matrix should contain the symbol combinations shown in Figure 2.

$$\begin{pmatrix} 0 & 0 \\ 0 & 1 \\ 1 & 0 \\ 1 & 1 \end{pmatrix}$$

Fig. 2. Symbol combinations expected in any pair of columns in an OA of strength 2 and alphabet 2.

Formally, an orthogonal array (OA), denoted by $OA_\lambda(N; t, k, v)$, can be defined as follows:

Definition 1. *An OA, denoted by $OA(N; t, k, v)$, is an $N \times k$ array on v symbols such that every $N \times t$ sub-array contains all the ordered subsets of size t from v symbols exactly λ times. Orthogonal arrays have the property that $\lambda = \frac{N}{v^t}$. When $\lambda = 1$ it can be omitted from the notation and the OA is optimal.*

Figure 3 shows another example of an $OA(9; 2, 4, 3)$; note that this time the alphabet is $v = 3$ and the combination of symbols $\{(0,0), (0,1), (0,2), (1,0), (1,1), (1,2), (2,0), (2,1), (2,2)\}$ appears only once in each pair of columns of the OA.

$$\begin{pmatrix} 0\ 0\ 0\ 0 \\ 1\ 1\ 1\ 0 \\ 2\ 2\ 2\ 0 \\ 0\ 1\ 2\ 1 \\ 1\ 2\ 0\ 1 \\ 2\ 0\ 1\ 1 \\ 0\ 2\ 1\ 2 \\ 1\ 0\ 2\ 2 \\ 2\ 1\ 0\ 2 \end{pmatrix}$$

Fig. 3. Example of an $OA(9; 2, 4, 3)$.

The OAs have some interesting properties, among them are the following ones:

1. The parameters of the OA satisfy $\lambda = N/v^t$;

2. An OA of strength t is also an OA of strength t', where $1 \leq t' \leq t$. The index λ' of an OA of strength t' is $\lambda' = \lambda \cdot v^{t-t'}$;

3. Let $A_i = \{0, 1, ..., r\}$ be a set of $OA(N_i; t_i, k, v)$, the juxtaposed array $A = \begin{bmatrix} A_0 \\ ... \\ A_r \end{bmatrix}$ is an

   $OA(N; t, k, v)$ where $N = N_1 + N_2 + ... + N_r$ and $t \geq \min\{t_0, t_1, ..., t_r\}$;

4. Any permutation of rows or columns in an OA, results in another OA with the same parameters;

5. Any subarray of size $N \times k'$ of an $OA(N; t, k, v)$, is an $OA(N, t', k', v)$ of strength $t' = \min\{k', t\}$;

6. Select the rows of an $OA(N; t, k, v)$ that starts with the symbol 0, and eliminate the first column; the resulting matrix is an $OA(N/v; t-1, k-1, v)$.

The following section presents some applications of OAs in the area of cryptography. These applications are related with the construction of difference schemes, universal hash functions, and in the authentication without secrecy.

3. Relevance of orthogonal arrays in cryptography

The purpose of this section is to present three applications that motivate the study of OAs in the area of cryptography. These applications have been described in (Gopalakrishnan & Stinson, 2008; Stinson, 1992a).

3.1 Authentication without secrecy

The use of authentication codes dates back to 1974, the time when they were invented by Gilbert et al. (1974). Most of the time, the transmission of information between two parts that are interested on keeping the integration of their information, is done through the use of *secrecy*, i.e. the practice of hiding information from certain group of individuals. However, sometimes it is important to transmit the information in areas that are insecure and where it is not necessary the secrecy. This part corresponds to the area of *Authentication Without Secrecy* (or AWS). An authentication code without secrecy is a code where an observed message can correspond to a unique source state.

Jones & Seberry (1986) described a situation in which two countries want to set transmission devices to monitor the activities of the other, such that possible compliance can be avoided.

The general model to define the use of the AWS can be described with three participants: a transmitter, a receiver, and an opponent. Let's call these participants Alice, Bob and Gabriel, respectively. Suppose that Alice wants to transmit a message to Bob in a public communication channel; however, they expect that the message must be transmitted integrally, i.e. without any changes in its composition. To do so, Alice encrypted the message and sent it through the channel. An encoding rule (based on a key scheme) ciphers the message; each encoding rule will be a one-to-one function from the source space to the message space. The key used to cipher the message has been sent to Bob (the receiver) through a secure channel, before the message has been encoded. Now, the third party member, Gabriel, has malicious intention of deforming the message. What is the chance of Gabriel to access the message of Alice and Bob and modify it conveniently to affect the final result?

Let's consider the following protocol of communication between Alice and Bob: a) Firstly, Alice and Bob choose the encoding code previously; b) Alice encode the message with a previously chosen key K; c) the message $m = (s, a)$ is sent over the communication channel; d) when Bob receives the message he verifies that $a = e_K(s)$ so that he ensures that it comes from Alice.

Let S be a set of k source states; let $\mathcal{M}$ be a set of v messages; and let $\mathcal{E}$ be a set of b encoding rules. Since each encoding rule is a one-to-one function from S to $\mathcal{M}$, the code can be represented by a $b \times k$ matrix, where the rows are indexed by encoding rules, the columns are indexed by source states, and the entry in row e and column s is $e(s)$. This matrix is called the encoding matrix. For any encoding rule $e \in \mathcal{E}$, define $M(e) = \{e(s) : s \in S\}$, i.e. the set of valid messages under encoding rule e. For an encoding rule e, and a message $m \in M(e)$, define $e^{-1}(m) = s$ if $e(s) = m$.

The types of damage that Gabriel can do to the message of Alice and Bob are impersonation, i.e. sending a message to one of them without the message even existed; and substitution, i.e. changing a message sent.

The application of OAs in *authentication without secrecy* is described by the following theorem:

Theorem 1. *Suppose that there is an authentication code without secrecy for k source states and having l authenticators, in which $P_{d_0} = P_{d_1} = 1/l$. Then*

1. $|\mathcal{E}| \geq l^2$, *and equality occurs if and only if the authentication matrix is an $OA(2, k, l)$ (with $\lambda = 1$) and the authentication rules are used with equal probability;*

2. $|\mathcal{E}| \geq k(l - 1) + 1$, *and equality occurs if and only if the authentication matrix is an $OA_\lambda(2, k, l)$ where*

$$\lambda = \frac{k(l - 1) + 1}{l^2}, \tag{1}$$

   and the authentication rules are used with equal probability.

This theorem has been proven by Stinson (1992a). It also show that this is the minimum probability expected for this case.

3.2 Universal hash function

Assume it is wanted to map keys from some universe U into m bins (labeled). The algorithm will have to handle some data set of $|S| = n$ keys, which is not known in advance. Usually, the goal of hashing is to obtain a low number of collisions (keys from S that land in the same bin). A deterministic hash function cannot offer any guarantee in an adversarial setting if the size of U is greater than m^2, since the adversary may choose S to be precisely the preimage of a bin. This means that all data keys land in the same bin, making hashing useless. Furthermore, a deterministic hash function does not allow for rehashing: sometimes the input data turns out to be bad for the hash function (e.g. there are too many collisions), so one would like to change the hash function.

The solution to these problems is to pick a function randomly from a family of hash functions. A universal hash function is a family of functions indexed by a parameter called the key with the following property: for all distinct inputs, the probability over all keys that they collide is small.

A family of functions $H = \{h : U \to [m]\}$ is called a universal family if Equation 2 holds.

$$\forall x, y \in U, x \neq y : Pr[h(x) = h(y)] \leq \frac{1}{m} \tag{2}$$

Any two keys of the universe collide with probability at most $\frac{1}{m}$ when the hash function h is drawn randomly from H. This is exactly the probability of collision we would expect if the hash function assigned truly random hash codes to every key. Sometimes, the definition is relaxed to allow collision probability $O(1/m)$. This concept was introduced by (Carter & Wegman, 1979; Wegman & Carter, 1981), and has found numerous applications in computer science.

A finite set H of hash functions is *strongly   universal₂* (or SU_2) if Equation 3 holds.

$$\{h \in H : h(x_1) = y_1, h(x_2) = y_2\}| = |H|/|B|^2, \forall x_1, x_2 \in A(x_1 \neq x_2), y_1, y_2 \in B \tag{3}$$

For practical applications, it is also important that $|H|$ is small. This is because $log_2|H|$ bits are needed to specify a hash function from the family. It is fairly straightforward to show that strongly universal hash functions are equivalent to orthogonal arrays. The following theorem can be found in (Stinson, 1994).

Theorem 2. *If there exists an* $OA_\lambda(2, k, n)$, *then there exists an* SU_2 *class H of hash functions from A to B, where* $|A| = k, |B| = n$ *and* $|H| = \lambda n^2$. *Conversely, if there exists an* SU_2 *class H of hash functions from A to B, where* $a = |A|$ *and* $b = |B|$, *then there exists an* $OA_\lambda(2, k, n)$, *where* $n = b, k = a$ *and* $\lambda = |H|/n^2$.

This theorem helps in establishing lower bounds on the number of hash functions and in constructing classes of hash functions which meet these bounds. It is straightforward to extend the definition and the theorem to SU_t class of universal hash functions.

3.3 Thresholds schemes

In a bank, there is a vault which must be opened every day. The bank employs three senior tellers; but it is not desirable to entrust the combination to any one person. Hence, we want to design a system whereby any two of the three senior tellers can gain access to the vault but no individual can do so. This problem can be solved by means of a threshold scheme.

Threshold schemes are actually a special case of secret sharing schemes. Stinson (1992b) presents a survey in this topic. Informally a (t, w)-threshold scheme is a method of sharing a secret key K among a finite set $\mathcal{P}$ of w participants, in such a way that any t participants can compute the value of K, but no group of $t - 1$ (or fewer) participants can do so. The value of K is chosen by a special participant called the *dealer*. The dealer is denoted by D and we assume $D \notin \mathcal{P}$. When D wants to share the key K among the participants in $\mathcal{P}$, he gives each participant some partial information called a *share*. The shares should be distributed secretly, so no participant knows the share given to another participant.

At a later time, a subset of participants $B \subseteq \mathcal{P}$ will pool their shares in an attempt to compute the secret key K. If $|B| \geq t$, then they should be able to compute the value of K as a function of the shares they collectively hold; if $|B| < t$, then they should not be able to compute K. In the example described above, we desire a $(2, 3)$-threshold scheme.

Often, we desire not only that an unauthorized subset of participants should be unable to compute the value of K by pooling their shares, but also they should be unable to determine anything about the value of K. Such a threshold scheme is called a *perfect threshold scheme*. Here, we will be concerned only about perfect threshold schemes.

We will use the following notation. Let $\mathcal{P} = \{P_i : 1 \leq i \leq w\}$ be the set of participants. $\mathcal{K}$ is the *key set* (i.e., the set of all possible keys); and S is the *share threshold schemes*.

Orthogonal arrays come into picture once again by means of the following theorem due to Dawson & Mahmoodian (1993).

Theorem 3. *An ideal (t, w) threshold scheme with $|\mathcal{K}| = v$ exists if and only if an $OA(t, w + 1, v)$ exists.*

The construction of the threshold scheme starting from the orthogonal array proceeds as follows. The first column of the OA corresponds to the dealer and the remaining w columns correspond to the w participants. To distribute a specific key K, the dealer selects a random row of the OA such that K appears in the first column and gives out the remaining w elements of the row as the shares. When t participants later pool their shares, the collective information will determine a unique row of the OA (as $\lambda = 1$) and hence they can compute K as the value of the first element in the row.

Can a group of $t - 1$ participants compute K? Any possible value of the secret along with the actual shares of these $t - 1$ participants determine a unique row of the OA. Hence, no value of the secret can be ruled out. Moreover, it is clear that the $t - 1$ participants can obtain no information about the secret.

4. Algorithms to construct OAs

This section presents some of the state-of-art algorithms for the construction of OAs. Special reference is done to the Bush's construction, which is benefited from the approach presented in this chapter because the efficient way of constructing the OAs using logarithm tables.

4.1 Rao-Hamming construction

The Rao-Hamming construction derived from the geniality of two scientists who independently elaborate procedures for the construction of OAs Hedayat et al. (1999). The following theorem describes the purpose of this construction.

Theorem 4. *If there is a prime power then an $OA(s^n, (s^n - 1)/(s - 1), 2)$ exists whenever $n \geq 2$.*

A simple way to obtain an orthogonal array with these parameters is the following. This construction always produces linear arrays. Form an $s^n \times n$ array whose rows are all possible n-tuples from $GF(s)$. Let $C_1, ..., C_n$ denote the columns of this array. The columns of the full orthogonal array then consist of all columns of the form shown in Equation 4.

$$z_1 C_1 + ... + z_n C_n = [C_1, ..., C_n]z \tag{4}$$

where $z = (z_1, ..., z_n)^T$ is an n-tuple from $GF(s)$, not all the z_i are zero, and the first nonzero z_i is 1. There are $(s^n - 1)/(s - 1)$ such columns, as required.

An alternative way to construct an OA using the Rao-Hamming Construction is by forming an $n \times (s^n - 1)/(s - 1)$ matrix whose columns are all nonzero n-tuples $(z_1, ..., z_n)^T$ from $GF(s)$ in which the first nonzero z_i is 1. The OA is then formed by taking all the linear combinations of the rows of this generator matrix.

An example of the construction of an OA, taken from Hedayat et al. (1999), is shown in Figure 4.

$$
\begin{array}{cc}
\text{(a)} & \text{(b)} \\[4pt]
\begin{pmatrix}
1 & 0 & 0 & 1 & 1 & 0 & 1 \\
0 & 1 & 0 & 1 & 0 & 1 & 1 \\
0 & 0 & 1 & 0 & 1 & 1 & 1
\end{pmatrix}
&
\begin{pmatrix}
0 & 0 & 0 & 0 & 0 & 0 & 0 \\
1 & 0 & 0 & 1 & 1 & 0 & 1 \\
0 & 1 & 0 & 1 & 0 & 1 & 1 \\
0 & 0 & 1 & 0 & 1 & 1 & 1 \\
1 & 1 & 0 & 0 & 1 & 1 & 0 \\
1 & 0 & 1 & 1 & 0 & 1 & 0 \\
0 & 1 & 1 & 1 & 1 & 0 & 0 \\
1 & 1 & 1 & 0 & 0 & 0 & 1
\end{pmatrix}
\end{array}
$$

Fig. 4. Example of the construction of an $OA(8; 2, 7, 2)$ using the Rao-Hamming construction. Figure 4(a) contains the generator matrix. Figure 4(b) shows the OA constructed from it.

4.2 Difference scheme algorithm

Difference schemes (DS), denoted by $D(r, c, s)$ are tables of r rows and c columns with s symbols such that the difference between each pair of columns yields all the symbols $\{0, 1, 2, ..., s - 1\}$.

If you have a difference scheme, you easily generate an orthogonal array by simply replicating the difference scheme s times and adding to each replication all symbols in turn modulo (s): if the sum exceeds s, you divide by s and keep the remainder.

So the problem becomes finding difference schemes. For instance, the multiplicative group of a Galois field is a difference scheme.

$$\begin{pmatrix} 0\ 0\ 0\ 0\ 0\ 0 \\ 0\ 1\ 2\ 1\ 2\ 0 \\ 0\ 2\ 1\ 1\ 0\ 2 \\ 0\ 2\ 2\ 0\ 1\ 1 \\ 0\ 0\ 1\ 2\ 2\ 1 \\ 0\ 1\ 0\ 2\ 1\ 2 \end{pmatrix}$$

Fig. 5. Example of a difference scheme $D(6,6,3)$.

An example is shown in Figure 5, as the multiplication table of $GF(2^2)$.

Given that the DS $D(r,c,s)$ is an array of size $r \times c$ based on the s elements of a group G so that for any two columns the element-wise differences contain every element of G equally often; clearly $r = \lambda s$ for some λ called the index.

If $D = D(r,c,s)$, then $\begin{bmatrix} D+0 \\ D+1 \\ \dots \\ D+(s-1) \end{bmatrix}$ is an $OA(rs;2,c,s)$. Figure 6 shows the construction of the $OA(16;2,4,4)$ from a $D(4,4,4)$.

(a)	(b)

$$\text{(a)}\quad\begin{pmatrix} 0\ 0\ 0\ 0 \\ 0\ 1\ 2\ 3 \\ 0\ 2\ 3\ 1 \\ 0\ 3\ 1\ 2 \end{pmatrix} \qquad \text{(b)}\quad \begin{pmatrix} 0\ 0\ 0\ 0 \\ 0\ 1\ 2\ 3 \\ 0\ 2\ 3\ 1 \\ 0\ 3\ 1\ 2 \\ 1\ 1\ 1\ 1 \\ 1\ 2\ 3\ 0 \\ 1\ 3\ 0\ 2 \\ 1\ 0\ 2\ 3 \\ 2\ 2\ 2\ 2 \\ 2\ 3\ 0\ 1 \\ 2\ 0\ 1\ 3 \\ 2\ 1\ 3\ 0 \\ 3\ 3\ 3\ 3 \\ 3\ 0\ 1\ 2 \\ 3\ 1\ 2\ 0 \\ 3\ 2\ 0\ 1 \end{pmatrix}$$

Fig. 6. Generated orthogonal array $OA(16;2,4,4)$ using the $D(4,4,4)$. Figure 6(a) presents the different scheme $D = (4,4,4)$. Figure 6(b) the OA constructed.

4.3 Hadamard matrix algorithms

Hadamard matrix is a DS with only two symbols: $\{-1,+1\}$. The interest in Hadamard matrices lies in the Hadamard conjecture which states that all multiples of 4 have a corresponding Hadamard matrix. Hadamard matrices are square matrices with a fixed column of just 1's. The smallest one is shown in Figure 7(a).

(a)

$$H_2 = \begin{pmatrix} 1 & 1 \\ 1 & -1 \end{pmatrix}$$

(b)

$$H_4 = \begin{pmatrix} 1 & 1 & 1 & 1 \\ 1 & -1 & 1 & -1 \\ 1 & 1 & -1 & -1 \\ 1 & -1 & -1 & 1 \end{pmatrix}$$

Fig. 7. Example of two Hadamard matrices H_2, H_4 of orders 2 and 4, respectively.

The Hadamard matrix H_4, that is shown in Figure 7(b), does not differ from the Rao-Hamming $OA(4; 2, 3, 2)$.

Figure 8 shows another example of a Hadamard matrix. This time it is shown its corresponding OA resulting after the removal of the first column and a symbol recoding.

(a)

$$\begin{pmatrix} 1 & 1 & 1 & 1 & 1 & 1 & 1 & 1 \\ 1 & -1 & 1 & -1 & 1 & -1 & 1 & -1 \\ 1 & 1 & -1 & -1 & 1 & 1 & -1 & -1 \\ 1 & -1 & -1 & 1 & 1 & -1 & -1 & 1 \\ 1 & 1 & 1 & 1 & -1 & -1 & -1 & -1 \\ 1 & -1 & 1 & -1 & -1 & 1 & -1 & 1 \\ 1 & 1 & -1 & -1 & -1 & -1 & 1 & 1 \\ 1 & -1 & -1 & 1 & -1 & 1 & 1 & -1 \end{pmatrix}$$

(b)

$$\begin{pmatrix} 1 & 1 & 1 & 1 & 1 & 1 & 1 \\ 0 & 1 & 0 & 1 & 0 & 1 & 0 \\ 1 & 0 & 0 & 1 & 1 & 0 & 0 \\ 0 & 0 & 1 & 1 & 0 & 0 & 1 \\ 1 & 1 & 1 & 0 & 0 & 0 & 0 \\ 0 & 1 & 0 & 0 & 1 & 0 & 1 \\ 1 & 0 & 0 & 0 & 0 & 1 & 1 \\ 0 & 0 & 1 & 0 & 1 & 1 & 0 \end{pmatrix}$$

Fig. 8. Figure 8(a) shows a Hadamard matrix of order 8; Figure 8(b) presents its equivalent $OA_2(2, 7, 2)$.

Not all Hadamard matrices can be generated by the Rao Hamming algorithm just by the addition of a column of 1's. Rao Hamming works if the number of levels is a power of a prime number. And this happens in a Hadamard matrix, where the number of levels is 2 (prime number). But not all Rao Hamming arrays are square after the addition of a single column of 1's. Moreover, the number of rows in a Rao Hamming OA is a power of the number of levels.

Remember the general form $OA(sn; 2, (sn - 1)/(s - 1), s)$, Hadamard matrices are square and the number of rows in the array need only to be a multiple of 4. For instance, 12 is a multiple of 4, it is not a prime power being the product 3. No Rao Hamming construction would yield a H_{12} matrix.

4.4 The Bush's construction

The Bush's construction is used to construct $OA(v^t; t, v + 1, v)$, where $v = p^n$ is a prime power. This construction considers all the elements of the Galois Field $GF(v)$, and all the polynomials $y_j(x) = a_{t-1}x^{t-1} + a_{t-2}x^{t-2} + \ldots + a_1 x + a_0$, where $a_i \in GF(v)$. The number of polynomials $y_j(x)$ are v^t, due to the fact that there are v different coefficients per each of the t terms.

Let's denote each element of $GF(v)$ as e_i, for $0 \leq i \leq v - 1$. The construction of an OA following the Bush's construction is done as follow:

1. Generate a matrix $\mathcal{M}$ formed by v^t rows and $v + 1$ columns;
2. Label the first v columns of $\mathcal{M}$ with an element $e_i \in GF(v)$;

3. Label each row of $\mathcal{M}$ with a polynomial $y_j(x)$;

4. For each cell $m_{j,i} \in \mathcal{M}$, $0 \le j \le v^t - 1, 0 \le i \le v - 1$, assign the value u whenever $y_j(e_i) = e_u$ (i.e. evaluates the polynomial $y_j(x)$ with $x = e_i$ and determines the result in the domain of $GF(v)$); and

5. Assign value u in cell $m_{j,i}$, for $0 \le j \le v^t - 1, i = v$, if e_u is the leading coefficient of $y_j(x)$, i.e. $e_u = a_{t-1}$ in the term $a_{t-1}x^{t-1}$ of the polynomial $y_j(x)$.

The constructed matrix $\mathcal{M}$ following the previous steps is an OA. We point out in this moment that the construction requires the evaluation of the polynomials $y_j(x)$ to construct the OA. The following subsection describes the general idea of the algorithm that does this construction with an efficient evaluation of these polynomials.

This section presented a survey of some construction reported in the scientific literature that are used to generate OAs. The following section will present an algorithm for the generation of logarithm tables of finite fields.

5. Algorithm for the construction of logarithm tables of Galois fields

In Barker (1986) a more efficient method to multiply two polynomials in $GF(p^n)$ is presented. The method is based on the definition of logarithms and antilogarithms in $GF(p^n)$. According with Niederreiter (1990), given a primitive element ρ of a finite field $GF(p^n)$, the discrete logarithm of a nonzero element $u \in GF(p^n)$ is that integer k, $1 \le k \le p^n - 1$, for which $u = \rho^k$. The antilogarithm for an integer k given a primitive element ρ in $GF(p^n)$ is the element $u \in GF(p^n)$ such that $u = \rho^k$. Table 1 shows the table of logarithms and antilogarithms for the elements $u \in GF(3^2)$ using the primitive element $x^2 = 2x + 1$; column 1 shows the elements in $GF(3^2)$ (the antilogarithm) and column 2 the logarithm.

Using the definition of logarithms and antilogarithms in $GF(p^n)$, the multiplication between two polynomials $\mathcal{P}_1(x)\mathcal{P}_2(x) \in GF(p^n)$ can be done using their logarithms $l_1 = log(\mathcal{P}_1(x)), l_2 = log(\mathcal{P}_2(x))$. First, the addition of logarithms $l_1 + l_2$ is done and then the antilogarithm of the result is computed.

Element $u \in GF(p^n)$	$\log_{2x+1}(u)$
1	0
x	1
$2x + 1$	2
$2x + 2$	3
2	4
$2x$	5
$x + 2$	6
$x + 1$	7

Table 1. Logarithm table of $GF(3^2)$ using the primitive element $2x + 1$.

Torres-Jimenez et al. (2011) proposed an algorithm for the construction of logarithm tables for Galois Fields $GF(p^n)$. The pseudocode is shown in Algorithm 5.1. The algorithm simultaneously finds a primitive element and constructs the logarithm table for a given $GF(p^n)$.

Algorithm 5.1: BUILDLOGARITHMTABLE(p, n)

for each $\rho \in GF(p^n) - 0$

$\quad$ **do** $\begin{cases} \mathcal{L} \leftarrow \varnothing \\ \mathcal{P}(x) \leftarrow 1 \\ k \leftarrow 0 \\ \textbf{while } (\mathcal{P}(x), k) \notin \mathcal{L} \textbf{ and } k < p^n - 1 \\ \quad \textbf{do} \begin{cases} \mathcal{L} \leftarrow \mathcal{L} \cup (\mathcal{P}(x), k) \\ k \leftarrow k + 1 \\ \mathcal{P}(x) \leftarrow p * \mathcal{P}(x) \end{cases} \\ \textbf{if } k = p^n - 1 \\ \quad \textbf{then } \{\textbf{return } (\rho) \end{cases}$

return $(\mathcal{L})$

Now, it follows the presentation of the core of this chapter, the efficient implementation of the Bush construction for OAs, based on a modification of the algorithm presented in this section.

6. Efficient construction of OAs

The idea that leads to an efficient construction of OAs through the Bush's construction relies on the algorithm proposed in (Torres-Jimenez et al., 2011). This algorithm computes the logarithm tables and the primitive element of a given Galois Field $GF(v)$. In this chapter, it is proposed an extension of this algorithm such that it can be used in combination with the Bush's construction to efficiently construct OAs of index unity. The result is an algorithm that uses only additions and modulus operations to evaluate the polynomials $y_j(x)$.

Let's show an example of this contribution. Suppose that it is wanted to construct the $OA\langle 4^3; 3, 5, 4 \rangle$. This array has an alphabet $v = p^n = 2^2 = 4$ and size 64×5. To construct it, it is required the polynomial $x + 1$ as the primitive element of $GF(2^2)$, and the logarithm table shown in Table 2(a) (both computed using the algorithm in (Torres-Jimenez et al., 2011)). Table 2(b) is a modified version of the logarithm table that contains all the elements $e_i \in GF(2^2)$ (this includes e_0, the only one which can not be generated by powers of the primitive element).

	(a)			(b)	
Power	**Polynomial in GF(2^2)**		**Element $e_i \in$ GF(2^2)**	**Polynomial in GF(2^2)**	
0	1		e_0	0	
1	x		e_1	1	
2	$x + 1$		e_2	x	
			e_3	$x + 1$	

Table 2. Logarithm table for $GF(2^2)$, with primitive element $x + 1$.

The following step in the construction of the OA is the construction of the matrix $\mathcal{M}$. For this purpose, firstly it is labeled its first v columns with the elements $e_i \in GF(2^2)$; after that, the rows are labeled with all the polynomials of maximum degree 2 and coefficients $e_j \in GF(2^2)$. Next, it is defined the integer value u for each cell $m_{j,i} \in \mathcal{M}$, where $0 \le j \le v^t - 1$ and

$0 \leq i \leq v - 1$, as the one satisfying $y_j(e_i) = e_u$. Finally, it is generated the values of cell $m_{j,i}$, where the column $i = v$, using the value of the leading coefficient of the polynomial $y_j(x)$, for each $0 \leq j \leq v^t - 1$. Table 3 shows part of the construction of the $OA(4^3; 3, 5, 4)$ through this method.

$\mathcal{M}$		Elements of $GF(2^2)$				
		e_0	e_1	e_2	e_3	
	$y_j(x)$ **Polynomial**	**0**	**1**	**x**	**x + 1**	
0	e_0	$\{u\|y_0(e_0) = e_u\}$	$\{u\|y_0(e_1) = e_u\}$	$\{u\|y_0(e_2) = e_u\}$	$\{u\|y_0(e_3) = e_u\}$	e_0
1	e_1	$\{u\|y_1(e_0) = e_u\}$	$\{u\|y_1(e_1) = e_u\}$	$\{u\|y_1(e_2) = e_u\}$	$\{u\|y_1(e_3) = e_u\}$	e_0
2	e_2	$\{u\|y_2(e_0) = e_u\}$	$\{u\|y_2(e_1) = e_u\}$	$\{u\|y_2(e_2) = e_u\}$	$\{u\|y_2(e_3) = e_u\}$	e_0
3	e_3	$\{u\|y_3(e_0) = e_u\}$	$\{u\|y_3(e_1) = e_u\}$	$\{u\|y_3(e_2) = e_u\}$	$\{u\|y_3(e_3) = e_u\}$	e_0
4	e_1x	$\{u\|y_4(e_0) = e_u\}$	$\{u\|y_4(e_1) = e_u\}$	$\{u\|y_4(e_2) = e_u\}$	$\{u\|y_4(e_3) = e_u\}$	e_0
5	$e_1x + e_1$	$\{u\|y_5(e_0) = e_u\}$	$\{u\|y_5(e_1) = e_u\}$	$\{u\|y_5(e_2) = e_u\}$	$\{u\|y_5(e_3) = e_u\}$	e_0
6	$e_1x + e_2$	$\{u\|y_6(e_0) = e_u\}$	$\{u\|y_6(e_1) = e_u\}$	$\{u\|y_6(e_2) = e_u\}$	$\{u\|y_6(e_3) = e_u\}$	e_0
7	$e_1x + e_3$	$\{u\|y_7(e_0) = e_u\}$	$\{u\|y_7(e_1) = e_u\}$	$\{u\|y_7(e_2) = e_u\}$	$\{u\|y_7(e_3) = e_u\}$	e_0
8	e_2x	$\{u\|y_8(e_0) = e_u\}$	$\{u\|y_8(e_1) = e_u\}$	$\{u\|y_8(e_2) = e_u\}$	$\{u\|y_8(e_3) = e_u\}$	e_0
9	$e_2x + e_1$	$\{u\|y_9(e_0) = e_u\}$	$\{u\|y_9(e_1) = e_u\}$	$\{u\|y_9(e_2) = e_u\}$	$\{u\|y_9(e_3) = e_u\}$	e_0
10	$e_2x + e_2$	$\{u\|y_{10}(e_0) = e_u\}$	$\{u\|y_{10}(e_1) = e_u\}$	$\{u\|y_{10}(e_2) = e_u\}$	$\{u\|y_{10}(e_3) = e_u\}$	e_0
11	$e_2x + e_3$	$\{u\|y_{11}(e_0) = e_u\}$	$\{u\|y_{11}(e_1) = e_u\}$	$\{u\|y_{11}(e_2) = e_u\}$	$\{u\|y_{11}(e_3) = e_u\}$	e_0
12	e_3x	$\{u\|y_{12}(e_0) = e_u\}$	$\{u\|y_{12}(e_1) = e_u\}$	$\{u\|y_{12}(e_2) = e_u\}$	$\{u\|y_{12}(e_3) = e_u\}$	e_0
13	$e_3x + e_1$	$\{u\|y_{13}(e_0) = e_u\}$	$\{u\|y_{13}(e_1) = e_u\}$	$\{u\|y_{13}(e_2) = e_u\}$	$\{u\|y_{13}(e_3) = e_u\}$	e_0
14	$e_3x + e_2$	$\{u\|y_{14}(e_0) = e_u\}$	$\{u\|y_{14}(e_1) = e_u\}$	$\{u\|y_{14}(e_2) = e_u\}$	$\{u\|y_{14}(e_3) = e_u\}$	e_0
15	$e_3x + e_3$	$\{u\|y_{15}(e_0) = e_u\}$	$\{u\|y_{15}(e_1) = e_u\}$	$\{u\|y_{15}(e_2) = e_u\}$	$\{u\|y_{15}(e_3) = e_u\}$	e_0
16	e_1x^2	$\{u\|y_{16}(e_0) = e_u\}$	$\{u\|y_{16}(e_1) = e_u\}$	$\{u\|y_{16}(e_2) = e_u\}$	$\{u\|y_{16}(e_3) = e_u\}$	e_1
17	$e_1x^2 + e_1$	$\{u\|y_{17}(e_0) = e_u\}$	$\{u\|y_{17}(e_1) = e_u\}$	$\{u\|y_{17}(e_2) = e_u\}$	$\{u\|y_{17}(e_3) = e_u\}$	e_1
18	$e_1x^2 + e_2$	$\{u\|y_{18}(e_0) = e_u\}$	$\{u\|y_{18}(e_1) = e_u\}$	$\{u\|y_{18}(e_2) = e_u\}$	$\{u\|y_{18}(e_3) = e_u\}$	e_1
19	$e_1x^2 + e_3$	$\{u\|y_{19}(e_0) = e_u\}$	$\{u\|y_{19}(e_1) = e_u\}$	$\{u\|y_{19}(e_2) = e_u\}$	$\{u\|y_{19}(e_3) = e_u\}$	e_1
20	$e_1x^2 + e_1x$	$\{u\|y_{20}(e_0) = e_u\}$	$\{u\|y_{20}(e_1) = e_u\}$	$\{u\|y_{20}(e_2) = e_u\}$	$\{u\|y_{20}(e_3) = e_u\}$	e_1
21	$e_1x^2 + e_1x + e_1$	$\{u\|y_{21}(e_0) = e_u\}$	$\{u\|y_{21}(e_1) = e_u\}$	$\{u\|y_{21}(e_2) = e_u\}$	$\{u\|y_{21}(e_3) = e_u\}$	e_1
22	$e_1x^2 + e_1x + e_2$	$\{u\|y_{22}(e_0) = e_u\}$	$\{u\|y_{22}(e_1) = e_u\}$	$\{u\|y_{22}(e_2) = e_u\}$	$\{u\|y_{22}(e_3) = e_u\}$	e_1
23	$e_1x^2 + e_1x + e_3$	$\{u\|y_{23}(e_0) = e_u\}$	$\{u\|y_{23}(e_1) = e_u\}$	$\{u\|y_{23}(e_2) = e_u\}$	$\{u\|y_{23}(e_3) = e_u\}$	e_1
24	$e_1x^2 + e_2x$	$\{u\|y_{24}(e_0) = e_u\}$	$\{u\|y_{24}(e_1) = e_u\}$	$\{u\|y_{24}(e_2) = e_u\}$	$\{u\|y_{24}(e_3) = e_u\}$	e_1
25	$e_1x^2 + e_2x + e_1$	$\{u\|y_{25}(e_0) = e_u\}$	$\{u\|y_{25}(e_1) = e_u\}$	$\{u\|y_{25}(e_2) = e_u\}$	$\{u\|y_{25}(e_3) = e_u\}$	e_1
26	$e_1x^2 + e_2x + e_2$	$\{u\|y_{26}(e_0) = e_u\}$	$\{u\|y_{26}(e_1) = e_u\}$	$\{u\|y_{26}(e_2) = e_u\}$	$\{u\|y_{26}(e_3) = e_u\}$	e_1
27	$e_1x^2 + e_2x + e_3$	$\{u\|y_{27}(e_0) = e_u\}$	$\{u\|y_{27}(e_1) = e_u\}$	$\{u\|y_{27}(e_2) = e_u\}$	$\{u\|y_{27}(e_3) = e_u\}$	e_1
28	$e_1x^2 + e_3x$	$\{u\|y_{28}(e_0) = e_u\}$	$\{u\|y_{28}(e_1) = e_u\}$	$\{u\|y_{28}(e_2) = e_u\}$	$\{u\|y_{28}(e_3) = e_u\}$	e_1
29	$e_1x^2 + e_3x + e_1$	$\{u\|y_{29}(e_0) = e_u\}$	$\{u\|y_{29}(e_1) = e_u\}$	$\{u\|y_{29}(e_2) = e_u\}$	$\{u\|y_{29}(e_3) = e_u\}$	e_1
30	$e_1x^2 + e_3x + e_2$	$\{u\|y_{30}(e_0) = e_u\}$	$\{u\|y_{30}(e_1) = e_u\}$	$\{u\|y_{30}(e_2) = e_u\}$	$\{u\|y_{30}(e_3) = e_u\}$	e_1
31	$e_1x^2 + e_3x + e_3$	$\{u\|y_{31}(e_0) = e_u\}$	$\{u\|y_{31}(e_1) = e_u\}$	$\{u\|y_{31}(e_2) = e_u\}$	$\{u\|y_{31}(e_3) = e_u\}$	e_1
$\vdots$		$\vdots$	$\vdots$	$\vdots$	$\vdots$	

Table 3. Example of a partial construction of the $OA(4^3; 3, 4, 5)$, using the Bush's construction.

During the definition of values e_u, the polynomials $y_j(e_i)$ must be evaluated. For example, the evaluation of the polynomial $y_{14} = e_3x + e_1$ at value $x = e_2$ yields $y_{14}(e_2) = e_3x + e_1 = e_3 \cdot e_2 + e_1 = e_0$. To obtain the result e_0 it is necessary to multiply the polynomials e_3 and e_2, and to add the result to e_1. Here is where lies the main contribution shown in this chapter, it is proposed to use the primitive element and the logarithm table constructed by the algorithm in (Torres-Jimenez et al., 2011) to do the multiplication through additions. To do that they are used equivalent powers of the primitive element of the elements $e_i \in GF(2^2)$ involved in the operation, e.g. instead of multiplying $(x + 1) \cdot (x)$ we multiply $x^2 \cdot x^1$. Then, the sum of indices does the multiplication, and the antilogarithm obtains the correct result in $GF(2^2)$. For the case of $x^2 \cdot x^1$ the result is $x^3 = x^0 = e_1$. Finally, we add this result to e_1 to complete the operation (this yield the expected value e_0). Note that whenever and operation yields a result outside of the field, a modulus operations is required.

The pseudocode for the construction of OAs using the Bush's construction and the logarithm tables is shown in Algorithm 6.1. The logarithm and antilogarithm table $\mathcal{L}_{i,j}$ is obtained through the algorithm reported by Torres-Jimenez et al. (2011). After that, each element e_i and each polynomial $y_j(x)$ in $GF(p^n)$ are considered as the columns and rows of $\mathcal{M}$, the OA that is being constructed. Given that the value of each cell $m_{i,j} \in \mathcal{M}$ is the index u of the element $e_u \in GF(p^n)$ such that $y_j(e_i) = e_u$, the following step in the pseudocode is the evaluation of the polynomial $y_j(x)$. This evaluation is done by determining the coefficient of each term $a_k \in y_j(x)$ and its index, i.e. the value of the element $e_l \in GF(p^n)$ that is the coefficient of a_k, and then adding it to $i \cdot d$ (the index of e_i raised to the degree of the term a_k). A modulus operation is applied to the result to obtained v, and then the antilogarithm is used over v such that the index it is able to get the value u of the element e_u. Remember that the algorithm `BuildLogarithmTable` simultaneously find the primitive element and computes the logarithm and antilogarithm tables.

Algorithm 6.1: BUILDORTHOGONALARRAY(p, n)

$\mathcal{L} \leftarrow$ BuildLogarithmTable(p, n)
$\mathcal{M} \leftarrow \varnothing$
for each element $e_i \in GF(p^n)$
do $\begin{cases} c \leftarrow i \\ \textbf{for each } \text{polynomial } y_j(x) \in GF(p^n) \\ \textbf{do} \begin{cases} r \leftarrow j \\ \textbf{for each } \text{term } a_k \in y_j(x) \\ \textbf{do} \begin{cases} d \leftarrow \texttt{GetDegree}(a_k) \\ l \leftarrow \texttt{GetIndexCoefficient}(a_k) \\ v \leftarrow (i \cdot d + l) \bmod (p^n - 1) \\ s \leftarrow \mathcal{L}_{v,1} \end{cases} \\ m_{r,c} \leftarrow s \end{cases} \end{cases}$
return $(\mathcal{M})$

Note that in the pseudocode the more complex operation is the module between integers, which can be reduced to shifts when $GF(p^n)$ involves powers of two. This fact makes the algorithm easy and efficient for the construction of OAs, requiring only additions to operate, and modulus operations when the field is over powers of primes different of two. After the construction of the OA, the number of operations required by the algorithm are bounded by $O(N \cdot t^2)$, due to it requires t operations for the construction of an OA matrix of size $N \times (t + 1)$.

7. Efficient constructions of CAs

This section analyzes the case when Covering Arrays can be constructed from cyclotomy by rotating a vector created from an OA(Colbourn, 2010). It is another process that can be benefited from the previously constructed logarithm tables. The cyclotomy process requires the test of different cyclotomic vectors for the construction of CAs. This vectors can be constructed using the logarithm table. The rest of the section details a bit more about CAs and this process of construction.

Definition 2 (Covering Array). *Let N, t, k, v be positive integers with $t \leq N$. A covering array $CA(N; t, k, v)$, with strength t and alphabet size v is an $N \times k$ array with entries from $\{0, 1, ..., k-1\}$ and the property that any $N \times t$ sub-array has all v^t possible t-tuples occurring at least once.*

Figure 9 shows the corresponding $CA(9; 2, 4, 3)$. The strength of this CA is $t = 2$ and the alphabet is $v = 3$, hence the combinations $\{0,0\}$, $\{0,1\}$, $\{0,2\}$, $\{1,0\}$, $\{1,1\}$, $\{1,2\}$, $\{2,0\}$, $\{2,1\}$, $\{2,2\}$ appear at least once in each subset of size $N \times 2$ of the CA. The CAs are commonly used instead of full experimental designs (FED) when constructing test sets, it is so because the relaxation produced by the use of a small interaction in a CA $t = 2$ (pair-wise) significantly reduce the number of test cases in a test set, implying in some cases savings of more than 90 percent in costs (time or other resources); the confidence level of the testing using combinatorial objects as CA increases with the interaction level involved (Kuhn et al., 2008).

When a CA contains the minimum possible number of rows, it is optimal and its size is called the *Covering Array Number* (CAN). The CAN is defined according to Equation 5.

$$CAN(t, k, v) = \min_{N \in \mathbb{N}} \{N : \exists\, CA(N; t, k, v)\}. \tag{5}$$

The trivial mathematical *lower bound* for a covering array is $v^t \leq CAN(t, k, v)$, however, this number is rarely achieved. Therefore determining achievable lower bounds is one of the main research lines for CAs; this problem has been overcome with the reduction of the known upper bounds. The construction of cyclotomic matrices can help to accomplish this purpose.

According to Colbourn (2010), a cyclotomic matrix (CM) is an array $\mathcal{O}$ of size $k \times k$ that is formed by k rotations of a vector of size k (called starter vector). Table 4 gives an example of a CM.

0	0	0	1	0	1	1
0	0	1	0	1	1	0
0	1	0	1	1	0	0
1	0	1	1	0	0	0
0	1	1	0	0	0	1
1	1	0	0	0	1	0
1	0	0	0	1	0	1

Table 4. CM of size 7×7 formed from the starter vector $\{0, 0, 0, 1, 0, 1, 1\}$. This matrix is a $CA(7; 2, 7, 2)$.

The strategy to construct a cyclotomic matrix involves the identification of a good vector starter. This task can be facilitated using the logarithm table derived from a Galois field. The construction is simple. The first step is the generation of the logarithm table for a certain $GF(p^n)$. After that, the table is transposed in order to transform it into a vector starter v. Then, by using all the possible rotations of it, the cyclotomic matrix is constructed. Finally, the validation of the matrix is done such that a CA can be identified.

$$\begin{pmatrix} 0\,0\,0\,0 \\ 0\,1\,1\,1 \\ 0\,2\,2\,2 \\ 1\,0\,1\,2 \\ 1\,1\,2\,0 \\ 1\,2\,0\,1 \\ 2\,0\,2\,1 \\ 2\,1\,0\,2 \\ 2\,2\,1\,0 \end{pmatrix}$$

Fig. 9. Covering array where $N = 9, t = 2, k = 4$ and $v = 3$.

Figure 10 shows an example of a cyclotomic matrix.

(a) Vector Starter

0	0	1	1	0	0	0	0	0	1	1	0

(b) Cyclotomic matrix

$$\begin{pmatrix} 0\,0\,1\,1\,0\,0\,0\,0\,0\,0\,1\,1\,0 \\ 0\,1\,1\,0\,0\,0\,0\,0\,1\,1\,0\,0 \\ 1\,1\,0\,0\,0\,0\,0\,0\,1\,1\,0\,0\,0 \\ 1\,0\,0\,0\,0\,0\,0\,1\,1\,0\,0\,0\,1 \\ 0\,0\,0\,0\,0\,0\,1\,1\,0\,0\,0\,1\,1 \\ 0\,0\,0\,0\,0\,1\,1\,0\,0\,0\,1\,1\,0 \\ 0\,0\,0\,0\,1\,1\,0\,0\,0\,1\,1\,0\,0 \\ 0\,0\,0\,1\,1\,0\,0\,0\,1\,1\,0\,0\,0 \\ 0\,0\,1\,1\,0\,0\,0\,1\,1\,0\,0\,0\,0 \\ 0\,1\,1\,0\,0\,0\,1\,1\,0\,0\,0\,0\,0 \\ 1\,1\,0\,0\,0\,1\,1\,0\,0\,0\,0\,0\,0 \\ 1\,0\,0\,0\,1\,1\,0\,0\,0\,0\,0\,0\,1 \\ 0\,0\,0\,1\,1\,0\,0\,0\,0\,0\,0\,1\,1 \end{pmatrix}$$

Fig. 10. Example of a cyclotomic vector V, or a vector starter, and the cyclotomic matrix formed with it. The matrix constitutes a $CA(13; 2, 13, 2)$.

The pseudocode to generate the cyclotomic vector and construct the CA is presented in Algorithm 7.1. There, the algorithm BuildLogarithmTable(p,n) is used to construct the table of logarithm and antilogarithms $\mathcal{L}$, where the ith row indicate the element $e_i \in GF(p^n)$, and the column 0 its logarithm, and the column 1 its antilogarithm. The first step is the construction of the vector starter $\mathcal{V}$, which is done by transposing the logarithm table $\mathcal{L}_{*,0}$, i.e. the first column of $\mathcal{L}$. After that, the cyclotomic matrix $\mathcal{M}$ is constructed by rotating the vector starter p^n times, each time the vector rotated will constituted a row of $\mathcal{M}$. Finally, the cyclotomic matrix $\mathcal{M}$ must be validated as a CA to finally return it; one strategy to do so is the parallel algorithm reported by Avila-George et al. (2010).

Algorithm 7.1: BUILDCOVERINGARRAY(p,n)

$\mathcal{L} \leftarrow$ BuildLogarithmTable(p,n)
for each $e_i \in GF(p^n)$
  do $\{\mathcal{V}_i \leftarrow \mathcal{L}_{i,0}$
for each $e_i \in GF(p^n)$
  do $\begin{cases} \textbf{for each } e_j \in GF(p^n) \\ \quad \textbf{do } \begin{cases} k \leftarrow (i+j)\mathrm{mod}(p^n) \\ m_{i,j} \leftarrow \mathcal{V}_k \end{cases} \end{cases}$
if IsACoveringArray($\mathcal{M}$)
  then $\{return\mathcal{M}$

  else $\{return\varnothing$

The following section presents some results derived from the research presented so far in this chapter.

8. Results

An example of one of the best known upper bounds for CAs constructed through the use of cyclotomic matrices is shown in Figure 11; the construction of such table was done with aid of the implementation proposed in this chapter.

The results from the experiment are found in the repository of CAs of Torres-Jimenez [1]. Some of the CAs matrices presented there are derived from the use of cyclotomic vectors constructed through the process described in the previous section, benefiting from the construction of the logarithm tables. Table 5 shows new upper bounds derived from this process.

---

[1] http://www.tamps.cinvestav.mx/~jtj/CA.php

Fig. 11. $CA(67; 4, 67, 2)$ generated through a cyclotomic matrix. This CA is the best known upper bound so far.

k	N	Algorithm
1231	1231	Cyclotomy
1283	1283	Cyclotomy
1319	1319	Cyclotomy
1361	1361	Cyclotomy
1367	1367	Cyclotomy
1373	1373	Cyclotomy
1381	1381	Cyclotomy
1423	1423	Cyclotomy
1427	1427	Cyclotomy
1429	1429	Cyclotomy
1439	1439	Cyclotomy
1447	1447	Cyclotomy
1459	1459	Cyclotomy
1483	1483	Cyclotomy
1487	1487	Cyclotomy
1493	1493	Cyclotomy
1499	1499	Cyclotomy
1511	1511	Cyclotomy
1523	1523	Cyclotomy
1549	1549	Cyclotomy
1559	1559	Cyclotomy
1567	1567	Cyclotomy
1571	1571	Cyclotomy
1579	1579	Cyclotomy
1583	1583	Cyclotomy
1597	1597	Cyclotomy
1601	1601	Cyclotomy
1607	1607	Cyclotomy
1609	1609	Cyclotomy
1613	1613	Cyclotomy
1619	1619	Cyclotomy
1621	1621	Cyclotomy
1627	1627	Cyclotomy
1997	1997	Cyclotomy
1999	1999	Cyclotomy
2003	2003	Cyclotomy
2503	2503	Cyclotomy

Table 5. New upper bounds for CAs obtained through cyclotomic matrices.

9. Conclusions

The main objective of this chapter was the presentation of a efficient implementation of the Bush's construction for Orthogonal Arrays (OAs). Also, it was presented a brief summary of the applications of OAs in cryptography, which could be benefited from the implementation. In addition, the algorithm was also applied for the construction of cyclotomy matrices that yielded new upper bounds of CAs.

Hence, the main contribution of this chapter consisted precisely in an algorithm that requires only additions and modulus operations over finite fields for the construction of OAs. To do so, it relies on a logarithm table constructed through a simple method reported in the literature. It is also presented the details for this construction through the code required to be implemented.

Additionally, the algorithm to construct logarithm table was also slightly modified to construct cyclotomy matrices for the construction of CAs. Here, it is presented the matrix of the $CA(67; 4, 67, 2)$ constructed from a cyclotomic matrix; it represents the best upper bound known so far for these parameters of the CA. Also, it is reported a set of 37 upper bounds of CAs obtained by the construction of the cyclotomy matrices constructed with

support of the algorithm reported here. These matrices are available on request in http:
//www.tamps.cinvestav.mx/~jtj/CA.php.

In addition to the efficient implementation of the Bush's construction through logarithm tables
of finite fields, this chapter also presents a brief summary of the combinatorial structures
called Orthogonal Arrays. The summary included formal definition, and basic notation
used in the scientific literature. Additionally, several applications of OAs in cryptography
were presented; and also, different methodologies to construct the combinatorial objects were
described; among them was the Bush's construction.

10. Acknowledgments

The authors thankfully acknowledge the computer resources and assistance provided by
Spanish Supercomputing Network (TIRANT-UV). This research work was partially funded
by the following projects: CONACyT 58554, Calculo de Covering Arrays; 51623 Fondo Mixto
CONACyT y Gobierno del Estado de Tamaulipas.

11. References

Avila-George, H., Torres-Jimenez, J., Hernández, V. & Rangel-Valdez, N. (2010). Verification
    of general and cyclic covering arrays using grid computing, *Data Management in Grid
    and Peer-to-Peer Systmes, Third International Conference, Globe 2010, Bilbao, Spain*, Vol.
    6265 of *Lecture Notes in Computer Science*, Springer, pp. 112–123.
Barker, H. A. (1986). Sum and product tables for galois fields, *International Journal of
    Mathematical Education in Science and Technology* 17: 473 – 485. http://dx.doi.
    org/10.1080/0020739860170409.
Bush, K. (1952). Orthogonal arrays of index unity, *Annals of Mathematical Statistics*
    23(3): 426–434.
    URL: *http://www.jstor.org/pss/2236685*
Carter, J. & Wegman, M. (1979). Universal classes of hash functions, *Journal of Computer and
    System Sciences* 18: 143–154. http://dx.doi.org/10.1016/0022-0000(79)
    90044-8.
Colbourn, C. J. (2010). Covering arrays from cyclotomy, *Designs, Codes and Cryptography*
    55: 201–219. http://dx.doi.org/10.1007/s10623-009-9333-8.
Dawson, E. & Mahmoodian, E. (1993). Orthogonal arrays and ordered threshold schemes,
    Australasian Journal of Combinatorics 8: 27–44.
    URL: *http://ajc.maths.uq.edu.au/pdf/8/ocr-ajc-v8-p27.pdf*
Gilbert, E., MacWilliams, F. & Sloane, N. (1974). Codes which detect deception, *The Bell System
    Technical Journal* 53: 405–424.
    URL: *http://www2.research.att.com/ njas/doc/detection.pdf*
Gopalakrishnan, K. & Stinson, D. R. (2008). Applications of orthogonal arrays to computer
    science, *Ramanujan Mathematical Society, Lecture Notes Series in Mathematics* 7: 149–164.
Hedayat, A., Sloane, N. & Stufken, J. (1999). *Orthogonal Arrays: Theory and Applications*,
    Springer-Verlag, New York.
Jones, T. & Seberry, J. (1986). Authentication without secrecy, *ARS Combinatoria* 21-A: 115–121.
Kuhn, R., Lei, Y. & Kacker, R. (2008). Practical Combinatorial Testing: Beyond Pairwise, *IT
    Professional* 10(3): 19–23. http://doi.ieeecomputersociety.org/10.1109/
    MITP.2008.54.

Niederreiter, H. (1990). A short proof for explicit formulas for discrete logarithms in finite fields, *Applicable Algebra in Engineering, Communication and Computing* 1(1): 55–57. http://dx.doi.org/10.1007/BF01810847.

Rao, C. (1946). Hypercube of strength 'd' leading to confounded designs in factorial experiments, *Bulletin of the Calcutta Mathematical Society* 38: 67–78.

Rao, C. (1947). Factorial experiments derivable from combinatorial arrangements of arrays, *Journal of the Royal Statistical Society* 9: 128–139.
URL: *http://www.jstor.org/pss/2983576*

Stinson, D. (1992a). Combinatorial characterizations of authentication codes, *Designs, Codes and Cryptography* 2: 175–187. http://dx.doi.org/10.1007/BF00124896.

Stinson, D. (1992b). An explication of secret sharing schemes, *Designs, Codes and Cryptography* 2: 357–390. http://dx.doi.org/10.1007/BF00125203.

Stinson, D. (1994). Combinatorial techniques for universal hashing, *Journal of Computer and System Sciences* 48: 337–346. http://dx.doi.org/10.1016/S0022-0000(05)80007-8.

Stinson, D. R. (2004). Orthogonal arrays and codes, *Combinatorial Designs*, Springer-Verlag, New York, chapter 10, pp. 225–255.

Taguchi, G. (1994). *Taguchi Methods: Design of Experiments*, American Supplier Institute.

Torres-Jimenez, J., Rangel-Valdez, N., Gonzalez-Hernandez, A. & Avila-George, H. (2011). Construction of logarithm tables for galois fields, *International Journal of Mathematical Education in Science and Technology* 42(1): 91–102. http://dx.doi.org/10.1080/0020739X.2010.510215.

Wegman, M. & Carter, J. (1981). New hash functions and their use in authentication and set equality, *Journal of Computer and System Sciences* 22: 265–279. http://dx.doi.org/10.1016/0022-0000(81)90033-7.

4

Malicious Cryptology and Mathematics

Eric Filiol

Laboratoire de Cryptologie et De Virologie Opérationnelles
ESIEA
France

1. Introduction

Malicious cryptology and malicious mathematics is an emerging domain initiated in Filiol & Josse (2007); Filiol & Raynal (2008;b). It draws its inspiration from crypto virology Young & Yung (2004). However this latter domain has a very limited approach of how cryptography can be perverted by malware. Indeed, their authors consider the case of extortion malware in which asymmetric cryptography is only used inside a malware payload to extort money in exchange of the secret key necessary to recover the file encrypted by the malware (e.g. a computer virus).

Malicious cryptology and malicious mathematics make in fact explode Young and Yung's narrow vision. This results in an unlimited, fascinating yet disturbing field of research and experimentation. This new domain covers several fields and topics (non-exhaustive list):

- Use of cryptography and mathematics to develop *"super malware"* (*über-malware*) which evade any kind of detection by implementing:
  - Optimized propagation and attack techniques (e.g. by using biased or specific random number generator) Filiol et al. (2007).
  - Sophisticated self-protection techniques. The malware code protects itself and its own functional activity by using strong cryptography-based tools Filiol (2005b).
  - Sophisticated auto-protection and code armouring techniques. Malware protect their own code and activity by using strong cryptography.
  - Partial or total invisibility features. The programmer intends to make his code to become invisible by using statistical simulability Filiol & Josse (2007).

- Use of complexity theory or computability theory to design undetectable malware.

- Use of malware to perform cryptanalysis operations (steal secret keys or passwords), manipulate encryption algorithms to weaken them on the fly in the target computer memory. The resulting encryption process will be easier to be broken Filiol (2011).

- Design and implementation of encryption systems with hidden mathematical trapdoors. The knowledge of the trap (by the system designer only) enables to break the system very efficiently. Despite the fact that the system is open and public, the trapdoor must remain undetectable. This can also apply to the keys themselves in the case of asymmetric cryptography Erra & Grenier (2009).

One could define malicious cryptology/mathematics as the interconnection of computer virology with cryptology and mathematics for their mutual benefit. The number of potential applications is almost infinite. In the context of this chapter, we could also define it – or a part of it – as the different mathematical techniques enabling to modify or manipulate reality and to reflect a suitable but false image of reality to the observer (may it be a human being or an automated system).

In this chapter we intend to present in more details a few of these techniques that are very illustrative of what malicious cryptography and malicious mathematics are. Section 2 first recalls a few definition and basic concepts in computer virology and in cryptology to make this chaper self-contained. In Section 3, we expose a detailed state-of-the-art of malicious cryptology and malicious mathematics. We then detail two of the most illustrative techniques in the two next sections. Section 4 addresses how mathematical reality can be perverted to design processor-dependent malware. Section 5 then exposes how malicious cryptosystems can be used to protect malware code against detection and analysis.

2. Basic definitions and concepts

2.1 Computer virology

A rather large definition of what malware (shortened for of *Malicious Software*) are, here follows.

Definition 1. *A malware is a malicious code or unwated piece of software like a virus, a worm, a spyware, a Trojan horse... whose aim is to undermine systems' confidentiality, integrity or availability.*

In a more formal approach, malware are programs that take data from the environment (computer, system, users..) as input argument and output one or more malicious actions: file erasing, data eavesdropping, denial of services... A detailed and technical presentation of what malware are, is availble in Filiol (2005).

We will address the problematic of anti-antiviral techniques that are used by malware. Indeed, most of the malicious cryptology and malicious mathematics techniques aims at providing such capabilities to malware. It is logical that the latter enforce techniques to prevent or disable functionalities installed by antiviral software or firewalls. Two main techniques can be put forward:

- *Stealth techniques.-* a set of techniques aiming at convincing the user, the operating system and security programs that there is no malicious code. Malware then aim to escape monitoring and detection

- *Polymorphism/metamorphism.-* As antiviral programs are mainly based on the search for viral signatures (scanning techniques), polymorphic techniques aim at making the analysis of files – only by their appearance as sequence of bytes – far more difficult. The basic principle is to keep the code vary constantly from viral copy to viral copy in order to avoid any fixed components that could be exploited by antiviral programs to identify the virus (a set of instructions, specific character strings).

  Polymorphic techniques are rather difficult to implement and manage and this is precisely where lies the critical aspect of designing powerful malicious techniques drawn from both mathematics and cryptology. Two following main techniques (a number of complex variants exist however) are to be considered:

- Code rewriting into an equivalent code. From a formal point of view any rewriting technique lies on one or more formal grammar. According to the class of the grammar considered, then the malware protection is more or less stronger.

- Applying encryption techniques to all or part of malware code. Generally, those encryption techniques consist in masking every code byte with a constant byte value (by means of XOR). Any valid encryption technique implies the use of a static key that eventually constitutes a true signature (or infection marker) when ill-implemented. Moreover any skilled reverse-engineer will always succeed in extracting this static key and hence will easily unprotect the malware source code.

• *Code armouring* Filiol (2005b) consists in writing a code so as to delay, complicate or even prevent its analysis. While polymorphism/metamorphism aims at limited/preventing automated (e.g. by an antivirus software) analysis, code armouring techniques's purposes is to limit or bar the reverse engineer (a human being) analysis.

2.2 Cryptology

2.2.1 Cryptosystems

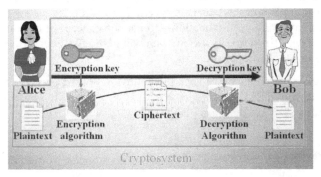

Fig. 1. General structure of a cryptosystem

A cryptosystem S (symmetric case) is defined as the set of an encryption/decryption algorithm E, a secret K, a plaintext message P and a ciphertext C. Let us recall that in the case of asymmetric cryptography (also well-known as public-key cryptography), the decryption and encryption algorithms are different, as well as the encryption and decryption keys. Asymmetric cryptography is mainly used for authentication and digital signature purposes but it can also be used to encrypt small quantities of information (a few dozen bytes). On the contrary, in the symmetric case, the key K and the algorithm E are the same. Symmetric cryptography is considered for encryption purposes. The plaintext is supposed to be secret while the cipher text is supposed to be accessed by any one. So with those notations, we have

$$C = E(K, P) \text{ and } P = E(K, C)$$

From a technical point of view, the internal operations (especially with respect to the key) may slightly differ according to the different classes of cryptosystems. But to summarize, any cryptosystem can be defined as a complex combination of substitutions and transpositions of bytes or string of bytes.

Cryptanalysis is the art of breaking cryptosystems; in other words, the attacker wants to access the plaintext P without the *a priori* knowledge of the key. This access can be performed directly through plaintext recovery or indirectly through key recovery which then enables the attacker to decipher the cipher text.

2.2.2 Entropy profile

Most of the problem regarding the use of cryptography for malicious purposes lies in the fact that code armouring and code mutation involve random data. These must be generated on-the-fly. In the context of metamorphism, the generator itself must be random too. For sake of simplicity, we shall speak of *Pseudo-Random Number Generator* (PRNG) to describe both a random number generator and an encryption system. The difference lies in the fact that in the latter case either random data produced from the expansion of the key are combined with the plaintext (stream ciphers) or they are the result of the combination of the key with the plaintext (block ciphers).

The whole issue lies in the generation of a so-called "good" randomness. Except that in the context of malicious cryptography Filiol (2007), the term "good" does not necessarily correspond to what cryptographers usually mean. In fact, it is better – yet a simplified but sufficient reduction as a first approximation – to use the concept of entropy Filiol & Raynal (2008). In the same way, the term of random data will indifferently describe the random data themselves or the result of encryption.

Consider a (malicious) code as an information source X. When parsed, the source outputs characters taking the possible values x_i $(i = 0, \ldots, 255)$, each with a probability $p_i = P[X = x_i]$. Then the entropy $H(X)$ of the source is the following sum[1]:

$$H(X) = \sum_{i=0}^{255} -p_i \log_2(p_i)$$

Random data, by nature will exhibit a high entropy value thus meaning that the uncertainty is maximal whenever trying to predict the next value output by the source X. On the contrary, non random data exhibit a low entropy profile (they are easier or less difficult to predict).

From the attacker's point of view the presence of random data means that something is hidden but he has to make the difference between legitimate data (e.g. use of packers to protect code against piracy) and illegitimate data (e.g. malware code). In the NATO terminology – at the present time it is the most precise and accurate one as far as InfoSec is concerned– random data relate to a COMSEC (*COMmunication SECurity*) aspect only.

For the attacker (automated software or human expert), the problem is twofold: first detect random data parts inside a code and then decrypt them. In this respect, any code area exhibiting a high entropy profile must be considered as suspicious. To prevent attention to be

---

[1] Let us note that here the entropy considers single characters or 1-grams only. A more accurate value would consider all the possible n-grams and would compute entropy when $n \to \infty$.

focused on those random parts, is it possible to add some TRANSEC (*TRANSmission SECurity*) aspect. The most famous one is steganography but for malware or program protection purposes it is not directly usable (data cannot be directly executed) and we have to find different ways. The other solution is to use malicious statistics as defined and exposed in Filiol & Raynal (2008). It is also possible to break randomness by using noisy encoding techniques like in Perseus technology.

Breaking randomness applies well on any data used for code mutation (e.g. junk code insertion), including specific subsets of code as CFGs (*Comtrol Flow Graphs*): randomly mutated CFG must exhibit the same profile as any normal CFG would. Otherwise, considering the COMSEC aspect only is bound to make the code detection very easy.

2.2.3 Key management

Encrypting a code or a piece of code implies its preliminary deciphering whenever it is executed. But in all of the cases – except those involving money extortion introduced Young and Yung Young & Yung (2004) – the key must be accessible to the code itself to decipher. Consequently in a way or another it is contained in a more or less obfuscated form inside the code. Therefore is it accessible to the analyst who will always succeed in finding and accessing it. Instead of performing cryptanalysis, a simple decoding/deciphering operation is sufficient.

It is therefore necessary to consider keys that are external to the encrypted code. Two cases are possible Filiol (2007):

- Environmental key management. The code gathers information in its execution environment and calculates the key repeatedly. The correct key will be computed when and only when the suitable conditions will be realized in the code environment – which is usually under the control of the code designer. The security model should prohibit dictionary attacks or environment reduction attacks (enabling reduced exhaustive search) by the code analyst. Consequently the analyst must examine the code in an controlled dynamic area (sandbox or virtual machine) and wait until suitable conditions are met without knowing when they will be. However it is possible to build more operational scenarii for this case and to detect that the code is being analyzed and controlled.

- Use of k-ary codes (Filiol (2007c)) in which a program is no longer a single monolithic binary entity but a set of binaries and non executable files (working in a serial mode or in a parallel mode) to produce a desired final (malicious or not) action. Then the analyst has a reduced view on the whole code only since generally he can access a limited subset of this k-set. In the context of (legitimate) code protection, one of the files will be a kernel-land module communicating with a userland code to protect. The code without the appropriate operating environment – with a user-specific configuration by the administrator – will never work. This solution has the great advantage of hiding (by outsourcing it), the encryption system itself. It is one particular instance with respect to this last solution that we present in this paper.

3. The state-of-the-art of malicious cryptology and malicious mathematics

As any recently emerging field, the history of malicious cryptology and malicious mathematics is rather short. Young and Yung seminal work Young & Yung (2004) has stirred up almost no further research in this area. The main reason is that this new field relates to techniques generally considered by the "bad guys", in other word the attackers (which include militaries, spies...).

Publishing such results is never easy since it addresses the critical issues of result reproducibility at least to enable the process of peer-review: any result whose reality must be verified and confirmed is likely to leak enough data and information allowing thus a misuse by the attacker. This situation hence does not ease the emergence of such a new research field. The first consequence is that the actual corpus of knowledge regarding malicious mathematics and malicious cryptography is likely to be far more extended that has been already published. Most of those techniques are known and used by the military and the intelligence domains. As a result, only a very few seminal papers (both theoretical and technical) are know at the present time. The second consequence is that most of the results are published in the most famous international hacking conferences which are far more reluctant at publishing theoretical and practical results in this area. In this respect, academics are losing interesting opportunities.

3.1 From mathematics and cryptology to computer virology

3.1.1 The origins

The mid 1930s could be reasonably considered as the starting point of the history of malicious mathematics. Indeed, the masterpiece Kleene's recursion theorem in essence contains much of the computer virology concepts Filiol (2005). Of course neither Kleene nor followers in recursion theory, calculability, complexity theory have ever imagined that their results could be used and interpreted in a malicous way.

During World War II then many studies have been performed that could be considered as first premises of malicious mathematics. Von Neuman's work, for exemple, dedicated to *Self-reproducing automata* – in other words viruses – is undoubtly the best case. As many such studies were at that time – due to the war[2] and then due to cold war era – it is very likely that many results were classified and still are nowadays. For instance, NSA released in 2010 only research works performed in computer virology. The case of cryptology – a subfield of mathematics and computer science – is probably even more emblematic since it has been considered as weapons, strictly controlled by governments and military until the early 2000s and is still under a strict control regarding for instance exports and knowledge dissemination (see the different national regulations and the Wassenaar Agreement Wassenaar Agreement (1996)). This the reason why seminal research works in the field of malicious mathematics and malicious cryptology are still very limited at least in the public domain.

Another famous case is the research work of Kraus (1980) which can be considered as the founding work of computer virology in 1980. The German government made suitable and efficient pressures to forbid the publication of this thesis. In this work, Kraus exposes theoretical and practical results in mathematics (recursive functions, computability and calculability theory) that actually has given birth to the modern computer virology Filiol

---

[2] von Neuman's results which were established in 1948-1949, have been published in 1966 only, by his student R. Burk.

(2005). The last copy of Krause's manuscript has been by chance discovered in a wet cellar of the University of Dortmund, translated into English and published in 2009 only Kraus (1980).

3.1.2 Early stages of modern malicious cryptology

From an academic point of view, malicious cryptology begins with Young & Yung (2004) but with a very narrow vision. In their approach, a malware encrypts user's data with asymmetric cryptology public keys and extort money from the user who wants the key to access his data again. In this approach the malware itself does not deploy any malicious mathematics or malicious cryptology techniques. Only the payload uses cryptology for money extorsion. Young & Yung contribution, while having the merit to initiate the issue does not propose more than a cryptography book.

In 2005, the first academic description of the use of cryptology in the viral mechanism itself is described in Filiol (2005b). In this case the symmetric cryptology combined with environmental key management enables, for specific operational conditions, to protect malware code against reverse engineering. The concept of total code armouring is defined and experimented.

3.1.3 Formalization results

3.1.3.1 Testing simulability

When dealing with malicious attacks, the main problem that any has to face is detection by security software. The issue is then first to understand how security software are working in order to infer or to identify ways to bypass detection efficiently. In Filiol & Josse (2007), a theoretical study – backed by numerous experiments – describes in a unified way any detection technique by means of statistical testing. From this model, the concept of statitical simulability is defined. Here the aim is to reverse the use of statistics to design powerful attack that mimic normal behaviour. In this respect, we can speak of malicious statistics.

Definition 2. *Simulating a statistical testing consists for an adversary, to introduce, in a given population P, a statistical bias that cannot be detected by an analyst by means of this test.*

There exist two different kinds of simulability:

- the first one does not depend on the testings (and their parameters) the defender usually considers. It is called *strong testing simulability*.

- on the contrary, the second one does depend on those testings that the attackers aims at simulating. It is called *weak testing simulability*.

Here we call "tester" the one who uses statistical testing in order to decide whether there is an attack or not, or whether a code is malicious or not...

Definition 3. *(Strong Testing Simulability) Let P be a property and T a (statistical) testing whose role is to decide whether P holds for given population P or not. Strongly simulating this testing consists in modifying or building a biased population P in such a way that T systematically decides that P holds on P, up to the statistical risks. But there exists a statistical testing T' which is able to detect that bias in P. In the same way, we say that t testings $(T_1, T_2, \ldots, T_t)$ are strongly simulated, if applying them* *results in deciding that P holds on $\mathcal{P}$ but does no longer hold when considering a $(t + 1)$-th testing T_{t+1}.*

In terms of security, strong simulability is a critical aspect in security analysis. In an antiviral context, strong simulability exists when the malware writer, who has identified any of the techniques used by one or more antivirus, writes malware that cannot be detected by the target antivirus but only by the malware writer. As a typical example, a viral database which contains t signatures is equivalent to t testings (see previous section) and any new malware corresponds to the testing T_{t+1}.

Definition 4. *(Weak Testing Simulability) Let P be a property and T a testing whose role is to decide whether P is valid for a given population $\mathcal{P}$ or not. To weakly simulate this testing means introducing in $\mathcal{P}$ a new property P' which partially modifies the property P, in such a way that T systematically decides that P holds on $\mathcal{P}$, up to the error risks.*

Weak simulability differs from strong simulability since the attacker considers the same testings as the tester does. The attacker thus introduces a bias that the tester is not be able to detect.

The property P' of Definition 4 is generally opposite to the property P. It precisely represents a flaw that the attacker aims at exploiting. Bringing weak simulability into play is somehow tricky. It requires to get a deep knowledge of the testings to be simulated.

The central approach consists in introducing the property P' in such a way that the estimators E_i in use remain in the acceptance region of the testing (generally that of the null hypothesis). Let us recall that during the decision step, the tester checks whether $E < S$ or not. Thus weak simulability consists in changing the value $S - E$ while keeping it positive. For that purpose, we use the intrinsic properties of the relevant sampling distribution.

3.1.3.2 Reversing calculability and complexity theory

There are two key issues as far as computer science is concerned:

- *Calculability.* Here the central concept is Turing machines. The aim is to decide whether there exists a Turing machine (e.g. a program) which can compute a given problem or not. Some problems are not computable (the corresponding Turing machine never stops). Consequently the problem has no solution! So calculability theory aims at determining which problems are computable and which are not (undecidable problems).

- *Complexity.* When dealing with computable programs, another issue arises: how efficiently a problem can be computed. Here the central tool is the number of operations to solve a problem. From that number, problems are split into complexity classes. To describe things simply Papadimitriou (1993), the *Polynomial class* (P) corresponds to problems that are "computationally easy"Âăto solve, *Non deterministic polynomial class* (NP) to "computationally hard" to solve problems while *NP-complete class* contains the hardest problems from the NP class ("computationally very hard" problems). In practice, only the P class is computable (from seconds to a few hours however!).

So, as exposed in Filiol (2008c), a clever attacker will consider problems that are either impossible to solve (undecidable problems) or computationally hard to solve in order to design his attack or his malware. In other words, he opposes these problems to the defender which must solve them (whenever possible).

In Filiol (2007b); Zbitskiy (2009) the formalization based on formal grammars is considered. Code mutation (polymorphism, metamorphism) is formally described and the authors demonstrate that the choice of formal grammar class (according to the Chomsky classification) can yield powerful attacks. This work has been later extended by Gueguen (2011) by using van Wijngaarden grammars.

Another field of mathematics provides a lot of complex problems: combinatorics and discrete mathematics. Powerful approaches also considers those parts of mathematics to design or model powerful attacks based on malicious mathematics. For instance, the concept of cover set from the graph theory has enabled to understand worms or botnets spreading mechanisms and hence to design powerful versions of those malicious codes Filiol et al. (2007).

The concept of k-ary malware Filiol (2007c) is directly inspired from combinatorics.

Definition 5. *A k-ary malware is a family of k files (some of them may be not executable) whose union constitues a computer malware and performs an offensive action that is equivalent to that of a true malware. Such a code is said* sequential (serial mode) *if the k constituent parts are acting strictly one after the another. It is said* parallel *if the k parts executes simultaneously (parallel mode).*

Detecting such codes becomes almost impossible due to the number of combinations that should be explored. It has been proved Filiol (2007c) that, provided that the program interactions are determistic, the detection of k-ary malware is NP-complete.

3.1.4 Miscellanous

Other techniques have been recently considered which cannot clearly be related to the previous approaches. They can be considered as exotic approaches and we have chosen to expose them in a detailed way. For instance, the attacker can exploit to his own benefit the difference that exists between theorerical reality and practical reality in mathematics. This different is a critical issue in computer science. In Section 4 we explain how processor-dependent malware can be designed.

Other approaches can also rely on malicious cryptanalysis techniques. These techniques have been initiated in Filiol (2006) with the concept of *Zero-knowledge-like proof of cryptanalysis*.

Definition 6. *(Zero-knowledge-like proof of cryptanalysis) Let be a cryptosystem S_K and a property $\mathcal{P}$ about the output sequence of length n produced by S denoted σ_K^n. No known method other than exhaustive search or random search can obtain property $\mathcal{P}$ for σ_K^n. Then, a zero-knowledge-like proof of cryptanalysis of S consists in exhibiting secret keys $K_1, K_2, \ldots, \ldots K_m$ such that the output sequences $(\sigma_{K_i}^n)_{1 \leq i \leq m}$ verify $\mathcal{P}$ and such that, checking it requires polynomial time complexity. Moreover, the property $\mathcal{P}$ does not give any information on the way it was obtained.*

It worth considering that the reader/verifier can bring up against the author/prover that some random keys has been taken, the keystream has been computed and afterwards been claimed that the keystreams properties have been desired. In other words, the author/prover tries to fool the verifier/reader by using exhaustive search to produce the properties that have been considered for the zero-knowledge-like proof protocol. Thus the relevant properties must be carefully chosen such that:

- the probability to obtain them by random search over the key space makes such a search untractable. On the contrary the verifier/reader would be able to himself exhibit secret keys producing keystream having the same properties by a simple exhaustive search;

- the known attacks cannot be applied to retrieve secret keys from a fixed keystream having the properties considered by the author/prover.

- to really convince the reader/verifier, a large number of secret keys must be produced by the author/prover, showing that "he was not lucky".

Since there do not exist any known method other than exhaustive search or random search to produce output sequences σ_K^n having property $\mathcal{P}$, and since the complexity of a successful search is too high in practice, anybody who is effectively able to exhibit a secret K producing such output sequences obviously has found some unknown weaknesses he used to obtain this result. The probability of realizing property $\mathcal{P}$ through an exhaustive search gives directly the upper bound complexity of the zero-knowledge-like proved cryptanalysis.

This technique has been used to design an efficient code armouring technique. We will detail it in Section 5.

3.2 From computer virology to cryptology: malware-based operationel cryptanalysis

While in the previous section we have exposed how cryptography and mathematics can be used for malicious purposes, the present section deals with the opposite view: how malware can help to solve difficult (in other words computationally hard) problems. As far as cryptology is concerned, it mainly relates to "how get secret quantities (e.g. cryptographic keys) in illegitimate way?"

In this respect, malware can help to solve this problem very efficiently in a technical field called *Applied cryptanalysis*. As an example, let us consider the case of the AES (Advanced Encryption Standard). Let us assume that we use a *Deep-crack*-like computer that can perform an exhaustive key search of 2^{56} keys per second (in real life, this computer does not exist; the best cryptanalysis allows exhaustive key search of 56-bit keys in roughly 3 hours). Then, any brute force attack on the different AES versions will require with such a machine:

- 1.5×10^{12} centuries for a 128-bit key,

- 2.76×10^{31} centuries for a 192-bit key,

- 5.1×10^{50} centuries for a 256 bit-key.

It is obvious that this approach which has been used for a long time, is no longer valid for modern systems. Moreover, the mathematical analysis of AES did not revealed exploitable weaknesses. Consequently, other techniques, called "*applied cryptanalysis*" must be considered. The purpose of these techniques is not to attack the system directly (via the algorithm) but rather to act at implementation or management levels. By way of illustration, it is as if you wanted to go into a room by making a hole in the bombproof door, when you need only walk through the paper-thin walls. One of these approaches consists in using computer viruses or other malware.

3.2.1 Circumventing IPSec-like network encryption

IPSec-based protocols are often presented by IT-experts as an efficient solution to prevent attacks against data exchange. More generally, the use of encryption to protect communication channels or to seclude sensitive networks is seen as the ultimate defence. Unfortunately, this confidence is illusory since such "armoured" protocols can be manipulated or corrupted by an attacker to leak information as soon as an access is managed with simple userâĂŹs permission. In Delaunay et al. (2008), the authors demonstrate how an attacker and/or a malware can subvert and bypass IPsec-like protocols (IPSec, WiFi, IP encryptors...) to make data evade from the accessed system illegitimately. By using a covert channel, they show how a malware can encode the information to be stolen, can insert it into the legitimate encrypted traffic and finally collect/decode the information on the attackerâĂŹs side. This attack is summarized in Figure 2 The malware uses efficient techniques from the error-correcting

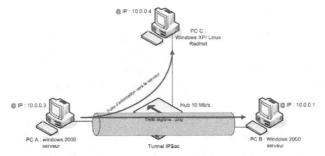

Fig. 2. General Scheme of IPSec-like protocol attacks by malware

theory to perform its attack. Moreover it adapts its behaviour to the encrypted traffic load in order to make its own activity totally invisible.

3.2.2 Dynamic cryptographic backdoors

A more efficient approach consists in exploiting implementation weaknesses in the environment (by means of a malware) or to change this latter as exposed in Filiol (2011). The first technique exploits the fact that many encryption algorithms rely on the operating system primitives to generate secret keys (e.g. Microsoft cryptographic API). The second solution is to modify the cryptographic algorithm on-the-fly in memory, and especially its mode of operation and/or its mathematical design. In fact the malware installs a dynamic trapdoor. The algorithm is not modified on the hard disk (no static forensics evidence). The trapdoor has a limited period of time and can be replayed more than once. In both cases, the encryption has been weakened in such a way that the attacker has just to intercept the ciphertext and perform the cryptanalysis. This technique has been efficiently applied to take control over the anonimity TOR network Filiol (2011b).

3.2.3 Anti-forensics cryptography

In the field of forensic analysis, encrypted data are particularly interesting when discovered on a hard disk. They are supposed to be a clear proof that a person has intended to protect data against analysis. When the forensics expert succeeds in one way or another to decrypt those encrypted data, the underlying plaintext clearly becomes very strong evidence for the judge. This means that in the process of digital proof, cryptography has a status of extremely high confidence.

In Filiol (2010a) it demonstrated how an attacker can use (malicious) cryptography in order to manipulate both the forensic analyst and the judge and thus fool them to incriminate an innocent people wrongly. The approach mainly lies in malicious cryptography techniques. The aim is to undermine a judgeâĂŹs blind faith in the value of cryptographic evidence and fool all those who rely heavily upon it. The paper shows with a fictional scenario how such an attack and manipulation can be performed. Hence it shows that the concept of (cryptographic) proof must be considered very cautiously and has no absolute value.

When coming back to the definition of a cryptosystem given in Section 2.2.1, the key point lies in the fact that any arbitrary cipher text C is defined relatively to a 3-tuple (P, K, E) only. In other words, you can do the following:

- **Technique 1**. Choose an arbitrary plaintext P, an arbitrary cipher text C and design accordingly a suitable pair (K, E) such that we obtain $C = E(K, P)$ and $P = E(K, C)$. This means that if we find random data on a hard disk and we do not have the algorithm E, we can assert almost anything. But worse, using malware we can replace any original pair (K, E) with a "malicious" one (K, E).

- **Technique 2**. Choose an arbitrary 3-tuple (E, C, P) and compute the key K such that we obtain $C = E(K, P)$. This approach has been partially addressed in Filiol (2006).

- **Technique 3**. Consider an arbitrary set of cipher texts $C_1, C_2...C_i...$ and an arbitrary encryption/decryption algorithm E thus relating to (legitimate) plaintexts $P_1, P_2...P_i...$ Thus we have for all i, for a key K i (possibly different for any i):

$$C_i = E(K, P_i) \text{ and } P_i = E(K, C_i)$$

For any additional arbitrary triplet (P, C, K), it is then possible to modify the cryptosystem E into the system E so that we obtain

$$C = E(K, P) \text{ and } P = E(K, C)$$

while we still have $C_i = E(K, P_i)$ and $P_i = E(K, C_i)$.

From a technical point of view, either the attacker modifies the system E on-the-fly or he simply replaces it with the modified one (e.g. with a virus). This technique is obviously the trickiest one but also the most convincing one.

Technically speaking, the difficulty depends on the kind of encryption system you intend to consider. While it is relatively easy for stream ciphers, the task becomes far more complex, yet not impossible, with block ciphers. Another aspect to take into consideration is the length (in bits) of the values C and P. The longer they are, the more difficult it will be to perform such rogue manipulation. However in the context of anti-forensics âĂŞ e.g. fooling an forensics expert âĂŞ those lengths can be relatively limited. The attacker will just have to build his attacking scenario carefully.

4. Processor-dependant malware

From the beginning of malware history (circa 1996), malware are:

- either operating system specific (Windows *.*, Unices, Mac, . . .);
- or application specific (e.g. macro viruses);
- or protocol dependent (e.g. *Conficker* versus *Slammer*).

At the present time, there are almost no hardware specific malware, even if some operating system are themselves hardware dependent (e.g. Nokia cell phones with *Symbian*). Recently, GPGPU malware Ioannidis (Polykronakis & Vasiliadis) have been proposed but they just exploit the fact that graphic cards are just distinct devices with almost the same features and capability as the system they are connected to. They do not really condition their action on new computing features. GPGPU malware strongly depend on the graphic card type (CUDA or OpenCL enabled).

We propose here to investigate the following critical issue: *is it possible to design malware – or more generally, any program – that operate beyond operating system and application types and varieties?* More precisely, we want:

- to operate beyond operating system and application types/varieties . . . ;
- while exploiting hardware specificities.

If such an approach would be possible, this would:

- enable far more precise and targeted attacks, at a finer level (surgical strikes) in a large network of heterogeneous machines but with generic malware;
- and represent a significant advantage in a context of cyberwarfare.

The recent case of the*StuxNet* worm shows that targeted attacks towards PLC components are nowadays a major concern in cyberattacks. However, while it can be very difficult to forecast and envisage which kind of applications is likely to be present on the target system (it can be a secret information), the variety in terms of hardware – and especially as far as processors are concerned – is far more reduced due to the very limited number of hardware manufacturers. We propose to consider *processor-dependent malware* and to rely on the onboard processor, which seems a good candidate to design hardware dependent software (a malware is nothing more than a software).

To design such *processor-dependent malware*, we need to identify the processor as precisely as possible. This is possible thanks to a different ways:

- by reversing existing binaries (but this provides a limited information since a given binary can indifferently execute on several processors like Intel x86s or AMDs chips),
- classical intelligence gathering...

There is a large spectrum of possibilities to collect this technical intelligence. But there is a bad news: deriving knowledge about processor internals is tricky and require a lot of work. Instead of analyzing processor logic gates architecture, we propose to work at the higher level: *to exploit mathematical perfection versus processor reality.*

4.1 Exploiting mathematical processor limitations

In order to use processors to discriminate programs' action and execution, we exploit the fact that first there is a huge difference between the mathematical reality and their implementation in computing systems and second that this difference is managed in various ways according to the processor brand, model and type.

4.1.1 Mathematical perfection versus processor reality

Let us begin with a very classical example: the algorithm given in Table 1. *what does this code (really) compute?*

Algorithm 1 : The $\sqrt{\ }$ problem
   Input: — a real A;
   Output: — a boolean B
   Begin:
      $B = \sqrt{A} * \sqrt{A}$;
      Return[A==B];
   End.

Table 1. The Square-root problem

Let us suppose we choose $A = 2.0$ as input for this *Square-root* algorithm, we then have two possible answers, that are *opposite*:

1. *Mathematically*: **True** is returned;

2. *Practically*: **False** is returned!

Let us now explain why we have these different outputs. This comes from the fact that processors:

- have an increasing (architecture) complexity and size,

- have bugs, known and unknown (not published),

- use floating point arithmetic,

- use generally "secret" algorithms for usual arithmetic functions like $1/x, \sqrt{x}, 1/\sqrt{x} \ldots$ that can be computed:
  1. at the *hardware* level;
  2. and/or at the *software* level.

As an example of a "secret algorithm", let us cite the famous Pentium Bugs *case* in 1994: Intel has never published neither the *correct* algorithm nor its bugged version used for the division but some researchers have tried reverse engineering techniques to understand which algorithm was programmed actually Coe et al. (1995).

Let us now consider the following problem: *can we define a set of (simple) tests to know on which processor we are?* As a practical example: *is it possible to know whether we are on a mobile phone or on a computer?*

The Intel Assembly Language instruction **CPUID** can be used both on Intel and AMD processors, but it has at least two severe drawbacks:

- it is easy to "find" it whenever scanning the file (malware detection issue);

- some other processors cannot recognize and process this instruction.

4.1.2 Processor bugs

Known or unknown bugs are good candidates to design such a set of tests and hence to discriminate processors:

- as an instance of such bug/test, it is easy determine whether we use a 1994 bugged Pentium or not: just use the numerical value that makes appear the *Pentium Division Bug*;

- but a lot of bugs will *freeze* the computer only (this can be used for processor-dependent denial of service [DoS] however);

- and it is not so simple to find a list of bugs, even if there are supposed to be "known".

The most interesting bugs to consider involve a floating point arithmetic operator. However it is worth keeping in mind that the knowledge of some other bugs (by the manufacturer, a Nation State...) can be efficiently used to target processors specifically and hence it represents a critical knowledge not to say a strategic one. Worse, hiding such bugs or managing floating arithmetics in a very specific way is more than interesting.

More generally let us consider some differences that exist event within the same type of processors but produced in two different versions: a national and an "export" version. As an example, we can consider the POPCOUNT function which compute the Hamming weight of an integer (the number of 1s in its binary form). Since it is a critical function in the context of cryptanalysis, the national version of a few processors have this function implemented in hardware while the export version just emulate it at the software level. Consequently a good way to discriminate national version from export version consists in computing Hamming weight a large number of times and then to record the computation time: it will be significantly higher for the export version which hence can be specifically targeted by a malware attack.

4.1.3 Using floating point arithmetics: the IEEE P754 standard

The IEEE P754 standard Overton (2011) has been approved as a norm by the IEEE ANSI in 1985. A lot of processors follow and comply to it but some processors do not (e.g. the CRAY 1 or the DEC VAX 780). Moreover, not all microcontrollers follow this standard either.

This norm does not impose algorithms to compute usual functions like $1/x, \sqrt{x}, 1/\sqrt{x}$ or e^x. It just gives a specification for the four basic operations: addition, substraction, multiplication and division. So, for all other functions, there is very likely to exist differences as far as their implementation as algorithms are concerned. But we have to find them!

For 32-bit, environments, we have (see Table 2):

- 1 bit for the sign;

- 23 bits for the mantissa;

sign(x)	mantissa(x)	exponent(x)
1 bit	23 bits	8 bits

Table 2. Structure of 32-bit float "numbers" in the IEEE P754 Standard

- 8 bits for the exponent (integer).

The floating point arithmetic has a lot of curiosities, let us see some of them. One can find in Kulisch & Miranker (1983) the following questions due to Rump:

- Evaluate the expression

$$F(X, Y) = \frac{(1682XY^4 + 3X^3 + 29XY^2 - 2X^5 + 832)}{107751}$$

  with $X = 192119201$ and $Y = 35675640$. The "exact" result is 1783 but numerically we can have a very different value like $-7.18056 \cdot 10^{20}$ (on a 32-bit IEEE P754 compliant processor).

- Evaluate the expression

$$P(X) = 8118X^4 - 11482X^3 + X^2 + 5741X - 2030$$

  with $X = 1/\sqrt{2}$ and $X = 0.707$. The "exact" result is 0 but numerically we can have a very different value like $-2.74822 \cdot 10^{-8}$ (on a 32-bit IEEE P754 compliant processor).

Let us recall that the numerical value of an algebraic expression depends (generally) on the compiler because a non basic numerical expression result depends strongly on the order of the intermediate computations.

If we want to know on which processor we are working, we need to find, before anything else, some critical information:

1. first the *base* value used to represent numbers;
2. second the *word length*, *i.e.* the number of bits the processor is used to work (with floating point numbers for example).

For the base value, it is easy to conjecture that the base is 2, at least for modern processors. As far as the the word length is concerned, we have not found any numerical algorithm that is able to answer this question but we have found something very close. The algorithm given in Table 3 called the *Gentleman Code* Gentleman & Marovitch (1974) is surprisingly very interesting for both problems. First we can again ask: *what does this code (really) compute?* Well, again, we have two possible answers:

1. *Mathematically*: the two loops are theoretically *infinite loops* so they are looping forever;
2. *Practically* (see Erra & Grenier (2009)):
   - $\log_2(A)$ gives the number of bits used by the mantissa of floating point numbers;
   - B is the base used by the floating point arithmetic of the environment (generally it is equal to 2).

Both values are of course *processor-dependent* constants. So, with a small program, which has a polynomial time complexity, we can compute the number of bits used to represent the *mantissa* of any floating point number and so, we can deduce the word length.

Algorithm 2 :   The Gentleman Code
  Input: — A=1.0 ; B=1.0;
  Output: — A, B
  Begin:
    A=1.0;
    B=1.0;
    While ((A+1.0)-A)-1.0==0 ;
      A=2*A;
    While ((A+B)-A)-B==0 ;
      B=B+1.0;
    Return[A,B];
  End.

Table 3. The Gentleman code

4.2 Implementation and experimental results

Let us present a few tests that enables to discriminate processors operationally (for more details refer to Erra & Grenier (2009)). Table 4 summarizes a first set of tests.   So these

Processor	Tests			
	1.2-0.8 == 0.4	0.1+0.1 == 0.2	0.1+0.1+0.1 == 0.3	0.1+...0.1 == 1.0
VAX 750	Yes	Yes	No	No
AMD 32	No	Yes	No	No
AMD 64	No	Yes	No	No
ATOM	No	Yes	No	No
INTEL DC	No	Yes	No	No
MIPS 12000	No	Yes	No	No
dsPIC33FJ21	No	Yes	Yes	No
IPHONE 3G	No	Yes	No	No

Table 4. A few easy computations

tests are interesting but not completely useful, this shows that we can simply know whether the processor follows the IEEE P754 arithmetic norm or not. For these simple expression, all processors that are IEEE P754 compliant will give the same answers..

With the following constant definitions in our test program in C, we obtain the results given in Tables 5 and 6.

- #define Pi1 3.141592653
- #define Pi2 3.141592653589

- #define Pi3 3.141592653589793

- #define Pi4 3.1415926535897932385

These results are more interesting, especially those in the third column (the numerical computation of $\sin(10^{37}\pi_1)$) in Table 5: a simple computation gives four subclasses of the set of processors (emphasized by a double horizontal lign between the subclasses).   To

Processor	$\sin(10^{10}\pi_1)$	$\sin(10^{17}\pi_1)$	$\sin(10^{37}\pi_1)$	$\sin(10^{17}\pi_1) == \sin(10^{17}\pi_2)$
IPHONE 3G	0.375...	0.423...	-0.837...	No
AMD 32	0.375...	0.424...	-0.837...	No
AMD 64	0.375..	0.424..	0.837...	No
ATOM	0.375..	0.423..	-0.832..	No
INTEL DC	0.375...	0.423...	-0.832...	No
MIPS 12000	0.375...	0.423...	-0.832...	No
dsPIC33	0.81...	0.62...	-0.44...	Yes

Table 5. Computation of $\sin(10^{10}\pi)$ for various numerical values of the constant π

Processor	$\sin(10^{37}\pi_1)$	$\sin(10^{37}\pi_2)$	$\sin(10^{37}\pi_3)$	$\sin(10^{37}\pi_4)$
IPHONE 3G	47257756	9d94ef4d	99f9067	99f9067
AMD 64	af545000	af545000	af545000	af545000
ATOM	47257756	9d94ef4d	99f9067	99f9067
INTEL DC	47257756	9d94ef4d	99f9067	99f9067
MIPS 12000	47257756	9d94ef4d	99f9067	99f9067
dsPIC33	bee5	bee5	bee5	bee5

Table 6. $\sin(10^{37}\pi)$ in hex for various numerical values of the constant π

conclude with this part, it is important to stress on the *Influence* of the Compiler. To illustrate this, let us give a last example. We want to compute the generalized sum

$$s(N) := \sum_{i=1}^{N} 10^N \tag{1}$$

The "exact" value is of course $N * 10^N$, but let us have a look at the Table 7 to see some values we can have when computing $s(N) - N * 10^N$. However we have to point out that the results of the Table 7) heavily depend of course of the processor but *also* of the compiler used, of the options used and so on . . . .

N	10	21	22	25	30	100
$s - N * 10^N$	0.0	0.0	$-8.05\,10^8$	$-6.71\,10^7$	$-4.50\,10^{15}$	$4.97\,10^{86}$

Table 7. Computation of $s(N) - \sum_{i=1}^{N} 10^N$ for different values of N

4.3 Open problems

More work has to be done to understand these aspects more deeply. Nonetheless, we have here new insights on how design more specific attacks when considering the processor type AND the compiler version/type as the same time.

Floating Point Arithmetic (FPA) looks promising to define a set of tests enabling to identify the processor or, more precisely, a subset of possible processors. In the context of the malicious use of mathematics, a lot of open problems are arising. Let us mention a few of them.

The first open problem relates to the following question: *can we find an numerical algorithm, with a linear complexity in time and space which computes a floating point expression to distinguish a given processor more precisely?* Beyond the examples presented here, a promising algorithm could be based on a variant of the famous *logistic equation*, thoroughly studied in the chaos theory, which is defined by:

$$x_{n+1} = r\,x_n\,(1 - x_n) \tag{2}$$

with $r \in [0, 4]$.

The sequence defined by Equation 2, for a chosen and fixed x_0, can exhibit very different behaviors:

- a *periodic* behavior for example for values of r less than 3.0;
- or a *chaotic* behavior for values of r slightly larger than 3.57.

Another open problem goes deeper into the misuse of mathematics by attackers: *find processor-dependent hash functions*. Generally, hash functions are defined as independent from the processor. But, in some cases (export control of the cryptography, countermeasures...), one can desire to get rid of this view. The aim then consists in taking the *opposite idea*. We consider a hash function that heavily depends of the processor used to compute it. For example, it can be interesting to design a specific hash function for a *smartphone* or a specific processor. The best way to design such a hash function seems to use the properties of the floating point arithmetic operators of the processor; more specifically some of the arithmetic functions implemented on the processor. Consequently, this second open problem evolves slightly towards the following question: *can we define, for a specific processor, hash functions that use the floating point arithmetic of the concerned processor that respect the classical requirements for such functions?*

5. Evading detection and analysis

Fighting against computer malware require a mandatory step of reverse engineering. As soon as the code has been disassemblied/decompiled (including a dynamic analysis step), there is a hope to understand what the malware actually does and to implement a detection algorithm. This also applies to protection of software whenever one wishes to analyze them.

In this section, we show how the techniques of malicious cryptography enable to implement total amoring of programs, thus prohibiting any reverse engineering operation. The main interest of that approach lies in the fact that TRANSEC properties are achieved at the same time. In other words, the protected binaries have the same entropy as any legitimate, unprotected code. This same technique can also achieve a certain level of polymorphism/metamorphism at the same time. For instance, a suitable 59-bit key stream cipher is sufficient to generate up to 2^{140} variants very simply. More interestingly, the old fashioned concept of decryptor which usually constitutes a potential signature and hence a weakness, is totally revisited.

To illustrate this approach, let us consider the case study presented in Filiol (2010b) (among many other similar approaches) in which only a very few instructions are protected against any disassembly attempt. Let us consider a piece of x86 assembly instructions to protect from analysis. These instructions are translated into an intermediate representation (IR) derived from the REIL language before a final translation into bytecode.

To evade analysis and detection, we intend to protect this final bytecode by using a malicious PRNG, e.g. the last line in the following extract of code:

```
[X86 ASM]        MOV EAX, 0x3 [B803000000]
[REIL IR]        STR (0x3, B4, 1, 0), (EAX, B4, 0, 0)
[BYTECODES]      0xF1010000 0x40004 0x3 0x0 0x6A
```

Let us now explore the different possible malicious PRNG we can use depending on the various operational conditions.

5.1 Malicious PRNG & protection scenarii

Sophisticated polymorphic/metamorphic or obfuscation techniques must rely on PRNG (Pseudo-Random Number Generator). In our context, the aim is to generate sequences of random numbers (here bytecode values) on-the-fly while hiding the code behavior.

Sequences are precomputed and we have to design a generator (the malicious PRNG) which will afterwards output those data. The idea is that any data produced by the resulting generator will be first used by the code as a valid address, and then will itself seed the PNRG to produce the next random data.

Three cases are to be considered:

1. the code is built from any arbitrary random sequence;
2. the sequence is given by a (non yet protected) instance of bytecode and we have to design an instance of PNRG accordingly;
3. a more interesting problem lies in producing random data that can be somehow interpreted by a PRNG as meaningful instructions like jump 0x89 directly.

This relates to interesting problems of PRNG cryptanalysis. We are going to address these three cases.

From a general point of view it is necessary to recall that for both three cases the malware author needs reproducible random sequences. By reproducible (hence the term of pseudo-random), we mean that the malware will replay this sequence to operate its course of execution. The reproducibility condition implies to consider a *deterministic Finite-State Machine* (dFSM). The general scheme of how this dFSM is working is illustrated as follows. Without the dFSM, any instruction data whenever executed produced a data used by the next instruction and so on (e.g. an address, an operand...).

$$I_0 \rightarrow D_0 \rightarrow I_1 \rightarrow D_1 \ldots \rightarrow D_i \rightarrow I_{(}i+1) \rightarrow \ldots$$

The problem lies in the fact that any analysis of the code easily reveals to the malware analyst all the malware internals since all instructions are hardcoded and unprotected. But if a few data/instructions are kept under an encrypted form, and are deciphered at execution only, the analysis is likely to be far more difficult (up to decryptor and the secret key protection issue). It is denied of *a priori* analysis capabilities. So to summarize, so we intend to have

$$I_0 \rightarrow D_0' \rightarrow I_1 \rightarrow D_1 \ldots \rightarrow D_i' \rightarrow I_{(}i+1) \rightarrow \ldots$$

where $dFSM(D_i') = D_i$ for all i. Upon execution, we just have to input data D_i' into the dFSM which will then output the data D_i.

A few critical points are worth stressing on

1. no key is neither required nor used;
2. instructions can similarly be protected as well.

Of course to be useful as a prevention tool against (static and dynamic) analysis, the dFSM must itself be obfuscated and protected against analysis. But this last point is supposed to be fulfilled Filiol (2010b).

5.2 (Malware) code built from an arbitrary sequence

In this case, the sequence is arbitrary chosen before the design of the code and hence the code is written directly from this arbitrary sequence. This case is the most simple to manage. We just have to choose carefully the dFSM we need. One of the best choice is to take a congruential generator since it implies a very reduced algorithm with simple instructions.

Let us consider X_0 an initial value and the corresponding equation

$$x_{(}i+1) = a * X_i + b \qquad mod(N)$$

where a is the multiplier, b is the increment and N is the modulus. Since the length of the sequence involved in the malware design is rather very short (up to a few tens of bytes), the choice of those parameters is not as critical as it would be for practical cryptographic applications. In this respect, one can refer to Knuth's reference book to get the best sets of parameters Knuth (1998).

Here are a few such examples among many others:

Standard minimal generator $a = 16,807 - b = 0 - N = 2^{31} - 1$.

VAX-Marsaglia generator $a = 16,645 - b = 0 - N = 2^{32}$.

Lavaux & Jenssens generator $a = 31,167,285 - b = 0 - N = 2^{48}$.

Haynes generator $a = 6,364,136,223,846,793,005 - b = 0 - N = 2^{64}$.

Kuth's generator $a = 22\,695\,477 - b = 1 - N = 2^{32}$ and $X_{n+1} >>= 16$.

Of course the choice of the modulus is directly depending on the data type used in the malware.

Another interesting approach is to consider hash functions and S/key. The principle is almost the same. We take a (m, n) hash function H which produces a n-bit output from a m-bit input with $m > n$. In our case we can build m in the following way

```
m = <data to protect><padding of random data><size of data>
```

or equivalently

```
m = D_i <random data> |D_i|
```

Then we choose a m-bit initialization vector (IV) and we compute the random sequence as follows

$$IV \rightarrow D_i = H(IV) \rightarrow x = H^{|D_i|}(D_i) \rightarrow y = H^{|x|}(x) \rightarrow H^{|y|}(y) \rightarrow$$

The iteration value $|D_i|$ can be used to get one or more required arbitrary value thus anticipating the next case. Of course the nature of the hash function is also a key parameter: you can either use existing hash function (e.g MD5, SHA-1, RIPEMD 160, SHA-2...) and keep only a subset of the output bit; or you can design your own hash function as explained in Knuth (1998).

5.3 Random sequence coming from an arbitrary (malware) code

In this slightly different case, the sequence is determined by a (non yet protected) instance of a code. This issue is then to design or use an instance of PRNG accordingly. This is of course a far more difficult issue which implies cryptanalytic techniques. To formalize the problem we have a sequence

$$X_0, X_1, X_2 \ldots x_i \ldots X_n$$

which represents critical data (addresses, ASM instructions, operands...) of a particular instance of a (malware) code. As for example let us consider three series of 32-bit integers describing bytecode values:

```
0x2F010000 0x040004 0x3 0x0 0x89        (1)
0x3D010000 0x040004 0x3 0x0 0x50        (2)
 0x5010000 0x040004 0x3 0x0 0x8D        (3)
```

They are just different instances of the same instruction Filiol (2010b). The aim is to have these data in the code under a non hardcoded but an obfuscated form, e.g.

$$K_0, K_1, K_2, \ldots K_i, \ldots K_n \ldots$$

We then have to find a dFSM such that

$$X_0 = dFSM(K_0), X_1 = dFSM(K_1) \ldots X_i = dFSM(K_i) \ldots$$

The notation K_i directly suggests that the quantity input to the dFSM is a key in a cryptographic context but these keys have to exhibit local low entropy profile at the same time. So the malicious PRNG must take this into account as well. In this case, we have to face a two-fold cryptanalytic issue:

- either fix the output value X_i and find out the key K_i which outputs X_i for an arbitrary dFSM,

- or for an arbitrary set of pairs (X_i, K_i) design a unique suitable dFSM for those pairs.

The first case directly relates to a cryptanalytic problem while the second refers more to the problem of designing cryptographic dFSMs with trapdoors. In our context of malicious cryptography, the trapdoors here are precisely the arbitrary pairs of values (X_i, K_i) while the dFSM behaves for any other pair as a strong cryptosystem Filiol (2010a). This second issue is far more complex to address and still is an open problem.

Let us focus on the first case which has been partially addressed for real-life cryptosystem like *Bluetooth* E0 Filiol (2007) in the context of zero knowledge-like proof of cryptanalysis. But in the present case we do not need to consider such systems and much simpler dFSM can be built conveniently for our purposes: sequences of data we use are rather short.

To fullfil all operational constraints Filiol (2010b) those dFSM have to exhibit additional features in order to

- be used for code mutation purposes,

- exhibit TRANSEC properties. In other words, if we have $Y = dFSM(X)$, then X and Y must have the same entropy profile. Replacing X with a Y having a higher entropy profile would focus the analyst's attention (or trigger security software alert by considering local entropy tests).

In Filiol (2010b) a 59-key bit stream cipher has been considered. This encryption system is a combination generator which ismade of three linear feedback shift register and a combining Boolean function. The value K_i initializes the content of registers R_1, R_2 and R_3 at time instant $t = 0$, and the stream cipher (our dFSM) outputs bits s^t which represent the binary version of values X_i.

To describe the general principle of this technique, we will use this dFSM in a procedure whose prototype is given by

```
void sco(unsigned long long int * X, unsigned long long int K)
  {
  /* K obfuscated value (input), X unobfuscated value (output) */
  /* (array of 8 unsigned char) by SCO                         */
  ...
  }
```

Now according to the level of obfuscation we need, different ways exist to protect critical data inside a code (series of integers (1), (2) and (3) above). We are going to detail two of them.

5.3.1 Concatenated bytecodes

The dFSM outputs critical data under a concatenated form to produce chunks of code corresponding to the exact entropy of the input value (K_i). This enables to prevent any local increase of the code entropy. For the dFSM considered, it means that we output series (1), (2) and (3) under the following form

```
1) --> 0x2F01000000040004000000030000000000000089
2) --> 0x3D01000000040004000000030000000000000050
3) --> 0x0501000000040004000000030000000000000008D
```

Let us detail the first output sequence (1). It will be encoded as three 59-bit outputs M_1, M_2 and M_3

```
M_1 =        0x0BC04000000LL;
M_2 = 0x080008000000060LL;
M_3 = 0x000000000000089LL;
```

To transform M_1, M_2 and M_3 back into five 32-bit values X_1, X_2, X_3, X_4 and X_5, we use the following piece of code:

```
/* Generate the M_i values */
sco(&M_1, K_1);
sco(&M_2, K_2);
sco(&M_3, K_3);

X_1 = M_1 >> 10;   /* X_1 = 0x2F010000L */
X_2 = ((M_2 >> 37) | (M_1 << 22)) & 0xFFFFFFFFL
                   /* X_2 = 0x00040004L */
X_3 = (M_2 >> 5) & 0xFFFFFFFFL; /* X_3 = 0x3 */
X_4 = ((M_3 >> 32) | (M_2 << 27)) & 0xFFFFFFFFL;
                   /* X_4 = 0x0 */
X_5 = M_3 & 0xFFFFFFFFL;         /* X_5 = 0x89 */
```

Values M_1, M_2 and M_3 will be stored in the code as the values K_1, K_2 and K_3 with $dFSM(K_i) = M_i$:

```
K_1 = 0x6AA00600000009LL;
K_2 = 0x500403000015DC8LL;
K_3 = 0x0E045100001EB8ALL;
```

Similarly we have for sequence (2)

```
M_1 =        0x0F404000000LL;    K_1 = 0x7514360000053C0LL;
M_2 = 0x080008000000060LL;       K_2 = 0x4C07A200000A414LL;
M_3 = 0x000000000000050LL;       K_3 = 0x60409500001884ALL;
```

and for sequence (3)

```
M_1 =        0x01404000000LL;    K_1 = 0x76050E00001F0B1LL;
M_2 = 0x080008000000060LL;       K_2 = 0x00000010C80C460LL;
M_3 = 0x00000000000008DLL;       K_3 = 0x000000075098031LL;
```

The main interest of that method is that the interpretation of code is not straightforward. Code/data alignment does not follow any logic (that is precisely why a 59-bit dFSM has been considered compared to a seemingly more obvious 64-bit dFSM ; any prime value is optimal).

Moreover, as we can notice, the K_i values are themselves sparse as unobfuscated opcodes are (structural aspect). Additionally, their entropy profile (quantitative aspect) is very similar to the M_i values (and hence the X_i ones). This implies that any detection techniques based on local entropy picks is bound to fail.

Due to the careful design of the 59-bit dFSM, the unicity distance obtained is greater than 59 bits (the unicity distance is the minimal size for a dFSM output to be produced by a single secret key). In the present case, a large number of different 59-bit keys can output an arbitrary output sequence. Here are the results for the three series (1), (2) and (3) (Table 8): This implies

Serie	M_i values	Number of K_i	M_i values	Number of K_i	M_i values	Number of K_i
(1)	M_1	314	M_2	2,755	M_3	8,177
(2)	M_1	319	M_2	2,755	M_3	26,511
(3)	M_1	9,863	M_2	2,755	M_3	3,009

Table 8. Number of possible keys for a given output value Filiol (2010b)

that the 9 M_i values can be randomly selected and thus we have

$$314 \times (2,755)^3 \times 8,177 \times 319 \times 26,511 \times 9,863 \times 3,009$$
$$= 13,475,238,762,538,894,122,655,502,879,250$$

different possible code variants. It is approximatively equal to 2^{103} variants. Details of implementation are described in Filiol (2010b).

5.3.2 Non concatenated bytecodes

In this second case, the dFSM outputs 59-bit chunks of data whose only the 32 least significant bits are useful. Then here five 59-bit chunks of data M_1, M_2, M_3, M_4 and M_5 are output. For sequence (1) we have

```
M_1 = 0x*******2F010000LL;
M_2 = 0x*******00040004LL;
```

```
M_3 = 0x********00000003LL;
M_4 = 0x********00000000LL;
M_5 = 0x********0000089LL;
```

where the symbol $*$ describes any random nibble.

The main interest of that method lies in the fact that it naturally and very simply provides increased polymorphism properties compared to the previous approach. Indeed about 2^{140} 5-tuples $(K_1, K_2, K_3, K_4, K_5)$ whenever they are input in the dFSM, produces 5-tuples $(X_1, X_2, X_3, X_4, X_5)$. Then a huge number of different instances of the same code can be produced by randomly choosing any possible 5-tuples. By increasing size of the memory of the FSM we even can arbitrarily increase the number of possible polymorphic instances.

6. Conclusion

The rise of malicious mathematics and malicious cryptography results in a number of critical issues.

For the first time, the advantage goes definitively to the attacker as soon as he uses malicious mathematics and malicious cryptology techniques. He has just to use most of the results of calculability theory and complexity theory for his own benefit. This shed a new light on the importance to answer to the famous question: *"does P = NP or not?"* But a positive solution would solve only the problem partly. Let us recall that modern cryptology for the first time in Mankind History was giving the advantage to the defender. Unfortunately this period of peace was short. The threat has just evolved, adapted and changed. We now have to face a very unsecure world again.

From that it follows that science can no be neutral and the question of science's dual use – and it corollary the control of knowledge – is more than ever into question.

Aside those society issues, malicious mathematics and malicious cryptology propose a new, stimulating, exciting research universe from a purely academic point of view. A huge number of open problems, both theoretical and practical have been identified. More are likely to come. in this respect, we can hope that meny good things can also arise from the research that will consider those problems.

7. References

Coe, T., Mathissen, T., Moler, C. & Pratt, V. (1995). Computational Aspects of the Pentium Affair. *IEEE Computational Science & Engineering*, 2(1): 18–30.

Delaunay, G., Filiol, E. & Jennequin, F. (2008). Malware-based Information Leakage over IPSEC Tunnels. *Journal of Information Warfare*, 7(3):11–22.

Erra, R. & Grenier, C. (2009). How to choose RSA Keys (The Art of RSA: Past, Present and Future)? *iAWACS 2009*, Laval, France. [online] http://www.esiea-recherche.eu/Slides09/slides_iAWACS09_Erra-Grenier_How-to-compute-RSA-keys.pdf

Filiol, E. (2005). *Computer Viruses: from Theory to Applications*, IRIS International Series, Springer Verlag France, ISBN-10: 2287239391.

Filiol. E. (2005). Strong Cryptography Armoured Computer Viruses Forbidding Code Analysis: the BRADLEY virus. *Proceedings of the 14th EICAR Conference*, ESAT Publishing, pp. 201–217.

Filiol, E (2006). Zero Knowledge-like proof of cryptanalysis of Bluetooth Encryption. *International Journal in Information Technology*, 3(4): 285–293.

Filiol, E., Franc, E., Gubbioli, A., Moquet, B. & Roblot, G. (2007). Combinatorial Optimisation of Worm Propagation on an Unknown Network. *International Journal in Computer Science*, 2(2): 124–130.

Filiol, E. & Josse, S. (2007). Statistical model for viral undecidability, *Journal of Computer Virology*, 3(2): 65–74, http://www.springer.com/computer/journal/11416

Filiol, E. (2007). Zero knowledge-like Proof of Cryptanalysis of Bluetooth Encryption. *International Journal in Information Theory*, 3(4): 40–51. [online] http://www.waset.org/journals/ijit/v3/v3-4-40.pdf

Filiol, E. (2007). *Techniques virales avancées*, IRIS Series, Springer Verlag France, ISBN 978-2-287-33887-8 (An English translation is due at the end of 2012).

Filiol, E. (2007). Metamorphism, Formal Grammars and Undecidable Code Mutation. *International Journal in Computer Science*, 2(1): 70–75.

Filiol, E. (2007). Formalisation and Implementation Aspects of K-ary (malicious) Codes. *Journal in Computer Virology*, 3(2): 75–86.

Filiol, E. & Raynal, F. (2008). Malicious Cryptography...reloaded, *CanSecWest Conference*, Vancouver, Canada. [online] http://cansecwest.com/csw08/csw08-raynal.pdf

Filiol, E & Raynal, F. (2008) Enciphered communications: a can of worms? *Revue de Défense Nationale*, Special Issue "From Crybercrime to Cyberwarfare", 5:86–97.

Filiol, E. (2008). Malware of the Future: When Mathematics Work for the Dark Side. *Hack.lu 2008*, Keynote Talk, Luxembourg, October 22nd. [Online] http://hack.lu/archives.

Filiol, E. (2010). Anti-forensics Techniques Based on Malicious Cryptography. *Proceedings of the 9th European Conference in Information Warfare ECIW 2010*, Thessaloniki, Greece, pp. 63 70, Academic Conferences International Press.

Filiol, E. (2010). Malicious Cryptography Techniques for Unreversable (malicious or not) binaries". *H2HC 2010 Conference* Sao Paulo, Brazil [online] http://arxiv.org/abs/1009.4000

Filiol, E (2011). Dynamic cryptographic backdoors, *CanSecWest Conference*, Vancouver, Canada.

Filiol, E (2011). Dynamic cryptographic backdoors - How to Take Control over the TOR Network, *H2HC Conference*, Sao Paulo, Brazil, October 2011.

Gentleman, W. & Marovitch, S. (1974). More on algorithms that reveal properties of floating point arithmetic units. *Communications of the ACM*, 17(5): 276–277.

Gueguen, G. (2011). Van Wijngaarden Grammars and Metamorphism. *6th International Workshop on Frontiers in Availability, Reliability and Security 2011 (ARES/FARES'11)*, Vienna, Austria.

Ioannidis, S., Polykronakis, M. & Vasiliadis, G. (2010). GPU-assisted Malware. *Malware 2010*. [online] http://dcs.ics.forth.gr/Activities/papers/gpumalware.malware10.pdf

Knuth, D. E., (1998). *The Art of Computer Programming: Seminumerical Algorithms*, Volume 2, Addison-Wesley.

Kraus, J. (1980). *Selbst Reproduzierende Programme*. Master Thesis in Computer Science, University of Dortmund. Translated from the German and edited by D. Bilar & E. Filiol, *Journal in Computer Virology*, 5(1): 9–87.

Kulisch, U. W. & Miranker, W. L. (1983). Arithmetic of computers, *Siam J. of computing*, 76:54–55.

Overton, M.-L. (2001). *Numerical Computing with IEEE Floating Point Arithmetic*, SIAM Publishing, ISBN-10: 0-89871-571-7.

Papadimitriou, C. H. (1993). *Computational Complexity*. Addison Wesley, ISBN-10 0201530821.

Perseus homepage. http://code.google.com/p/libperseus/

The Wassenaar Arrangement in Export Control for Conventional Arms and Dual-Use Goods and Technologies http://www.wassenaar.org

Young, A. & Yung, M. (2004). *Malicious Cryptography: Exposing Cryptovirology*, Wiley, ISBN 0-7645-4975-8.

Zbitskiy, P. V. (2009). Code Mutation Techniques by Means of Formal Grammars and Automata. *Journal in Computer Virology*, 5(3): 199–207.

5

Elliptic Curve Cryptography and Point Counting Algorithms

Hailiza Kamarulhaili and Liew Khang Jie

School of Mathematical Sciences, Universiti Sains Malaysia, Minden, Penang
Malaysia

1. Introduction

Elliptic curves cryptography was introduced independently by Victor Miller (Miller, 1986) and Neal Koblitz (Koblitz, 1987) in 1985. At that time elliptic curve cryptography was not actually seen as a promising cryptographic technique. As time progress and further research and intensive development done especially on the implementation side, elliptic curve cryptography is now being implemented widely. Elliptic curves cryptography offers smaller key size, bandwidth savings and faster in implementations when compared to the RSA (Rivest-Shamir-Adleman) cryptography which based its security on the integer factorization problem. The most interesting feature of the elliptic curves is the group structure of the points generated by the curves, where points on the elliptic curves form a group. The security of elliptic curves cryptography relies on the elliptic curves discrete logarithm problem. The elliptic curve discrete logarithm problem is analogous to the ordinary algebraic discrete logarithm problem, $l = g^x$, where given the l and g, it is infeasible to compute the x. Elliptic curve discrete logarithm problem deals with solving for n the relation $P = nG$. Given the point P and the point G, then it is very hard to find the integer n. To implement the discrete logarithm problem in elliptic curve cryptography, the main task is to compute the order of group of the curves or in other words the number of points on the curve. Computation to find the number of points on a curve, has given rise to several point counting algorithms. The Schoof and the SEA (Schoof-Elkies-Atkin) point counting algorithms will be part of the discussion in this chapter. This chapter is organized as follows: Section 2, gives some preliminaries on elliptic curves, and in section 3, elliptic curve discrete logarithm problem is discussed. Some relevant issues on elliptic curve cryptography is discussed in section 4, in which the Diffie-Hellman key exchange scheme, ElGamal elliptic curve cryptosystem and elliptic curve digital signature scheme are discussed here accompanied with some examples. Section 5 discussed the two point counting algorithms, Schoof algorithm and the SEA (Schoof-Elkies-Atkin) algorithm. Following the discussion in section 5, section 6 summaries some similarities and the differences between these two algorithms. Section 7 gives some brief literature on these two point counting algorithms. Finally, section 8 is the concluding remarks for this chapter.

2. Elliptic curves

Elliptic curves obtained their name from their relation to elliptic integrals that arise from the computation of the arc length of ellipses (Lawrence & Wade, 2006). Elliptic curves are different from ellipses and have much more interesting properties when compared to ellipses. An elliptic curve is simply the collection of points in x-y plane that satisfy an equation $y^2 + a_1xy + a_3y = x^3 + a_2x^2 + a_4x + a_6$, and this equation could either be defined on real, rational, complex or finite field. This equation is called the Weierstrass equation.

Definition 2.1: An elliptic curve E, defined over a field K is given by the Weierstrass equation:

$$E: \ y^2 + a_1xy + a_3y = x^3 + a_2x^2 + a_4x + a_6, \ \text{where} \ a_1,a_2,a_3,a_4,a_6 \in K \tag{1}$$

In other words, let K be any field, then we assume $a_1,a_2,a_3,a_4,a_6 \in K$ and the set of K-rational points:

$$E(K) = \{(x,y) \mid x,y \in K, y^2 + a_1xy + a_3y = x^3 + a_2x^2 + a_4x + a_6\}.$$

If one is working with characteristic, char $(K) \neq 2,3$, then admissible changes of variables will transform the above equation (1) into the following form:

$$y^2 = x^3 + ax + b \ \text{where} \ a,b \in K \tag{2}$$

But when one works with $char(K) = 2$ or 3, then the general form of equation is given by (3) and (4) respectively.

$$y^2 + xy = x^3 + a_2x^2 + a_6 \tag{3}$$

$$y^2 = x^3 + a_2x^2 + a_6 \tag{4}$$

2.1 Case for real numbers

This case allows us to work with graphs of E. The graph of E has two possible forms, whether the cubic polynomial has only one real root or three real roots. Now, we consider the following examples. Take the equations $y^2 = x(x+1)(x-1)$ and $y^2 = x^3 + 73$. The graphs are as follows:

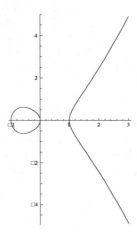

Fig. 1.1. $y^2 = x(x+1)(x-1)$

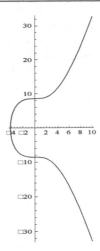

Fig. 1.2. $y^2 = x^3 + 73$.

Looking at the curves, how do you create an algebraic structure from something like this. Basically, one needs to figure out how to find a way to define addition of two points that lie on the curve such that the sum is another point which is also on the curve. If this could be done, together with an identity element, O_∞, group structure can be constructed from points on the curves. The following are some formulas for points operations on the curves which is defined by the equation (2).

1. $P + O_\infty = P$, for all points P.

2. $-P = \cap_\omega -(P)$

3. The opposite point, $-P = (x, -y)$

4. $P = (x_1, y_1)$ & $Q = (x_2, y_2)$, then $P + Q = R = (x_3, y_3)$, with

$$x_3 = m^2 - x_1 - x_2,$$
$$y_3 = m(x_1 - x_3) - y_1,$$
$$m = \frac{y_2 - y_1}{x_2 - x_1} \quad \text{if} \quad Q \neq \pm P$$

or

$$m = \frac{3x_1^2 + a}{2y_1} \quad \text{if} \quad P = Q.$$

It can be shown that the addition law is associative, that is

$$(P + Q) + R = P + (Q + R).$$

It is also commutative,

$$P + Q = Q + P.$$

When several points are added, it does not matter in what order the points are added or how they are grouped together. Technically speaking, the points on the curve, E form an abelian group. The point O_∞ is the identity element of this group.

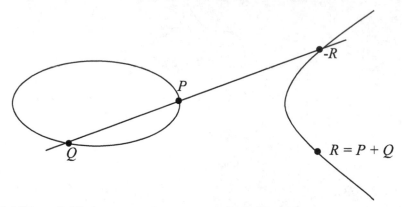

Fig. 1.3. Addition of elliptic curve points over a real number curve

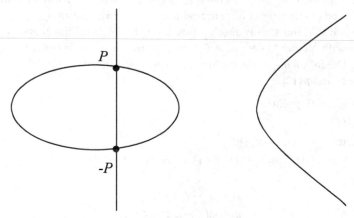

Fig. 1.4. Arbitrary points P and $-P$

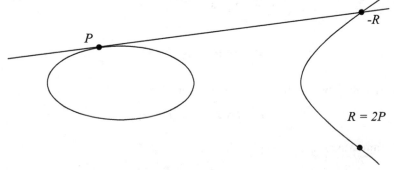

Fig. 1.5. Addition of a point to itself (point doubling)

2.2 Case for integer mod *p* (prime field)

The operations of points on elliptic curves indicated in the previous section are fascinating and it is applicable to the area of cryptography. It so happen that similar formulas work if real numbers are replaced with finite field. An elliptic curve defined over prime field is cryptographically good if the curve is non-singular. This happens when the discriminant, $-16(4a^3 + 27b^2) \neq 0$. That means, the polynomial $x^3 + ax + b$ has no multiple roots.

Now define an elliptic curve mod *p*, where *p* is a prime. For the rest of this section several examples are shown to exhibit its cryptographic use.

Example 2.1: Let *E* be given by $y^2 \equiv x^3 + 2x - 1 \pmod 5$. First of all, compute and list all the points on the curve by letting *x* run through the values 0, 1, 2, 3, 4 and solve for *y*. Substitute each of these into the equation and find the values of *y* that solve the equation.

$$x \equiv 0 \Rightarrow y^2 \equiv -1 \equiv 4 \quad \Rightarrow \quad y \equiv 2,3 \pmod 5$$
$$x \equiv 1 \Rightarrow y^2 \equiv 2 \quad \Rightarrow \quad \text{no solution}$$
$$x \equiv 2 \Rightarrow y^2 \equiv 11 \equiv 1 \equiv 16 \quad \Rightarrow \quad y \equiv 1,4 \pmod 5$$
$$x \equiv 3 \Rightarrow y^2 \equiv 32 \equiv 2 \quad \Rightarrow \quad \text{no solution}$$
$$x \equiv 4 \Rightarrow y^2 \equiv 71 \equiv 1 \equiv 16 \quad \Rightarrow \quad y \equiv 1,4 \pmod 5$$

Therefore, yield the following points along with point at infinity, the identity element:

$$(0,2), (0,3), (2,1), (2,4), (4,1), (4,4), (\infty,\infty)$$

Elliptic curves mod *p* generates finite sets of points and it is these elliptic curves that are useful in cryptography. For cryptographic purposes, the polynomial $x^3 + ax + b$ is assumed not to have multiple roots, as it will lead to weak curves and vulnerable to attack. Computation of points on elliptic curve can also be obtained by using the *Mathematica* software. Now we demonstrate how it can be done. First we need to choose the base point *G*, and the coefficient *a*. Then choose the coefficient *b*, so that *G* lies on the curve $y^2 \equiv x^3 + ax + b \pmod 5$. Now say the point *G* = (1, 3) and choose *a* = 2. Then substitute this into the equation, give the value of *b* = 1. Thus we have $y^2 \equiv x^3 + 2x + 1 \pmod 5$. The following points are generated using the *Mathematica* programming software. The command **multsell** is used to generate points from the curve and was fully written by Lawrence Washington (Lawrence & Wade, 2006). The following are the points generated using the **multsell** command. Thus the following points are generated.

$$(1,3),(3,2),(0,4),(0,1),(3,3),(1,2),(\infty,\infty)$$

2.2.1 Points addition and doubling on elliptic curves

As it was shown earlier in the formulations of points on an elliptic curve, adding points on elliptic curve is not the same as adding points in the plane. Scalar multiplication of a point on the curve for which we have say, *mP* with *m* = 2185, will be evaluated as 2(2(2(2(2(2(2(2(2(2(2(2P))) + P)))) + P))) + P. This is called doubling operation. The following examples show us how addition and doubling operation exactly works using the formulation in section 2.1.

Example 2.2 (point addition) : Suppose E is defined by $y^2 = x^3 + 2x + 1 \pmod 5$. Now add the point (1, 2) and the point (3, 2). The slope $m = \dfrac{2-2}{3-2} \equiv 0 \pmod 5$. Then, we have the following formulas to obtain the third point on the curve.

$$x_3 = -1 - 3 = -4 \equiv 1 \pmod 5$$
$$y_3 = -2 \equiv 3 \pmod 5$$

This means that (1, 2) + (3, 2) = (1, 3), which is also on the curve. This can be verified using the *Mathematica* function, **addell** which was also developed by Lawrence C. Washington (Lawrence & Wade, 2006).

Example 2.3 (point doubling):   Using the same E as in example 1.2, compute $2P = P + P$, where $P = (1, 3)$. This operation is called doubling.

$$m = \frac{3(1) + 2}{2(3)} = \frac{5}{6} \equiv 5 \cdot 6 \equiv 0 \pmod 5$$
$$\therefore m \equiv 0 \pmod 5$$

$$x_3 = -1 - 1 = -2 \equiv 3 \pmod 5$$
$$y_3 = -3 \equiv 2 \pmod 5$$

Thus we have $x_3 = 3, y_3 = 2$. Hence $(1,3) + (1,3) = (3,2)$. This also can be verified using the *Mathematica* command, **addell**. For the ordinary scalar multiplication, say, 3P, is evaluated as 2P + P.

3. Elliptic curve discrete logarithm problem

The term, elliptic curve discrete logarithm problem (ECDLP) comes from the classical discrete logarithm problem, $x \equiv g^k \pmod p$, where we want to find k. In the context of elliptic curve, suppose that the points P, Q on an elliptic curve are made known and $Q = kP$ for some k, then find the k. The difficulty of finding the k is what makes the elliptic curves an area which is cryptographically worth exploring for. In other words, elliptic curves cryptosystem rely its security on the difficulty of the discrete logarithm problem and the available efficient algorithms that can solve the discrete logarithm problem.

Solving the elliptic curve discrete logarithm problem is very hard and until now there is no good and efficient algorithm available to solve the problem. Nevertheless there are a few algorithms being widely discussed, which is popular amongst the cryptanalysts. They are analog of Pohlig-Hellman attack, index calculus attack and baby step-giant step attack. The baby-step giant-step attack on discrete logarithm problem works for elliptic curves although it requires too much memory to be practical. Generally speaking, there is no algorithm available to solve the discrete logarithm problem in sub-exponential time.

4. Elliptic curve cryptography

More than twenty years ago, when elliptic curve cryptography was first introduced independently by

Neal Koblitz and Victor Miller, researchers never thought that elliptic curve cryptography could be implemented efficiently and securely. During those times the arithmetic operations on elliptic curves were difficult to perform. The arithmetic on the elliptic curves was not very efficient and it was only meant for academic interest. Since then, a great deal of effort has been put on the study of elliptic curve and its implementation in cryptography. By the late 1990s the implementations were ten times more efficient and this has made the elliptic curves cryptography as a challenge to the RSA (Rivest- Shamir-Adleman) cryptography.

In recent years, the bit length for secure RSA use has increased and this has increased the processing load on applications using RSA. This is due to the development of the integer factorization algorithms which runs in sub-exponential time and as a result, RSA had to choose a very large key for it to sustain the intractability of the system, where as the elliptic curves cryptosystem require fewer bits or shorter key lengths for the same security level, since the security of the elliptic curve cryptography relies on the discrete logarithm problem and the best known algorithm to solve those problems is fully exponential time. Thus reduction in the time, cost as well as the size or bandwidth and memory requirements, which is crucial factor in some applications such as designs of smart cards, where both memory and processing power are limited but requiring high security. For an example, 160 bits in elliptic curve cryptosystem is around 1024 bits in RSA cryptosystem. Nowadays, elliptic curve cryptosystem is one of the important components in Microsoft Windows, email applications, bank cards and in mobile phones.

As it was mentioned earlier that elliptic curves cryptosystem based its security on the hardness of the discrete logarithm problem. One of the most important aspects in elliptic curve cryptosystem is choosing the right curve that preserved the hardness of discrete logarithm problem. One way to ensure this is to avoid singular curves as the discrete logarithm problem for these types of curves can reduce the hardness of the discrete logarithm problem. The arithmetic on these curves can be much faster over these curves and this is due to the fact that several terms vanished and these types of curves are considered weak and the system will no longer be intractable. Therefore, as mentioned earlier in the previous section, elliptic curves suitable for cryptographic use are of type non-singular curves.

4.1 Embedding plaintext on an elliptic curve

Before messages can be encrypted, those messages need to be embedded on the points of the elliptic curve (Lawrence & Wade, 2006). The embedding process encoded the message m, which is already in a number form, as a point on the curve. Let K be a large positive integer so that a failure rate of $1/2^K$ is acceptable in the decoding process, where $K \in Z$. Assume now that m satisfies $(m+1)K < p$. The message m is presented by a number $x = mK + j$, where K is an integer and $0 \leq j < K$. For $j = 0,1,2,.....,K-1$, compute $x^3 + ax + b \pmod{p}$ and calculate the square root of it. If there is a square root y, then embedded point, $P_m = (x,y)$. Otherwise, increase the j by one and again compute the new x.

Repeat this step until either the square root is found or $j = K$. For the case where j equals K, the mapping of the message to a point failed. In order to recover the message from the embedded point, $P_m = (x, y)$. m can be recovered by computing $\lfloor x / K \rfloor$. Once the messages have been encoded as points on an elliptic curve, then those points can be manipulated arithmetically to hide away those messages. This process is called encryption process. The reverse of the encryption process is called decryption process. There are three versions of classical algorithms, where arithmetic of elliptic curves is being adopted. They are the elliptic curve Diffie-Hellman key exchange, ElGamal elliptic curve cryptosystem and ElGamal elliptic curve digital signature algorithm.

4.2 Elliptic curve diffie-hellman key exchange

Elliptic curve Diffie-Hellman key exchange was first introduced by Diffie and Hellman in the year 1976 (Hellman, 1976). Now we exhibit the implementation of elliptic curve Diffie-Hellman key exchange. Alice and Bob want to exchange a key. Thus, they agreed on a public point generator or the base point G on an elliptic curve $y^2 \equiv x^3 + ax + b \pmod{p}$. Now choose $p = 7211$ and $a = 1$ and the point $G = (3, 5)$. This gives $b = 7206$. Alice chooses a random integer $k_A = 12$ and Bob chooses random integer $k_B = 23$. Alice and Bob keep these private to themselves but publish the $k_A G$ and $k_B G$. In this case we have

$$k_A G = (1794, 6375) \text{ and } k_B G = (3861, 1242).$$

Alice now takes $k_B G$ and multiples by k_A to get the:

$$k_A (k_B G) = 12(3861, 1242) = (1472, 2098).$$

Similarly, Bob takes $k_A G$ and multiples by k_B to get the key:

$$k_B (k_A G) = 23(1794, 6375) = (1472, 2098).$$

Notice that Alice and Bob have the same key.

4.3 Elliptic curve Elgamal cryptosystem

Assuming we have a situation where there are two parties communicating through an insecure channel. The communication is between Alice and Bob. The following example exhibits the use of elliptic curves to encrypt and decrypt messages.

Example 4.1: Firstly, we must generate a curve. Choose the prime $p = 8831$, the point $G = (x, y) = (3, 7)$ and $a = 1$. To make G lie on the curve $y^2 \equiv x^3 + ax + b \pmod{p}$, we then obtain $b = 19$. Alice has a message, represented as a point $P_m = (5, 1743)$ and she wants to send it to Bob. Bob has chosen a random number $a_b = 5$ and published the point $a_b G = (7335, 7164)$. Alice then chooses a random number $k = 4$. She sends Bob $kG = (254, 2386)$ and $P_m + k(a_b G) = (269, 1803)$. Bob then first calculate $a_b kG = 5(254, 2386) = (4217, 7788)$. Bob then subtract this from $(269, 1803)$:

$$(269,1803) - (4217,7788) = (269,1803) + (4217,-7788) = (5,1743)$$

Now Bob recovered the message $P_m = (5,1743)$ that Alice sent.

4.4 ElGamal elliptic curve digital signature algorithm

A digital signature is an electronic analogue of a hand written signature that allows a receiver to convince a third party that the message is in fact originated from the sender. ElGamal elliptic curve digital signature algorithm is an analogue to the digital signature algorithm proposed earlier by ElGamal in 1985 where some modifications were done to deal with points on an elliptic curve.

Now suppose that Alice wants to sign a message m. assuming that m is an integer, Alice fixes an elliptic curve $E(\bmod p)$, where p is a large prime and a point A on E. We assume that the number of points n on E has been calculated and $0 \le m < n$. Alice also has to choose a private integer a and compute $B = aA$. The prime p, the curve E, the integer n, and the points A and B are made public. To sign the message m, Alice does the following procedure:

1. Alice chooses a random integer k with $1 \le k < n$ and gcd (k, n) = 1, and computes $R = kA = (x, y)$,
2. Now, Alice computes $s \equiv k^{-1}(m - ax)(\bmod n)$ and
3. Sends the signed message (m, R, s) to Bob.

Note that R is a point on F, and m and s are integers. Next, Bob verifies the signature as follows:

1. Bob now downloads Alice's public information p, E, n, A, B, and
2. Computes $V_1 = xB + sR$ and $V_2 - mA$.
3. Declares the signature valid if $V_1 = V_2$.

We can verify that the verification procedure works because we have the following:

$$V_1 = xB + sR = xaA + k^{-1}(m - ax)(kA) = xaA + (m - ax)A = mA = V_2$$

5. Point counting for E (mod p)

Let $E : y^2 = x^3 + bx + c(\bmod p)$ be an elliptic curve. Then the number of points on E denoted as $\#E(F_p)$, satisfies Hasse's theorem (Jacobson & Hammer, 2009),(Lawrence & Wade,2006). According to Hasse's theorem, the number of points on E, $\#E(F_p)$, satisfy the following inequality.

$$p + 1 - 2\sqrt{p} \le \#E\left(F_p\right) \le p + 1 + 2\sqrt{p}$$

Number of points on the curve E is called the order of the curve. The order of a point is defined by the number of times the point added to itself until the infinity is obtained. The order of any point on the curve E, will divide the order of the curve E. If the order of the curve has many factors or smooth, then this curve is not cryptographically good. For cryptography, it is best if the order of the curve is a large prime number. Generally finding order of a curve is not trivial. In a situation where $p \geq 5$ is a prime, for small p, points can be listed by letting $x = 0,1,2,....,p-1$ and seeing when $x^3 + ax + b$ is a square mod p. When p is large, it is infeasible to count the points on the curve by listing them. There are several algorithms that can deal with this problem, They are Schoof's algorithm and Schoof-Elkies-Atkin (SEA) algorithm (Lawrence &Wade, 2006). In principal, there are approximately p points on the curve E and inclusive of the point at infinity, a total of $p + 1$ points is expected to be on the curve. The order of a curve is called 'smooth' if the order of the curve is divisible by many small factors, where this can brings point multiplications to identity (point at infinity). The type of curve which is desirable is of type 'non-smooth' order, where the order of the curve is divisible by a large prime number. The Schoof-Elkies-Atkin point counting method has become sufficiently efficient to find cryptographic curves of prime order over F_p with heuristic time $O(\log^6 p)$. In the next section, we will discuss the two counting point algorithms, the Schoof counting point algorithm and the Schoof-Elkies-Atkins counting point algorithm.

5.1 Schoof and Schoof-Elkies-Atkin (SEA) point counting algorithms

To determine the $\#E(F_p)$, one needs to compute $z = y^2 = x^3 + ax + b$ for each x in F_p and then test if z has a square root in F_p. If there exists $y \in F_p$ such that $y^2 = z$, then we have $2p +$ (a point of infinity) that is $2p + 1$ elements in the group because each x value will produce two values of y. However, according to the theorem of finite fields, there is around ½ of the non-zero elements of F_p are quadratic residues. So, there is approximately $p + 1$ number of points. There are a few point counting algorithms and in this section, we focus only on two point counting methods. They are Schoof and Schoof-Elkies-Atkin (SEA) point counting algorithms. In this chapter, we will describe the two algorithms in a brief manner. Readers are required to have some backgrounds in number theory and algebraic geometry. For more details on arithmetic of elliptic curves, one needs to refer to (Silverman, 1986) and for the introduction on Schoof algorithm, refer to (Schoof, 1985).

5.1.1 Schoof's algorithm

René Schoof (Schoof, 1985) had introduced a deterministic polynomial time algorithm to compute the number of F_p-points of elliptic curve defined over a finite field F_p which was given by Weierstrass form in (2). Schoof algorithm has managed to compute the group order of over 200 digits. In the Schoof algorithm, the characteristic polynomial of Frobenius endomorphism is critical to the development of Schoof's algorithm. Another crucial part in this algorithm is to compute the division polynomials in order to carry out the computation of the order of the group of elliptic curve. If the division polynomials have low degree, then the division polynomials is said to be efficiently computable.

Let E be an elliptic curve defined over F_p denoted as E / F_p, where F_p is a prime field of characteristic $p > 3$. Define the Frobenius endomorphism ϕ_p as the following:

$$\phi_p : E(\overline{F}_p) \to E(\overline{F}_p)$$

$$(x,y) \mapsto (x^p, y^p)$$

The Frobenius map or endomorphism ϕ_p satisfies the characteristic equation (5)

$$\phi_p^2 - t\phi_p + p = 0, \forall P \in (\overline{F}_p) \tag{5}$$

where $\overline{F}_p$ is the algebraic closure of the prime field F_p. Let t is the trace of Frobenius endomorphism, then the number of points, $\#E(F_p)$ is given in (6) as follows:

$$\#E(F_p) = p + 1 - t, |t| \le 2\sqrt{p} \tag{6}$$

Obviously from equation (5), we have for all points, $P = (x,y) \in E(\overline{F}_p)$ satisfying the following equation (7):

$$(x^{p^2}, y^{p^2}) + p(x,y) = t(x^p, y^p) \tag{7}$$

where scalar multiplication by p or t signifies adding a point to itself p or t times respectively. For $(x,y) \in \overline{E}[l]$, where $E[l] = \{P = (x,y) \in E(\overline{F}_p) \mid [l]P = O_\infty\}$, here each $P \in E[l]$ is called l-torsion point. If $t(x^p, y^p) \equiv \overline{t}(x^p, y^p)$ where $\overline{t}$ is t mod l and $\overline{p}$ known as p mod l where l is a prime. Now, the equation of (7) is reduced as following:

$$(x^{p^2}, y^{p^2}) + \overline{p}(x,y) = \overline{t}(x^p, y^p)$$

To determine t (mod l) for primes $l > 2$, we need to compute the division polynomials.

Definition 5.1.1 (Division Polynomial)

Division polynomial (McGee, 2006) is a sequence of polynomials in $\psi_m \in \mathbb{Z}[x,y,a,b]$ and goes to zero on points of particular order. Let E be the elliptic curve given by (2). The division polynomials $\psi_m(x, y) = 0$ if and only if $(x, y) \in E[n]$. These polynomials are defined recursively as follows (Schoof, 1985):

$\Psi_{-1} = -1$

$\Psi_0 = 0$

$\Psi_1 = 1$

$\Psi_2 = 2y$

$\Psi_3 = 3x^4 + 6ax^2 + 12bx - a^2$

$\Psi_4 = 4y (x^6 + 5xa^4 + -20bx^3 - 5a^2x^2 - 4abx - 8b^2 - a^3)$

$\Psi_{2m} = \Psi_m (\Psi_{m+2} \Psi^2_{m-1} - \Psi_{m-2} \Psi^2_{m+1}) / 2y \qquad m \in \mathbb{Z}, m \ge 3$

$\Psi_{2m+1} = \Psi_{m+2} \Psi^3_m - \Psi^3_{m+1} \Psi_{m-1} \qquad m \in \mathbb{Z}, m \ge 2$

For simplicity, the polynomials are suppressed to Ψ_n. which is called the nth division polynomial.

Let us derive the $\Psi_3 = 3x^4 + 6ax^2 + 12bx - a^2$. In division polynomial Ψ_3, we must have a point $P = (x,y) \in E[3]$ which is a point with order 3 such that $[3]P = \infty$. Therefore, we have $2P = -P$ and we know the x- coordinate for point $2P$ and P is the same. The formula for the x-coordinate in $2P$ is given in the earlier section.

$$x = \lambda^2 - 2x$$

$$= \left(\frac{3x^2 + a}{2y}\right)^2 - 2x$$

$$= \left(\frac{9x^4 + 6ax^2 + a^2}{4y^2}\right) - 2x$$

$$3x(4y^2) = 9x^4 + 6ax^2 + a^2$$
$$12xy^2 = 9x^4 + 6ax^2 + a^2$$
$$12x(x^3 + ax + b) = 9x^4 + 6ax^2 + a^2$$
$$\Psi_3 = 12x^4 + 12ax^2 + 12bx - 9x^4 - 6ax^2 - a^2 = 0$$
$$\therefore \Psi_3 = 3x^4 + 6ax^2 + 12bx - a^2$$

We can replace y^2 by $(x^3 + ax + b)$ to eliminate the y term. The polynomial $f_n(x) \in F_p[x]$ is defined as follows:

$$f_n(x) = \psi_n(x,y) \text{ if } n \text{ is odd}$$

$$f_n(x) = \frac{\psi_n(x,y)}{y} \text{ if } n \text{ is even}$$

If n is odd, then the degree of $f_n(x)$ is $\dfrac{n^2 - 1}{2}$ whereas if n is even, then the degree of $f_n(x)$ is $\dfrac{n^2 - 4}{2}$.

The following proposition shows point additions relates to the division polynomials.

Proposition 5.1.1

Let $(x, y) \in E(\overline{F_p})$, with $\overline{F_p}$, the algebraic closure of F_p. Let $n \in \mathbb{Z}$, then for $[n]P = P + P + P +...+ P$ is given by

$$[n]P = (x - \frac{\psi_{n-1}\psi_{n+1}}{\psi_n^2}, \frac{\psi_{n+2}\psi_{n-1}^2 - \psi_{n-2}\psi_{n+1}^2}{4y\psi_n^3})$$

5.1.1.1 Computation of number of points, #E(Fp) using Schoof's algorithm

Here, we present briefly the Schoof's algorithm. For E as defined in (2) over F_p and the Hasse's theorem,

$$\#E\ (F_p) = p + 1 - t \text{ where } |\ t\ | \leq 2\sqrt{p}\ .$$

Input : Elliptic curve $y^2 = x^3 + ax + b$ over prime field F_p .

Output: Number of points, $\#E(F_p)$.

1.   Create a set of small primes not equal to the char $(F_p) = p$,

$$S = \{l_1, l_2,..., l_L\}, = \{2, 3, 5, 7, 11,... l_L\} \text{ such that } \prod_{i=1}^{L} l_i > \left\lceil 4\sqrt{p}\ \right\rceil.$$

a.   For case when the prime l = 2:
2.   gcd $(x^3 + ax + b, x^p - x) \neq 1$, then $t \equiv 0$ (mod 2), else $t \equiv 1$ (mod 2).

This is to test whether E has point of order 2, $(x, 0) \in F[2]$ or precisely roots of E.

If gcd $(x^3 + ax + b, x^p - x) = \gcd(x^3 + ax + b, x_p - x) = 1$, then $x^3 + ax + b$ has no root in F_p, else it has at least one such root.

3.   To test whether which case is to be used, we have to compute the following relation:

$$\gcd\left((x^{p^i} - x)\psi_{p_l}^2 - \psi_{p_l-1}\psi_{p_l+1}(mod\,\psi_l, p), \psi_l\right)$$

If the gcd $= 1$, proceed to (B), else proceed to (C) .

b.   For the case when $(x^{p^2}, y^{p^2}) \neq \pm p_l(x, y)$
4.   For each $l \in S$, compute $p_l \equiv p$ (mod l)

5.   For case $(x^{p^2}, y^{p^2}) \neq \pm p_l(x, y)$

6.   Compute $(x', y') = (x^{p^2}, y^{p^2}) + p_l(x, y) \neq \infty$

7.   For each $1 \leq \tau \leq \dfrac{l-1}{2}$, compute the x-coordinate, x_τ of $\tau(x, y) = (x_\tau, y_\tau)$

8.   If $x' - x_\tau \neq 0 (mod\,\psi_l)$ then try next τ, else compute y' and y_τ .

9.   If $\dfrac{y' - y_\tau}{y} \equiv 0 (mod\,\psi_l)$, then $t \equiv \tau(mod\,l)$, else $t \equiv -\tau(mod\,l)$

10.   If all values $1 \leq \tau \leq \dfrac{l-1}{2}$ fail, then proceed to case (C).

c.   For the case when $(x^{p^2}, y^{p^2}) = \pm p_l(x, y)$
11.   Compute w such that $w^2 \equiv p$ (mod l)
12.   If w^2 does not exist, then $t \equiv 0$ (mod l), else
13.   Compute $(x^p, y^p) = \pm w(x, y) = \pm(x_w, y_w) = (x_w, \pm y_w)$

14. If gcd(numerator($(x^p - x_w)$), ψ_l) = 1, then $t \equiv 0 (\mathrm{mod}\, l)$

15. Else compute gcd(numerator($(y^p - y_w) / y$), ψ_l)

16. If gcd(numerator($(y^p - y_w) / y$), ψ_l) = 1, then $t \equiv -2w (\mathrm{mod}\, l)$, else $t \equiv 2w (\mathrm{mod}\, l)$

Recover t via Chinese Remainder Theorem (CRT)

17. At this point we have computed t (mod l) for any $l \in S$.

18. $T \equiv t$ (mod N) where $N = \prod_{i=1}^{L} l_i$:

19. If T is in Hasse's bounds, then $t = T$, else $t \equiv - T$ (mod N)

20. $\#E\,(F_p) = p + 1 - t$.

5.1.2 Schoof-Elkies-Atkin (SEA) algorithm

Schoof's algorithm is not practical because of the exponential growth in the degree of the division polynomial and hence it is not suitable for cryptographic purposes. Atkin and Elkies has improved the Schoof's algorithm by analyzing the method to restrict the characteristic polynomial of elliptic curve such that

$$\chi(\phi_p) = \phi_p^2 - t\phi_p + p \tag{8}$$

where the Frobenius splits over F_l. The discussion will follow the literature found in (Cohen et al., 2006). In 1988, Atkin devised an algorithm to the order of ϕ_p in projective general linear group dimension 2 of F_l, whereas Elkies in 1991 introduced a mean to replace the division polynomial which has degree $(l^2 - 1)/2$ by a kernel polynomial with degree $(l - 1)/2$ in Elkies prime procedures. To differentiate between the Elkies prime and Atkin prime, one can calculate the discriminant from (8), so we get $\Delta = t^2 - 4p$. If Δ is a square then the prime l is Elkies prime, else it is Atkin prime. However, we need to classify the primes at the beginning stage and there is no information of t. Therefore this method is not suitable. However, Atkin proved that l-modular polynomial, $\Phi_l(x, y) \in \mathbb{Z}[x, y]$ can be used to differentiate the prime at the early stage of SEA algorithm. SEA algorithm is one of the fastest algorithms for counting the number of points on E over a large prime field. The following part of this section follows the text from (Chen, 2008), (Cohen et al., 2006), and (Galin, 2007).

5.1.2.1 Modular polynomial

Modular polynomial comes from the theory of modular form and the interpretation of elliptic curves over the complex field as lattices. A moderately comprehensive development of the theory can be found in (Silverman, 1986). Before we proceed with the SEA algorithm, we know the modular polynomial. The detail proof of this theorem can be obtained in (Cox, 1989). These polynomials will be used in Elkies and Atkin procedures.

Theorem 5.1.2.1 (modular polynomial)

Let m be a positive integer.

i. $\Phi_m(x,y) \in \mathbb{Z}[x,y]$

ii. $\Phi_m(x,y)$ is irreducible when regarded as polynomial in x.

iii. $\Phi_m(x,y) = \Phi_m(y,x)$ if $m > 1$.

iv. If m is a prime, l then, $\Phi_l(x,y) \equiv (x^l - y)(x - y^l) \bmod l\mathbb{Z}[x,y]$

Let l be the prime different from characteristic p, then the classical modular polynomial has $(l^2 + 3l + 4)/2$ coefficients. Here are examples of the classical modular polynomials taken from (Galin, 2007).

For $l = 3$, we have the modular polynomial as follows:

$$\Phi_3(x,y) = x^4 - x^3y^3 + y^4 + 2232(x^3y^2 + x^2y^3) - 1069956(x^3y + xy^3) + 36864000(x^3 + y^3)$$
$$+2587918086x^2y^2 + 8900222976000(x^2y + xy^2) + 452984832000000(x^2 + y^2)$$
$$-770845966336000000xy + 1855425871872000000000(x + y)$$

For $l = 5$, we have the following modular polynomial:

$$\Phi_5(x,y) = x^6 - x^5y^5 + y^6 + 3720(x^5y^4 + x^4y^5) - 4550940(x^5y^3 + x^3y^5) + 2028551200(x^5y^2 + x^2y^5)$$
$$-246683410950(x^5y + xy^5) + 1963211489280(x^5 + y^5) + 1665999364600x^4y^4$$
$$+107878928185336800(x^4y^3 + x^3y^4) + 383083609779811215375(x^4y^2 + x^2y^4)$$
$$+128541798906828816384000(x^4y + xy^4) + 1284733132841424456253440(x^4 + y^4)$$
$$-441206965512914835246100x^3y^3 + 26898488858380731577417728000(x^3y^2 + x^2y^3)$$
$$-192457934618928282996551082311680000(x^3y + xy^3)$$
$$+280244777828439527804321565297868800(x^3 + y^3)$$
$$+5110941777552418083110765199360000x^2y^2$$
$$+36554736583949629295706472332656640000(x^2y + xy^2)$$
$$+6692500042627997708487149415015068467200(x^2 + y^2)$$
$$-264073457076620596259715790247978782949376xy$$
$$+53274330803424425450420160273356509151232000(x + y)$$
$$+14135994715472135869775347469107136275100467200.$$

We now give some backgrounds needed for SEA algorithm. These information might have some gaps and readers are suggested to refer to (Silverman, 1986) and (Cox, 1989) for further details.

5.1.2.2 Elliptic curve over complex field

The theory of elliptic curves over complex field is corresponding to the lattice and thus equivalently to the torus that is the mapping of $E(\mathbb{C}) \rightarrow \mathbb{C}/\Lambda$ and $\mathbb{C}/\Lambda \rightarrow E(\mathbb{C})$. Lattice, $\Lambda = w_1\mathbb{Z} + w_2\mathbb{Z}$ where $w_1, w_2 \in \mathbb{C}$ are $\mathbb{R}$-linearly independent, then an elliptic function $f(z)$ defined on $\mathbb{C}$ except for isolated singularities, satisfies two conditions: $f(z)$ is meromorphic on $\mathbb{C}$ and $f(z + w_1) = f(z + w_2) = f(z)$. This indicates a doubly periodic meromorphic function (Cox, 1989). An example of elliptic function is the Weierstrass $\wp$-function defined in the following theorem. Proofs for all the theorems, lemma and propositions are omitted.

Theorem 5.1.2.2

Let $\Lambda \subset \mathbb{C}$ be a lattice. The Weierstrass $\wp$-function relative to Λ is given by

$$\wp(z) = \wp(z, \Lambda) = \frac{1}{z^2} + \sum_{w \in \Lambda \setminus \{0\}} \left(\frac{1}{(z-w^2)} - \frac{1}{(w^2)} \right)$$

Then,

i.   The sum defining $\wp(z)$ converges absolutely and uniformly on compact set not containing elements of Λ.

ii. $\wp(z)$ is meromorphic in $\mathbb{C}$ and has a double pole at each $w \in \Lambda$.

iii. $\wp(-z) = \wp(z)$, $\forall z \in \mathbb{C}$ which is an even function.

iv. $\wp(z+w) = \wp(z), \forall w \in \Lambda$

Therefore, the Weierstrass $\wp$-function relative to Λ is a doubly periodic function with periods w_1 and w_2 which is known as the basis of Λ.

Theorem 5.1.2.3.

The relation between Weierstrass $\wp$-function and its first derivative is given by $\wp'(z)^2 = 4\wp(z)^3 - g_2\wp(z) - g_3$. Then there is lattice, Λ such that $g_2(\Lambda) = 60G_4$ and $g_3(\Lambda) = 140G_6$ where $G_4 = \sum_{w \in \Lambda \setminus \{0\}} \frac{1}{w^4}$ and $G_6 = \sum_{w \in \Lambda \setminus \{0\}} \frac{1}{w^6}$. Hence, there is an isomorphism between points on elliptic curve over the complex field and points on the complex modulo a suitable lattice Λ that is $E(\mathbb{C}) \simeq \mathbb{C} / \Lambda$

5.1.2.3 j-invariant, $j(\tau)$

Elliptic function depends on the lattice being used. Let $\Lambda = w_1\mathbb{Z} + w_2\mathbb{Z}$ and $\tau = \frac{w_1}{w_2}$. Since $w_1, w_2 \in \mathbb{C}$ are

$\mathbb{R}$-linearly independent, therefore the τ is not in $\mathbb{R}$. Now, τ belongs to Poincaré upper half plane,

$$\mathcal{H} = \{ x + iy \in \mathbb{C} \mid y > 0 \}.$$

By restricting to Λ_τ, we have $g_2(\Lambda) = g_2(\Lambda_\tau)$, $g_3(\Lambda) = g_3(\Lambda_\tau)$ and $D = g_2^3 - 27g_3^2$ which is closely related to the discriminant of the polynomial $4x^3 - g_2x - g_3$. Then,

$$j(\tau) = 1728 \frac{g_2(\tau)^3}{g_2(\tau)^3 - 27g_3(\tau)^2}.$$

If lattice $\Lambda \in \mathbb{C}$, there exists a nonzero $\lambda \in \mathbb{C}$ such that $\Lambda_\tau = \lambda\Lambda$ for some $\tau \in F$ where F is the standard fundamental region.

Two lattices, Λ and $\Lambda' \in \mathbb{C}$ is homothetic, then there exist nonzero $\lambda \in \mathbb{C}$ such that $\Lambda' = \lambda\Lambda$.

Theorem 5.1.2.4.

If Λ and Λ' are lattices in $\mathbb{C}$, then $j(\Lambda) = j(\Lambda')$ if and only if Λ and Λ' are homothetic.

$j(\tau)$ is a holomorphic function on the Poincaré upper half plane, $\mathcal{H} = \{x + iy \in \mathbb{C} \mid y > 0\}$. The properties of $j(\tau)$ are related to the action on the special linear group, $SL(2, \mathbb{Z})$ with determinant one on $\mathcal{H}$. This is defined as such that $z \in \mathcal{H}$ and $\gamma = \begin{pmatrix} a & b \\ c & d \end{pmatrix} \in SL(2,\mathbb{Z})$ then

$\gamma\tau = \dfrac{a\tau + b}{c\tau + d}$, $\gamma\tau \in \mathcal{H}$. If τ and τ' in $\mathcal{H}$, then $j(\tau) = j(\tau')$ if and only if $\tau' = \gamma\tau$ for some $\gamma \in SL(2,\mathbb{Z})$

For classical modular polynomial and any $n > 0$.

$$S_n^* = \{\begin{pmatrix} a & b \\ 0 & d \end{pmatrix} \mid a,b,d \in \mathbb{Z}, 0 \le b < d, ad = n, \gcd(a,b,d) = 1\}$$

For $\alpha - \begin{pmatrix} a & b \\ 0 & d \end{pmatrix} \in S_n^*$, define the map

$$j \circ \alpha(\tau) = j(\frac{a\tau + b}{d})$$

Hence, the n-th modular polynomial can also defined as

$$\Phi_n(x, j) = \prod_{\alpha \in S_n^*} (x \quad j \circ \alpha(\tau)).$$

5.1.2.4 Computation of modular polynomial

Let l be a prime, we now discuss the method to compute modular polynomial, $\Phi_l(x,y)$. According to previous theorem, we have $\Phi_l(x,y) = \Phi_l(y,x)$ and $\Phi_l(x,y) \equiv (x^l - y)(x - y^l) \bmod l\mathbb{Z}[x,y]$. Besides, $\Phi_l(x,y)$ is a monic polynomial with degree l +1 as polynomial in x and therefore we can write

$$\Phi_l(x,y) = (x^l - y)(x - y^l) + l\sum_{0 \le i \le l} c_{ii}x^i y^i + l\sum_{0 \le i < j \le l} c_{ij}(x^i y^j + x^j y^i)$$

where the coefficient $c_{ij} \in \mathbb{Z}$ which can found by q-expansion of j–function. We also have the identity

$$\Phi_p(j(l\tau), j(\tau)) = 0.$$

Substituting the q-expansion for $j(\tau)$ and $j(l\tau)$ into $\Phi_l(x,y)$, we have the following:

$$((j(l\tau)^l - j(\tau))(j(l\tau) - j(\tau)^l) + l \sum_{0 \leq i \leq l} c_{ii} j(l\tau)^i j(\tau)^i + l \sum_{0 \leq i < j \leq l} c_{ij}(j(l\tau)^i j(\tau)^j + j(l\tau)^j j(\tau)^i) = 0.$$

This is obtained by equating the coefficients of the different powers of infinite number of linear equations in the variable c_{ij}. However, the finite number of linear equations can be obtained by equating the coefficients of negative powers of q which is a unique solution. It is suffices to calculate those coefficients of the q-expansions which contribute to negative powers of $j(\tau)$ and only need the first $l^2 + l$ coefficients of the q-expansion of the j-function. Computing on modular polynomial becomes tedious as when prime l getting bigger, the number of digit for the coefficient do increase rapidly. Previously, we have listed the two modular polynomial $\Phi_3(x,y)$ and $\Phi_5(x,y)$. For $\Phi_{11}(x,y)$, its coefficients are more than 120 digits and is not shown here.

Lemma 5.1.2.1

Let $E_1/\mathbb{C}$ and $E_2/\ \mathbb{C}$ be two elliptic curves with j-invariants j_{E_1} and j_{E_2} respectively, then $\Phi_n(j_{E_1}, j_{E_2}) = 0$ if and only if there is an isogeny from E_1 to E_2 whose kernel is cyclic of degree n.

Theorem 5.1.2.5

Let E an elliptic curve defined over F_p with $p \neq l$, then the $l + 1$ zeroes $\tilde{j} \in F_p$ of the polynomial $\Phi_l(x, j(E)) = 0$ are the j-invariants of the isogenous curves $\tilde{E} = E/C$ with C one of the $l + 1$ cyclic subgroups of $E[l]$.

Theorem 5.1.2.6 (Atkin classification).

Let E be an ordinary elliptic curve defined over F_p with j-invariant $j \neq 0$, 1728. Let $\Phi_l(x, j) = h_1 h_2 ... h_s$ be the factorization of $\Phi_l(x, j) \in F_p[x]$ as a product of irreducible polynomials. Then there are the following possibilities for the degrees of $h_1, ..., h_s$:

i. $(1, l)$ or $(1, 1, ..., 1)$. In either case we have $\Delta = t^2 - 4p \equiv 0 \pmod{l}$. In the former case we set $r = l$ and the later case $r = 1$.

ii. $(1, 1, r, r, ..., r)$. In this case $\Delta = t^2 - 4p$ is square modulo l, r divides $l - 1$ and ϕ_p acts on

$E[l]$ as a diagonal matrix $\begin{pmatrix} \lambda & 0 \\ 0 & \mu \end{pmatrix}$ with $\lambda, \mu \in F_l^*$.

iii. $(r, r, ..., r)$ for some $r > 1$. In this case $\Delta = t^2 - 4p$ is a nonsquare modulo l, r divides $l + 1$ and the restriction of ϕ_p to $E[l]$ has an irreducible characteristic polynomial over F_l

In all these 3 cases, r is the order of ϕ_p in $PGL_2(F_p)$ and the trace t satisfies $t^2 \equiv p(\xi + \xi^{-1})^2 \pmod{l}$ for some r-th root of unity $\xi \in \overline{F_l}$. The number of irreducible factors s satisfies $(-1)^s = (\frac{p}{l})$.

Proof: Refer to (Galin, 2007).

To determine the type of prime, it suffices to compute $g(x) = \gcd(\Phi_l(x,j), x^p - x)$. If $g(x) \neq 1$, l is an Elkies prime else it is an Atkin prime.

Example 5.1.2.1

Let an elliptic curve, E defined over F_{113} with the equation given by $y^2 = x^3 - 15x + 13$

$S = \{2, 3, 5, 7\}$ such that $\prod_{i=1}^{4} l_i = 210 > \lceil 4\sqrt{p} \rceil = 43$. Let us check $l = 3$ and 5.

For $l = 3$. check whether it is an Elkies or Atkin prime. The j- invariant, $j_E = 28$.

$$\Phi_3(x,28) = x^4 - x^3(28)^3 + (28)^4 + 2232(x^3(28)^2 + x^2(28)^3) - 1069956(x^3(28) + x(28)^3)$$
$$+36864000(x^3 + (28)^3) + 2587918086x^2(28)^2 + 8900222976000(x^2(28) + x(28)^2)$$
$$+452984832000000(x^2 + (28)^2) - 770845966336000000x(28)$$
$$+1855425871872000000000(x + 28).$$

$$\Phi_3(x,28) \equiv x^4 + 81x^3 + 111x^2 + 65x + 52 (\text{mod}\,113)$$

$$\gcd(\Phi_3(x,28), x^{113} - x) = 1$$

Hence 3 is an Atkin prime.

For $l = 5$. Check whether it is an Elkies or Atkin prime. The j- invariant, $j_F = 28$.

$$\Phi_5(x,28) \equiv x^6 + 90x^3 + 81x^4 + 65x^3 + 49x^2 (\text{mod } 113)$$

$$\gcd(\Phi_5(x,28), x^{113} - x) = x^2 + 94x + 63 \neq 1$$

Hence 5 is an Elkies prime.

Definition 5.1.2.1

Let the discriminant of the characteristic equation, $\Delta = t^2 - 4p$. If Δ is a square in F_l then the prime l is an Elkies prime else l is an Atkin prime.

5.1.2.5 Atkin primes procedures

Since $t^2 = p(\xi + \xi^{-1})^2$ over F_l, each pair (ξ, ξ^{-1}) determines one value of t^2 or at most two values of t.

The number of the possible values of t_l is Euler totient function, $\varphi(r)$ and $r \leq l + 1$.

Let recall the reduced characteristic polynomial $\chi_l(T) = T^2 - t_l T + p_l = (T - \lambda)(T - \mu)$

$$(T - \lambda)(T - \mu) = T^2 - (\lambda\mu)T + (\lambda\mu)$$

Therefore $\lambda + \mu \equiv t \pmod{l}$ and $\lambda\mu \equiv p \pmod{l}$

Then $\dfrac{\lambda}{\mu}$ is an element of order exactly r in F_{l^2} Find r such that which $\gcd(\Phi_l(x), x^{p^r} - x) \neq 1$.

$\gamma = \dfrac{\lambda}{\mu}$ where $\gamma \in F_{l^2}$ is a primitive r-th root of unity. Now let g be a generator of $F_{l^2}^*$ and

$\gamma_i = g^{\left(\frac{i(l^2-1)}{r}\right)}$ for $\gcd(i, r) = 1$ and satisfying $1 \leq i < r$.

Next, for nonsquare $d \in F_l$, we have $\lambda = x_1 + x_2\sqrt{d}$ and $\mu = x_1 - x_2\sqrt{d}$ for some $x_i \in F_l$.

Similarly we have $\gamma_i = g_{i_1} + g_{i_2}(\sqrt{d}) = \dfrac{\lambda}{\mu} = \dfrac{\lambda^2}{\lambda\mu} = \dfrac{x_1^2 + x_2^2 d + 2x_1 x_2\sqrt{d}}{p}$ where $g_{i_1}, g_{i_2} \in F_l$

Compare both sides,

$$g_{i_1} \equiv \frac{x_1 x_2 + x_2^2 d}{p} \pmod{l} \qquad \Rightarrow p g_{i_1} \equiv x_1^2 + x_2^2 d \pmod{l}$$

$$g_{i_2}\sqrt{d} \equiv \frac{2x_1 x_2\sqrt{d}}{p} \pmod{l} \quad \Rightarrow p g_{i_2} \equiv 2x_1 x_2 \pmod{l}$$

Also, $p \equiv \lambda\mu \equiv x_1^2 + dx_2^2 \pmod{l}$, so it follows that $x_1^2 = \dfrac{p(g_{i_1} + 1)}{2}$. If x_1^2 is not a square in F_l, γ_i is discarded and move to the next one. Else, we have the following.

$$\therefore t \equiv \lambda + \mu \equiv 2x_1 \pmod{l}$$

5.1.2.6 Elkies primes procedures

Determine for the isogenous elliptic curve. Then recall the reduced characteristic polynomial $\chi_l(T) = T^2 - t_l T + p_l = (T - \lambda)(T - \mu)$

$$(T - \lambda)(T - \mu) = T^2 - (\lambda\mu)T + (\lambda\mu).$$

Therefore, $\lambda + \mu \equiv t \pmod{l}$ and $\lambda\mu \equiv p \pmod{l}$.

Notice that $t_l \equiv \lambda + \mu = \lambda + \dfrac{p}{\lambda} \pmod{l}$, so once we get the value of λ then we can find t_l.

If $\lambda = \mu$, then $t_l \equiv 2\lambda \equiv 2\sqrt{p} \pmod{l}$.

If $\lambda \neq \mu$, $E[l]$ has two subgroups C_1, C_2 that are stable under ϕ_p, we need to replace the division polynomial with degree $(l^2 - 1)/2$ by finding a kernel polynomial with degree $(l-1)/2$ whose roots are the x-coordinate of the subgroup C_1 or C_2. The kernel polynomial is defined by

$$F_l(x) = \prod_{\pm P \in C_L \setminus \{0\}} (x - x(P))$$

One can obtain the value of λ by using the relation $(x^p, y^p) = \lambda(x, y)$.

We find λ such that $\gcd(\psi_\lambda^2(x^p - x) + \psi_{\lambda-1}\psi_{\lambda+1}, F_l(x)) \neq 1$. It suffices to check the value $1 \leq \lambda \leq (l-1)/2$. Then compute $t_l \equiv \lambda + \mu = \lambda + \frac{p}{\lambda} \pmod{l}$.

To combine Elkies and Atkin prime, we apply the concept of Chinese Remainder Theorem, and then we obtain the t in the final step by using the elementary method (baby-steps giant-steps which is not covered in this chapter, and one should refer to (Galin, 2007) for further details). Next, we summarize these two algorithms into making some comparison between them.

6. Compare and contrast between Schoof's algorithm and Schoof-Elkies-Atkin (SEA) algorithm

i.   Similarities between Schoof's algorithm and SEA algorithm
*   Polynomial time and deterministic point counting algorithms for elliptic curve with characteristic $K \neq 2, 3$
*   Using Hasse's theorem or specifically Hasse's interval as a boundary to determine $\#E(F_p)$.
*   Using a specific type of polynomial which is essential for the computation steps.
*   Classified as l-adic point counting algorithms.
*   Begin by letting $S = \{2, 3, 5, ..., L\}$ be a set of primes not including char (F_p) such that $\prod_{l \in S} l > 4\sqrt{n}$
*   Both algorithms is to find the trace of the Frobenius endomorphism, t.
*   Making use of the Frobenius endomorphism, ϕ_p and the characteristic equation is such that:

$$\chi_l(T) = T^2 - t_l T + p_l = (T - \lambda)(T - \mu), \text{ so } t \equiv \lambda + \mu \pmod{l} \text{ and } p \equiv \lambda\mu \pmod{l}.$$

ii. Differences between Schoof's algorithm and SEA algorithm
*   Practicality
i.   Schoof's algorithm: Most successful general point counting algorithm but not practical because the degree of division polynomial will grow exponentially when l becomes larger.
ii. SEA algorithm: Most practical version of point counting algorithm. However the use of classical modular polynomial will lead to the increasing of number of coefficients when l becomes larger. This problem is overcome by using canonical modular polynomial, Müller modular polynomial and Atkin modular polynomial which have similar construction like classical modular polynomial.
*   Complexity
i.   Schoof's algorithm: $O(\log^8 p)$ bit operations.

ii.   SEA algorithm: O (log $^6 p$) bit operations due to the replacement of division polynomial $(l^2 - 1) / 2$ by its factor that is kernel polynomial with degree $(l-1) / 2$.

*   Classification of prime, p
i.   Schoof's algorithm: No classification of prime. However, two cases are considered such that :

$$(x^{p^2}, y^{p^2}) \neq \pm p_l(x,y) \text{ or } (x^{p^2}, y^{p^2}) = \pm p_l(x,y)$$

ii.   SEA algorithm: for $p > 2$, p is classified as Elkies primes or Atkin primes by using modular polynomial such that $\gcd(\Phi_l(x, j(E)), x^p - x) = 1$, then l is an Atkin prime, else l is an Elkies prime.

*   Polynomial involved
i.   Schoof's algorithm: division polynomial, ψ_l with degree $(l^2 - 1)/2$. To construct division polynomial, concept of torsion point is applicable.
ii.   SEA algorithm: modular polynomial with degree $l +1$ is used to differentiate Atkin and Elkies prime. The construction of modular polynomial works in complex field and also need to deal with j-function and q-expansion (Cox, 1989) but the result can be applied in finite field, F_p.

*   Method to combine the t_l (mod l)
i.   Schoof's algorithm: Recover the t from t_l (mod l) from Chinese Remainder Theorem.
ii.   SEA algorithm:

For Elkies primes: Recover the t_E from t_l (mod l) from Chinese Remainder Theorem. For Atkin primes: Divide the primes into two sets that each in equal numbers by using Chinese Remainder Theorem. Finally this theorem is used again and then the exact t is found by using baby-steps giant steps.

7. Some literature on Schoof and Schoof-Elkies-Atkin (SEA) point counting algorithms

In this section, we will give some brief literature of these two algorithms. As we have mentioned earlier, René Schoof (Schoof, 1985) had proposed the Schoof's algorithm in 1985. In (Cohen et al, 2006), Atkin and Elkies had further improved the Schoof's algorithm in 1991. In Elkies procedure, Elkies had replaced the division polynomial with degree $(l^2 - 1) / 2$ by a kernel polynomial with degree $(l-1)/2$ whereas Atkin developed an algorithm to evaluate the order of ϕ_p in $PGL_2(F_l)$ and hence shown that the number of point can be counted on $E(F_p)$ and this thus lead to the Schoof-Elkies-Atkin (SEA) algorithm which was practical.

In (Menezes et al., 1993), elliptic curves which defined over field of characteristic 2 are attractive because the arithmetic easier for implementation. They have employed some heuristic to improve the running time and able to compute $\#E(F_{2^m})$ for $m \leq 155$. For the Schoof's part, they were able to compute t modulo l for $l = 3, 5, 7, 11, 13, 17, 19, 23, 31, 64, 128, 256, 512$ and 1024. The computation on $\#E(F_{2^{155}})$ takes roughly 61 hours on a SUN-2

SPARC station. Then, it was also mentioned that the information obtained from Schoof's algorithm and the heuristics can be combined with the information from Atkin's method to compute $\#E(F_{2^m})$ for large values of m.

In (Couveignes & Morain, 1994), they had shown how to use the powers of good prime in an efficient way by computing the isogenies between curves over the ground field. They had investigated the properties of new structure which is known as isogeny cycle.

In (Lercier & Morain, 1995), they mentioned that when l was an Elkies prime, the cost of computation turn out to be greater than that computation of Atkin prime and hence suggested that it is better to treat an Elkies prime as an Atkin prime and hence motivate their dynamic strategy. The implementation result shown that Schoof's algorithm in characteristic 2 was faster than in large characteristic at least for small fields. The large prime case was faster due to the polynomial arithmetic was faster for F_{2^n} since squaring was an easy operation in characteristic 2. However, when n increased, the computing cost of the isogeny took much time than in large prime case.

In (Lercier, 1997), mentioned the improvement made by Elkies and Atkin and worked in any finite field. The computation of isogeny is only worked in finite fields of large characteristic. However this problem was solved by Couveignes, by taking in the formal group and had implemented it. The computation of isogenies then turned out to be the major cost while counting the point. Lercier had proposed better algorithm for characteristic 2 case which based on algebraic properties. The slight change in Schoof's algorithm sped up the randomly search of elliptic curves with order nearly prime instead of specific curves such as supersingular curves or curves obtained from complex multiplication.

In (Izu et al., 1998), they wanted to find elliptic curve which had prime order and believed that curve with this order was secure for cryptographic application. In calculating the order, they combined efficiently the Atkin and Elkies method, the isogeny cycles method and trial search by match-and-sort techniques and implemented them for elliptic curve over prime field, F_p in a reasonable time where p is a prime number whose size around 240-bits. As a result, it had increased the speed of the process almost 20%. They managed to find elliptic curves with prime order in a reasonable time for characteristic p of base field is around 240-bits.

In SEA algorithm, the classical modular polynomials with degree $l+1$ will increase the size of coefficient as l increases, as well as their degree in y also is very high. Therefore canonical modular polynomials achieve small coefficient and lower degree in y. Details can be obtained in (Cohen et al., 2006). Besides, according to the work from (Blake et al., n.d.), their approach shown that classical modular polynomial can be replaced by Müller modular polynomial or Atkin modular polynomial. This experiment had been done for $l = 197$. The result shows that Müller modular polynomial has less number of coefficients compared to the classical one. However the Atkin modular polynomial has the least number of coefficients compared with the classical modular polynomial and Müller modular polynomial.

8. Conclusion

This chapter gives some backgrounds on elliptic curve cryptography. The mathematical preliminaries on elliptic curve, basic definitions, group operations on an elliptic curve, the addition law as well as the doubling operations are part of the discussion topics in this chapter. This chapter also includes the arithmetic of elliptic curves defined over the real numbers as well as on a finite field and some examples are shown to enhance understanding. Several schemes such as elliptic curve Diffie-Hellman key exchange scheme, elliptic curve ElGamal cryptosystem and elliptic curve digital signature scheme are discussed along with some examples. Concept of point counting algorithms is also treated quite rigorously in terms of the mathematical aspects, and the discussion is restricted to two types of algorithms, the Schoof and the Schoof-Elkies-Atkin (SEA) point counting algorithms. Building on the discussion of the point counting algorithms, several comparisons are derived along with some literatures on the development of these two point counting algorithms especially on the Schoof-Elkies-Atkin (SEA) algorithm. This chapter has shown the procedures in the Schoof and the Schoof-Elkies-Atkin (SEA) algorithms. Extensive mathematical concepts explaining these two algorithms are displayed in this chapter. The Schoof point counting algorithm is regarded as an initiative effort towards producing efficient point counting algorithm, where several modification has emerges from the idea of this algorithm, and the immediate improvement were produced by Elkies and Atkin. The most recent known modification build on Schoof algorithm is the one from Pierrick Gaudry, David Kohel, Benjamin Smith (Schoof-Pila algorithm), presented in the Elliptic Curve Cryptography workshop, held in Nancy, France, in September 2011.

The arithmetic on elliptic curve plays a very important role in cryptography and this chapter has highlighted some mathematical aspects needed in the development of elliptic curve cryptography. Many studies have been devoted to finding fast algorithms on performing group operations on elliptic curves as well as algorithms to compute number of points on elliptic curves. So far elliptic curve cryptography seems to out perform other cryptographic schemes. Interest groups working on elliptic curve cryptography are seen to have more ideas to explore as most directions are on the higher genus curves or hyperelliptic curves instead of the ordinary curves that are being treated in this chapter. Genus 2 curve for instance, is a hyperelliptic curve, which possesses different properties from the ordinary elliptic curve. Points on hyperelliptic curves do not forms a group, instead the corresponding jacobian takes the role. Some properties in the ordinary curves could be extended to those higher genus curves. In the future, we might probably have a situation where hyperelliptic curve cryptography comes into play.

9. Acknowledgment

This article was written under the funding of the Universiti Sains Malaysia Short Term Grant, 2010-2012, account number 304/PMaths/6310075.

10. References

Blake, I. F., Csirik, J. A., Rubinstein, M., & Seroussi, (n.d.), G. On the Computation of Modular Polynomials for Elliptic Curves. *HP Laboratories Technical Report.*

Chen, R. J. (2008). Lecture Notes on Elliptic Curve Crytography. Department of Computer Science, National Chiao Tung University.

Cohen, H., Frey, G., Avanzi, R., Doche, C., Lange, T., Kim, N., et al. (2006). *Handbook of Elliptic Curve and Hyperelliptic Curve Cryptography*, Taylor & Francis Group, LLC., ISBN:1-58488-518-1 , New York.

Couveignes, J., & Morain, F. (1994). Schoof's Algorithm and Isogeny Cycles. In: *Algorithmic Number Theory*, L. M. Adleman & M. D. Huang, pp. 43-58, Springer Berlin/Heidelberg, ISBN:978-3-540-58691-3, New York.

Cox, D. A. (1989). *Primes of the Form x^2 + ny^2: Fermat, Class Field Theory and Complex Multiplication*, John Wiley & Sons, Inc., ISBN: 0-471-50654-0, USA.

Diffie, W., & Hellman, M. (1976). New directions in cryptography. *IEEE Transactions on information Theory*, Vol 22, No 6, (November 1976), pp. 644-654, ISSN: 0018-9448.

Galin, B. (2007). *Schoof-Elkies-Atkin Algorithm*, Senior thesis, Department of Mathematics, Stanford University, USA.

Izu, T., Kogure, J., Noro, M., & Yokoyama, K. (1998). Efficient Implementation of Schoof's Algorithm, In: *Advances in Cryptology — ASIACRYPT'98 International Conference on the Theory and Application of Cryptology and Information Security*, Kazuo Ohta & Dingyi Pei, pp. 66-79, Springer Berlin / Heidelberg, ISBN: 978-3-540-65109-3, New York.

Jacobson, M. J., Jr., Erickson S., Hammer, J. , Scheidler, R., Shang, N., Shen, S. & Stein, A. (2009). Cryptographic Aspects of Real Hyperelliptic Curves, In: *13th Elliptic Curves Cryptosystem Workshop*, Calgary, Canada.

Koblitz, N. (1987) Elliptic Curve Cryptosystems. Mathematics of Computation, Vol. 48, No. 177, (January 1987), pp. 203-209.

Lawrence, C. W. & Wade, T.(2006). *Introduction to Cryptography with Coding Theory, 2nd edition*, Pearson Prentice Hall, ISBN: 0-13-186239-1, USA.

Lercier, R. (1997), Finding Good Random Elliptic Curves for Cryptosystems Defined over F_{2n}, *EUROCRYPT '97 International Conference on the Theory and Application of Cryptographic Techniques* , ISBN: 3-540-62975-0, Konstanz, Germany, May 11–15, 1997.

Lercier, R., & Morain, F. (1995). Counting the Number of Points on Elliptic Curves over Finite Fields: Strategies and Performances, *EUROCRYPT'95 Proceedings of the 14th Annual International Conference on Theory and Application of Cryptographic Techniques*, ISBN: 3-540-59409-4, Saint-Malo, France, May 21-25, 1995.

McGee, J. J. (2006). *René Schoof's Algorithm for Determining the Order of the Group of Points on an Elliptic Curve over a Finite Field*. Virginia Polytechnic Institute and State University, USA.

Miller, V. (1986). Use of Elliptic Curves in Cryptography, Advances in Cryptology — CRYPTO '85 Proceedings, Hugh C. Williams, pp. 417-426, Springer Berlin / Heidelberg, ISBN: 978-3-540-16463-0, New York.

Menezes, A., Vanstone, S., & Zuccherato, R. (1993). Counting Points on Elliptic Curves over F_{2m}. Mathematics of Computation, Vol. 60, No. 201, (January 1993), pp. 407-420, DOI 10.1090/S0025-5718-1993-1153167-9.

Schoof, R. (1985). Elliptic Curves over Finite Fields and the Computation of Square Roots Mod *p*, *Mathematics of Computation, Volume* 44, No. 170, (April 1985), pp. 483-494.

Silverman, J. H. (1986). *Graduate Texts in Mathematics*: *The Arithmetic of Elliptic Curves*, Springer-Verlag, ISBN: 0-387-96203-4, USA.

6

Division and Inversion Over Finite Fields

Abdulah Abdulah Zadeh
Memorial University of Newfoundland,
Canada

1. Introduction

Arithmetic operation such as addition, multiplication, division and inversion are widely used in data communication systems, coding and cryptography particularly public key cryptography.

Since 1976, when the principles of public key cryptography were introduced (by Whitfield Diffie and Martin Hellman) (Diffie & Hellman 1976), RSA was the most well-known public key cryptographic system. Rivest, Shamir and Adleman (RSA) algorithm composes a public key considered sufficiently long enough to be recognized as secure. The security of RSA is based on difficulty of factoring large numbers to its prime components. For many years, RSA was the leading method for industrial encryption. RSA cryptographic algorithm includes addition, squaring and multiplication operations. Addition and squaring are two simple operations over finite fields; hence, the most important arithmetic operation for RSA based cryptographic systems is multiplication.

With the advances of computer computational power, RSA is becoming more and more vulnerable. In 1985, Victor S. Miller (Miller 1985) and Neal Koblitz (Koblitz 1987) proposed Elliptic Curve Cryptography (ECC), independently. ECC offer higher security in compare with RSA.

The security of ECC relies on the difficulty of solving Elliptic Curve Discrete Logarithm Problem or ECDLP. So far not any efficient method has been offered to solve ECDLP and its complexity is higher than factoring large numbers to its prime components (where the security of RSA relies on that). Hence, ECC can offer higher security with smaller key size and designers can use it to save storage space, consumed power in the circuit and increase the bandwidth.

Elliptic Curve Cryptographic algorithm includes addition, squaring, multiplication and division (or inversion). Many research and studies have been done on multiplication. However, division and inversion research are becoming more relevant to cryptographic systems. In the terms of implementation area, complexity and executing time; division (or inversion) is the most costly operation in public key cryptography. For many years hardware implementations of division or inversion were an ambitious goal. However, recent advances in technology of ASIC circuits and the ability to provide high capacity FPGAs, let circuit designers to achieve this goal.

In this chapter we study two main classes of proposed algorithms for division (and inversion). The first class of dividers is based on Fermat's little theorem. This class of dividers also called as multiplicative based dividers. In the next chapter we introduce the principles of these algorithms and the proposed methods to improve their efficiency.

Chapter three is about the other class of dividers, called Euclidian based dividers. We review the principles and all proposed algorithms based on Euclidian algorithm.

2. Dividers based on Fermat's little theorem

The most simple and primary dividers were based on Fermat's little theorem. These kinds of dividers are also known as multiplicative based dividers, because in these algorithms, division is performed by sequence of multiplication operations (and squaring). Squaring in finite fields are simple operations, which are usually perform in a simple clock cycle. However multiplication is more complicated operation and in terms of time and implementation area is more costly.

Based on Fermat's little theorem, if P is a prime number for any integer a, we can write:

$$a^P \equiv a \ (mod \ P)$$

Dividing two side to a, we get

$$a^{P-1} \equiv 1 \ (mod \ P) \quad or \quad a \times a^{P-2} \equiv 1 \ (mod \ P)$$

Hence we can conclude the inversion of any integer a over $GF(P)$ is a^{P-2}.

Example.1: For example inversion of 4 over $GF(7)$ is $4^{-1} \equiv 4^5 \equiv 2 \ (mod \ 7)$.

$$2 \times 4 \equiv 8 \equiv 1 \ (mod \ 7)$$

Expanding this technique to $GF(2^m)$, we can write

$$a^{2^m-1} = a \times a^{2^m-2} = 1 \ (over \ GF(2^m)).$$

Hence, $a^{-1} = a^{2^m-2}$, in which $a \in GF(2^m)$.

To compute a^{2^m-2}, the most primary method is "square and multiplication" algorithm. In square and multiplication algorithm instead of $2^m - 3$ multiplications, we calculate a^{2^m-2}, with at most $m - 1$ squaring and $m - 2$ multiplications.

Alg.1: *Square and Multiplication Algorithm*

Input $a \in GF(2^m)$

Output $A = a^{2^m-2}$

1. $b = 2^m - 2$
2. $A = a$
3. while $b \neq 1$
    3.1.   if (b is even)
        3.1.1. $b = b/2$
        3.1.2. $A = A \times A$
    3.2.   else
        3.2.1. $b = b - 1$
        3.2.2. $A = A \times a$
4. Return A

To better understand of square and multiplication algorithms, we review the following equations. As we know, we can decompose 2^{m-2} in the following form.

$$2^m - 2 = 2(2^{m-1} - 1)$$

$$= 2(2^{m-1} - 2 + 1)$$

$$= 2(1 + 2(2^{m-2} - 1))$$

$$\vdots$$

$$= 2(1 + 2(1 + 2(1+..)))$$

Hence, we can use the above equations to decompose a^{2^m-2} to:

$$a^{2^m-2} = a^{2(2^{m-1}-1)} = (a^{(2^{m-1}-1)})^2$$

$$= (a^{(2^{m-1}-2+1)})^2 = (a \times a^{(2^{m-1}-2)})^2$$

$$(a \times a^{2(2^{m-2}-1)})^2 = (a \times (a^{(2^{m-2}-1)})^2)^2$$

$$\vdots$$

$$= (a(a(\dots a(aa^2)^2 \dots)^2)^2)^2$$

The square and multiplication algorithm use the same principle to calculate a^{2^m-2}.

2.1 Itoh and Tsujii algorithm

Itoh and Tsujii (Itoh & Tsujii 1988) offered a more efficient algorithm over normal basis; however it is applicable over polynomial and other basis. Their algorithm was based on multiplication which can be applied on some values of m. In their algorithm, they reduced the number of multiplications, significantly. Many efforts have been done to improve Itoh and Tsujii algorithm and make it more general for all values of m (Guajardo & C. Paar 2002; Henriquez, et. al. 2007). Here we review the general form of this algorithm.

To describe Itoh and Tsujii algorithm, we introduce a new term, called addition chain.

Definition *addition chain*: Addition chain for an integer value such as $m - 1$, is a series of integers with t elements such that, $u_0 = 1$ and $u_t = m - 1$, and $u_i = u_{ki} + u_{ji}$.

Where ki and ji are two integer values between 0 and i.

Example.2: If $m = 193$, then the addition chain could be

1, 2, 3, 6, 12, 24, 48, 96, 192

In this addition chain for all elements of sequence we have $u_i = u_{i-1} + u_{i-1}$ except for u_2, which $u_2 = u_1 + u_0$.

u_0	u_1	u_2	u_3	u_4
	$u_0 + u_0$	$u_1 + u_0$	$u_2 + u_2$	$u_3 + u_3$
1	2	3	6	12

u_5	u_6	u_7	u_8
$u_4 + u_4$	$u_5 + u_5$	$u_6 + u_6$	$u_7 + u_7$
24	48	96	192

Let's define a function $\beta_k(a) = a^{2^k-1}$, which $a \in GF(2^m)$. We know that $\beta_m(a) = a^{2^m-1} = a^{-1}$. The other characteristic of this function is enlisted as follow:

$$\beta_{j+k} = \beta_k^{2^j} \times \beta_j$$

$$\beta_{2k} = \beta_k^{2^k+1} \text{ or } \beta_k^{2^k} \times \beta_k$$

Hence, to compute a^{-1}, we should use the equations above and using addition chaining to achieve $\beta_m(a) = a^{2^m-1}$.

Example.3: for $m = 193$, and above addition chain, we can write the following calculations

$u_0 = 1$	$\beta_1 = a^{2^1-1}$
$u_1 = 2$	$\beta_2 = (\beta_1)^{2^2-1} = a^{2^2-1}$
$u_2 = 3$	$\beta_3 = (\beta_2)^{2^1-1} \times \beta_1$
$u_3 = 6$	$\beta_6 = (\beta_3)^{2^3} \times \beta_3$
$u_3 = 12$	$\beta_{12} = (\beta_6)^{2^6} \times \beta_6$
$u_3 = 24$	$\beta_{24} = (\beta_{12})^{2^{12}} \times \beta_{12}$
$u_4 = 48$	$\beta_{48} = (\beta_{24})^{2^{24}} \times \beta_{24}$
$u_4 = 96$	$\beta_{96} = (\beta_{48})^{2^{48}} \times \beta_{48}$
$u_4 = 192$	$\beta_{192} = (\beta_{96})^{2^{96}} \times \beta_{96}$

It has been shown that the maximum number of multiplication in this method is t and the required number of square operation is $m - 1$. The size of addition chain or t is estimated as $\lfloor log_2(m - 1) \rfloor + HW(m - 1) + 1$, where $HW(m - 1)$ is the hamming weight of $m - 1$.

For more information and more details, the readers may refer to (Guajardo & C. Paar 2002; Henrıquez, et. al. 2007).

Itoh and Tsujii algorithm is presented in Alg.2.

After calculating inversion, division simply becomes a multiplication operation.

The advantage of Fermat's little theorem based inversion algorithm is that, it can be implemented just by using multiplication and square arithmetic operators. This eliminates the need to add any extra components, such as dividers. When ECC was proposed, the dividers were not as advanced as they are now; hence, multiplicative based dividers were the best candidates for hardware implementation of ECC, particularly over FPGAs. Also it is possible to use these dividers for reconfigurable cryptosystems, which are designed to perform both RSA and ECC algorithms. Since the sizes of these cryptosystems are becoming larger, dropping a big component such as divider is a huge saving on implemented area for designers. The main drawback of the cipher cores without dividers is the longer computational time.

Alg.2: *Itoh and Tsujii Algorithm to compute inversion*

Input $a \in GF(2^m)$

Output a^{-1}

1. $\beta_{u0}(a) = a$
2.   For $i = 1$ to t do

    2.1. $\beta_{ui}(a) = \left(\beta_{uki}(a)\right)^{2^{uji}} \times \beta_{uji}(a)$

3.   Return $\beta_{ut}^2(a)$

---

3. Euclidian based dividers

Euclid's algorithm is an old algorithm to calculate the greatest common divider (GCD) of two integers. The basic principle of Euclid's algorithm is that, the greatest common divider of a and b, $GCD(a,b)$, is equal to the greatest common divider of a and $a \pm b$ or in other word $GCD(a,b) = GCD(a, a \pm b) = GCD(a \pm b, b)$.

Example.4: $GCD(18,30) = 6,$

$$GCD(18,30) =$$

$$GCD(30 - 18,18) = GCD(12,18) =$$

$$GCD(18 - 12,12) = GCD(6,12) =$$

$$GCD(12 - 6,6) = GCD(6,6) = 6$$

We can apply the above principle more than once and rewrite this theorem as $GCD(a,b) = GCD(a, n \times a \pm m \times b) = GCD(\acute{n} \times a \pm \acute{m} \times b, b)$.

Example.5: GCD(90,525)=15

$$GCD(90,525 - 5 \times 90) = GCD(90,525 - 450) =$$

$$GCD(90,75) = GCD(75,90 - 75) =$$

$$GCD(75,15) = GCD(15,75 - 3 \times 15) =$$

$$GCD(15,0) = 15$$

To reduce the calculation time, we can offer the Alg.3.

Alg.3: *Euclidian algorithm to calculate Greatest Common Divider (GCD)*

Input a, b

Output $GCD(a, b)$

1. While $(b \neq 0)$
   1.1. $t = b$
   1.2. $b = a \bmod b$
   1.3. $a = t$
2. Return (a)

The above algorithm can be made more compact using a recursive approach. Alg. 4 presents the recursive and more compact version of Alg. 3.

Alg.4: *Euclidian algorithm to calculate Greatest Common Divider (Recursive Approach)*

Input a, b

Output $GCD(a, b)$

1. if $(b = 0)$
   1.1.   Return (a)
2. else
   2.1.   Return $(GCD(a, a \bmod b))$

We provide a useful theorem below which will be used this section, to make the Euclidian algorithm more general for our purpose.

Theorem: let's assume $b = a \times q + r$. Then $GCD(a, b) = GCD(a, r)$

$$GCD(a, b) = GCD(a, b - a \times q)$$

$$= GCD(a, r)$$

The simple proof for this theorem is by applying Euclid's theorem $(GCD(a, b) = GCD(a, b - a))$ for q times, to give the same relationship.

In order to use Euclid's theorem for division or inversion, assume two values such as a and b. We have already seen how to compute $d = GCD(a, b)$. We know that there are two variables, x and y, which satisfies the following equation

$$a \times x + b \times y = d$$

If we can design an algorithm which accepts a and b, and produces x and y; we can use that algorithm to find inversion. Assume P is a prime value and a is an integer where $0 < a < P - 1$. We know $v = GCD(a, P) = 1$. Hence, applying the above algorithm, we can find x and y which $a \times x + P \times y = 1$.

If we use that algorithm over the finite field, $GF(P)$, we can calculate the inverse of a which is x (i.e. $a^{-1} = x$). Using the algorithm above, it gives us x and y such that it satisfy the equation: $a \times x + P \times y = 1$. Over the finite field, $GF(P)$, $P \times y = 0$. Then $a \times x + P \times y = 1$ over $GF(P)$ could be simplified to $a \times x = 1$. Then x is the inversion of a over $GF(P)$.

Let's $GCD(a_i, b_i) = d$. We know there are two integer values, x_i and y_i such that (where one of the values is smaller than zero):

$$a_i \times x_i + b_i \times y_i = d.$$

Based on Euclid's theorem, we can write $GCD(a_i, b_i - a_i q_i) = d$. Hence, the equation above can be rewritten as:

$$a_i \times x_{i+1} + (b_i - a_i q_i) \times y_{i+1} = d.$$

By rearranging this equation, we can write:

$$a_i \times x_{i+1} - a_i q_i \times y_{i+1} + b_i \times y_{i+1} =$$

$$a_i \times (x_{i+1} - q_i \times y_{i+1}) + b_i \times y_{i+1} = d$$

Then we can conclude:

$$x_i = x_{i+1} - q_i \times y_{i+1}$$

$$y_i = y_{i+1}.$$

(1)

Similarly, for $GCD(a_i - b_i q_i, b_i) = d$, we can write the same equations and conclude

$$y_i = y_{i+1} - q_i \times x_{i+1}$$

$$x_i = x_{i+1}.$$

(2)

If we perform the Euclidian algorithm to calculate d, at the final step or loop $GCD(a_n, b_n) = GCD(a_n, a_n q_n) = a_n = d$. The above relationship for this step will be

$$a_n \times x_n + b_n \times y_n =$$

$$a_n \times x_n + a_n q_n \times y_n = a_n = d$$

So $x_n = 1$ and $y_n = 0$.

Example.6: Let's $a = 37$ and $b = 17$

$$37x_0 + 17y_0 = 1$$

$$(37 - 2 \times 17)x_0 + 17y_0 = 1 \qquad q_0 = 2$$

$$3x_1 + 17y_1 = 1$$

$$3x_1 + (17 - 5 \times 3)y_1 = 1 \qquad q_1 = 5$$

$$3x_2 + 2y_2 = 1$$

$$(3 - 1 \times 2)x_2 + 2y_2 = 1 \qquad q_2 = 1$$

$$x_3 + 2y_3 = 1$$

$$x_3 + (2 - 2 \times 1)y_3 = 1 \qquad q_3 = 2$$

$$x_4 = 1$$

Using (1) and (2) for the above relation in backward (start from x_4, y_4 and q_3), we can calculate x_0 and y_0.

$$y_3 = y_4 = 0 \qquad x_3 = x_4 - q_3 y_4 = 1$$

$$x_2 = x_3 = 1 \qquad y_2 = y_3 - q_2 x_3 = -1$$

$$y_1 = y_2 = -1 \qquad x_1 = x_2 - q_1 y_2 = 6$$

$$x_0 = x_1 = 6 \qquad y_0 = y_1 - q_0 x_1 = -13$$

Then finally:

$$37 \times 6 + 17 \times (-13) = 1$$

Hence, one way of finding x and y is to execute Euclidian algorithm. Then calculate x_i and y_i based on the equations above. Alg.5 is based on this idea.

<u>Alg.5: *Algorithm of Finding x and y*</u>

Input: a, b $(b \geq a)$

Output: $GCD(a, b), x, y$

1. $y_1 = 1$
2. $y_2 = 0$
3. $x_1 = 1$
4. $x_2 = 0$
5. While $(a \neq 1)$
   - 5.1. $q = \lfloor \frac{b}{a} \rfloor$; $r = b - qa$; $x = x_2 - qx_1$; $y = y_2 - qy_1$;
   - 5.2. $b = a$; $a = r$; $x_2 = x_1$; $x_1 = x$; $y_2 = y_1$; $y_1 = y$;
6. $d = b$;
7. $x = x_2$;
8. $y = y_2$;
9. Return (d, x, y)

In order to get better impression about the role of x_1, x_2, y_1 and y_2 in Alg.5 (and Alg.6) we recommend to extend the last two equations of example.6 (i.e. y_0 and x_0) and rewrite them with q_i, y_4 and x_4.

All the substitutions at step 5.1 and 5.2 of Alg.5 should be executed at the same time.

We can simplify this algorithm for a and P (where $0 \le a < P$, and P is a prime number) to calculate a^{-1} over $GF(P)$ (Alg.6).

Alg.6: *Algorithm of Computing Inversion Over $GF(P)$*

Input: $P, a \in GF(P)$

Output: a^{-1}

1. $y_1 = 1$
2. $y_2 = 0$
3. While $(a \ne 1)$
   3.1. $q = \left\lfloor \dfrac{P}{a} \right\rfloor$
   3.2. $a = P - qa; \; P = a; \; y_2 = y_1; y_1 = y_2 - qy_1$
4. Return (y_1)

All the operations on Alg.6 are performs over $GF(P)$. All the substitutions at step 3.2 of Alg.6 should be done simultaneously.

In the algorithm above, we should perform a division at each loop (step 3.1.). To avoid division, we can assume if $P \ge a$ then $q = 1$ and if $P < a$ then $q = 0$ or swap a and P and y_1 and y_2 values. Then we can compute $GCD(a, b - a)$, instead of computing $GCD(a, b) = GCD(a, b - aq)$. This technique increases the number of iterations.

Modifying the above algorithms for polynomial basis, we have Alg.7. All operations in Alg.7 should be done over $GF(2^m)$. In Alg.7, P represents the irreducible polynomial of $GF(2^m)$.

Alg.7: *Algorithm of Computing Inversion Over $GF(2^m)$*

Input: $a \in GF(2^m)$

Output: a^{-1}

1. $y_1 = 1$
2. $y_2 = 0$
3. While $(a \ne 1)$
   3.1. $a = P + a; \; P = a; \; y_2 = y_1; y_1 = y_2 + y_1$
4. Return (y_1)

Example.7: let's assume we want to calculate $1/7$ over $GF(17)$

$$y_1 = 1 \quad y2 = 0 \quad a = 7 \quad P = 17$$

$$y_1 = -1 \quad y2 = 1 \quad a = 10 \quad P = 7$$

$$y_1 = 1 \quad y2 = -1 \quad a = 7 \quad P = 10$$

$$y_1 = -2 \quad y2 = 1 \quad a = 3 \quad P = 7$$

$$y_1 = 3 \quad y2 = -2 \quad a = 4 \quad P = 3$$

$$y_1 = -2 \quad y2 = 3 \quad a = 3 \quad P = 4$$

$$y_1 = 5 \quad y2 = -2 \quad a = 1 \quad P = 3$$

Then $7^{-1} = 5$ over $GF(17)$.

The reviewed algorithm, so far, calculates inversion. After an inversion is calculated, simply multiply y_1 to create a division. In (Takagi 1998), N. Takagi offered an algorithm which directly calculates division.

This algorithm is based on two concepts:

(1) If a is even and P is odd, then $GCD(a, P) = GCD(a/2, P)$;

(2) If both a and P are odd, then $GCD(a, P) = GCD((a - P)/2, a) = GCD(\frac{a-P}{2}, P)$; Where in the proposed algorithm, we choose the minimum of a and P (i.e. $GCD(a, P) = GCD((a - P)/2, \min\{a, P\})$).

The proposed algorithm over $GF(P)$ is presented as Alg.8. In Alg.8, b_0 represents the least significant bit (LSB) of b. Also all operation are performed over $GF(P)$.

Alg.8: _Algorithm of Computing Division Over GF(P)_

Input: $P, a \in GF(P), b \in GF(P)$

Output: a/b

1. $v = 0$
2.   While $(b > 0)$
    2.1.   While $(b_0 = 0)$
        2.1.1. $b = b/2$; $a = a/2$;
    2.2.   If $(b \geq P)$
        2.2.1. $b = b - P$; $a = a - v$;
    2.3.   else
        2.3.1. $b = P - b$; $P = b$;
        2.3.2. $a = v - a$; $v = a$;
3.   Return (v)

P values decrease at each step. At the final step, b and P are zero and one, respectively. This algorithm will finish at most after $2m - 1$ iterations, where $2^{m-1} < P < 2^m$.

Alg.9: *Algorithm of Computing Division Over* $GF(2^m)$

Input: $P(x), a \in GF(2^m), b \in GF(2^m)$

Output: a/b

1. $v = 0$;
2. While $((a \neq 0)$ and $(P \neq 1))$
    2.1.   If $(b_0 = 1)$
        2.1.1.   If $(b \geq P)$
            2.1.1.1. $b = b + P$; $a = a + v$;
        2.1.2.   else
            2.1.2.1. $b = P + b$; $P = b$;
            2.1.2.2. $a = v + a$; $v = a$;
    2.2. $b = b/2$;
    2.3. $a = a/2$;
3. Return (v)

To extend this algorithm to be applicable over $GF(2^m)$, the following changes should be applied; Assume $P(x)$ as irreducible polynomial (It is known that P_0 is always 1) and substitute $P(x)$ with P. The degrees of the most significant nonzero bit of $b(x)$ and $P(x)$ will distinguish which variable is larger (in step 2.2). Hence, the algorithm will be as Alg.9.

Alg.10: *Modified Algorithm of Computing Division Over* $GF(2^m)$

Input: $P(x), a \in GF(2^m), b \in GF(2^m)$

Output: a/b

1. $v = 0$;
2. While $((a \neq 0)$ and $(P \neq 1))$
    2.1.   If $(b_0 = 1)$
        2.1.1. If $(\delta < 0)$
            2.1.1.1. $b = b + P$; $P = b$;
            2.1.1.2. $a = a + v$; $v = a$;
            2.1.1.3. $\delta = -\delta$;
        2.1.2.   else
            2.1.2.1. $b = P + b$;
            2.1.2.2. $a = v + a$;
    2.2. $b = b/2$;
    2.3. $a = a/2$;
    2.4. $\delta = \delta - 1$;
3. Return (v)

This algorithm, takes at most $2m - 1$ iterations to finish. Checking the degree of b and P, is a costly operation in hardware implementation. In (Brent & Kung 1983), Brent and Kung reduced this complexity by adopting a new idea. They used a new variable, δ, to represent the difference of upper bounds of degree b and $P(x)$. In (Brent & Kung 1983) they use this method to calculate the Greatest Common Divisor of two variables. However this method can be used to calculate division.

At the initialization step, δ should be equal to -1. Then the above algorithm has to be changed as Alg.10.

Example.8: Let's $a = 1101$, $b = 0111$ and the irreducible polynomial is $P(x) = x^4 + x + 1$.

$$\delta = -1 \quad b = 0111 \quad P = 1\,0011 \quad a = 1101 \quad v = 0$$

$$\delta = 0 \quad b = 1010 \quad P = 0\,0111 \quad a = 1111 \quad v = 1101$$

$$\delta = -1 \quad b = 0101 \quad P = 0\,0111 \quad a = 1110 \quad v = 1101$$

$$\delta = 0 \quad b = 0001 \quad P = 0\,0101 \quad a = 1000 \quad v = 1110$$

$$\delta = -1 \quad b = 0010 \quad P = 0\,0101 \quad a = 0011 \quad v = 1110$$

$$\delta = -2 \quad b = 0001 \quad P = 0\,0101 \quad a = 1000 \quad v = 1110$$

$$\delta = -1 \quad b = 0010 \quad P = 0\,0001 \quad a = 0011 \quad v = 1000$$

The final step to improve the algorithm above is applied within the loop. Hardware implementation of "*while*" statement is difficult. This is because the number of iterations is an unknown variable, making it inappropriate for cryptographic cores and particularly systolic implementations. We know that this algorithm takes at most $2m - 1$ iterations. Hence, instead of a "*while*" loop, we implement a "*for*" loop. This modification can be done by a simple change in Alg.10. In step.2, instead of "While $((a \neq 0)\ and\ (P \neq 1))$" we should write "For $i = 1$ to $2m - 1$".

So far we have presented very general forms of divider algorithms. We reviewed all the proposed algorithms because each one has a unique characteristic that makes it more efficient for a specific design of a core. Many research papers have been done to improve the above algorithms and make them more efficient for hardware implementations. For example, in (Wu, Shieh & Hwang 2001), the designers proposed a new algorithm. In their algorithms, they eliminate δ and use two other variables to Instead of comparing δ relationship to zero, they only check two bits of their new adopted variables in their algorithm; thus making the new algorithms more efficient for hardware (by eliminating step 2.1.1 in Alg.10). Another example can be seen in (Zadeh 2007), where the number of iterations is reduced from $2m - 1$ to m by combining two loop iterations. The paper explores how a number of modifications can reduce the number of conditional statements.

Other similar classes of dividers have been proposed such as Dual Field Modular dividers or Unified Modular Division (UMD). These classes perform division on two finite field (over $GF(P)$ and $GF(2^m)$). Unified Modular Dividers have been applied in some applications such as network servers (Wolkerstorfer 2002; Tenca & Tawalbeh 2004).

Euclidian algorithm is the most efficient algorithm for division in terms of area and time. Until now, not many hardware platforms were able to implement this algorithm. Advances in technology of ASIC offer many high capacity reconfigurable platforms such as FPGA. It gives hardware designers the ability of using these dividers in real applications. It is foreseeable that Euclidian dividers will be more widely implemented in the future.

4. Conclusion

In this chapter, we have reviewed two common classes of dividers which are widely used for cryptographic purpose. The most common dividers to be implemented in Elliptic Curve Cryptography and other cryptographic cores are multiplicative based dividers (based on Fermat's little theorem) and Euclidian based dividers.

To perform division over finite field, some other dividers have been proposed such as "Wiener-Hopf equation" based dividers. In Wiener-Hopf based dividers, the divisor (b) should expand to an $m \times m$ matrix, B, then the linear equation $B \times v = a$ should be solved to get v. v can be calculated using Gaussian elimination algorithm (Morii, Kasahara & Whiting 1989; Hasan & Bhargava 1992). The hardware efficiency of these dividers are not comparable with multiplicative and Euclidian based dividers.

In terms of implementation area multiplicative based dividers are very efficient. Since they don't need any extra component on the circuit and they can perform division using embedded components of the cipher cores. Also in term of speed, Euclidian based dividers are very fast.

5. References

Brent R. P., Kung H. T., (Aug. 1983), "Systolic VLSI arrays for linear time GCD computation", in VLSI-83, pp: 145 − 154, Amsterdam.

Chen C., Qin Z., (June 2011), "Efficient algorithm and systolic architecture for modular division", International Journal of Electronics, vol. 98, No. 6, pp: 813 − 823.

Diffie W., Hellman M. E., (Nov. 1976), "New directions in cryptography", IEEE Transactions on Information Theory, vol. IT-22, pp: 644-654.

Dormale G. M. D., Quisquater J. , (2006), "Iterative modular division over GF(2^m): novel algorithm and implementations on FPGA", Applied Reconfigurable Computing – ARC 2006, pp: 370 − 382.

Guajardo Jorge, Paar Christof, (2002), "Itoh-Tsujii inversion in standard basis and its application in cryptography and codes", Designs, Codes and Cryptography, vol. 25, pp: 207 − 216.

Hankerson, Darrel, Menezes, Alfred J., Vanstone, Scott, (2004), "Guide to elliptic curve cryptography", Springer-Verlag, ISBN: 978 0 387 95273 4.

Hasan M.A., Bhargava V.K., (Aug. 1992), "Bit-serial systolic divider and multiplier for finite fields GF(2^m)", IEEE Transaction on Computers, vol. 41, No. 8, pp: 972 − 980.

Itoh T., Tsujii S., (1988), "A fast algorithm for computing multiplicative inverses in GF(2^m) using normal basis", Information and computing, vol. 78, pp: 171-177.

Kim Chang Hoon, Hong Chun Pyo, (July 2002), "High speed division architecture for GF(2^m)", Electronics Letters, vol. 38, No.15, pp: 835 − 836.

Koblitz N., (1987), "Elliptic curve cryptosystems", Mathematics of Computation, vol. 48, pp: 203–209.

Miller V. S., (1985), "Use of elliptic curves in cryptography", H.C. Wiliams, Ed., Advances in Cryptology, CRYPTO 85, LNCS, vol. 218, pp: 417–426.

Morii M., Kasahara M., Whiting D. L., (Nov. 1989), "Efficient bit serial multiplication and the discrete time Wiener Hopf equation over finite fields", IEEE Transaction on Information Theory, vol. 35, pp:1177 – 1183.

Rodrıguez-Henrıquez Francisco, Morales-Luna Guillermo, Saqib Nazar A., Cruz-Cortes Nareli, (2007), "Parallel Itoh-Tsujii multiplicative inversion algorithm for a special class of trinomials", Des. Codes Cryptography, pp: 19 – 37.

Takagi N., (May 1998), "a vlsi algorithm for modular division based on the binary GCD algorithm", IEICE Transaction on Fundamentals, vol. E81-A, No.5, pp: 724 – 728.

Takagi N., Yoshika J., Takagi K., (May 2001), "A fast algorithm for multiplicative inversion in $GF(2^m)$ using normal basis", IEEE Transaction on Computers, vol. 50, No. 5, pp: 394 – 398.

Tawalbeh L. A., Tenca A. F., (Sep. 2004), "An algorithm and hardware architecture for integrated modular division and multiplication in GF(P) and $GF(2^n)$", Application Specific Systems, Architectures and Processors 2004, IEEE, pp: 247 – 257.

Tenca A. F., Tawalbeh L.A., (March 2004), "Algorithm for unified modular division in GF(P) and $GF(2^m)$ suitable for cryptographic hardware", Electronics Letters, vol. 40, No. 5, pp: 304 – 306.

Wolkerstorfer Johannes, (2002), "Dual-field arithmetic unit for GF(P) and $GF(2^m)$", International Workshop on Cryptographic Hardware and Embedded Systems CHES 2002, LNCS, vol. 2523, pp: 500 – 514.

Wu C., Wu C., Shieh M., Hwang Y., (2001), "Systolic VLSI realization of a novel iterative division algorithm over $GF(2^m)$: a high-speed, low-complexity design", ISCAS, pp: 33 – 36.

Wu C., Wu C., Shieh M., Hwang Y., (2004), "High speed, low complexity systolic designs of novel iterative division algorithms in $GF(2^m)$", IEEE Transaction on Computers, pp: 375 – 380.

Wu C. H., Wu C. M., Shieh M. D., Hwanng Y. T. , (Aug 2000), "Novel iterative division algorithm over $GF(2^m)$ and its systolic VLSI realization", Circuits and Systems, pp: 280 – 283.

Zadeh Abdulah Abdulah, (2007), "High speed modular divider based on GCD algorithm", Information and Communications Security, ICICS, LNCS, pp: 189 – 200.

Part 2

Applications of Cryptographic Algorithms and Protocols

7

Scan-Based Side-Channel Attack on the RSA Cryptosystem

Ryuta Nara, Masao Yanagisawa and Nozomu Togawa
Waseda University
Japan

1. Introduction

Individual authentication increases in importance as network technology advances. IC passport, SIM card and ID card used in entering and leaving management systems are dependent on a cryptography circuit for keeping their security. LSI chips used there usually include cryptography circuits and encrypt/decrypt important data such as ID numbers and electronic money information. However, there is a threat that a secret key may be retrieved from the cryptography LSI chip. Recently, side-channel attacks against a cryptosystem LSI has been reported (Boneh et al., 1997; Brier et al., 2004; Kocher, 1996; Kocher el al., 1999; Schramm el al., 2003). For example, scan-based side-channel attacks which retrieve secret keys in a cryptography LSI have attracted attention over the five years. A scan path is one of the most important testing techniques, where registers are connected in serial so that they can be controlled and observed directly from outside the LSI. Test efficiency can be increased significantly. On the other hand, one can have register data easily by using a scan path, which implies that one can retrieve a secret key in a cryptography LSI. This is a *scan-based side-channel attack*.

One of the difficulties in the scan-based side-channel attack is how to retrieve a secret key from obtained scanned data from a cryptosystem LSI. In a scan path, registers inside a circuit have to be connected so that its interconnection length will be shortened to satisfy timing constraints. This means that no one but a scan-path designer knows correspondence between registers and scanned data. To succeed a scan-based side-channel attack against a cryptography LSI, an attacker needs to retrieve secret keys from the scanned data almost "randomly" connected.

Symmetric-key cryptosystems such as DES and AES are very popular and widely used. They make use of the same secret key in encryption and decryption. However, it may be difficult to securely share the same secret key, such as in communicating on the Internet. Public-key cryptosystems, on the other hand, make use of different keys to encrypt and decrypt. One of the most popular public-key cryptography algorithms is RSA (Rivest et al., 1978), which is used by many secure technologies such as secure key agreement and digital signature.

Yang et al. first showed a scan-based side-channel attack against DES in 2004 and retrieved a secret key in DES (Yang et al., 2004). They also proposed a scan-based side-channel attack against AES in 2006 (Yang et al., 2006). Nara et al. proposed an improved scan-based side-channel attack method against AES in 2009 (Nara et al., 2009). A scan-based side-channel attack against elliptic curve cryptography (Koblitz, 1987; Miller, 1986) was proposed by Nara et al. (Nara et al., 2011). On the other hand, any scan-based side-channel attacks against RSA have not been proposed yet in spite of the fact that RSA is a de-facto standard for a public-key cryptosystem. Since public-key cryptosystems have complicated algorithm compared with that of symmetric-key cryptosystems such as DES and AES, we cannot apply the scan-based side-channel attacks against symmetric-key cryptosystems to an RSA circuit. An elliptic curve cryptography algorithm is completely different from an RSA algorithm although they both are public-key algorithms. We cannot apply the scan-based side-channel attacks against elliptic curve cryptosystem to RSA, either.

In this paper, we propose a scan-based side-channel attack against an RSA circuit, which is almost independent of a scan-path structure. The proposed method is based on detecting intermediate values calculated in an RSA circuit. We focus on a 1-bit time-sequence which is specific to some intermediate value. We call it a *scan signature* because its value shows their existence in the scanned data obtained from an RSA circuit. By checking whether a scan signature is included in the scanned data or not, we can retrieve a secret key in the target RSA circuit even if we do not know a scan path structure, as long as a scan path is implemented on an RSA circuit and it includes at least 1-bit of each intermediate value.

The purpose of our proposed method is, not to make secure scan architecture ineffective but to retrieve a secret key using scanned data in an RSA circuit with as few limitations as possible. In fact, our scan-based side-channel attack method without any modification might not work against RSA circuits using some secure scan architecture. Several secure scan architectures without consideration of our proposed scan signature cannot protect our method as discussed in Section 6.

This paper is organized as follows: Section 2 introduces RSA encryption and decryption algorithms; Section 3 shows an algorithm of retrieving a secret key in an RSA circuit using intermediate values and explains problems to retrieve a secret key using a scan path; Section 4 proposes our scan-based side-channel attack method based on a *scan signature*; Section 5 demonstrates experimental results and performance analysis; Section 7 gives several concluding remarks.

2. RSA algorithm

RSA cryptography (Rivest et al., 1978) was made public in 1978 by Ronald Linn Rivest, Adi Shamir, Leonard Max Adleman. The RSA is known as the first algorithm which makes public-key cryptography practicable. It is commonly used to achieve not only encryption/decryption but also a digital signature and a digital authentication, so that most cryptography LSIs in the market implement and calculate the RSA cryptography.

The security of an RSA cryptography depends on the difficulty of factoring large numbers. To decrypt a ciphertext of an RSA cryptography will be almost impossible on the assumption that no efficient algorithm exists for solving it.

2.1 Encryption and decryption

An RSA algorithm encrypts a plaintext with a public key (n, e) and decrypts a ciphertext with a secret key (n, d). Let us select two distinct prime numbers p and q. We calculate n by

---

Algorithm 1 Binary method (MSB to LSB).

Input: c, d, and n.
Output: $c^d \bmod n$.
  $i = L - 1$.
  $m = 1$.
  while $i \geq 0$ **do**
    $m = m^2 \bmod n$.
    if $d_i = 1$ **then**
      $m = m \times c \bmod n$.
    end if
    $i = i - 1$.
  end while
  return m.

---

multiplying p by q, which is used as the modulus for both a public key and a secret key. To determine exponents of them, we calculate $\varphi(pq)$[1] for multiplying $(p - 1)$ by $(q - 1)$.

Let us select an integer e satisfying the conditions that $1 < e < \varphi(pq)$ and, e and $\varphi(pq)$ is coprime, where e is an exponent of a public key. Let us determine an integer d satisfying the congruence relation $de \equiv 1 \bmod \varphi(pq)$. That is to say, the public key consists of the modulus n and the exponent e. The private key consists of the modulus n and the exponent d.

Let us consider that Alice secretly sends a message m to Bob. First, Alice receives his public key (n, e). Second, she calculates the ciphertext c with Equation 1.

$$c = m^e \quad \bmod n \tag{1}$$

Then Alice transmits c to Bob. Bob decrypts c by using his private key and receive her message m. Equation 2 represents a decryption computation.

$$m \equiv c^d \quad \bmod n \tag{2}$$

2.2 Binary method

The bit length of an RSA key must be more than 1,024 bits because its security depends on its key length. It is currently recommended that n be at least 2,048 bits long (Silverman, 2002). This means that the exponent d in Equation 2 is at least 1,024 bits long. When we decrypt a cyphertext, its computation amount becomes quite large without modification. Since modulo exponentiation dominates the execution time of decrypting a cyphertext, efficient algorithms have been proposed. The binary method (Stein, 1967), as shown in Algorithm 1, is one of the most typical exponent algorithms. In Algorithm 1, the exponent d is represented by $d = d_{L-1}2^{L-1} + d_{L-2}2^{L-2} + \cdots + d_1 2 + d_0$, where L shows the maximum key bit length. Fig. 1 shows an example of the binary method in case of $d = 1011_2$.

3. Scan-based attack against RSA

A scan path connects registers in an circuit serially and makes us access to them directly so that a tester can observe register values inside the circuit easily. A scan path model is shown

---

[1] $\varphi()$ is Euler's totient function.

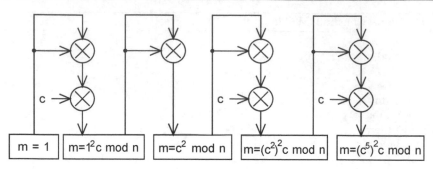

Fig. 1. Binary method example ($d = 1011_2$).

in Fig. 2. A scan path test is widely used in recent circuit implementations due to its testability and easiness of implementation.

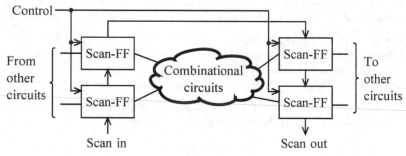

Fig. 2. Scan path model.

The purpose of a scan-based attack against RSA is to retrieve a secret exponent d from scanned data in an RSA circuit. Scan-based attack here requires several assumptions as in the previous researches in (Nara et al., 2009; 2011; Yang et al., 2004; 2006), which are summarized as shown below:

1. Attackers can encrypt/decrypt arbitrary data using the secret key on a target RSA circuit.

2. Attackers can obtain scanned data from a target RSA circuit.

3. Scanned data is not modified with compactors aimed at test efficiency.

4. Attackers know that the binary method in Algorithm 1 is used in a target RSA circuit.

5. Attackers also know the modulus n used in a target RSA circuit.[2]

In addition to these, they need to be able to predict the intermediate values of the binary method using an off-line simulation.

In this section, we explain the scan-based attack against an RSA circuit (Section 3.1) and its problems in a practical case (Section 3.2).

---

[2] Note that, since the public key consists of the modulus n and the public exponent e, attackers can easily know the modulus n.

3.1 Retrieving a secret exponent using intermediate values (Messerges et al., 1999)

In order to retrieve a secret exponent d, we have to solve the integer factorization in RSA. If the bit length of a secret exponent d is more than 1,024 bits or more than 2,048 bits, it is impossible to solve this problem within a realistic time. However, if we know all the "intermediate values" during the binary method shown in Algorithm 1, we can retrieve a secret exponent d in a polynomial time (Messerges et al., 1999).

Let $d = d_{L-1}2^{L-1} + d_{L-2}2^{L-2} + \cdots + d_1 2 + d_0$, where L is the maximum key bit length of d. Assume that all the intermediate values in Algorithm 1 are obtained. Let $m(i)$ be the intermediate value of m at the end of loop i in Algorithm 1. Assume also that $d_{L-1}, d_{L-2}, \cdots, d_{i+1}$ are already retrieved. An attacker tries to reveal the next bit d_i. In this case, $m(i)$ is equal to Equation 3 below, if and only if $d_i = 0$:

$$c^{\sum_{j=i+1}^{L-1} d_j 2^{j-i}} \quad \mod n. \tag{3}$$

Similarly, $m(i)$ is equal to Equation 4 below, if and only if $d_i = 1$:

$$c^{\sum_{j=i+1}^{L-1} d_j 2^{j-i}+1} \quad \mod n. \tag{4}$$

Based on the above discussion, we employ $SF(i)$ defined by Equation 5 as a *selective function* for RSA:

$$SF(i) = c^{\sum_{j=i+1}^{\ell-1} d_j 2^{j-i}+1} \quad \mod n. \tag{5}$$

ℓ represents a significant key length, or key length in left-align representation, i.e., the secret exponent can be represented by

$$d - d_{L-1}2^{L-1} \mid \cdots \mid d_1 2 \mid d_0 \Big|_{d_{L-1}=0,\ldots,d_\ell=0}$$
$$= d_{\ell-1}2^{\ell-1} + \cdots + d_1 2 + d_0. \tag{6}$$

When using the selective function for RSA above, we have to know in advance $d_{\ell-1}, d_{\ell-2}, \cdots, d_{i+1}$.

$SF(i) \neq SF(j)$ always holds true for $i \neq j$ for $0 \leq i, j \leq \ell - 1$. Given a message c and bit values of secret component $d_{\ell-1}, d_{\ell-2}, \cdots, d_{i+1}$, we assume that $d_i = 1$ and check whether $SF(i)$ appears somewhere in intermediate values. If it appears in them, we really determine d_i as one. If not, we determine d_i as zero.

Example 1. *Let us consider that the public key $(n, e) = (101111001, 1011)$ and the secret key $(n, d) = (101111001, 10111)$. The maximum key length L is 8 bits and the secret exponent $d = 10111$, i.e, $d_7 = 0, d_6 = 0, d_5 = 0, d_4 = 1, d_3 = 0, d_2 = 1, d_1 = 1, d_0 = 1$. We assume that we do not know d and a significant key length ℓ. The intermediate values in Algorithm 1 are summarized in Table 2 when we use a message $c = 10011100$, whose parameters are shown in Table 1.*

Now we try to retrieve the 8-bit secret exponent d using intermediate values.

First we try to retrieve the first bit $d_{\ell-1}$ ($i = \ell - 1$). We find $d_{\ell-1} = 1$ by the definition of a significant key length ℓ. Then $SF(\ell - 1)$ is calculated as $SF(\ell - 1) = c = 10011100$. Since 10011100 appears in Table 2, we confirm that $d_{\ell-1}$ is retrieved as one. Now we assume that the secret exponent $d = \underline{1}$. We *compare* $m(\ell - 1) = (c^1 \mod n) = 10011100$ *with the binary method result* 10001111. *Since they are not equal,* $d \neq 1$.

Next, we try to retrieve the second bit $d_{\ell-2}$ ($i = \ell - 2$). *We have already known that* $d_{\ell-1} = 1$. *We assume here that* $d_{\ell-2} = 1$. *In this case,* $SF(\ell - 2)$ *is calculated as* $SF(\ell - 2) = 11010$. *Since* 11010 *does not appear in Table 2, then* $d_{\ell-2}$ *is retrieved not as one but as zero, i.e.,* $d_{\ell-2} = 0$. *Now we assume that* $d = 1\underline{0}$. *We compare* $m(\ell - 2) = (c^{10} \mod n) = (m(\ell-1)^2 \mod n) = 11010000$ *with the binary method result* 10001111. *Since they are not equal,* $d \neq 10$.

Next, we try to retrieve the third bit $d_{\ell-3}$ ($i = \ell - 3$). *We have already known that* $d_{\ell-1} = 1$ *and* $d_{\ell-2} = 0$. *We assume here that* $d_{\ell-3} = 1$. *In this case,* $SF(\ell - 3)$ *is calculated as* $SF(\ell - 3) = 10000010$. *Since* 10000010 *appears in Table 2, then* $d_{\ell-3}$ *is retrieved as one, i.e.,* $d_{\ell-3} = 1$. *Now we assume that* $d = 10\underline{1}$. *We compare* $m(\ell - 3) = (c^{101} \mod n) = SF(\ell - 3) = 10000010$ *with the binary method result* 10001111. *Since they are not equal,* $d \neq 101$.

Next, we try to retrieve the fourth bit $d_{\ell-4}$ ($i = \ell - 4$). *We have already known that* $d_{\ell-1} = 1$, $d_{\ell-2} = 0$ *and* $d_{\ell-3} = 1$. *We assume here that* $d_{\ell-4} = 1$. *In this case,* $SF(\ell - 4)$ *is calculated as* $SF(\ell - 4) = 100111$. *Since* 100111 *appears in Table 2, then* $d_{\ell-1}$ *is retrieved as one, i.e.,* $d_{\ell-4} = 1$. *Now we assume that* $d = 101\underline{1}$. *We compare* $m(\ell - 4) = (c^{1011} \mod n) = SF(\ell - 4) = 100111$ *with the binary method result* 10001111, $d \neq 1011$.

We have already known that $d_{\ell-1} = 1$, $d_{\ell-2} = 0$, $d_{\ell-3} = 1$ *and* $d_{\ell-4=1}$. *We assume here that* $d_{\ell-5} = 1$. $SF(\ell - 5)$ *is calculated as* $SF(\ell - 5) = 10001111$ ($i = \ell - 5$). *Since* 10001111 *appears in Table 2, then* $d_{\ell-5}$ *is retrieved as one, i.e.,* $d_{\ell-5} = 1$. *Now we assume that* $d = 1011\underline{1}$. *We compare* $m(\ell - 5) = (c^{10111} \mod n) = SF(\ell - 5) = 10001111$ *with the binary method result* 10001111. *Since they are equal to each other, we find that the secret exponent* d *is* 10111 *and a significant bit* ℓ *is five.*

3.2 Problems to retrieve a secret key using scan path

If we retrieve an L-bit secret exponent d using an exhaustive search, we have to try 2^L possible values to do it. On the other hand, the method explained in Section 3.1 retrieves a secret exponent one-bit by one-bit from MSB to LSB. It tries at most $2L$ possible values to retrieve an L-bit secret exponent. Further, the method just checks whether $SF(i)$ exists in the intermediate value $m(i)$ in Algorithm 1.

In order to apply this method to a scan-based attack, we have to know which registers store intermediate values, i.e., we have to know correspondence between scanned data and $SF(i)$.

However, scan paths are usually designed automatically by EDA tools so that nearby registers are connected together to shorten the scan path length. Only designers can know the correspondence between scanned data and registers and thus retrieved scanned data can be considered to be "random" for attackers. Therefore, it is very difficult to find out the values of $SF(i)$ in scanned data for attackers.

Messerges (Messerges et al., 1999) only shows the correspondence between intermediate values and a bit of a secret exponent. It does not indicate the method how to discover the intermediate value from scanned data. For that reason, its analysis method cannot directly apply to scan-based attacks against an RSA LSI.

We have to find out only $SF(i)$ somehow in the scanned data to retrieve a secret exponent d using the method in Section 3.1.

Maximum key length L	8 bits
Modulus n	101111001
Public exponent e	1011
Secret exponent d	10111

Table 1. Example parameters in Algorithm 1.

i	d_i	m^2	m
7	0	1	1
6	0	1	1
5	0	1	1
4	1	1	10011100
3	0	11010000	11010000
2	1	100011110	10000010
1	1	100111000	100111
0	1	1101	10001111

Table 2. Intermediate values at the end of i-th loop of Algorithm 1 (message $c = 10011100_2$).

4. Analysis scanned data

In order to solve the problem that attackers do not know the correspondence between registers of the scanned data and ones storing intermediate values during the binary method, we focus on the general property on scan paths: *a bit position of a particular register r in a scanned data when giving one input data is exactly the same as that when giving another input data*. This is clearly true, since a scan path is fixed in an LSI chip and the order of connected registers in its scan path is unchanged.

If we execute the binary method for each of N messages on an RSA circuit, a bit pattern of a *particular* bit position in scanned data for these N messages gives N-bit data. Based on the above property, this N-bit data may give a bit pattern of a particular bit in an intermediate value when we give each of these N messages to the RSA circuit.

We can calculate $SF(i)$ from the same N messages and $d_{\ell-1}$ down to d_0 of the secret exponent d by using an off-line simulation. By picking up a particular bit (LSB, for example) in each of $SF(i)$ values for N messages, we also have an N-bit data (see Fig. 3). If N is large enough, this N-bit data gives information completely unique to $SF(i)$. We can use this N-bit data as a *scan signature* SS_i to $SF(i)$ in scanned data.

Our main idea in this section is that we find out a scan signature SS_i to $SF(i)$ in scanned data (see Fig. 4) to retrieve the secret exponent d from $d_{\ell-1}$ down to d_0. If an N-bit scan signature SS_i appears in the scanned data for N messages, d_i is determined as one. If not, it is determined as zero.

In the rest of this section, we firstly propose a scan signature SS_i to $SF(i)$. Secondly we propose an overall method to retrieve a secret exponent d using scan signatures. Thirdly we analyze the probabilities of successfully retrieving a secret exponent by using our method.

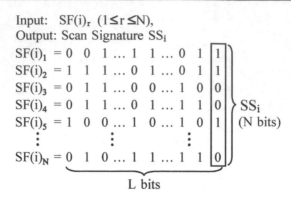

Fig. 3. Scan signature SS_i.

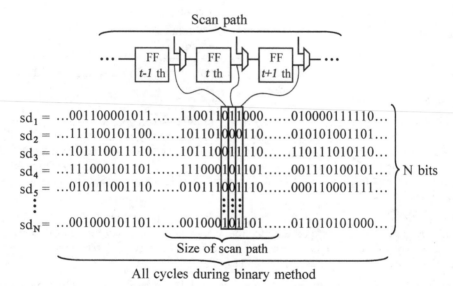

All cycles during binary method

Fig. 4. Scanned data.

4.1 Calculating a scan signature to $SF(i)$

Assume that N messages $c_1, \cdots, c_N$ are given. Also assume that we have already known $d_{\ell-1}, \cdots, d_{i+1}$ for a secret exponent d. Let $SF(i)_r$ be the selective function for RSA when giving the message c_r for $1 \leq r \leq N$. Assuming that $d_i = 1$, we can calculate $SF(i)_r$ for $1 \leq r \leq N$.

Let us focus on a particular bit of $SF(i)_r$. If N is large enough, a set of these bits for $SF(i)_r$ ($1 \leq r \leq N$) gives information unique to $SF(i)_r$. By using it, we can check whether $SF(i)_r$ are calculated or not in the target. As Fig. 3 shows, we define a *scan signature* SS_i to be a set of $SF(i)_r$ LSBs for the sake of convenience.

If SS_i appears in scanned data, d_i is determined as one. If not, d_i is determined as zero. After d_i is correctly determined, we can continue to determine the next bit of the secret exponent d in the same way.

Our proposed method has an advantage compared to conventional scan-based attacks (Yang et al., 2004; 2006). Our method is effective in the case of partial scan architecture. As long as a scan path includes at least 1-bit of each intermediate value, we can check whether the scan signature exists or not in the scanned data.

4.2 Scanned data analysis method

First we prepare N messages $c_1, \cdots, c_N$ and give them to an RSA circuit. For each of these messages, we obtain all the scanned data from the scan out of the RSA circuit until it outputs the binary method result. As Fig. 4 shows, the size of scanned data for each of these messages is ("scan path length" × "number of binary method cycles.")

Now we check whether a scan signature SS_i to $SF(i)$ appears in the obtained scanned data under the assumption that we do not know a secret exponent d in the RSA circuit as follows:

Step 1: Prepare N messages $c_1, c_2, \cdots, c_N$, where $c_r \neq c_s$ for $1 \leq r, s \leq N$ and $r \neq s$.

Step 2: Input c_r ($1 \leq r \leq N$) into the target RSA circuit and obtain scanned data every one cycle while the binary method works, until the RSA circuit outputs the result. Let sd_r denote the obtained scanned data for the message c_r ($1 \leq r \leq N$).

Step 3: From the definition, we have $d_{\ell-1} = 1$. Compare $m(\ell - 1) = (c_1 \mod n)$ with its binary method result. If they are equal, then we find that the secret exponent d is one and stop. If not, go to the next step.

Step 4: Calculate $SF(\ell - 2)_r$ assuming $d_{\ell-2} = 1$ for each c_r ($1 \leq r \leq N$) and obtain the scan signature $SS_{\ell-2}$.

Step 5: Check whether the scan signature $SS_{\ell-2}$ exists in the scanned data $sd_1, \cdots, sd_N$, which includes the scanned data in all the cycles while the binary method runs. If it exists, then we can find out that $d_{\ell-2}$ is equal to 1, and if it does not exist, then we can find out that $d_{\ell-2}$ is equal to 0.

Step 6: Calculate $m(\ell - 2) = ((c_1)^{d_{\ell-1} \times 2 + d_{\ell-2}} \mod n)$ and compare it with its binary method result. If they are equal, then we find that the secret exponent d is retrieved and terminate the analysis flow.

Step 7: We determine $d_{\ell-3}, d_{\ell-4}, \cdots$ in the same way as Step 4–Step 6 until the analysis flow is terminated at Step 6.

We show the example below to explain how the method above works.

Example 2. *As in Example 1, let us consider that the public key $(n, e) = (101111001, 11)$ and the secret key $(n, d) = (101111001, 10111)$. The maximum key length L is 8 bits and the secret exponent $d = 10111_{10} = 10111_2$, i.e, $d_7 = 0, d_6 = 0, d_5 = 0, d_4 = 1, d_3 = 0, d_2 = 1, d_1 = 1, d_0 = 1$. We assume that we do not know d and a significant key length ℓ. The parameters are shown in Table 1. Assume that the cycle counts of binary method are 16 and the size of the scan path is 128 in the target RSA circuit.*

(Step 1) First we prepare 8 messages $c_1, c_2, \cdots, c_8$, where $c_r \neq c_s$ for $1 \leq r, s \leq 8$ and $r \neq s$. The target RSA circuit executes the binary method as in Table 2.

(Step 2) *We input c_r ($1 \leq r \leq 8$) into the target RSA circuit and obtain scanned data every one cycle while the binary method works, until the RSA circuit outputs the result. Let sd_r denote the obtained scanned data for the messages c_r ($1 \leq r \leq 8$). The total size of scanned data is $16 \times 128 = 2,048$ (see Fig. 5).*

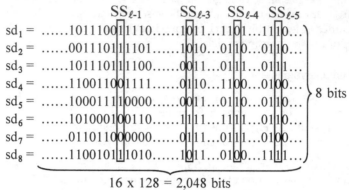

Fig. 5. Scanned data example.

(Step 3) *Let us start to determine $d_{\ell-1}$. We find $d_{\ell-1} = 1$ by the definition of ℓ. It is not necessary to check whether $d_{\ell-1} = 1$ or not, but we can check it as follows: we calculate $SF(\ell-1)_r = c_r$ for each c_r ($1 \leq r \leq 8$) and obtain the scan signature $SS_{\ell-1}$ (see Fig. 6). As Fig. 6 (a) shows, the scan signature $SS_{\ell-1}$ becomes "11101001". Since we find out that the scan signature $SS_{\ell-1}$ exists in bit patterns of scanned data sd_r ($1 \leq r \leq 8$) in Fig. 5, we confirm that $d_{\ell-1}$ is retrieved as one, i.e., $d_{\ell-1} = 1$. Now we assume that $d = \underline{1}$. We compare $m(\ell-1) = ((c_1)^1 \mod n)$ with its binary method result. In case they are not equal, $d \neq 1$.*

(Step 4, Step 5, Step 6, and Step 7) *Next let us determine $d_{\ell-2}$. We calculate $SF(\ell-2)_r$ assuming $d_{\ell-2} = 1$ for each c_r ($1 \leq r \leq 8$) and obtain the scan signature $SS_{\ell-2}$ (see Fig. 6 (b)). As Fig. 6 (b) shows, the scan signature $SS_{\ell-2}$ becomes "01111100". Since we find out that the scan signature $SS_{\ell-2}$ does not exist in bit patterns of scanned data sd_r ($1 \leq r \leq 8$) in Fig. 5, we can determine that $d_{\ell-2}$ is equal to zero, i.e., $d_{\ell-2} = 0$. Now we assume that $d = 1\underline{0}$. We compare $m(\ell-2) = (m(\ell-1)^2 \mod n)$ with its binary method result. In case they are not equal, $d \neq 10$.*

(Step 4, Step 5, Step 6, and Step 7) *Next let us determine $d_{\ell-3}$. We calculate $SF(\ell-3)_r$ assuming $d_{\ell-3} = 1$ for each c_r ($1 \leq r \leq 8$) and obtain the scan signature $SS_{\ell-3}$ (see Fig. 6 (c)). As Fig. 6 (c) shows, the scan signature $SS_{\ell-3}$ becomes "00010110". Since we find out that the scan signature $SS_{\ell-3}$ exists in bit patterns of scanned data sd_r ($1 \leq r \leq 8$) in Fig. 5, we can determine that $d_{\ell-3}$ is equal to one, i.e., $d_{\ell-3} = 1$. Now we assume that $d = 10\underline{1}$. We compare $m(\ell-3) = (m(\ell-2)^2 \times c_1 \mod n) = SF(\ell-3)_1$ with its binary method result. In case they are not equal, $d \neq 101$.*

(Step 4, Step 5, Step 6, and Step 7) *Next let us determine $d_{\ell-4}$. We calculate $SF(\ell-4)_r$ assuming $d_{\ell-4} = 1$ for each c_r ($1 \leq r \leq 8$) and obtain the scan signature $SS_{\ell-4}$ (see Fig. 6 (d)). As Fig. 6 (d) shows, the scan signature $SS_{\ell-4}$ becomes "01101110". Since we find out that the scan signature $SS_{\ell-4}$ exists in bit patterns of scanned data sd_r ($1 \leq r \leq 8$), we can determine that $d_{\ell-4}$ is equal to one, i.e., $d_{\ell-4} = 1$. Now we assume that $d = 101\underline{1}$. We compare $m(\ell-4) = (m(\ell-3)^2 \times c_1 \mod n) = SF(\ell-4)_1$ with its binary method result. In case they are not equal, $d \neq 1011$.*

(Step 4, Step 5, Step 6, and Step 7) *Finally let us determine $d_{\ell-5}$. We calculate $SF(\ell-5)_r$ assuming $d_{\ell-5} = 1$ for each c_r ($1 \leq r \leq 8$) and obtain the scan signature $SS_{\ell-5}$ (see Fig. 6 (e)). As Fig. 6*

Input: $SF(\ell\text{-}1)_r$ $(1 \leq r \leq 8)$
Output: Scan signature $SS_{\ell\text{-}1}$

$$
\begin{array}{l}
SF(\ell\text{-}1)_1 = 1 \ 0 \ 1 \ 1 \ 0 \ 0 \ 1 \ \boxed{1} \\
SF(\ell\text{-}1)_2 = 1 \ 0 \ 0 \ 1 \ 1 \ 0 \ 0 \ \boxed{1} \\
SF(\ell\text{-}1)_3 = 0 \ 0 \ 1 \ 0 \ 1 \ 1 \ 0 \ \boxed{1} \\
SF(\ell\text{-}1)_4 = 0 \ 1 \ 0 \ 1 \ 0 \ 0 \ 1 \ \boxed{0} \\
SF(\ell\text{-}1)_5 = 1 \ 0 \ 1 \ 0 \ 1 \ 1 \ 0 \ \boxed{1} \\
SF(\ell\text{-}1)_6 = 0 \ 0 \ 0 \ 1 \ 0 \ 0 \ 1 \ \boxed{0} \\
SF(\ell\text{-}1)_7 = 1 \ 1 \ 1 \ 1 \ 1 \ 0 \ 0 \ \boxed{0} \\
SF(\ell\text{-}1)_8 = 0 \ 0 \ 0 \ 1 \ 1 \ 0 \ 0 \ \boxed{1}
\end{array} \Bigg\} SS_{\ell\text{-}1}
$$

(a) Scan signature $SS_{\ell\text{-}1}$.

Input: $SF(\ell\text{-}2)_r$ $(1 \leq r \leq 8)$
Output: Scan signature $SS_{\ell\text{-}2}$

$$
\begin{array}{l}
SF(\ell\text{-}2)_1 = 0 \ 0 \ 0 \ 0 \ 1 \ 0 \ 1 \ \boxed{0} \\
SF(\ell\text{-}2)_2 = 1 \ 1 \ 1 \ 1 \ 0 \ 1 \ 0 \ \boxed{1} \\
SF(\ell\text{-}2)_3 = 0 \ 1 \ 1 \ 0 \ 0 \ 1 \ 1 \ \boxed{1} \\
SF(\ell\text{-}2)_4 = 1 \ 1 \ 0 \ 0 \ 1 \ 1 \ 0 \ \boxed{1} \\
SF(\ell\text{-}2)_5 = 1 \ 1 \ 0 \ 0 \ 1 \ 0 \ 1 \ \boxed{1} \\
SF(\ell\text{-}2)_6 = 0 \ 0 \ 1 \ 1 \ 1 \ 0 \ 1 \ \boxed{1} \\
SF(\ell\text{-}2)_7 = 0 \ 1 \ 1 \ 0 \ 0 \ 1 \ 1 \ \boxed{0} \\
SF(\ell\text{-}2)_8 = 0 \ 1 \ 1 \ 1 \ 0 \ 1 \ 0 \ \boxed{0}
\end{array} \Bigg\} SS_{\ell\text{-}2}
$$

(b) Scan signature $SS_{\ell\text{-}2}$.

Input: $SF(\ell\text{-}3)_r$ $(1 \leq r \leq 8)$
Output: Scan signature $SS_{\ell\text{-}3}$

$$
\begin{array}{l}
SF(\ell\text{-}3)_1 = 0 \ 1 \ 1 \ 0 \ 0 \ 1 \ 1 \ \boxed{0} \\
SF(\ell\text{-}3)_2 = 1 \ 1 \ 1 \ 1 \ 1 \ 0 \ 0 \ \boxed{0} \\
SF(\ell\text{-}3)_3 = 0 \ 1 \ 1 \ 0 \ 0 \ 1 \ 0 \ \boxed{0} \\
SF(\ell\text{-}3)_4 = 1 \ 0 \ 0 \ 1 \ 0 \ 0 \ 1 \ \boxed{1} \\
SF(\ell\text{-}3)_5 = 0 \ 0 \ 0 \ 0 \ 1 \ 1 \ 0 \ \boxed{0} \\
SF(\ell\text{-}3)_6 = 0 \ 0 \ 0 \ 1 \ 0 \ 0 \ 1 \ \boxed{1} \\
SF(\ell\text{-}3)_7 = 0 \ 1 \ 1 \ 1 \ 0 \ 0 \ 0 \ \boxed{1} \\
SF(\ell\text{-}3)_8 = 0 \ 0 \ 0 \ 1 \ 1 \ 0 \ 0 \ \boxed{0}
\end{array} \Bigg\} SS_{\ell\text{-}3}
$$

(c) Scan signature $SS_{\ell\text{-}3}$.

Input: $SF(\ell\text{-}4)_r$ $(1 \leq r \leq 8)$
Output: Scan signature $SS_{\ell\text{-}4}$

$$
\begin{array}{l}
SF(\ell\text{-}4)_1 = 1 \ 1 \ 0 \ 0 \ 1 \ 0 \ 1 \ \boxed{0} \\
SF(\ell\text{-}4)_2 = 0 \ 1 \ 0 \ 1 \ 1 \ 1 \ 0 \ \boxed{1} \\
SF(\ell\text{-}4)_3 = 1 \ 1 \ 1 \ 0 \ 0 \ 1 \ 1 \ \boxed{1} \\
SF(\ell\text{-}4)_4 = 0 \ 1 \ 1 \ 0 \ 0 \ 1 \ 0 \ \boxed{0} \\
SF(\ell\text{-}4)_5 = 1 \ 1 \ 0 \ 1 \ 1 \ 0 \ 1 \ \boxed{1} \\
SF(\ell\text{-}4)_6 = 1 \ 0 \ 1 \ 1 \ 0 \ 0 \ 1 \ \boxed{1} \\
SF(\ell\text{-}4)_7 = 0 \ 1 \ 1 \ 0 \ 0 \ 1 \ 1 \ \boxed{1} \\
SF(\ell\text{-}4)_8 = 1 \ 0 \ 1 \ 1 \ 0 \ 0 \ 0 \ \boxed{0}
\end{array} \Bigg\} SS_{\ell\text{-}4}
$$

(d) Scan signature $SS_{\ell\text{-}4}$.

Input: $SF(\ell\text{-}5)_r$ $(1 \leq r \leq 8)$
Output: Scan signature $SS_{\ell\text{-}5}$

$$
\begin{array}{l}
SF(\ell\text{-}5)_1 = 0 \ 0 \ 1 \ 0 \ 1 \ 1 \ 1 \ \boxed{1} \\
SF(\ell\text{-}5)_2 = 0 \ 0 \ 0 \ 1 \ 1 \ 0 \ 0 \ \boxed{1} \\
SF(\ell\text{-}5)_3 = 0 \ 0 \ 1 \ 0 \ 0 \ 1 \ 0 \ \boxed{1} \\
SF(\ell\text{-}5)_4 = 0 \ 1 \ 1 \ 1 \ 0 \ 1 \ 0 \ \boxed{0} \\
SF(\ell\text{-}5)_5 = 0 \ 1 \ 1 \ 1 \ 1 \ 0 \ 1 \ \boxed{1} \\
SF(\ell\text{-}5)_6 = 1 \ 0 \ 1 \ 0 \ 0 \ 0 \ 0 \ \boxed{1} \\
SF(\ell\text{-}5)_7 = 0 \ 1 \ 1 \ 0 \ 1 \ 1 \ 1 \ \boxed{0} \\
SF(\ell\text{-}5)_8 = 1 \ 0 \ 1 \ 1 \ 1 \ 0 \ 1 \ \boxed{1}
\end{array} \Bigg\} SS_{\ell\text{-}5}
$$

(e) Scan signature $SS_{\ell\text{-}5}$.

Fig. 6. Example of scan signatures.

(e) shows, the scan signature $SS_{\ell-5}$ becomes "11101101". Since we find out that the scan signature $SS_{\ell-5}$ exists in bit patterns of scanned data sd_r $(1 \leq r \leq 8)$, we can determine that $d_{\ell-5}$ is equal to one, i.e., $d_{\ell-5} = 1$. Now we assume that $d = 1011\underline{1}$. We compare $m(\ell - 5) = (m(\ell - 4)^2 \times c_1 \bmod n) = SF(\ell - 5)_1$ with its binary method result. In case they are equal to each other, we find that the secret exponent d is 10111 and a significant bit ℓ is five.

4.3 Possibility of successfully retrieving a secret key

Given that the scan size is α bits and the cycle counts to obtain the binary method result is T. Assume that scanned data are completely random data.

Even though $SF(i)_r$ for $1 \leq r \leq N$ is not calculated in the target RSA circuit, its scan signature may exist in scanned data. When $\alpha T < 2^N$, the probability that the scan signature SS_i to $SF(i)_r$ exists in somewhere in bit patterns of scanned data sd_r $(1 \leq r \leq N)$ is $\alpha T / 2^N$ despite we do not calculate $SF(i)_r$.

Sufficiently large N can decrease the probability that we mistakenly find out the scan signature SS_i in scanned data. For instance, if α is 3,072, T is 1,024, and N is 30^3, then the probability that we mistakenly find out the scan signature SS_i in scanned data is $3,072 \times 1,024/2^{30} \simeq 2.93 \times 10^{-3}$. If α is 6,144, T is 2,048, and N is 35, then the probability that we mistakenly find out the scan signature SS_i in scanned data is $6,144 \times 2,048/2^{35} \simeq 3.66 \times 10^{-4}$.

5. Experiments and analysis

We have implemented our analysis method proposed in Section 4 in the C language on Red Hat Enterprise Linux 5.5, AMD Opteron 2360SE 2.5GHz, and 16GB memories and performed the following experiments:

1. First, we have generated secret exponents randomly. Thousand of them have a bit length of 1,024 and 2,048, respectively. The other hundred of them have a bit length of 4,096.

2. Next, we have given each of the secret exponents into the target RSA circuit based on Algorithm 1 and obtained scanned data. The target RSA circuit obtains binary method results in 1,024 cycles for a 1,024-bit secret exponent, in 2,048 cycles for a 2,048-bit secret exponent, and in 4,096 cycles for a 4,096-bit secret exponent. Scan path length for a 1,024-bit secret exponent is 3,072 bits, that for a 2,048-bit secret exponent is 6,144 bits, and that for a 4,096-bit secret exponent is 12,192 bits. Then total size of the obtained scanned data for 1,024-bit secret exponent is $3,072 \times 1,024 = 3,145,728$ bits, that for 2,048-bit secret exponent is $6,144 \times 2,048 = 12,582,912$ bits, and that for 4,096-bit secret exponent is $12,192 \times 4,096 = 49,938,432$ bits

3. Finally, we have retrieved each of the secret exponents by our proposed analysis method using the obtained scanned data.

Fig. 7 and Table 4 show the results. Fig. 7 shows the number N of required messages to retrieve each secret exponent when giving each of the secret exponents. For example, the 4th 1,024-bit secret exponent is shown in Table 3. In order to retrieve this secret exponent, we need 29 messages, i.e., $n = 29$. In this case, we can successfully retrieve the 4th secret exponent using 29 messages but fail to retrieve it using 28 messages or less.

Throughout this experiment, the required number of messages is approximately 29.5 on average for 1,024-bit secret exponents and is approximately 32 for 2,048-bit secret exponents and is approximately 37 for 4,096-bit secret exponents. A running time is 98.3 seconds to retrieve a 1,024-bit secret exponent and 634.0 seconds to retrieve a 2,048-bit secret exponent.

---

[3] These values are derived from the experiments in Section 5.

	4-th secret exponent d
1,024 bits	0x3AD29CF2FC6CB6B0C010B17DF98C5081
	4E4585225AC42E8ECB7BB1847498D62F
	BA696CDD226EE9195F4E58A89321721F
	021C4511E6C994301363706058FF3765
	E29EEBA03E370A201BA5B60A356682A5
	1D05EE10DF8CB75D7B4578B3D29A515E
	2F86DEC487AB6BCD88C7351908D71851
	6C11B2419BD8C05739214E6CF44D12F

Table 3. Secret exponent example.

Key bit length bit	1,024	2,048	4,096
# of retrieving secret exponents	1,000	1,000	100
# of required messages (average)	29.5	32	37

Table 4. Experimental results.

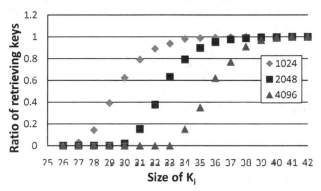

Fig. 7. Number of required messages to retrieve secret exponents.

6. Discussions

We consider secure scan architecture proposed so far against our proposed scan-based attack.

Firstly, the secure scan architecture proposed in (Sengar et al., 2007) cannot protect our proposed method from retrieving a secret key. (Sengar et al., 2007) inserts some inverters into a scan path to invert scanned data. However, since inverted positions of scanned data are always fixed, the value of a 1-bit register sequence is only changed to its inverted value. By checking whether SS_i or inverted SS_i exist in the scanned data, our proposed method can easily make it ineffective.

Inoue's secure scan architecture (Inoue et al., 2009) adds unrelated data to scanned data to confuse attackers. A sequence of scanned data to which unrelated data are added is fixed and it is not always true that they confuse all the bits to protect the scanned data in order to reduce area overhead. If the register storing scan signature SS_i is not confused, our proposed method can easily make it ineffective, too.

Secondly, (Chandran & Zhao, 2009; Gomułkiewicz et al., 2006; Hely et al., 2005; 2006; 2007; Lee et al., 2006; 2007; Paul et al., 2007; Yang et al., 2006) require authentication to transfer between system mode and test mode, and their security depends on authentication methods. If authentication would be broken-through and attackers could obtain scanned data, a secret key in an RSA circuit could be retrieved by using our proposed method. We consider that authentication strength is a different issue from the purpose of this chapter.

Finally, (Mukhopadhyay, et al.; Sengar et al., 2007; Shi el al., 2008) use a compactor so as not to output scanned data corresponding to registers directly. (Doulcier el al., 2007) proposes AES-based BIST, whereby there is no need for scan path test. However, applying these methods effectively to an RSA circuit is quite unclear because these methods are implemented only on an AES circuit or just on a sample circuit not for cryptography.

7. Concluding remarks

Our proposed scan-based attack can effectively retrieve a secret key in an RSA circuit, since we just focus on the variation of 1-bit of intermediate values named a scan signature. By monitoring it in the scan path, we can find out the register position specific to intermediate values. The experimental results demonstrate that a 1,024-bit secret key can be retrieved by using 29.5 messages, a 2,048-bit secret key by using 32 input, and a 4,096-bit secret key can be retrieved by using 37 messages.

In the future, we will develop a new scan-based side-channel attack against compressed scan data for RSA. In this paper, we only pick up one RSA LSI implementation but there can be other implementations available such as in (Miyamoto et al., 2008). We will attack these RSA implementations and successfully retrieve a secret key. Developing countermeasures against the proposed scan-based side-channel attacking method is another future work.

8. References

Boneh, D.; DeMillo, R. A. & Lipton, R. J. (1997). On the importance of checking cryptographic protocols for faults, *Proceedings of Advances in Cryptology - EUROCRYPTO '97*, Lecture Notes in Computer Science, Vol. 1233, pp. 37–51.

Brier, E.; Clavier, C. & Olivier, F. (2004). Correlation power analysis with a leakage model, *Proceedings of Cryptography Hardware Embedded Systems 2004*, Lecture Notes in Computer Science, Vol. 3156, pp. 16–29.

Chandran, U. & Zhao, D. (2009). SS-KTC: a high-testability low-overhead scan architecture with multi-level security integration, *Proceedings of 27th IEEE VLSI Test Symposium*, pp. 321–326.

Doulcier, M.; Flottes, M. L. & Rouzeyre, B. (2007). AES-based BIST: self-test, test pattern generation and signature analysis, *Proceedings of 25th IEEE VLSI Test Symposium*, pp. 94–99.

Gomułkiewicz, M.; Nikodem, M. & Tomczak, T. (2006). Low-cost and universal secure scan: a design-architecture for crypto chips, *Proceedings of International Conference on Dependability of Computer Systems*, pp. 282–288.

Hely, D.; Bancel, F.; Flottes, M. L. & Rouzeyre, B. (2005), Test control for secure scan designs, *Proceedings of European Test Symposium*, pp. 190–195.

Hely, D.; Bancel, F.; Flottes, M. L. & Rouzeyre, B. (2006). Secure scan techniques: a comparison, *Proceedings of 12th IEEE International On-Line Testing Symposium*, pp. 119–124.

Hely, D.; Bancel, F.; Flottes, M. L. & Rouzeyre, B. (2007). Securing scan control in crypto chips, *Journal of Electron Test*, pp. 457–464.

Inoue, M.; Yoneda, T.; Hasegawa, M. & Fujiwara, H. (2009). Partial scan approach for secret information protection, *Proceedings of European Test Symposium*, pp. 143–148.

Kocher, P. C. (1996). Timing attacks on implementations of Diffie-Hellman, RSA, DSS, and other systems, *Proceedings of Advances in Cryptology - Crypto '96*, Lecture Notes in Computer Science, Vol. 1109, pp. 104–113.

Koblitz, N. (1987). Elliptic curve cryptosystems, *Mathematics of Computation*, Vol. 48, pp. 203–209.

Kocher, P. C.; Jaffe, J. & Jun, B. (1999). Differential power analysis, *Proceedings of 19th Annual International Cryptology Conference on Advances in Cryptology*, pp. 388–397.

Lee, J.; Tehranipoor, M. & Plusquellic, J. (2006). A low-cost solution for protecting IPs against scan-based side-channel attacks, *Proceedings of 24th IEEE VLSI Test Symposium*, pp. 94–99.

Lee, J.; Tehranipoor, M.; Patel, J. & Plusquellic, J. (2007). Securing designs against scan-based side-channel attacks, *IEEE Transactions on Dependable and Secure Computing*, pp. 325–336.

Messerges, T. S.; Dbbish, E. A. & Sloan, R. H. (1999). Power analysis attacks of modular exponentiation in smartcards, *Proceedings of Workshop on Cryptographic Hardware and Embedded Systems*, Lecture Notes in Computer Science, Vol. 1717, pp. 144–157.

Miller, V. (1986). Uses of elliptic curves in cryptography, *the Advances in Cryptology*, ed. H. Williams, pp. 417–426.

Miyamoto, A.; Homma, N.; Aoki, T. & Satoh, A. (2008). Systematic design of high-radix montgomery multipliers for RSA processors, *Proceedings of IEEE International Conference on Computer Design (ICCD 2008)*, pp. 416–421.

Mukhopadhyay, D.; Banerjee, S.; RoyChowdhury, D. & Bhattacharya, B. B. (2005). CryptoScan: a secured scan path architecture, *Proceedings of 14th Asian Test Symposium*, pp. 348–358.

Nara, R.; Togawa, N.; Yanagisawa, M. & Ohtsuki, T. (2009). A scan-based side-channel attack based on scan signatures for AES cryptosystems, *IEICE Transactions on Fundamentals of Electronics, Communications and Computer Sciences*, Vol. E92–A, No. 12, pp. 3229–3237.

Nara, R.; Togawa, N.; Yanagisawa, M. & Ohtsuki, T. (2011). Scan vulnerability in elliptic curve cryptosystems, *IPSJ Transactions on System LSI Design Methodology*, Vol. 4, Sep., pp. 47–59.

Paul, S.; Chakraborty, R. S. & Bhunia, S. (2007). Vim-scan: a low overhead scan design approach for protection of secret key in scan-based secure chips, *Proceedings of the 25th IEEE VLSI Test Symposium* pp. 455–460.

Rivest, R. L.; Shamir, A. & Adelman, L. (1978). A method for obtaining digital signature and public-key cryptosystems, *Communications of the ACM*, Vol. 21, pp. 120–126.

Schramm, K.; Wollinger, T. & Paar, C. (2003). A new class of collision attacks and its application to DES, *T. Johansson (ed.) FSE 2003*, Lecture Notes in Computer Science, Vol. 2887, pp. 206–222.

Sengar, G.; Mukhopadhyay, D. & Chowdhury, D. R. (2007). Secured flipped scan-path model for crypto-architecture, *IEEE Transactions on Very Large Scale Integration System*, Vol. 26, No. 11, pp. 2080–2084.

Sengar, G.; Mukhopadhyay, D. & RoyChowdhury, D. (2007). An efficient approach to develop secure scan tree for crypto-hardware, *Proceedings of 15th International Conference of Advanced Computing and Communications*, pp. 21–26.

Shi, Y.; Togawa, N.; Yanagisawa, M. & Ohtsuki, T. (2008). A secure test technique for pipelined advanced encryption standard, *IEICE Transactions on Information and Systems*, Vol. E91–D, No. 3, pp. 776–780.

Silverman, R. D. (2002). Has the RSA algorithm been compromised as a result of Bernstein's Paper?
http://www.rsa.com/rsalabs/node.asp?id=2007, RSA Laboratories, April 8.

Stein, J. (1967). Computational problems associated with Racah algebra, *Journal of Computational Physics*, Vol. 1, pp. 397–405.

Yang, B.; Wu, K. & Karri, R. (2004). Scan based side-channel attack on dedicated hardware implementations of data encryption standard, *Proceedings of The International Test Conference*, pp. 339–344.

Yang, B.; Wu, K. & Karri, R. (2006). Secure scan: a design-for-test architecture for crypto chips, *IEEE Transactions on Computer-Aided Design of Integrated Circuits and Systems*, Vol. 25, No. 10, pp. 2287–2293.

8

PGP Protocol and Its Applications

Hilal M. Yousif Al-Bayatti[1],
Abdul Monem S. Rahma[2] and Hala Bhjat Abdul Wahab[2]
[1]Applied Science University, Kingdom of Bahrain
*[2]Computer Science Depart , University of Technology, Baghdad,
Iraq*

1. Introduction

Every few years, computer security has to re-invent itself. New technologies and new application bring new threats, especially with the ever-increasing growth of data communication, the need for security and privacy has become a necessity. Cryptography and data security are an essential requirement for communication privacy. One of the newest hot spots in security research is curve security. The forms produced by graphic systems are much harder to counterfeit, especially when the counterfeiter has no information about algorithm and the data that are used in design the shape.

The main goal of this chapter is combining the curve security methods with cryptography algorithms in order to increase the capability of cryptography. The weakness of the cryptographic key generated from normal color image is clear due to the nearest pixel values of image. This led to propose in this chapter a new method in order to generate a cryptographic key depending on generated (2D & 3D) mathematical models (digital image) and clipping the key according to algorithm and the data of curve generation.

2. Key management cryptographic systems

2.1 Conventional encryption

Conventional encryption has benefits; most notably speed. It is especially useful for encrypting data which will not be transmitted. However, conventional encryption alone, as a means for transmitting secure data, can be expensive simply due to the difficulty of secure key distribution (Droste, 1996). For a sender and recipient to communicate securely using conventional encryption, they must agree upon a key and keep it secret between themselves. If they are in different physical locations, they must trust a courier or some other secure communications medium to prevent the disclosure of the secret key during transmission (Sauer & Chandy, 1981).

2.2 Public-key cryptography

The concept of public-key cryptography was introduced in 1976 by Whitfield Diffie and Martin Hellman and, independently, by Ralph Markle, to solve the key management problem in secret-key cryptography. Each person receives a pair of different but related keys; the public-key and the private key (Schneir, 1996). The public key is published, while the private key is kept secret. Anyone can send a confidential message using public information, but the message can only decrypted by someone who has the private key. It is not possible to determine the secret key from the public key.

Public-key cryptography is based on the idea of a trapdoor function:

- $f : X \rightarrow Y$
- f is one-to-one,
- f is easy to compute,
- f^{-1} is difficult to compute, and
- f^{-1} becomes easy to compute if a trapdoor is known.

Public-key cryptography ensures a secret key exists between communicating parties, without the need to distribute secret keys. The most famous public-key cryptosystem is that devised by Rivest et al. (RSA). The RSA scheme relies on the inability to factor n where n=pq; p and q are large strong prime numbers, and when p and q are of roughly equal length, the modules become harder to factor. Factoring is assumed to be a difficult problem upon which several public-key cryptosystems are based. However, no known polynomial time algorithm can decipher the keys using the public information.

In RSA, algorithm encryption and decryption take the following forms:

$$C = M^e \bmod n$$

$$M = C^d \bmod n$$

Where M: plain text, C: cipher text, e: encryption key, and d: decryption key. Finding the factors of an RSA modulus depends on finding the encryption key. If an adversary discovers the factors of n, he or she can easily compute the decryption key using the following steps (Guan, 1987):

$$n = p \times q$$

$$\theta(n) = (p-1)(q-1) \text{, then}$$

$$d = e^{-1}(\theta(n)) \bmod n$$

The RSA algorithm has the following characteristics (Menezes et al.,1996):

- It is computationally infeasible to determine the decryption key given only knowledge of the algorithm and the encryption key.
- Either of the two keys can be used for encryption, with the other used for decryption.

2.3 Use of multi keys (huge) in a public-key cryptography system

One of the major roles of public-key encryption has been to address the problem of key distribution. There are two distinct aspects involving the use of public-key cryptography in this regard:

1. The distribution of public keys
2. The use of public-key encryption to distribute secret keys
3. A hybrid schema

2.3.1 Distribution of public keys

Several techniques have been proposed for the distribution of public keys. Almost all these proposals can be grouped within the following general schemes:

1. Public announcement
2. Publicly available directory
3. Public-key authority
4. Public-key certificates

For more details see (Stalings,2005).

2.3.2 Distribution of secret keys using public-key cryptography

Once public keys have been distributed or have become accessible, secure communication that thwarts eavesdropping, tampering, or both is possible. However, few users will wish to make exclusive use of public-key encryption for communication because of the relatively slow data rates that can be achieved. Accordingly, public-key encryption allows the distribution of secret keys to be used for conventional encryption.

1. Simple Secret Key Distribution
2. Secret Key Distribution with Confidentiality and Authentication.

2.3.3 A hybrid schema

A further application of public-key encryption used to distribute secret keys is a hybrid approach based on IBM mainframes .This scheme retains the use of a key distribution centre (KDC) that shares a secret master key with each user and distributes secret session keys encrypted with the master key. A public key scheme is used to distribute the master keys. The following rationale is provided for using this three-level approach:

Performance: There are many applications, especially transaction-oriented applications, in which the session keys change frequently. Distribution of session keys by public-key encryption could degrade overall system performance because of the relatively high computational load of public-key encryption and decryption. With a three-level hierarchy, public-key encryption is used only occasionally to update the master key between a user and the KDC.

Backward compatibility: The hybrid scheme is easily overlaid on an existing KDC scheme, with minimal disruption or software changes. The addition of a public-key layer provides a secure, efficient means of distributing master keys. This is of advantage in a configuration where a single KDC serves a widely distributed set of users.

3. Cryptographic protocol (Pretty Good Privacy)

Pretty Good Privacy (PGP) is a public key system for encrypting electronic mail using the RSA public key cipher (Schaefer, 1999). PGP is a hybrid cryptosystem and combines some of the best features of both conventional and public-key cryptography. When a user encrypts plaintext, PGP first compresses that plaintext. Data compression saves modem transmission time and disk space and, more importantly, strengthens cryptographic security. The majority of cryptanalysis techniques exploit patterns found in the plaintext to crack the cipher. Compression reduces these patterns in the plaintext, thereby greatly enhancing resistance to cryptanalysis (files which are too short to compress or which do not compress well are not compressed). PGP then creates a session key, which is a one-time-only secret key. This key is a random number generated from the random movements of the mouse and the keystrokes. The session key works with a very secure, fast conventional encryption algorithm to encrypt the plaintext; the result is ciphertext. Once the data is encrypted, the session key is then encrypted to the recipient's public key. This public key-encrypted session key is transmitted along with the ciphertext to the recipient. Figure (1) shows the send process.

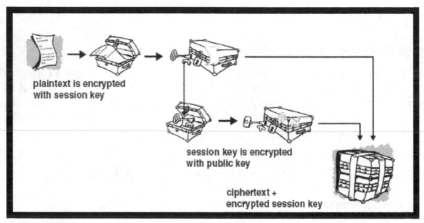

Fig. 1. Send Process.

Decryption works in the reverse way. The recipient's copy of PGP uses his or her private key to recover the session key, which PGP then uses to decrypt the conventionally encrypted ciphertext. Figure (2) shows the receiving process.

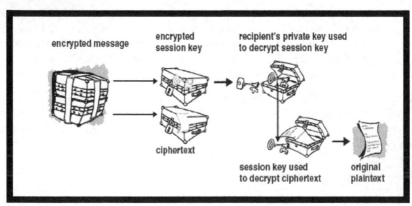

Fig. 2. Received Process

The combination of the two encryption methods combines the convenience of public-key encryption with the speed of conventional encryption. Conventional encryption is approximately 10,000 times faster than public-key encryption. Public-key encryption in turn provides a solution to key distribution and data transmission issues. Used together, performance and key distribution are improved without any compromise in security.

4. Generate randomness digital images

4.1 Introduction

Computer graphics is a topic of rapidly growing importance in the field of information technology. It has always been one of the most visually spectacular branches of computer technology, producing images whose appearance and motion make them quite unlike any other form of computer output . Computer graphics are also an extremely effective medium for communication between man and computer; the human eye can absorb the information content of a diagram or perspective view much faster than it can scan a table of numbers (Demel & Miller, 1984).

It is important to achieve consensus about what *computer graphics* and *visualisation* are. The word *graphics* is associated with charts, graphs, images, pictures and patterns, often in the context of art, design or animation; *visualisation* is the process of converting data into images (Gomes & Velho, 1997) .In order to understand computer graphics, we must study the methods used to create and structure data in the computer, as well as the methods for turning these into images. These two steps correspond to the two main areas of research in computer graphics: modelling and visualisation (Egerton & Hall,1998). Computer graphics are pictures generated by a computer (Hill, 2000)

4.2 Curve fitting generation

There are two main classes of curve generation algorithms:

Firstly, algorithms that interpolate the control points: the algorithm returns points along a curve which pass exactly through the control points at specific instants and form a smooth curve for points in between.

Secondly, algorithms that approximate the control points: this algorithm returns points from a curve that are attracted toward each control point in turn, but do not actually pass through all of them (Hill, 2000).

4.3 Interpolation techniques

Interpolation techniques are of great importance in numerical analysis since they are widely used in a variety of science and engineering domains where numerical methods are the only way to predict the value of tabulated functions for new input data. There are three reasons for using interpolation: firstly, interpolation methods are the basis of many other procedures, such as numerical differentiation, integration and solution methods for ordinary and partial-differential equations. Secondly, these methods demonstrate important theories about polynomials and the accuracy of numerical methods. Thirdly, interpolating with polynomials serves as an excellent introduction to techniques for drawing smooth curves .

Several methods of interpolation and approximation exist, some of which are:-

4.3.1 Lagrangian polynomials

The Lagrange polynomial is the simplest way to exhibit the existence of a polynomial for interpolation with unevenly spaced data. The Lagrange interpolating polynomial $L_{N,K}$ has degree N and is one at $x=x_k$ and $j \neq k$ zero at $x=x_j$ where

$$L_{N,K}(x) = \frac{(x-x_0)(x-x_1)...(x-x_{K-1})(x-x_{K+1})...(x-x_N)}{(x_K-x_0)(x_K-x_1)...(x_K-x_{K+1})...(x_K-x_N)}$$
$$= \frac{\prod_{\substack{j=0 \\ j \neq K}}^{N}(x-x_j)}{\prod_{\substack{j=0 \\ j \neq K}}^{N}(x_K-x_j)} \tag{1}$$

Note that $\prod_{K=1}^{N} K = 1.2.3...N$.

=The interpolating polynomial may be written:

$$P_N(x) = \sum_{K=0}^{N} y_k L_{N,K}(x) = y_0 L_{N,0}(x) + y_1 L_{N,1}(x) + ... + y_N L_{N,N}(x) \tag{2}$$

It is just a linear combination of the Lagrange interpolation polynomials $L_{N,K}(x)$ with the y_K as the coefficients (Goldman, 2002).

4.3.2 B-spline polynomials

Although Bezier curves and surfaces are well suited to many shape-modelling problems, complex geometric constructions are required to guarantee continuity when piecing curves together (Harrington, 1987). The use of spline functions avoids this by using mathematical constraints to allow only those curves that possess the required continuity at joints. The B-spline function generates a curve section which has continuous slopes so that they fit together smoothly: see figure (3).

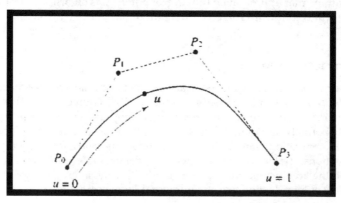

Fig. 3. B-Spline curve segment.

A B-spline of order k=3 consisting of n-k+2 segments is defined by a linear combination of basic functions C_i using n+1

Control points v_i

$$C_i(u) = b_{-1}(u)v_{i-1} + b_0(u)v_i + b_1(u)v_{i+1} + b_2(u)v_{i+2} \qquad (3)$$

Where the base functions are defined by (Pham, 1988):

$$b_{-1}(u) = 1/6(-u^3 + 3u^2 - 3u + 2)$$
$$b_0(u) = 1/6(3u^3 - 6u^2 + 4)$$
$$b_1(u) = 1/6(-3u^3 + 3u^2 + 3u + 1)$$
$$b_2(u) = 1/6u^3$$

A B-spline curve exhibits local control- a control point is connected to four segments (in the case of a cubic) and moving a control point can influence only these segments. In figure (4) that shows the effect of changing control points P1. This pulls the segments of curve in the appropriate direction and also affects, to a lesser extent, parts of the curve, thus demonstrating the important locality property of B-spline (Watt, 1999).

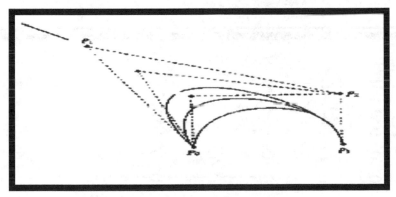

Fig. 4. The effect of changing the position of control point P1.

5. Generating 2D and 3D digital images using curve fitting techniques

A new method is proposed to generate 2D and 3D images using the parametric Lagrange curve and rolling circle movement.

5.1 Generating 2D images using the parametric lagrange curve and rolling circle movement

In this section a new method is proposed for generating a 2D image (digital image); it involves using a rolling circle moved around the parametric Lagrange curve as a tool for generating the digital image.

The image generated must have the following properties:-

a.   The image must not be regular; i.e. does not contain identifiable objects or pattern and cannot be described to anyone by anybody.
b.   Reproduction of the image by counterfeiters will be difficult or infeasible unless all the algorithms used to generate the image are known, as well as all the parameter values.
c.   The image must have the property of random colour (pixel values), allowing the image to be used in the security field.

The process to generate such a 2D image consists of the following stages:

Stage One

•   Initialise a 2D mesh of control points to generate a curve.
•   Initialising a 2D mesh is achieved by selecting a set of control points according to a determined increment value between control points. This increment value, as well as those of the x-coordinate and y- coordinate, may be fixed or variable. These choices were all studied and the conclusion drawn was that the increment value plays an important role in the generated image, since any change in its value generates a new mesh of control points and will lead to a new image with new features. This property gives security to the image, because counterfeiters would have difficulty guessing the starting control points and the increment values of the x- or y-coordinates. Figure (5) shows an example of a 2D mesh of control points with equal increments to the x- and y-coordinates.

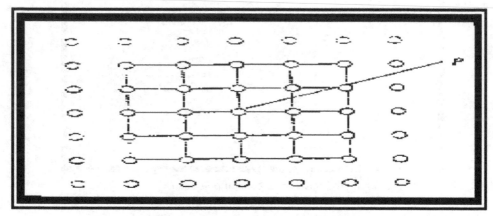

Fig. 5. Mesh of control points (p).

Stage Two

The generated curve is then moved according to algorithm (1) through the 2D mesh initialised in stage one. This process is achieved by marking the control points on the mesh using a simple method , for example 1, 2, 3... etc, and entering the number of control points from the 2D mesh into a simple pseudo-random generator. The pseudo-random generator produces a set of numbers represented as addresses of the control points in the 2D mesh; it does this in a random way and these are used to generate (interpolate) the curve. Figure (6) shows two examples of marking a 2D mesh; figure (2a) shows a mesh of size (4×4) with control points, and figure (2b) shows a mesh of size (5×5).

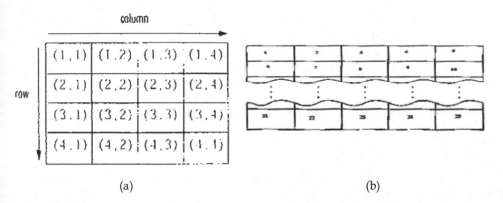

Fig. 6. Examples for marking meshes of control points.

Stage Three

After executing stage two, the generated image boundaries are determined. A large number of recursive pixels will be obtained and spread across the computer screen according to the isolation movement of the generated curve. Determining the image boundaries is achieved by deleting all the pixels outside the fixed boundaries of the image. The size of the image (boundaries) is kept secret between the sender and the receiver.

Described below are the proposed complete algorithms for generating a 2D image using a parametric Lagrange curve with a rolling circle moved around it.

5.1.1 Algorithm (1): Generate a 2D image

Input: Input a first control point, increment value (Inc), size of mesh control points (N×N) and the image size desired.

Output: Generate a 2D digital image.

Process:

Step 1.   Initialise the mesh of control points according to the start control points; increment the value and the size of the mesh.

Step 2.   Mark the control points of the mesh.

Step 3.   Enter the number of marks to simple pseudo-random generator.

Step 4.   Take the sequence of output from the generator to represent the addresses of the set of control points in the mesh.

Step 5.   draw the parametric Lagrange curve   with rolling circle.

Step 6.   Repeat step 4 with new sequence of numbers and step 5 until obtaining the recursive pixels that covers the image size that need to generate.

Step 7.   Clip the image according to the size the user entered.

Step 8.   Obtain the 2D generated image.

Step 9.   End.

Example:

In the following example a 2D image is generated using a mesh size of (25×25) with the same increment value of x- and y-coordinates equal to (10), using a radius for the rolling circle equal to (15), and the image size required to be generated is equal to (256×256) pixels. Figure (7a) shows the random oscillation curve movement through the 2D mesh is due to the movement of the curve path out of the mesh boundary. Figure (7b) shows the final stage of generating the 2D image by clipping the image size to (256×256) pixels.

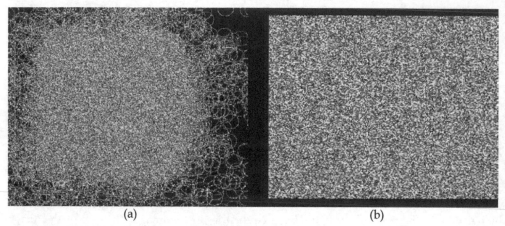

(a)   (b)

Fig. 7. (a) The random oscillation curve movement through the 2D mesh, (b) image of size (256x256) pixels

5.2 Generating a 3D image

This section introduces a new idea for generating a 3D image by inserting a third coordinate (z) to all the mathematical equations that were used to generate the 2D image. Generating a 3D image is very useful for increasing the key space and thus renders the process of estimating the key infeasible. This is because searching in 3D increases the number of possible control points the counterfeiter needs to estimate. In order to imagine working with 3D, it is suggested that the image be viewed as an empty cube which is to be filled completely with random colour pixels, then slides from the cube will be clipped in different ways. The clipped slide from the three-dimensional image can be used directly as a secret key, or by clipping a curve from this slide according to a secret set of control points by using a parametric Bezier curve (control curve) to represent the secret key between the sender and receiver.

5.2.1 Proposed algorithm to move a 3D rolling circle around a 3D parametric Lagrange curve

To create a parametric form from a 3D curve, it is necessary to invent three functions, $x(.)$, $y(.)$, $z(.)$, and say that the curve is "at" $P(t)=(x(t),y(t),z(t))$ at time t (Hill, 2000). The circular helix is given parametrically by: $x(t) = \cos(t)$, $y(t) = \sin(t)$ and $z(t)=bt$. For some constant b. The curve is illustrated in figure (8):

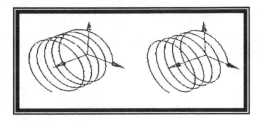

Fig. 8. Circular helix.

Many variations on the circular helix are possible. For example, the conical helix, with equation P (t) = (t cos (t), t sin (t), bt). Any 2D curve (x(t), y(t)) can, of course, be converted into a helix by appending z(t)= bt, or some other form for z(t).

5.2.2 Algorithm2: (Move a 3D rolling circle around a 3D parametric Lagrange curve)

Input: Take the triple data (New-x_i, New-y_i, New-z_i), i= 0,…,h-1, that was computed in algorithm (1) to represent the circle centre coordinates (x-c, y-c, z-c),and the radius circle value.

Output: Moving a 3D rolling circle around the 3D parametric Lagrange curve that generated in algorithm (1).

Process:

Step 1.   Set radius=15, b=10
Step 2.   For i= 0 to h-1
            Set x-c= New-x, y-c=New-y, z-c=New-z
            For index=0 to 360
             X=radius*cos (index) +x-c
             Y=radius*sin (index) +y-c
             Z=index*b+z-c
Step 3.   Plot (X, Y, Z)
Step 4.   Next index
Step 5.   Next i
Step 6.   End.

5.2.3 Generating 3D image stages

In section (7.2.1) the method for generating the 3D image by using 3D mathematical models was described and the algorithms needed to perform this generation were explained. In addition, it was suggested that the 3D image resembles an empty cube and the aim is to fill the cube completely with random colour pixels. This process involved a set of different stages, including: initialising a 3D mesh of control points; marking the control points to produce a sequence of control points by using a pseudo-random generator; implementation of algorithm (2) to move the 3D Lagrange curve with a 3D rolling circle through the 3D mesh of control points; deleting all the pixels outside the cube; and the final stage is obtaining the cube (image) which is completely filled with random colour pixels. The following illustrates the stages for generating a 3D image:-

Stage One

3D shape is to be divided into slides (planes) as each slide takes a 2D matrix, its axes are x and y, and the number of their slides will be equal to the depth z-axis of the shape. Figure (9 shows an example of an initialised 3D mesh.

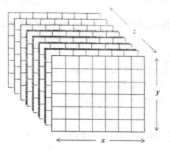

Fig. 9. Initialised 3D mesh.

The initialising of a 3D mesh is achieved using the same algorithm that was used to generate the 2D mesh of control points, but by inserting the third coordinate (z) to the control point coordinates, and determining the increment values of the x-, y-, and z-coordinates. In addition, when changing the increment values of the x-, y-, and z-coordinates, we obtain different types of 3D mesh control points, which makes the process of estimating the mesh more difficult for counterfeiters. Figure (10) shows an example of the cubic mesh (3D mesh) with equal increment values (x, y and z) between the control points.

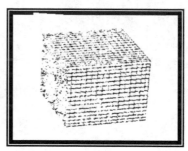

Fig. 10. Example of cube mesh.

Stage Two

Marking the 3D mesh is achived by counting the 3D mesh control points. The cube mesh can be visualised as resembling a set of 2D mesh slides marked with page numbers (z-coordinates), or an array of three dimensional coordinates.

Stage Three

A pesudo-random generator is used to produce the random addresses of control points from the 3D mesh, which are then used as a set of control points to implement algorithm (2) for moving the 3D curve (parametric Lagrange curve) with the 3D rolling circle through the 3D mesh. Figure (11) shows an example of the curve moving through the 3D cube.

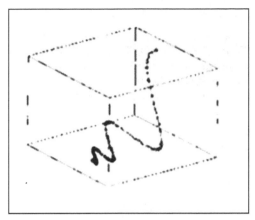

Fig. 11. Example of moving curve through cube.

Stage Four

This stage eliminates all the pixels drawn out of the cube due to the isolation of the moving Lagrange curve. The deleting process aims to remove all the pixels outside the 3D shape, and this is implicitly implemented in the algorithm which computes pixels and tests whether their coordinates are outside the boundaries of the 3D coordinates.

The complete algorithm below shows how to generate a 3D image using 3D mathematical models.

Algorithm 3: Generating a 3D Image Using 3D Mathematical Model

Input: Identify the first control point, increment value, size of mesh control points (N×N×N) and size of the 3D image that need to be generated.

Output: Generate 3D image and save the colour values in 3D array size (N×N×N).

Process:

Step 1. Initialise a 3D mesh of control points according to the starting control point; increment the value and the size of the 3D mesh.

Step 2. Mark the control points of the 3D mesh.

Step 3. Enter the number of marks from 3D mesh into a simple pseudo-random generator.

Step 4. Take a sequence of numbers from the pseudo-random generator to represent the addresses of the control points in the mesh.

Step 5. Execute algorithms (1) and (2) to draw the parametric Lagrange curve with a rolling circle and save the resulting colour pixel values for points in 3D array size (N×N×N).

Step 6. Repeat step4 with a new sequence of control point numbers and step 5 until the cube is completely filled with recursive pixels.

Step 7. Delete all the pixels which were placed outside the cube due to the isolation-moving curve.

Step 8. Obtain 3D generated image.

Step 9. End.

Example

To explain the work of the algorithm, figure (5) shows the implementation of algorithm (8). This example used the 3D size (100×100×10), (i.e. the 3D consisted of 100,000 random colour pixels) that was used to generate a 3D mesh of control points, and the 3D mesh of size (50×50×50), (i.e. the mesh consisted of 125,000 control points), and equal increment values between the control points. Figure (12) shows the results:

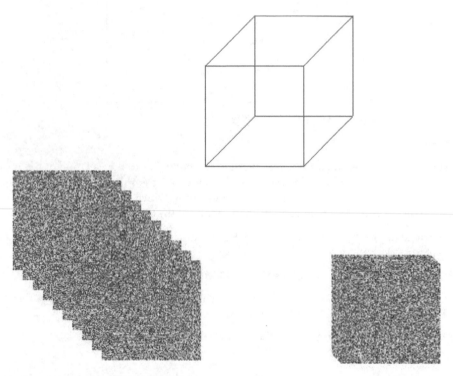

Fig. 12. Example to generate 3D-image

6. Clipping symmetric keys from the 2D and 3D images using the bezier curve method

The weakness of a key that is generated from a normal colour image is clear due to the nearest pixel values of the image. A new method for generating a symmetric cryptographic key is proposed which works by generating 2D and 3D images according to mathematical curve equations which will make the key sufficiently robust. A symmetric key is a string of random bits, and the number of random bits in it determine the key's variability and strength. Cryptographers recommend that to be reasonably secure, keys should be at least 90 bits long. The world standard is 128 bits because this is a convenient size for computers; there is no technical reason to use a shorter key. The second type of encryption is the public key or asymmetric systems, which uses separate keys for encryption and decryption: private key and the public key.

6.1 Proposed algorithm for clipping symmetric key from the (2D and 3D) images using the bezier curve method

Control points play an important role in curve generation as well as in clipping cryptography keys from 2D images and from the slides of 3D images. Control points are used to clip a curve or part of the generated images (2D & 3D). For this reason the control point must remain secret between the sender and receiver, (i.e. control points represent the master key used to clip the secondary key formed by a curve from random pixel colour values).

According to cryptography principles, it is assumed that all algorithms used are public to the attacker and only the key is secret. The secret key consists of a number of control points used to clip the key, and the coordinates of the control points; for example (4,10,10,20,15,30,60,100) which means using 4 control points to clip the curve and use the coordinates respectively (10,10),(20,15),(15,30),(60,100). Additionally, we can change any one of the parameters for the secret key to obtain a new secret key; this makes the process of generating the key more flexible and efficient.

There are different ways to select the control points from a 2D mesh or from a 3D mesh with different increment values between the control points and the control points themselves; this makes the counterfeiter's process of estimating the primary key infeasible. Figure (13) shows an example for selecting a set of control points to clip the curve of points using the Bezier method.

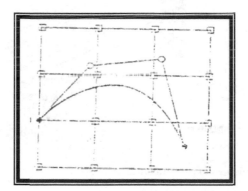

Fig. 13. Example for clip key from 2D mesh using Bezier Curve.

The size of the clipped key from the generated image is flexible depending on the flexibility of the generated image size; for example in the 2D image, the image size used is 256×256 pixels, which is equal to 65,536 pixels with each pixel represented by 24 bits (i.e. the key size is 1,572,864 bits), and the key space used in the 3D image is (100×100×100) pixels, which is equal to 1,000,000 pixels (i.e. the key space size is 24,000,000 bits).

In this example, samples of different key sizes were clipped, and the randomness of the keys was tested according to the five popular tests for randomness mentioned above.

Figure (14) shows an example of how to clip slides from a 3D image; figure (15) shows how to clip a curve as a key from a 3D slide.

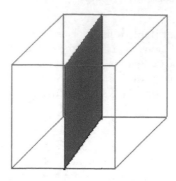

Fig. 14. Example of clipping slides from a 3D image.

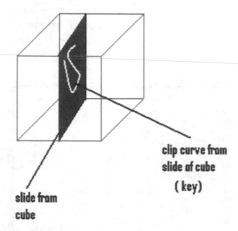

Fig. 15. Example of clipping a curve from slide of cube.

The following illustrates the algorithm for clipping a key from a 2D image and clipping a key from slides of a 3D image.

6.1.1 Algorithm(4): Generating key from generated image using Bezier curve method or by clipping parts of the generated images directly

Input: The sender inputs the number of control points to be used for the generation of the key (N), then inputs the chosen set of control point coordinates (x,y,z) from the mesh of the 2D or 3D image according to the boundaries of the images (i.e. the sender must know the boundaries of the generated image before clipping the keys).

Output: Clip stream of colour pixels from generated image (2D or 3D) using the Bezier Curve method or clip part (slide) from the generated image directly.

Process:

Step 1.   Assignment of the set of control points entered by sender to two arrays x (.), y (.).

Step 2.   The user inputs his choice for clipping key from 2D or 3D and using curve equations for clipping the key or clipping part from the generated image directly.
            If (clipped the key from 2D-image) then go to (A)
            Otherwise, go to (B)
            (A) (Clipped Key From 2D-Generated Image).
             If (Clipped Key Using Bezier Curve Equation) then go to step3.
             Otherwise, go to step 12.

Step 3.   (Clipped Key Using Bezier Curve Generation).
            Set i=0
            i<= N-1 do
            For u= 0 to 1 step 0.01

Step 4.   Let $X = (1-u)^3 x_i + 3(1-u)^2 u x_{i+1} + 3(1-u)u^2 x_{i+2} + u^3 x_{i+3}$

            Let $Y = (1-u)^3 y_i + 3(1-u)^2 u y_{i+1} + 3(1-u)u^2 y_{i+2} + u^3 y_{i+3}$

Step 5.   Get Pixel (X, Y),

Step 6.   Open file (Clip.txt) to save the pixel colour for pairs (X, Y).

Step 7.   Next u

Step 8.   i=i-1,
            Loop

Step 9.   Convert the Contents the files (Clip.txt) to the binary digits   (Bin.txt), which represent stream of bits (symmetric key).

Step 10. Execute the five-randomness test on the binary files (Bin.txt) for checking the randomness of the key (i.e. Step10 is an optional step the user can cancel this step).

Step 11. End

Step 12. (Clipped   part   from   generated   image   to   represent   the   key).
            {When the sender decides to clip directly from the 2D-generated image, he chooses only two corner coordinates from the mesh that represent the two corners of a rectangle}.

Step 13. Input the two control points (x1, y1) and (x2, y2).

Step 14. For i= x1 to x2
               For j= y1 to y2
               Get pixel (i,j)

Step 15. Open file (Clip-p.txt) to save the pixel colour for pairs (i,j).

Step 16. Next j
            Next i

Step 17. Convert the Contents of files (Clip-p.txt) to binary digits (Bin.txt), which represent stream of bits (symmetric key).

Step 18. End.

(Clipped Key From 3D-generated Image)

            {Work with a 3D image requires user to determine the level of (z)- coordinate from the cube, which is represented in this case by the slide number from the cube to clip 2D slide from 3D image.}

Step 19. Step19: Input the level of z-coordinate (z-coordinate), and the two control points (x_1, y_1) and (x_2, y_2) from z-slide, and clipped slide of colour pixels from the three dimensions array (3D).

Step 20. Set z= z-coordinate
   For i= x_1 to x_2
   For   j= y1 to y2
   slide (i, j) =3D(i , j, z)
   Next j,   Next i.

Step 21. Go to (A).

6.2 Tests of randomness for the clipped keys

Different sizes of keys are used in these tests and the results prove that the keys have the randomness property and can be used as a symmetric key in the cryptography field.

Tests		Key5= 1024 bit	Key6= 2604 bit	Key7= 3844 bit	Key 8= 5084 bit	Pass value
Frequency test		0.098	0.498	1.000	0.964	Must be ≤ 3.84
Run test	T_0	9.289	13.028	20.680	13.249	Must be ≤ 22.362
	T_1	6.656	3.867	5.475	8.127	
Poker test		7.409	1.568	3.077	3.497	Must be ≤ 11.1
Serial test		4.016	1.705	6.504	5.899	Must be ≤5.99
Auto correlation test for ten bits	Shift 1	0.079	0.031	0.075	0.087	Must be ≤3.48
	Shift 2	3.068	3.086	1.268	2.240	
	Shift 3	0.024	0.019	0.094	0.044	
	Shift 4	0.004	0.886	1.667	1.196	
	Shift 5	0.048	0.010	0.115	0.884	
	Shift 6	0.035	0.006	0.104	0.911	
	Shift 7	0.048	0.003	0.284	0.640	
	Shift 8	0.476	0.006	0.652	0.013	
	Shift 9	0.616	0.420	1.102	0.331	
	Shift 10	0.063	1.124	0.104	0.133	

Table 1. the results of randomness test for the keys clipped from 2D & 3D images.

6.3 Using generated digital images to modify cryptography protocol (PGP)

The strong cryptography employed by PGP is the best available today. The PGP protocol is a hybrid cryptosystem that combines some of the best features of both conventional and public-key cryptography. In this section, we propose to insert the generated digital image capability into the PGP protocol stages in order to increase protocol robustness in the face of counterfeiters. According to the tests in the previous sections, the generated 2D or 3D images have the randomness property and can clip many keys with different sizes. These properties make the generated images very useful as a source of clipping randomness session keys, and there is the capability to generate many keys from the images. We propose to use the generated (3D or 3D) images facility to generate a session key instead of using movement of the mouse or keystrokes. The session key clipped from the generated image in this case consists of two session keys; a *primary session key* and a *secondary session key*. The primary session key represents the Bezier curve coordinates and the secondary session key represents the stream of randomness bits sequence that is clipped according to curve equations. The work with New-PGP begins when a user encrypts plaintext. *Firstly,* the plaintext is compressed. *Secondly,* a session key is created by generating 2D or 3D images according to the proposed algorithms. *Thirdly,* the user enters the primary session key to the clip secondary key from the digital image. *Fourthly,* the user XOR the stream of bits sequence (secondary session key) with the plaintext after the compression process. *Fifthly,* the sender uses the public key from the RSA algorithm to encrypt the primary session key. *Sixthly,* the sender transmits the encrypt primary session key along with the ciphertext to the recipient. Decryption works in the reverse order. The recipient's copy of new-PGP uses his or her private key from the RSA algorithm to recover the primary session key which is used to generate the secondary key from the generated image to decrypt the conventionally encrypted ciphertext. Figures (16) and (17) show the send and receive process according to new-PGP protocol.

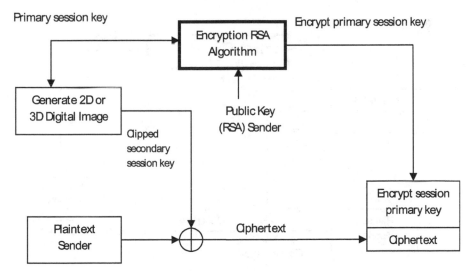

Fig. 16. Send Process

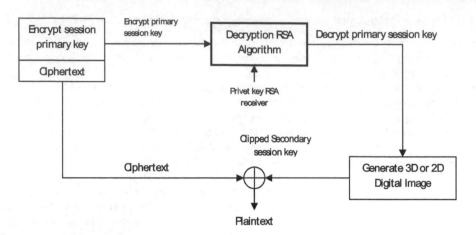

Fig. 17. Receive Process.

Example:-

To explain how the New-Protocol works and indicate the protocol behaviour, we proposed to generate a 3D-image size (100×100 ×100) pixels, by using a mesh size of (50×50×50) control points, and a primary session key (PSK) that consists of (4) control points with the coordinates (10,10), (20,20), (30,30), (40,40), with increment step u equal to 0.01. According to the primary session key, we clipped a secondary session key size (SSK) equal to 260 random bits. According to the randomness tests in table (1), the public key (PK) of RSA algorithm consists of (n=997517,e=193) where (secret p=977) and (secret q=1021), and the private key of RSA algorithm equals (d=727297).

Figures (18) and (19) illustrate the proposed protocol with the example values:

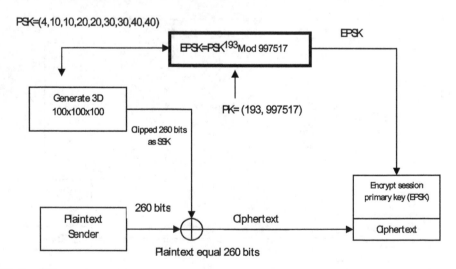

Fig. 18. Send Process.

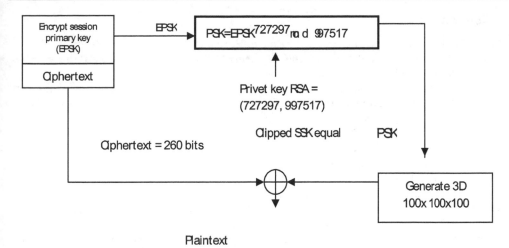

Plaintext

Fig. 19. Receive Process.

7. Conclusions

The proposed methods in this chapter are starts by studying most of the curve fitting methods and selects the curve fitting methods that are suitable to the work. Secondly developing the curve security algorithm and proposed algorithm to generate (2D & 3D) digital images, thirdly producing algorithm to clipping symmetric cryptographic key from 2D or 3D generated image, fourthly proposing algorithm to modify PGP cryptographic protocol by using 2D or 3D generated images.

Finally implementing the proposed generated digital image in image cryptography technique and then testing the results according to the authorized measures that are used in this field.

In this chapter proved a combine curve security with cryptography algorithms increase the cryptography capability. The proposed methods gives reasonable results in generating many randomness keys with different sizes. The 2D & 3D mathematical models succeed to generate randomness digital images that can play important role in cryptography according to the results that obtain from authorized randomness tests and from image cryptography tests, which gave reasonable tests.

From the New-PGP method, we obtained the following information:-

1. The process of guessing the primary session key from the secondary key is infeasible, because there is no correlation between the two session keys.
2. If the counterfeiter succeed in solving the factorisation problem from RSA and found the private key from public key, the key obtained would not help him to recover the plaintext from the primary session key unless the secondary session key was known.
3. All the secondary session keys have the property of randomness according to the randomness tests.
4. The New-PGP increased the security of the PGP protocol, making the protocol more robust and efficient.

8. References

Watt, A. (1999). *3D Computer Graphics (3rd edition)*, Addison Wesley, ISBN 978-0201398557

Demel, J. & Miller, M. (1984). *Introduction to Computer Graphics*, Brook/Cole Pub Co, ISBN 978-0534030537, USA

Droste, S. (1996). *New Result on Visual Cryptography*, CRYPTO 96, Proceedings of the 16th Annual International Cryptology Conference, pp. 401-415, Santa Barbara, CA, USA, August 18-22, 1996

Egerton, P.A. & Hall, W.S. (1998). *Computer Graphics: Mathematical First Steps*, Prentice Hall, ISBN 978-0135995723, London, UK

Goldman, R. (2002). *Lagrange Interpolation and Neville's Algorithm*, Department of Computer Science, Rice University, Available from www.clear.rice.edu/comp360/lectures/lagra.pdf

Gomes, J.; Velho, L. (1997). *Image Processing for Computer Graphics*, Springer-Verlag, ISBN 0-387-94854-6, New York, USA

Guan, P. C. (1987). *Cellular Automaton Public-key Cryptosystem*, Complex Systems, Vol1, Issue 1, (1987), pp.51-57, Available from,www.complex-systems.com/pdf/01-1-4.pdf

Harrington, S. (1987). *Computer Graphics a Programming Approach*, McGraw-Hill, ISBN 978-0070267534

Hill, F. S. (2000). *Computer Graphics Using OPENGL (2nd edition)*, Prentice Hall, ISBN 978-0023548567

Menezes, A.; Van Oorschot, P. & Vanstone, S. (1996). *Handbook of Applied Cryptography (1st edition)*, CRC Press, ISBN 978-0849385230

Pham B. (1988). *Offset Approximation of Uniform B-splines*, Computer Aided design, Vol 20, Issue 8, (October 1988), Elsevier Ltd, pp. 471-474

Stallings, W. (2005). *Cryptography and Network Security: Principles and Practice (4th edition)*, Prentice-Hall, ISBN 978-0131873162, USA

Sauer, C.; Chandy, K. (1981). *Computer Systems Performance Modeling*, Prentice-Hall, ISBN 978-0131651753

Schaefer, E. (1999). *An introduction to Cryptography and Cryptanalysis*, Santa Clara University, Available from http://math.scu.edu/-eschaefe/crylec.pdf-united states

Schneir, B. (1996). *Applied Cryptography (2nd edition)*, John Wiley & Sons, ISBN 978-0471117094

Secure and Privacy-Preserving Data Aggregation Protocols for Wireless Sensor Networks

Jaydip Sen

Innovation Lab, Tata Consultancy Services Ltd.
India

1. Introduction

In recent years, wireless sensor networks (WSNs) have drawn considerable attention from the research community on issues ranging from theoretical research to practical applications. Special characteristics of WSNs, such as resource constraints on energy and computational power and security have been well-defined and widely studied (Akyildiz et al., 2002; Sen, 2009). What has received less attention, however, is the critical privacy concern on information being collected, transmitted, and analyzed in a WSN. Such private and sensitive information may include payload data collected by sensors and transmitted through the network to a centralized data processing server. For example, a patient's blood pressure, sugar level and other vital signs are usually of critical privacy concern when monitored by a medical WSN which transmits the data to a remote hospital or doctor's office. Privacy concerns may also arise beyond data content and may focus on context information such as the location of a sensor initiating data communication. Effective countermeasure against the disclosure of both data and context-oriented private information is an indispensable prerequisite for deployment of WSNs in real-world applications (Sen, 2010a; Bandyopadhyay & Sen, 2011).

Privacy protection has been extensively studied in various fields such as wired and wireless networking, databases and data mining. However, the following inherent features of WSNs introduce unique challenges for privacy preservation of data and prevent the existing techniques from being directly implemented in these networks.

- *Uncontrollable environment*: sensors may have to be deployed in an environment that is uncontrollable by the defender, such as a battlefield, enabling an adversary to launch physical attacks to capture sensor nodes or deploy counterfeit ones. As a result, an adversary may retrieve private keys used for secure communication and decrypt any communication eavesdropped by the adversary.
- *Sensor-node resource constraints*: battery-powered sensor nodes generally have severe constraints on their ability to store, process, and transmit the sensed data. As a result, the computational complexity and resource consumption of public-key ciphers is usually considered unsuitable for WSNs.

- *Topological constraints*: the limited communication range of sensor nodes in a WSN requires multiple hops in order to transmit data from the source to the base station. Such a multi-hop scheme demands different nodes to take diverse traffic loads. In particular, a node closer to the base station (i.e., data collecting and processing server) has to relay data from nodes further away from base station in addition to transmitting its own generated data, leading to higher transmission rate. Such an unbalanced network traffic pattern brings significant challenges to the protection of context-oriented privacy information. Particularly, if an adversary has the ability to carry out a global traffic analysis, observing the traffic patterns of different nodes over the whole network, it can easily identify the sink and compromise context privacy, or even manipulate the sink node to impede the proper functioning of the WSN.

The unique challenges for privacy preservation in WSNs call for development of effective privacy-preserving techniques. Supporting efficient in-network data aggregation while preserving data privacy has emerged as an important requirement in numerous wireless sensor network applications (Acharya et al., 2005; Castelluccia et al., 2009; Girao et al., 2005; He et al., 2007; Westhoff et al., 2006). As a key approach to fulfilling this requirement of private data aggregation, *concealed data aggregation* (CDA) schemes have been proposed in which multiple source nodes send encrypted data to a sink along a *converge-cast tree* with aggregation of cipher-text being performed over the route (Acharya et al., 2005; Armknecht et al., 2008; Castelluccia et al., 2009; Girao et al., 2005; Peter et al., 2010; Westhoff et al., 2006).

He et al. have proposed a *cluster-based private data aggregation* (CPDA) scheme in which the sensor nodes are randomly distributed into clusters (He et al., 2007). The cluster leaders carry out aggregation of the data received from the cluster member nodes. The data communication is secured by using a shared key between each pair of communicating nodes for the purpose of encryption. The aggregate function leverages algebraic properties of the polynomials to compute the desired aggregate value in a cluster. While the aggregation is carried out at the aggregator node in each cluster, it is guaranteed that no individual node gets to know the sensitive private values of other nodes in the cluster. The intermediate aggregate value in each cluster is further aggregated along the routing tree as the data packets move to the sink node. The privacy goal of the scheme is two-fold. First, the privacy of data has to be guaranteed end-to-end. While only the sink could learn about the final aggregation result, each node will have information of its own data and does not have any information about the data of other nodes. Second, to reduce the communication overhead, the data from different source nodes have to be efficiently combined at the intermediate nodes along the path. Nevertheless, these intermediate nodes should not learn any information about the individual nodes' data. The authors of the CPDA scheme have presented performance results of the protocol to demonstrate the efficiency and security of the protocol. The CPDA protocol has become quite popular, and to the best of our knowledge, there has been no identified vulnerability of the protocol published in the literature so far. In this chapter, we first demonstrate a security loophole in the CPDA protocol and then proceed to show how the protocol can be made more secure and efficient.

Some WSN application may not require privacy of the individual sensor data. Instead, the data aggregation scheme may need high level of security so that no malicious node should be able to introduce any fake data during the execution of the aggregation process. This requirement introduces the need for design of secure aggregation protocols for WSNs.

Keeping this requirement in mind, we also present a secure and robust aggregation protocol for WSNs where aggregation algorithm does not preserve the privacy of the individual sensor data but guarantees high level of security in the aggregation process so that a potential malicious insider node cannot inject false data during the aggregation process.

The rest of this chapter is organized as follows. Section 2 provides a brief background discussion on the CPDA scheme. In Section 3, we present a cryptanalysis on CPDA and demonstrate a security vulnerability of the scheme. In Section 4, we present some design modifications of the CPDA scheme. Section 4.1 presents an efficient way to compute the aggregation operation so as to make CPDA more efficient. Section 4.2 briefly discusses how the identified security vulnerability can be addressed. Section 5 presents a comparative analysis of the overhead of the original CPDA protocol and its proposed modified version. Section 5.1 provides a comparison of the communication overheads in the network, and Section 5.2 provides an analysis of the computational overheads in the sensor nodes in the sensor nodes. Section 6 discusses the importance of security in designing aggregation schemes for WSNs. Section 7 presents some related work in the field of secure aggregation protocols in WSNs. In Section 8, a secure aggregation algorithm for WSNs is proposed. Section 9 presents some simulation results to evaluate the performance of the proposed secure aggregation protocol. Section 10 concludes the chapter while highlighting some future directions of research in privacy and security in WSNs.

2. The CPDA scheme for data aggregation in WSNs

The basic idea of CPDA is to introduce noise to the raw data sensed by the sensor nodes in a WSN, such that an aggregator can obtain accurate aggregated information but not individual sensor data (He et al., 2007). This is similar to the *data perturbation* approach extensively used in privacy-preserving data mining. However, unlike in privacy-preserving data mining, where noises are independently generated (at random) leading to imprecise aggregated results, the noises in CPDA are carefully designed to leverage the cooperation between different sensor nodes, such that the precise aggregated values can be obtained by the aggregator. The CPDA protocol classifies sensor nodes into two types: cluster leaders and cluster members. There is a one-to-many mapping between the cluster leaders and cluster members. The cluster leaders are responsible for aggregating data received from the cluster members. For security, the messages communicated between the cluster leaders and the cluster members are encrypted using different symmetric keys for each pair of nodes.

The details of the CPDA scheme are provided briefly in the following sub-sections.

2.1 The network model

The sensor network is modeled as a connected graph $G(V, E)$, where V represents the set of senor nodes and E represents the set of wireless links connecting the sensor nodes. The number of sensor nodes is taken as $|V| = N$.

A data aggregation function is taken that aggregates the individual sensor readings. CPDA scheme has focused on additive aggregation function: $f(t) = \sum_{i=1}^{N} d_i(t)$, where $d_i(t)$ is the individual sensor reading at time instant t for node i. For computation of the aggregate functions, the following requirements are to be satisfied: (i) privacy of the individual sensor data is to be protected, i.e., each node's data should be known to no other nodes except the node itself, (ii) the number of messages transmitted within the WSN for the purpose of data aggregation should be kept at a minimum, and (iii) the aggregation result should be as accurate as possible.

2.2 Key distribution and management

CPDA uses a random key distribution mechanism proposed in (Eschenauer & Gligor, 2002) for encrypting messages to prevent message eavesdropping attacks. The key distribution scheme has three phases: (i) key pre-distribution, (ii) shared-key discovery, and (iii) path-key establishment. These phases are described briefly as follows.

A large key-pool of K keys and their identities are first generated in the key pre-distribution phase. For each sensor nodes, k keys out of the total K keys are chosen. These k keys form a *key ring* for the sensor node.

During the key-discovery phase, each sensor node identifies which of its neighbors share a common key with itself by invoking and exchanging discovery messages. If a pair of neighbor nodes share a common key, then it is possible to establish a secure link between them.

In the path-key establishment phase, an end-to-end path key is assigned to the pairs of neighboring nodes who do not share a common key but can be connected by two or more multi-hop secure links at the end of the shared-key discovery phase.

At the end of the key distribution phase, the probability that any pair of nodes possess at least one common key is given by (1).

$$p_{connect} = 1 - \frac{((K-k)!)^2}{(K-2k)!K!}$$
(1)

If the probability that any other node can overhear the encrypted message by a given key is denoted as $p_{overhear}$, then $p_{overhear}$ is given by (2).

$$p_{overhear} = \frac{k}{K}$$
(2)

It has been shown in (He et al., 2007) that the above key distribution algorithm is efficient for communication in a large-scale sensor network and when a limited number of keys are available for encryption of the messages to prevent eavesdropping attacks.

2.3 Cluster-based private data aggregation (CPDA) protocol

The CPDA scheme works in three phases: (i) cluster formation, (ii) computation of aggregate results in clusters, and (ii) cluster data aggregation. These phases are described below.

Cluster formation: Fig. 1 depicts the cluster formation process. A query server Q triggers a query by sending a *HELLO* message. When the *HELLO* message reaches a sensor node, it elects itself as a cluster leader with a pre-defined probability p. If the value of p is large, there will be more number of nodes which will elect themselves as cluster leaders. This will result in higher number of clusters in the network. On the other hand, smaller values of p will lead to less number of clusters due to fewer number of cluster leader nodes. Hence, the value of the parameter p can be suitably chosen to control the number of clusters in the network. If a node becomes a cluster leader, it forwards the *HELLO* message to its neighbors; otherwise, it waits for a threshold period of time to check whether any *HELLO* message arrives at it from any of its neighbors. If any *HELLO* message arrives at the node, it decides to join the cluster formed by its neighbor by broadcasting a *JOIN* message as shown in Fig. 2. This process is repeated and multiple clusters are formed so that the entire WSN becomes a collection of a set of clusters.

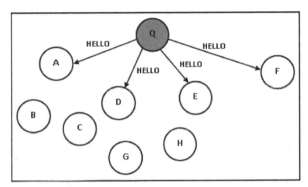

Fig. 1. The query server Q sends *HELLO* messages for initiating the cluster formation procedure to its neighbors A, D, E and F. The query server is shaded in the figure.

Computation within clusters: In this phase, aggregation is done in each cluster. The computation is illustrated with the example of a simple case where a cluster contains three members: A, B, and C, where A is the assumed to be the cluster leader and the aggregator node, whereas B and C are the cluster member nodes. Let a, b, c represent the private data held by the nodes A, B, and C respectively. The goal of the aggregation scheme is to compute the sum of a, b and c without revealing the private values of the nodes.

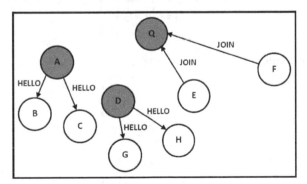

Fig. 2. A and D elect themselves as the cluster leaders randomly and in turn send *HELLO* messages to their neighbors. E and F join the cluster formed by Q. B and C join the cluster formed with A as the cluster leader, while G and H join the cluster with D as the cluster leader. All the cluster leaders and the query server are leader.

As shown in Fig. 3, for the privacy-preserving additive aggregation function, the nodes A, B, and C are assumed to share three public non-zero distinct numbers, which are denoted as x, y, and z respectively. In addition, node A generates two random numbers r_1^A and r_2^A, which are known only to node A. Similarly, nodes B and C generate r_1^B, r_2^B and r_1^C, r_2^C respectively, which are private values of the nodes which have generated them.

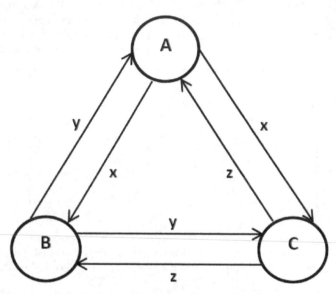

Fig. 3. Nodes A, B and C broadcast their distinct and non-zero public seeds x, y and z respectively

Node A computes v_A^A, v_B^A, and v_C^A as shown in (3).

$$
\left.
\begin{aligned}
v_A^A &= a + r_1^A x + r_2^A x^2 \\
v_B^A &= a + r_1^A y + r_2^A y^2 \\
v_C^A &= a + r_1^A z + r_2^A z^2
\end{aligned}
\right\}
\tag{3}
$$

Similarly, node B computes v_A^B, v_B^B, and v_C^B as in (4).

$$
\left.
\begin{aligned}
v_A^B &= b + r_1^B x + r_2^B x^2 \\
v_B^B &= b + r_1^B y + r_2^B y^2 \\
v_C^B &= b + r_1^B z + r_2^B z^2
\end{aligned}
\right\}
\tag{4}
$$

Likewise, node C computes v_A^C, v_B^C, and v_C^C as in (5).

$$
\left.
\begin{aligned}
v_A^C &= c + r_1^C x + r_2^C x^2 \\
v_B^C &= c + r_1^C y + r_2^C y^2 \\
v_C^C &= c + r_1^C z + r_2^C z^2
\end{aligned}
\right\}
\tag{5}
$$

Node A encrypts $v_B{}^A$ and sends it to node B using the shared key between node A and node B. Node A also encrypts $v_C{}^A$ and sends it to node C using the shared key between node A and node C. In the same manner, node B sends encrypted $v_A{}^B$ to node A and $v_C{}^B$ to node C; node C sends encrypted $v_A{}^C$ and $v_B{}^C$ to node A and node B respectively. The exchanges of these encrypted messages are depicted in Fig. 4. On receiving $v_A{}^B$ and $v_A{}^C$, node A computes the sum of $v_A{}^A$ (already computed by node A), $v_A{}^B$ and $v_A{}^C$. Now, node A computes F_A using (6).

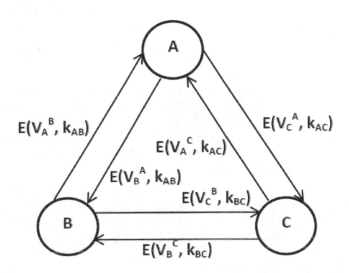

Fig. 4. Exchanges of encrypted messages among nodes A, B and C using shared keys

$$F_A = v_A^A + v_A^B + v_A^C = (a+b+c) + r_1 x + r_2 x^2 \tag{6}$$

In (6), $r_1 = r_1^A + r_1^B + r_1^C$ and $r_2 = r_2^A + r_2^B + r_2^C$. Similarly, node B and node C compute F_B and F_C respectively, where F_B and F_C are given by (7) and (8) respectively.

$$F_B = v_B^A + v_B^B + v_B^C = (a+b+c) + r_1 y + r_2 y^2 \tag{7}$$

$$F_C = v_C^A + v_C^B + v_C^C = (a+b+c) + r_1 z + r_2 z^2 \tag{8}$$

Node B and node C broadcast F_B and F_C to the cluster leader node A, so that node A has the knowledge of the values of F_A, F_B and F_C. From these values the cluster leader node A can compute the aggregated value $(a + b + c)$ as explained below.

The equations (6), (7), and (8) can be rewritten as in (9).

$$U = G^{-1} F \tag{9}$$

In (9), $G = \begin{bmatrix} 1 & x & x^2 \\ 1 & y & y^2 \\ 1 & z & z^2 \end{bmatrix}$, $U = \begin{bmatrix} a+b+c \\ r_1 \\ r_2 \end{bmatrix}$ and $F = \begin{bmatrix} F_A & F_B & F_c \end{bmatrix}^T$.

Since x, y, z, F_A, F_B, and F_C are known to the cluster leader node A, it can compute the value of $(a + b + c)$ without having any knowledge of b and c.

In order to avoid eavesdropping attack by neighbor nodes, it is necessary to encrypt the values of $v_B{}^A$, $v_C{}^A$, $v_A{}^B$, $v_C{}^B$, $v_A{}^C$, and $v_B{}^C$. If node B overhears the value of $v_C{}^A$, then node B gets access to the values of $v_C{}^A$, $v_B{}^A$ and F_A. Then node B can deduce: $v_A^A = F_A - v_B^A - v_C^A$. Having the knowledge of $v_A{}^A$, node B can further obtain the value of a if x, $v_A{}^A$, $v_A{}^B$ and $v_A{}^C$ are known. However, if node A encrypts $v_C{}^A$ and sends it to node C, then node B cannot get $v_C{}^A$. With the knowledge of $v_B{}^A$, F_A, and x from node A, node B cannot deduce the value of a. If node B and node C collude and reveal node A's information (i.e., $v_B{}^A$ and $v_C{}^A$), to each other, then node A's privacy will be compromised and its private value a will be revealed. In order to reduce the probability of such collusion attacks, the cluster size should be as large as possible, since in a cluster of size m, at least $(m - 1)$ nodes should collude in order to successfully launch the attack. Higher values of m will require larger number of colluding nodes thereby making the attack more difficult.

Cluster data aggregation The CPDA scheme has been implemented on top of a protocol known as *Tiny Aggregation* (TAG) protocol (Madden et al., 2002). Using the TAG protocol, each cluster leader node routes the sum of the values in the nodes in its cluster to the query server through a TAG routing tree whose root is situated at the server.

3. An Attack on the CPDA scheme

In this section, we present an efficient attack (Sen & Maitra, 2011) on the CPDA aggregation scheme. The objective of the attack is to show the vulnerability of the CPDA scheme which can be suitably exploited by a malicious participating sensor node. The intention of the malicious node is to participate in the scheme in such a way that it can get access to the private values (i.e., a, b and c) of the participating sensor nodes. For describing the attack scenario, we use the same example cluster consisting of three sensor nodes A, B and C. Node A is the cluster leader whereas node B and node C are the cluster members. We distinguish two types of attacks: (i) attack by a malicious cluster leader (e.g., node A) and (ii) attack by a malicious cluster member (e.g., either node B or node C). These two cases are described in detail in the following sub-sections.

3.1 Privacy attack by a malicious cluster leader node

Let us assume that the cluster leader node A is malicious. Node A chooses a very large value of x such that $x \gg y, z$. Since y and z are public values chosen by node B and node C which are broadcast in the network by node B and node C respectively, it is easy for node A to choose a suitable value for x.

Nodes A, B and C compute the values of $v_A{}^A$, $v_B{}^A$, $v_C{}^A$, $v_A{}^B$, $v_B{}^B$, $v_C{}^B$, $v_A{}^C$, $v_B{}^C$, and $v_C{}^C$ using (3), (4) and (5) as described in Section 2.3. As per the CPDA scheme, node A receives:

$v_A^B = b + r_1^B x + r_2^B x^2$ from node B. Since x is very large compared to b and r_1^B node A can derive the value of r_2^B using (10) where we consider integer division.

$$\frac{v_A^B}{x^2} = \frac{b}{x^2} + \frac{r_1^B}{x} + r_2^B = 0 + 0 + r_2^B = r_2^B \tag{10}$$

Using the value of r_2^B as derived in (10), and using $v_A^B = b + r_1^B x + r_2^B x^2$, node A can now compute the value of r_1^B by solving (11).

$$\frac{v_A^B - r_2^B x^2}{x} = \frac{b}{x} + r_1^B = 0 + r_1^B = r_1^B \tag{11}$$

In the same manner, node A derives the values of r_1^C and r_2^C from v_A^C received from node C. Since $r_1 = r_1^A + r_1^B + r_1^C$, and $r_2 = r_2^A + r_2^B + r_2^C$, as shown in (6), (7) and (8), node A can compute the values of r_1 and r_2 (r_1^B, r_2^B, r_1^C, and r_2^C are derived as shown above, and r_1^A and r_2^A were generated by node A).

At this stage, node A uses the values of F_B and F_C received from node B and node C respectively as shown in (7) and (8). Node A has now two linear simultaneous equations with two unknowns: b and c, the values of y and z being public. Solving (7) and (8) for b and c, the malicious cluster leader node A can get the access to the private information.

3.2 Privacy attack by a malicious cluster member node

In this scenario, let us assume that the cluster member node B is malicious and it tries to access the private values of the cluster leader node A and the cluster member node C. Node B chooses a very large value of y so that $y >> x, z$. Once the value of F_B is computed in (7), node B derives the value of r_2 and r_1 using (12) and (13).

$$\frac{F_B}{y^2} = \frac{(a+b+c)}{y^2} + \frac{r_1}{y} + r_2 = 0 + 0 + r_2 \tag{12}$$

$$\frac{F_B - r_2 y^2}{y} = \frac{(a+b+c)}{y} + r_1 = 0 + r_1 = r_1 \tag{13}$$

As per the CPDA scheme, node B receives $v_B^C = c + r_1^C y + r_2^C y^2$ from node C. Since the magnitude of y is very large compared to c, r_1^C and r_2^C, it is easy for node B to derive the values of r_2^C and r_1^C using (14) and (15) respectively.

$$\frac{v_B^C}{y^2} = \frac{c}{y^2} + \frac{r_1^C}{y} + r_2^C = 0 + 0 + r_2^C = r_2^C \tag{14}$$

$$\frac{v_B^C - r_2^C y^2}{y} = \frac{c}{y} + r_1^C = 0 + r_1^C = r_1^C \tag{15}$$

Using (12), (13), (14) and (15) node B can compute $r_1^A = r_1 + r_1^B - r_1^C$ and $r_2^A = r_2 - r_2^B - r_2^C$. Now, node B can compute the value of a using $v_A^B = a + r_1^A y + r_2^A y^2$ (received from node A), in which the values of all the variables are known except that of a. In a similar fashion, node B derives the value of c using $v_B^C = c + r_1^C y + r_2^C y^2$ (received from node C).

Since the private values of the nodes A and C are now known to node B, the privacy attack launched by participating cluster member node B is successful on the CPDA aggregation scheme.

4. Modification of the CPDA Scheme

In this section, we present two modifications of CPDA scheme: one towards making the protocol more efficient and the other for making it more secure.

4.1 Modification of CPDA scheme for enhanced efficiency

In this section, a modification is proposed for the CPDA protocol for achieving enhanced efficiency in its operation. The modification is based on suitable choice for the value of x (the public seed) done by the aggregator node A.

Let us assume that the node A chooses a large value of x such that the following conditions in (16) and (17) are satisfied.

$$r_2 x^2 >> r_1 x \tag{16}$$

$$r_1 x >> (a+b+c) \tag{17}$$

In (16) and (17), $r_1 = r_1^A + r_1^B + r_1^C$ and $r_2 = r_2^A + r_2^B + r_2^C$. Now, node A has computed the value of F_A as shown in (6). In order to efficiently compute the value of $(a + b + c)$, node A divides the value of F_A by x^2 as shown in (18).

$$\frac{F_A}{x^2} = \frac{(a+b+c)}{x^2} + \frac{r_1 x}{x^2} + r_2 = 0 + 0 + r_2 = r_2 \tag{18}$$

Using (18), node A derives the value of r_2. Once the value of r_2 is deduced, node A attempts to compute the value of r_1 using (19) and (20).

$$F_A - r_2 x^2 = (a+b+c) + r_1 x \tag{19}$$

$$r_1 = \frac{(F_A - r_2 x^2)}{x} - \frac{(a+b+c)}{x} = \frac{(F_A - r_2 x^2)}{x} - 0 = \frac{(F_A - r_2 x^2)}{x} \tag{20}$$

Since, the values of F_A, r_2 and x are all known to node A, it can compute the value of r_1 using (20). Once the values of r_1 and r_2 are computed by node A, it can compute the value of $(a + b + c)$ using (6). Since the computation of the sum $(a + b + c)$ by node A involves two division operations (involving integers) only (as done in (18) and (20)), the modified CPDA scheme is light-weight and it is much more energy-efficient hence much more energy- and time-efficient as compared to the original CPDA scheme. The original CPDA scheme involved additional computations of the values of F_B and F_C, and an expensive matrix inversion operation as described in Section 2.3.

4.2 Modification of the CPDA scheme for resisting the attack

In this section, we discuss the modifications required on the existing CPDA scheme so that a malicious participant node cannot launch the attack described in Section 3.

It may be noted that, the vulnerability of the CPDA scheme lies essentially in the unrestricted freedom delegated on the participating nodes for generating their public seed values. For example, nodes A, B and C have no restrictions on their choice for values of x, y and z respectively while they generate these values. A malicious attacker can exploit this freedom to generate an arbitrarily large public seed value, and can thereby launch an attack as discussed in Section 3.

In order to prevent such an attack, the CPDA protocol needs to be modified. In this modified version, the nodes in a cluster make a check on the generated public seed values so that it is not possible for a malicious participant to generate any arbitrarily large seed value. For a cluster with three nodes, such a constraint may be imposed by the requirement that the sum of any two public seeds must be greater than the third seed. In other words: $x + y > z$, $z + x > y$, and $y + z > x$. If these constraints are satisfied by the generated values of x, y and z, it will be impossible for any node to launch the attack and get access to the private values of the other participating nodes.

However, even if the above restrictions on the values of x, y and z are imposed, the nodes should be careful in choosing the values for their secret random number pairs. If two nodes happen to choose very large values for their random numbers compared to those chosen by the third node, then it will be possible for the third node to get access to the private values of the other two nodes. For example, let us assume that nodes A and C have chosen the values of r_1^A, r_2^A and r_1^C, r_2^C such that they are all much larger than r_1^B and r_2^B - the private random number pair chosen by node B. It will be possible for node B to derive the values of a and c: the private values of nodes A and C respectively. This is explained in the following.

Node B receives $v_B^A = a + r_1^A y + r_2^A y^2$ from node A and computes the values of r_1^A and r_2^A using (21) and (22).

$$\frac{v_B^A}{y^2} = \frac{a}{y^2} + \frac{r_1^A}{y} + r_2^A = 0 + 0 + r_2^A \tag{21}$$

$$\frac{v_B^A - r_2^A y^2}{y} = \frac{a}{y} + r_1^A = 0 + r_1^A = r_1^A \tag{22}$$

In a similar fashion, node B derives the values of r_1^C and r_2^C from v_B^C received from node C. Now, node B computes $r_1 = r_1^A + r_1^B + r_1^C$ and $r_2 = r_2^A + r_2^B + r_2^C$, since it has access to the values of all these variables. In the original CPDA scheme in (He et al., 2007), the values of F_B and F_C are broadcast by nodes B and C in unencrypted from. Hence, node B has access to both these values. Using (7) and (8), node B can compute the values of a and c, since these are the only unknown variables in the two linear simultaneously equations.

In order to defend against the above vulnerability, the CPDA protocol needs further modification. In this modified version, after the values v_A^A, v_A^B, and v_A^C are generated and shared by nodes A, B and C respectively, the nodes check whether the following constraints are satisfied: $v_A{}^A + v_A{}^B > v_A{}^C$, $v_A{}^B + v_A{}^C > v_A{}^A$, and $v_A{}^C + v_A{}^A > v_A{}^B$. The nodes proceed for further execution of the algorithm only if the above three inequalities are satisfied. If all three inequalities are not satisfied, there will be a possibility that the random numbers generated by one node is much larger than those generated by other nodes - a scenario which indicates a possible attack by a malicious node.

5. Performance analysis

In this section, we present a brief comparative analysis of the overheads of the original CPDA protocol and the proposed modified CPDA protocols that we have discussed in Section 4.1 and Section 4.2. Our analysis is based on two categories of overheads: (i) overhead due to message communication in the network and (ii) computational overhead at the sensor nodes.

5.1 Communication overhead

We compare communication overheads of three protocols - the *tiny aggregation protocol* (TAG), the original CPDA protocol and the proposed modified CPDA protocols. In TAG, each sensor node needs to send 2 messages for the data aggregation protocol to work. One *HELLO* message communication from each sensor node is required for forming the aggregation tree, and one message is needed for data aggregation. However, this protocol only performs data aggregation and does not ensure any privacy for the sensor data. In the original CPDA protocol, each cluster leader node sends 4 messages and each cluster member node sends 3 messages for ensuring that the aggregation protocol works in a privacy-preserving manner. In the example cluster shown in Fig. 3, the 4 messages sent by the cluster leader node A are: one *HELLO* message for forming the cluster, one message for communicating the public seed x, one message for communicating $v_B{}^A$ and $v_C{}^A$ to cluster member nodes B and C respectively, and one message for sending the aggregate result from the cluster. Similarly, the 3 messages sent by the cluster member node B are: one message for communicating its public seed y, one message for communicating $v_A{}^B$ and $v_C{}^B$ to cluster leader node A and cluster member node C respectively, and one message for communicating the intermediate result F_B to the cluster leader node A.

In contrast to the original CPDA protocol, the modified CPDA protocol in Section 4.1 involves 3 message communications from the cluster leader node and 2 message communications from each cluster member node. The 3 messages sent by the cluster leader node A are: one *HELLO* message for forming the cluster, one message for broadcasting its public seed x, and one message for sending the final aggregate result. It may be noted that in this protocol, the cluster leader node A need not send $v_B{}^A$ and $v_C{}^A$ to the cluster member nodes B and C respectively. Each cluster member node needs to send 2 messages. For example, the cluster member node B needs to broadcast its public seed y, and also needs to send $v_A{}^B$ to the cluster leader node A. Unlike in the original CPDA protocol, the cluster member node B does not send F_B to the cluster leader. Similarly, the cluster member node C does not send F_C to the cluster leader node A. In a cluster consisting of three members, the original CPDA protocol would involve 10 messages (4 messages from the cluster leader and 3 messages from each cluster member). The modified CPDA protocol presented in Section 4.1, on the other hand, would involve 7 messages (3 messages from the cluster leader and 2 messages from each cluster member) in a cluster of three nodes. Therefore, in a cluster of three nodes, the modified CPDA protocol presented in Section 4.1 will involve 3 less message communications. Since in a large-scale WSN the number of clusters will be quite high, there will be an appreciable reduction in the communication overhead in the modified CPDA protocol presented in Section 4.1.

The secure version of the modified CPDA protocol presented in Section 4.2 involves the same communication overhead as the original CPDA protocol. However, if any node chooses abnormally higher values for its public seed or its private random numbers, the secure version of the modified CPDA protocol will involve 2 extra messages from each of the participating sensor nodes. Therefore, in a cluster of three nodes, the secure version of the modified CPDA protocol will involve 6 extra messages in the worst case scenario when compared with the original CPDA protocol.

If p_c is the probability of a sensor node electing itself as a cluster leader, the average number of messages sent by a sensor node in the original CPDA protocol is: $4p_c + 3(1 - p_c) = 3 + p_c$. Thus, the message overhead in the original CPDA is less than twice as that in TAG. However, in the modified CPDA protocol presented in Section 4.1, the average number of messages communicated by a sensor node is: $3p_c + 2(1 - p_c) = 2 + p_c$. As mentioned in Section 2.3, in order to prevent collusion attack by sensor nodes, the cluster size in the CPDA protocol should be as large as possible. This implies that the value of p_c should be small. Since the value of p_c is small, it is clear that the message overhead in the modified CPDA protocol presented in Section 4.1 is almost the same as that in TAG and it is much less (one message less for each sensor node) than that of the original CPDA protocol. In the secure version of the protocol in Section 4.2, the communication overhead, in the average case, will be the same as in the original CPDA protocol. However, in the worst case, the number of messages sent by a sensor node in this protocol will be: $6p_c + 5(1 - p_c) = 5 + p_c$. This is 2.5 times the average communication overhead in the TAG protocol and 1.67 times the average communication overhead in the original CPDA protocol. The secure protocol, therefore, will involve 67% more overhead in the worst case scenario (where a malicious participant sensor node chooses abnormally higher values for its public seed as well as for its private random numbers).

5.2 Computational overhead

In this section, we present a comparative analysis of the computational overheads incurred by the sensor nodes in the original CPDA protocol and in the proposed efficient version of the protocol.

Computational overhead of the original CPDA protocol: The computational overhead of the CPDA protocol can be broadly classified into four categories: (i) computation of the parameters, (ii) computation for encrypting messages, (iii) computation of the intermediate results, and (iv) computation of the final aggregate result at the cluster leader node. The details of these computations are presented below:

i.   *Computation of the parameters at the sensor nodes:* Each sensor node in a three member cluster computes three parameters. For example, the cluster leader node A computes $v_A{}^A$, $v_B{}^A$, $v_C{}^A$. Similarly, the cluster member node B computes $v_A{}^B$, $v_B{}^B$ and $v_C{}^B$. We first compute the overhead due these computations.

Since $v_A^A = a + r_1^A x + r_2^A x^2$, for computation of $v_A{}^A$, node A needs to perform 2 addition, 2 multiplication and 1 exponentiation operations. Hence, for computing $v_A{}^A$, $v_B{}^A$ and $v_C{}^A$, node A needs to perform 6 addition, 6 multiplication and 3 exponentiation operations. Therefore, in a cluster consisting of three members, for computation of all parameters, the original CPDA protocol requires 18 addition, 18 multiplication and 9 exponentiation operations.

ii.   *Computations for encrypting messages*: Some of the messages in the CPDA protocol need to be communicated in encrypted form. The encryption operation involves computational overhead. For example, node A needs to encrypt $v_B{}^A$ and $v_C{}^A$ before sending them to nodes B and C respectively. Therefore, 2 encryption operations are required at node A. For a cluster consisting of three members, the CPDA protocol will need 6 encryption operations.

iii. *Computations of intermediate results*: The nodes A, B, and C need to compute the intermediate values F_A, F_B and F_C respectively for computation of the final aggregated result. Since $F_A = v_A^A + v_A^B + v_A^C = (a + b + c) + r_1 x + r_2 x^2$ and $r_1 = r_1^A + r_1^B + r_1^C$ and $r_2 = r_2^A + r_2^B + r_2^C$, for computing F_A, node A will need to perform 4 addition operations. Therefore, for a cluster of three members, 12 addition operations will be needed.

iv.   *Aggregate computation at the cluster leader*: For computing the final aggregated result in a privacy-preserving way, the cluster leader node A needs to perform one matrix inversion operation and one matrix multiplication operation.

The summary of various operations in the original CPDA protocol are presented in Table 1.

Operation Type	No. of operations
Addition	30
Multiplication	18
Exponentiation	3
Encryption	6
Matrix multiplication	1
Matrix inversion	1

Table 1. Operation in the CPDA protocol

Computational overhead of the modified CPDA protocol: The overhead of the efficient version of the CPDA protocol presented in Section 4.1 are due to: (i) computation of the parameters at the sensor nodes, (ii) computation of the intermediate result at the cluster leader node, and (iii) computation of the aggregated result at the cluster leader node. The details of these computations are presented below.

i.   *Computation of the parameters at the sensor nodes*: In the modified version of the CPDA protocol, the nodes A, B and C need to only compute $v_A{}^A$, $v_A{}^B$, and $v_A{}^C$ respectively. As shown earlier, each parameter computation involves 2 addition, 2 multiplication and 1 exponentiation operations. Therefore, in total, 6 addition, 6 multiplication, and 3 exponentiation operations will be needed.

ii.   *Computations for encrypting messages*: The nodes B and C will need to encrypt the messages $v_A{}^B$ and $v_A{}^C$ respectively before sending them to the cluster leader node A. Therefore, 2 encryption operations will be required.

iii. *Computation of intermediate result*: The cluster leader node A will only compute F_A in the modified CPDA. The cluster member nodes B and C need not perform any computations here. As discussed earlier, computation of F_A needs 4 addition operations.

iv.   *Aggregate computation at the cluster leader*: For computation of the final result at the cluster leader node, 2 integer division and 2 subtraction operations will be required.

v.   The summary of various operations in the modified CPDA protocol are presented in Table 2.

Operation Type	No. of operations
Addition	10
Subtraction	2
Multiplication	6
Division	2
Exponentiation	3
Encryption	2

Table 2. Operation in the proposed modified CPDA protocol

It is clearly evident from Table 1 and Table 2 that the modified version of the CPDA protocol involves much less computational overhead than the original version of the protocol.

6. Security requirements in data aggregation protocols for WSNs

The purpose of any WSN deployment is to provide the users with access to the information of interest from the data gathered by spatially distributed sensor nodes. In most applications, users require only certain aggregate functions of this distributed data. Examples include the average temperature in a network of temperature sensors, a particular trigger in the case of an alarm network, or the location of an event. Such aggregate functions could be computed under the end-to-end information flow paradigm by communicating all relevant data to a central collector node. This, however, is a highly inefficient solution for WSNs which have severe constraints in energy, memory and bandwidth, and where tight latency constraints are to be met. As mentioned in Section 1 of this chapter, an alternative solution is to perform in-network computations (Madden et al., 2005). However, in this case, the question that arises is how best to perform the distributed computations over a network of nodes with wireless links. What is the optimal way to compute, for example, the average, min, or max of a set of statistically correlated values stored in different nodes? How would such computations be performed in the presence of unreliability such as noise, packet drops, and node failures? Such questions combine the complexities of multi-terminal information theory, distributed source coding, communication complexity, and distributed computation. This makes development of an efficient in-network computing framework for WSNs very challenging.

Apart from making a trade-off between the level of accuracy in aggregation and the energy expended in computation of the aggregation function, another issue that needs serious attention in WSN is security. Unfortunately, even though security has been identified as a major challenge for sensor networks (Karlof & Wagner, 2003), most of the existing proposals for data aggregation in WSNs have not been designed with security in mind. Consequently, these schemes are all vulnerable to various types of attacks (Sen, 2009). Even when a single sensor node is captured, compromised or spoofed, an attacker can often manipulate the value of an aggregate function without any bound, gaining complete control over the computed aggregate. In fact, any protocol that computes the average, sum, minimum, or maximum function is insecure against malicious data, no matter how these functions are computed. To defend against these critical threats, in this chapter, an energy-efficient aggregation algorithm based on distributed estimation approach. The algorithm is secure and robust against malicious attacks in WSNs. The main threat that has been considered while designing the proposed scheme is the *injection of malicious data* in the network by an adversary who has compromised a sensor's sensed value by subjecting it to unusual temperature, lighting, or other spoofed environmental conditions. In designing the proposed algorithm, a WSN is considered as a collective entity that performs a sensing task and have proposed a distributed estimation algorithm that can be applied to a large class of aggregation problems.

In the proposed scheme (Sen, 2011), each node in a WSN has complete information about the parameter being sensed. This is in contrast to the snapshot aggregation, where the sensed parameters are aggregated at the intermediate nodes till the final aggregated result reaches the root. Each node, in the proposed algorithm, instead of unicasting its sensed information to its parent, broadcasts its estimate to all its neighbors. This makes the protocol more fault-tolerant and increases the information availability in the network. The scheme is an extension of the one suggested in (Boulis et al., 2003). However, it is more secure and reliable even in presence of compromised and faulty nodes in a WSN.

In the following section, we provide a brief discussion on some of the well-known secure aggregation schemes for WSNs.

7. Overview of some aggregation protocols for WSNs

Extensive work has been done on aggregation applications in WSNs. However, security and energy- two major aspects for design of an efficient and robust aggregation algorithm have not attracted adequate attention. Before discussing some of the existing secure aggregation mechanisms, we present a few well-known aggregation schemes for WSNs.

In (Heidemann, 2001), a framework for flexible aggregation in WSNs has been presented following snapshot aggregation approach without addressing issues like energy efficiency and security in the data aggregation process. A cluster-based algorithm has been proposed in (Estrin et al., 1999) that uses *directed diffusion* technique to gather a global perspective utilizing only the local nodes in each cluster. The nodes are assigned different level – level 0 being assigned to the nodes lying at the lowest level. The nodes at the higher levels can communicate with the nodes in the same cluster and the cluster head node. This effectively enables *localized cluster computation*. The nodes at the higher level communicate the local information of the cluster to get a global picture of the network aggregation. In (Madden et al., 2002), the authors have proposed a mechanism called TAG – a generic data aggregation scheme that involves a language similar to SQL for generating queries in a WSN. In this scheme, the *base station* (BS) generates a query using the query language, and the sensor nodes send their reply using routes constructed based on a *routing tree*. At each point in the routing tree, the data is aggregated using some aggregation function that was defined in the initial query sent by the BS. In (Shrivastava et al., 2004), a summary structure for supporting fairly complex aggregate functions, such as median and range quires have been proposed. Computation of relatively easier function such as min/max, sum, and average are also supported in the proposed framework. However, more complex aggregates, such as the most frequently reported data values are not supported. The computed aggregate functions are approximate but the estimate errors are statistically bounded. There are also propositions based on programmable sensor networks for aggregation based on snapshot algorithms (Jaikaeo et al., 2000). In (Zhao et al., 2002), the authors have focussed their attention into the problem of providing a residual energy map of a WSN. They have proposed a scheme for computing the equi-potential curves of residual energy with certain acceptable margin of error. A simple but efficient aggregation function is proposed where the location approximation of the nodes are not computed. A more advanced aggregate function can be developed for this purpose that will encompass an accurate convex curve. For periodic update of the residual energy map, the authors have proposed a naïve scheme of incremental updates. Thus if a node changes its value beyond the tolerance limit its value is transmitted and aggregated again by some nodes before the final change reaches the user. No mechanism exists for prediction of changes or for estimation of correlation between sensed values for the purpose of setting the tolerance threshold. In (Goel & Imielinski, 2001), a scheme has been proposed for the purpose of monitoring the sensed values of each individual sensor node in a WSN. There is no aggregation algorithm in the scheme; however, the spatial-temporal correlation between the sensed data can be extrapolated to fit an aggregation function. The authors have also attempted to modify the techniques of MPEG-2 for sensor network monitoring to optimize communication overhead and energy. A central node computes predictions and transmits them to all the nodes. The nodes send their update only if their sensed data deviate significantly from the predictions. A distributed computing framework is developed by establishing a hierarchical dependency among the nodes. An energy efficient aggregation algorithm is proposed by the authors in (Boulis et al., 2003), in which each node in a WSN senses the parameter and there is no hierarchical dependency among the nodes. The nodes in a neighbourhood periodically broadcast their information based on a threshold value.

As mentioned earlier in this section, none of the above schemes consider security aspects in the aggregation schemes. Security in aggregation schemes for WSNs has also attracted attention from the researchers and a considerable number of propositions exist in the literature in this perspective. We discuss some of the well-known mechanisms below.

A *secure aggregation* (SA) protocol has been proposed that uses the $\mu TESLA$ protocol (Hu & Evans, 2003). The protocol is resilient to both intruder devices and single device key compromises. In the proposition, the sensor nodes are organized into a tree where the internal nodes act as the aggregators. However, the protocol is vulnerable if a parent and one of its child nodes are compromised, since due to the delayed disclosure of symmetric keys, the parent node will not be able to immediately verify the authenticity of the data sent by its children nodes.

Przydatek et al. have presented a *secure information aggregation* (SIA) framework for sensor networks (Przydatek et al., 2003; Chan et al., 2007). The framework consists of three categories of node: a home server, base station and sensor nodes. A base station is a resource-enhanced node which is used as an intermediary between the home server and the sensor nodes, and it is also the candidate to perform the aggregation task. SIA assumes that each sensor has a unique identifier and shares a separate secret cryptographic key with both the home server and the aggregator. The keys enable message authentication and encryption if data confidentiality is required. Moreover, it further assumes that the home server and the base station can use a mechanism, such as *μTESLA*, to broadcast authenticated messages. The proposed solution follows *aggregate-commit-prove* approach. In the *first phase*: *aggregate-* the aggregator collects data from sensors and locally computes the aggregation result using some specific aggregate function. Each sensor shares a key with the aggregator. This allows the aggregator to verify whether the sensor reading is authentic. However, there is a possibility that a sensor may have been compromised and an adversary has captured the key. In the proposed scheme there is no mechanism to detect such an event. In the *second phase*: *commit-* the aggregator commits to the collected data. This phase ensures that the aggregator actually uses the data collected from the sensors, and the statement to be verified by the home server about the correctness of computed results is meaningful. One efficient mechanism for committing is a *Merkle hash-tree* construction (Merkle, 1980). In this method, the data collected from the sensors is placed at the leaves of a tree. The aggregator then computes a binary hash tree staring with the leaf nodes. Each internal node in the hash tree is computed as the hash value of the concatenation of its two children nodes. The root of the tree is called the commitment of the collected data. As the hash function in use is collision free, once the aggregator commits to the collected values, it cannot change any of the collected values. In the *third and final phase*, the aggregator and the home server engage in a protocol in which the aggregator communicates the aggregation result. In addition, aggregator uses an interactive proof protocol to prove correctness of the reported results. This is done in two logical steps. In the first step, the home server ensures that the committed data is a good representation of the sensor data readings collected. In the second step, the home server checks the reliability of the aggregator output. This is done by checking whether the aggregation result is close to the committed results. The interactive proof protocol varies depending on the aggregation function is being used. Moreover, the authors also presented efficient protocols for secure computation of the median and the average of the measurements, for the estimation of the network size, and for finding the minimum and maximum sensor reading.

In (Mahimkar & Rappaport, 2004), a protocol is proposed that uses elliptic curve cryptography for encrypting the data in WSNs. The scheme is based on clustering where all nodes within a cluster share a secret cluster key. Each sensor node in a cluster generates a partial signature over its data. Each aggregator aggregates its cluster data and broadcasts the aggregated data in its cluster. Each node in a cluster checks its data with the aggregated data broadcast by the aggregator. A sensor node puts its partial signature to authenticate a message only if the difference between its data and aggregated data is less than a threshold. Finally, the aggregator combines all the partially signed message s to form a full signature with the authenticated result.

Deng et al. proposed a collection of mechanisms for *securing in-network processing* (SINP) for WSNs (Deng et al., 2003). Security mechanisms have been proposed to address the downstream requirement that sensor nodes authenticate commands disseminated from parent aggregators and the upstream requirement that aggregators authenticate data produced by sensors before aggregating that data. In the downstream stage, two techniques are involved: one way functions and *μTESLA*. The upstream stage requires that a pair-wise key be shared between an aggregator and its sensor nodes.

Cam et al. proposed an *energy-efficient secure pattern-based data aggregation* (ESPDA) protocol for wireless sensor networks (Cam et al., 2003; Cam et al., 2005; Cam et al., 2006a). ESPDA is applicable for hierarchy-based sensor networks. In ESPDA, a cluster-head first requests sensor nodes to send the corresponding pattern code for the sensed data. If multiple sensor nodes send the same pattern code to the cluster-head, only one of them is permitted to send the data to the cluster-head. ESPDA is secure because it does not require encrypted data to be decrypted by cluster-heads to perform data aggregation.

Cam et al. have introduced another *secure differential data aggregation* (SDDA) scheme based on pattern codes (Cam et al., 2006b). SDDA prevents redundant data transmission from sensor nodes by implementing the following schemes: (1) SDDA transmits differential data rather than raw data, (2) SDDA performs data aggregation on pattern codes representing the main characteristics of the sensed data, and (3) SDDA employs a sleep protocol to coordinate the activation of sensing units in such a way that only one of the sensor nodes capable of sensing the data is activated at a given time. In the SDDA data transmission scheme, the raw data from the sensor nodes is compared with the reference data and the difference of them is transmitted in the network. The reference data is obtained by taking the average of previously transmitted data.

In (Sanli et al., 2004), a *secure reference-based data aggregation* (SRDA) protocol is proposed for cluster-based WSNs, in which raw data sensed by sensor nodes are compared with reference data values and then only difference data is transmitted to conserve sensor energy. Reference data is taken as the average of a number of historical (i.e. past) sensor readings. However, a serious drawback of the scheme is that does not allow aggregation at the intermediate nodes.

To defend against attacks by malicious aggregator nodes in WSNs which may falsely manipulate the data during the aggregation process, a cryptographic mechanism has been proposed in (Wu et al., 2007). In the proposed mechanism, a *secure aggregation tree* (SAT), is constructed that enables monitoring of the aggregator nodes. The child nodes of the aggregators can monitor the incoming data to the aggregators and can invoke a voting scheme in case any suspicious activities by the aggregator nodes are observed.

A *secure hop-by-hop data aggregation protocol* (SDAP) has been proposed in (Yang et al., 2006), in which a WSN is dynamically partitioned into multiple logical sub-trees of almost equal sizes using a probabilistic approach. In this way, fewer nodes are located under a high-level sensor node, thereby reducing potential security threats on nodes at higher level. Since a compromised node at higher level in a WSN will cause more adverse effect on data aggregation than on a lower-level node, the authors argue that by reducing number of nodes at the higher level in the logical tree, aggregation process becomes more secure.

In (Ozdemir, 2007), a secure and reliable data aggregation scheme – SELDA- is proposed that makes use of the concept of web of trust. Trust and reputation based schemes have been extensively used for designing security solutions for multi-hop wireless networks like *mobile ad hoc networks* (MANETs), *wireless mesh networks* (WMNs) and WSNs (Sen, 2010b; Sen, 2010c; Sen 2010d). In this scheme, sensor nodes exchange trust values in their neighborhood to form a *web of trust* that facilitates in determining secure and reliable paths to aggregators. Observations from the sensor nodes which belong to a web of trust are given higher weights to make the aggregation process more robust.

A *data aggregation and authentication* (DAA) protocol is proposed in (Cam & Ozdemir, 2007), to integrate false data detection with data aggregation and confidentiality. In this scheme, a monitoring algorithm has been proposed for verifying the integrity of the computed aggregated result by each aggregator node.

In order to minimize false positives (a scenario where an alert is raised, however there is no attack), in a WSN, a dynamic threshold scheme is proposed in (Parkeh & Cam, 2007), which dynamically varies the threshold in accordance with false alarm rate. A data aggregation algorithm is also proposed to determine the detection probability of a target by fusing data from multiple sensor nodes.

Du et al. proposed a *witness-based data aggregation* (WDA) scheme for WSNs to assure the validation of the data fusion nodes to the base station (Du et al., 2003). To prove the validity of the fusion results, the fusion node has to provide proofs from several witnesses. A witness is one who also conducts data fusion like a data fusion node, but does not forward its result to the base station. Instead, each witness computes the MAC of the result and then provides it to the data fusion node, which must forward the proofs to the base station. This scheme can defend against attacks on data integrity in WSNs.

Wagner studied secure data aggregation in sensor networks and proposed a mathematical framework for formally evaluating their security (Wagner, 2004). The robustness of an aggregation operator against malicious data is quantified. Ye et al. propose a *statistical en-route filtering mechanism* to detect any forged data being sent from the sensor nodes to the base station of a WSN using multiple MACs along the path from the aggregator to the base station (Ye et al., 2004; Ye et al., 2005).

8. The proposed distributed secure aggregation protocol

In this section, we propose a distributed estimation algorithm that is secure and resistant to insider attack by compromised and faulty nodes. There are essentially two categories of aggregation functions (Boulis et al., 2003):

- Aggregation functions that are dependent on the values of a few nodes (e.g., the *max* result is based on one node).
- Aggregation functions whose values are determined by all the nodes (e.g., the average function).

However, computation of both these types of functions are adversely affected by wrong sensed result sent by even a very few number of compromised nodes. In this chapter, we consider only the first case, i.e., aggregation function that find or approximate some kind of boundaries (e.g., maxima, minima), and hence the aggregation result is determined by the values of few nodes. However, the proposed algorithm does not assume any knowledge about the underlying physical process.

8.1 The proposed secure aggregation algorithm

In the proposed distributed estimation algorithm, a sensor node instead of transmitting a partially aggregated result, maintains and if required, transmits an estimation of the global aggregated result. The global aggregated description in general will be a vector since it represents multi-dimensional parameters sensed by different nodes. A global estimate will thus be a probability density function of the vector that is being estimated. However, in most of the practical situations, due to lack of sufficient information, complex computational requirement or unavailability of sophisticated estimation tools, an estimate is represented as: (*estimated value, confidence indication*), which in computational terms can be represented as: (*average of estimated vector, covariance matrix of estimated vector*). For the sake of manipulability with tools of estimation theory, we have chosen to represent estimates in the form of (A, P_{AA}) with A being the mean of the aggregated vector and P_{AA} being the covariance matrix of vector A. For the *max* aggregation function, vector A becomes a scalar denoting the mean of the estimated max, and P_{AA} becomes simply the variance of A.

In the snapshot aggregation, a node does not have any control on the rate at which it send information to its parents; it has to always follow the rate specified the user application. Moreover, every node has little information about the global parameter, as it has no idea about what is happening beyond its parent. In proposed approach, a node accepts estimations from all of its neighbors, and gradually gains in knowledge about the global information. It helps a node to understand whether its own information is useful to its neighbors. If a node realizes that its estimate could be useful to its neighbors, it transmits the new estimate. Unlike snapshot aggregation where the node transmits its estimate to its parent, in the proposed scheme, the node broadcasts its estimate to all its neighbors. Moreover, there is no need to establish and maintain a hierarchical relationship among the nodes in the network. This makes the algorithm particularly suitable for multiple user, mobile users, faulty nodes and transient network partition situations.

The proposed algorithm has the following steps:

1. Every node has an estimate of the global aggregated value (global estimate) in the form of (mean, covariance matrix). When a node makes a new local measurement, it makes an aggregation of the local observation with its current estimate. This is depicted in the block *Data Aggregation 1* in Fig. 5. The node computes the new global estimate and decides whether it should broadcast the new estimate to its neighbors. The decision is based on a threshold value as explained in Section 8.4.
2. When a node receives a global estimate from a neighbor, it first checks whether the newly received estimate differs from its current estimate by more than a pre-defined threshold.
    a. If the difference does not exceed the threshold, the node makes an aggregation of the global estimates (its current value and the received value) and computes a new global estimate. This is depicted in the block *Data Aggregation 2* in Fig. 5. The node then decides whether it should broadcast the new estimate.

    b.   If the difference exceeds the threshold, the node performs the same function as in step (a). Additionally, it requests its other neighbors to send their values of the global estimate.

    c.   If the estimates sent by the majority of the neighbors differ from the estimate sent by the first neighbor by a threshold value, then the node is assumed to be compromised. Otherwise, it is assumed to be normal.

3.   If a node is identified to be compromised, the global estimate previously sent by it is ignored in the computation of the new global estimate and the node is isolated from the network by a broadcast message in its neighborhood.

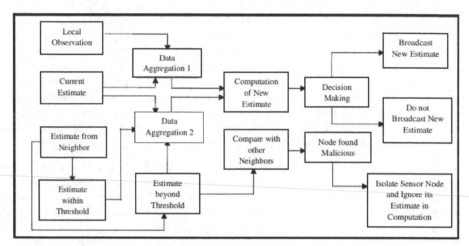

Fig. 5. A Schematic flow diagram of the proposed aggregation algorithm

8.2 Aggregation of two global estimates

In Fig. 5, the block *Data Aggregation 1* corresponds to this activity. For combining two global estimates to produce a single estimate, *covariance intersection* (CI) algorithm is used. CI algorithm is particularly suitable for this purpose, since it has the capability of aggregating two estimates without requiring any prior knowledge about their degree of correlation. This is more pertinent to WSNs, as we cannot guarantee statistical independence of observed data in such networks.

Given two estimates (A, P_{AA}) and (B, P_{BB}), the combined estimate (C, P_{CC}) by CI is given by (23) and (24):

$$P_{CC} = (\omega * P_{AA}^{-1} + (1-\omega)P_{BB}^{-1})^{-1} \tag{23}$$

$$C = P_{CC}(\omega * P_{AA}^{-1} * A + (1-\omega)P_{BB}^{-1} * B) \tag{24}$$

Here, P_{AA}, P_{BB}, and P_{CC} represent the covariance matrices associated with the estimates A, B, and C respectively. The main computational problem with CI is the computation of ω. The value of ω lies between 0 and 1. The optimum value of ω is arrived at when the trace of the determinant of P_{CC} is minimized.

For *max* aggregation function, covariance matrices are simple scalars. It can be observed from (23) and (24) that in such a case ω can be either 1 or 0. Subsequently, P_{CC} is equal to the minimum of P_{AA} and P_{BB}, and C is equal to either A or B depending on the value of P_{CC}. Even when the estimates are reasonably small-sized vectors, there are efficient algorithms to determine ω.

8.3 Aggregation of a local observation with a global estimate

This module corresponds to the block *Data Aggregation 2* in Fig. 5. Aggregation of a local observation with a global estimate involves a statistical computation with two probability distributions.

Case 1: Mean of the local observation is greater than the mean of the current global estimate: In case of *max* aggregation function, if the mean of the local observation is greater than the mean of the current global estimate, the local observation is taken as the new estimate. The distribution of the new estimate is arrived at by multiplying the distribution of the current global estimate by a positive fraction (w_1) and summing it with the distribution of the local observation. The fractional value determines the relative weight assigned to the value of the global estimate. The weight assigned to the local observation being unity.

Case 2: Mean of the local observation is smaller than the mean of the current global estimate: If a node observes that the mean of the local observation is smaller than its current estimate, it combines the two distributions in the same way as in *Case 1* above, but this time a higher weight (w_2) is assigned to the distribution having the higher mean (i.e. the current estimate). However, as observed in (Boulis et al., 2003), this case should be handled more carefully if there is a sharp fall in the value of the global maximum. We follow the same approach as proposed in (Boulis et al., 2003). If the previous local measurement does not differ from the global estimate beyond a threshold value, a larger weight is assigned to the local measurement as in *Case 1*. In this case, it is believed that the specific local measurement is still the global aggregated value.

For computation of the weights w_1 and w_2 in *Case 1* and *Case 2* respectively, we follow the same approach as suggested in (Boulis et al., 2003). Since all the local measurements and the global estimates are assumed to follow Gaussian distribution, almost all the observations are bounded within the interval $[\mu \pm 3*\sigma]$. When the mean of the local measurement is larger than the mean of the global estimate, the computation of the weight (w_1) is done as follows. Let us suppose that $l(x)$ and $g(x)$ are the probability distributions for the local measurement and the global estimate respectively. If $l(x)$ and $g(x)$ can take non-zero values in the intervals $[x_1, x_2]$ and $[y_1, y_2]$ respectively, then the weight $w_1(x)$ will be assigned a value of 0 for all $x \leq \mu_1 - 3*\sigma$ and $w_1(x)$ will be assigned a value of 1 for all $x > \mu_1 - 3*\sigma$. Here, x_1 is equal to $\mu_1 - 3*\sigma_1$, where μ_1 and σ_1 are the mean and the standard deviation of $l(x)$ respectively.

When the mean of the local measurement is smaller than the mean of the global estimate, the computation of the weight w_2 is carried out as follows. The value of $w_2(x)$ is assigned to be 0 for all $x \leq max \{\mu_1 - 3*\sigma_1, \mu_2 - 3*\sigma_2\}$. $w_2(x)$ is assigned a value of 1 for all $x > max \{\mu_1 - 3*\sigma_1, \mu_2 - 3*\sigma_2\}$. Here, y_1 is equal to $\mu_2 - 3*\sigma_2$, where μ_2 and σ_2 represent the mean and the standard deviation of $g(x)$ respectively.

In all these computations, it assumed that the resultant distribution after combination of two bounded Gaussian distributions is also a Gaussian distribution. This is done in order to maintain the consistency of the estimates. The mean and the variance of the new Gaussian distribution represent the new estimate and the confidence (or certainty) associated with this new estimate respectively.

8.4 Optimization of communication overhead

Optimization of communication overhead is of prime importance in resource constrained and bandwidth-limited WSNs. The block named *Decision Making* in Fig. 5 is involved in this optimization mechanism of the proposed scheme. This module makes a trade-off between energy requirement and accuracy of the aggregated results.

To reduce the communication overhead, each node in the network communicates its computed estimate only when the estimate can bring a significant change in the estimates of its neighbors. For this purpose, each node stores the most recent value of the estimate it has received from each of its neighbors in a table. Every time a node computes its new estimate, it checks the difference between its newly computed estimate with the estimates of each of its neighbors. If this difference exceeds a pre-set threshold for any of its neighbors, the node broadcasts its newly computed estimate. The determination of this threshold is crucial as it has a direct impact on the level of accuracy in the global estimate and the energy expenditure in the WSN. A higher overhead due to message broadcast is optimized by maintaining two-hop neighborhood information in each node in the network (Boulis et al., 2003). This eliminates communication of redundant messages. This is illustrated in the following example.

Suppose that nodes A, B and C are in the neighborhood of each other in a WSN. Let us assume that node A makes a local measurement and this changes its global estimate. After combining this estimate with the other estimates of its neighbors as maintained in its local table, node A decides to broadcast its new estimate. As node A broadcasts its computed global estimate, it is received by both nodes B and C. If this broadcast estimate changes the global estimate of node B too, then it will further broadcast the estimate to node C, as node B is unaware that the broadcast has changed the global estimate of node C also. Thus the same information is propagated in the same set of nodes in the network leading to a high communication overhead in the network.

To avoid this message overhead, every node in the network maintains its two-hop neighborhood information. When a node receives information from another node, it not only checks the estimate values of its immediate neighbors as maintained in its table but also it does the same for its two-hop neighbors. Thus in the above example, when node B receives information from node A, it does not broadcast as it understands that node C has also received the same information from node A, since node C is also a neighbor of node A. The two-hop neighborhood information can be collected and maintained by using algorithms as proposed in (McGlynn & Borbash, 2001).

The choice of the threshold value is vital to arrive at an effective trade-off between the energy consumed for computation and the accuracy of the result of aggregation. For a proper estimation of the threshold value, some idea about the degree of dynamism of the physical process being monitored is required. A more dynamic physical process puts a greater load on the estimation algorithm thereby demanding more energy for the same level of accuracy (Boulis et al., 2003). If the user has no information about the physical process, he can determine the level of accuracy of the aggregation and the amount of energy spent dynamically as the process executes.

8.5 Security in aggregation scheme

The security module of the proposed scheme assumes that the sensing results for a set of sensors in the same neighborhood follows a normal (Gaussian) distribution. Thus, if a node receives estimates from one (or more) of its neighbors that deviates from its own local estimate by more than three times its standard deviation, then the neighbor node is suspected to have been compromised or failed. In such a scenario, the node that first detected such an anomaly sends a broadcast message to each of its neighbors requesting for the values of their estimates. If the sensing result of the suspected node deviates significantly (i.e., by more than three times the standard deviation) from the observation of the majority of the neighbor nodes, then the suspected node is detected as malicious. Once a node is identified as malicious, a broadcast message is sent in the neighborhood of the node that detected the malicious node and the suspected node is isolated from the network activities.

However, if the observation of the node does not deviate significantly from the observations made by the majority of its neighbors, the suspected node is assumed to be not malicious. In such a case, the estimate sent by the node is incorporated in the computation of the new estimate and a new global estimate is computed in the neighborhood of the node.

9. Simulation results

In this section, we describe the simulations that have been performed on the proposed scheme. As the proposed algorithm is an extension of the algorithm presented in (Boulis et al., 2003), we present here the results that are more relevant to our contribution, i.e., the performance of the security module. The results related to the energy consumption of nodes and aggregation accuracy for different threshold values (discussed in Section 8.4) are presented in detail in (Boulis et al., 2003) and therefore these are not within the scope of this work.

In the simulated environment, the implemented application accomplishes temperature monitoring, based on network simulator (ns-2) and its sensor network extension Mannasim (Mannasim, 2002). The nodes sense the temperature continuously and send the maximum sensed temperature only when it differs from the last data sent by more than 2%.In order to simulate the temperature behaviour of the environment, random numbers are generated following a Gaussian distribution, taking into consideration standard deviation of 1°C from an average temperature of 25°C. The simulation parameters are presented in Table 3.

To evaluate the performance of the security module of the proposed algorithm, two different scenarios are simulated. In the first case, the aggregation algorithm is executed in the nodes without invoking the security module to estimate the energy consumption of the aggregation algorithm. In the second case, the security module is invoked in the nodes and some of the nodes in the network are intentionally compromised. This experiment allows us to estimate the overhead associated with the security module of the algorithm and its detection effectiveness.

Parameter	Value
No. of nodes	160
Simulation time	200 s
Coverage area	120 m * 120 m
Initial energy in each node	5 Joules
MAC protocol	IEEE 802.11
Routing protocol	None
Node distribution	Uniform random
Transmission power of each node	12 mW
Transmission range	15 m
Node capacity	5 buffers
Energy spent in transmission	0.75 W
Energy spent in reception	0.25 mW
Energy spent in sensing	10 mW
Sampling period	0.5 s
Node mobility	Stationary

Table 3. Simulation parameters

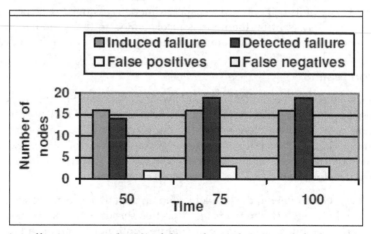

Fig. 6. Detection effectiveness with 10% of the nodes in the network faulty

It is observed that *delivery ratio* (ratio of the packets sent to the packets received by the nodes) is not affected by invocation of the security module. This is expected, as the packets are transmitted in the same wireless environment, introduction of the security module should not have any influence on the delivery ratio.

Regarding energy consumption, it is observed that the introduction of the security module has introduced an average increase of 105.4% energy consumption in the nodes in the network. This increase is observed when 20% of the nodes chosen randomly are compromised intentionally when the aggregation algorithm was executing. This increase in energy consumption is due to additional transmission and reception of messages after the security module is invoked.

To evaluate the detection effectiveness of the security scheme, further experiments are conducted. For this purpose, different percentage of nodes in the network is compromised and the detection effectiveness of the security scheme is evaluated. Fig. 6 and Fig. 7 present the results for 10% and 20% compromised node in the network respectively. In these diagrams, the false positives refer to the cases where the security scheme wrongly identifies a sensor node as faulty while it is actually not so. False negatives, on the other hand, are the cases where the detection scheme fails to identify a sensor node which is actually faulty. It is observed that even when there are 20% compromised nodes in the network the scheme has a very high detection rate with very low false positive and false negative rate. The results show that the proposed mechanism is quite effective in detection of failed and compromised nodes in the network.

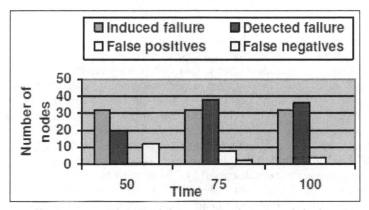

Fig. 7. Detection effectiveness with 20% of the nodes in the network faulty

10. Conclusion and future research issues

In-network data aggregation in WSNs is a technique that combines partial results at the intermediate nodes en route to the base station (i.e. the node issuing the query), thereby reducing the communication overhead and optimizing the bandwidth utilization in the wireless links. However, this technique raises privacy and security issues of the sensor nodes which need to share their data with the aggregator node. In applications such as health care and military surveillance where the sensitivity of the private data of the sensors is very high, the aggregation has to be carried out in a privacy-preserving way, so that the sensitive data are not revealed to the aggregator. A very popular scheme for this purpose exists in the literature which is known as CPDA. Although CPDA is in literature for quite some time now, no vulnerability of the protocol has been identified so far. In this chapter, we have first demonstrated a security vulnerability in the CPDA protocol, wherein a malicious sensor node can exploit the protocol is such a way that it gets access to the private values of its neighbors while participating in data aggregation process. A suitable modification of the CPDA protocol is further proposed so as to plug the identified vulnerability and also to make the protocol computationally more efficient. We have also made an analysis of the communication and computational overhead in the original CPDA protocol and the proposed modified version of the CPDA protocol. It has been found from the analysis that the modified version of the protocol involves appreciably less message communication overhead in the network and computational load on the sensor nodes.

We have also presented a comprehensive discussion on the existing secure aggregation protocols for WSNs and proposed a secure aggregation protocol for defending against attacks by malicious insider nodes that may introduce fake messages/data or alter data of honest nodes in the network. The performance of the proposed scheme has been evaluated on a network simulator and results have shown that the scheme is effective for defending attacks launched by malicious insider nodes in a WSN.

It may be noted that over the past few years, several schemes have been proposed in the literature for privacy preserving data aggregation in WSNs. A very popular and elegant approach in this direction is *homomorphic encryption* (Fontaine & Galand, 2007). Westhoff et al. have proposed additive privacy homomorphic functions that allow for end-to-end encryption between the sensors and the sink node and simultaneously enable aggregators to apply aggregation functions directly over the ciphertexts (Westhoff et al., 2006). This has the advantage of eliminating the need for intermediate aggregators to carry out decryption and encryption operations on the sensitive data. Armknecht et al. have presented a symmetric encryption scheme for sensor data aggregation that is homomorphic both for data and the keys (Armknecht et al., 2008). This is called *bi-homomorphic encryption*, which is also essentially an additive homomorphic function. Castellucia et al. have proposed an approach that combines inexpensive encryption techniques with simple aggregation methods to achieve efficient aggregation of encrypted data in WSNs (Castelluccia et al., 2009). The method relies on end-to-end encryption of data and hop-by-hop authentication of nodes. Privacy is achieved by using additive homomorphic functions. A very simple approach for privacy-preserving multi-party computation has been discussed by Chaum (Chaum, 1988). The protocol is known as *Dining Cryptographers Problem* which describes the way a channel is created so that it is difficult to trace (i.e. identify) the sender of any message through that channel.

The approaches based on privacy homomorphic functions are more elegant than CPDA for the purpose of carrying out sensor data aggregation in a privacy preserving way. However, they involve large computational overhead due to complexities involved in computing the homomorphic encryption functions and the associated key management related issues. Most of the existing public key cryptography-based privacy homomorphic functions are too heavy for resource-constrained battery-operated sensor nodes. Some secure data aggregation schemes use elliptic curve cryptography (Westhoff et al., 2006). However, these schemes work only for some specific query-based aggregation functions, e.g., sum, average etc. A more elegant scheme that works for all types of functions is clearly in demand. In (Gentry, 2009), a fully homomorphic function has been presented. However, this scheme is too complex and heavy-weight for deployment in WSNs. In addition, in some WSN environment, symmetric cryptography-based privacy homomorphic encryption schemes are more suitable (Castelluccia, 2005; Castelluccia, 2009; Ozdemir, 2008). However, most of the current homomorphic encryption schemes are based on public key encryption. Hence, exploration of symmetric key cryptography based privacy homomorphism functions is an interesting research problem. Another emerging research problem is the use of *digital watermarking* schemes in place of privacy homomorphic encryption functions (Zhang et al., 2008). However, this method allows only one-way authentication of sensor data at the base station only. To defend against *rogue base station attacks* on sensor nodes, this scheme would not be applicable. Design of mutual authentication scheme using watermarking techniques for secure and privacy-preserving data aggregation protocols is another research problem that needs attention of the research community.

11. References

Acharya, M.; Girao, J. & Westhohh, D. (2005). Secure Comparison of Encrypted Data in Wireless Sensor Networks. *Proceedings of the 3rd International Symposium on Modelling and Optimization in Mobile, Ad Hoc, and Wireless Networks (WIOPT)*, pp. 47-53, Washington, DC, USA, 2005.

Akyildiz, I. F.; Su, W.; Sankarasubramaniam, Y. & Cayirci, E. (2002). Wireless Sensor Networks: A Survey. *IEEE Computer*, Vol 38, No 4, pp. 393-422, March 2002.

Armknecht, F.; Westhoff, D.; Girao, J. & Hessler, A. (2008). A Lifetime-Optimized End-to-End Encryption Scheme for Sensor Networks Allowing In-Network Processing. *Computer Communications*, Vol 31, No 4, pp. 734-749, March 2008.

Bandyopadhyay, D. & Sen, J. (2011). Internet of Things: Applications and Challenges in Technology and Standardization. *International Journal of Wireless Personal Communications- Special Issue; Distributed and Secure Cloud Clustering (DISC)*, Vol 58, No 1, pp. 49-69, May 2011.

Boulis, A.; Ganeriwal, S. & Srivastava, M. B. (2003). Aggregation in Sensor Networks: An Energy-Accuracy Trade-Off. *Ad Hoc Networks*, Vol 1, No 2-3, pp. 317-331, September 2003.

Cam, H.; Muthuavinashiappan, D. & Nair, P. (2003). ESPDA: Energy-Efficient and Secure Pattern-Based Data Aggregation for Wireless Sensor Networks. *Proceedings of IEEE International Conference on Sensors*, pp. 732-736, Toronto, Canada, October 2003.

Cam, H.; Muthuavinashiappan, D. & Nair, P. (2005). Energy-Efficient Security Protocol for Wireless Sensor Networks. *Proceedings of the IEEE Vehicular Technology Conference (VTC'05)*, pp. 2981-2984, Orlando, Florida, October 2005.

Cam, H. & Ozdemir, S. (2007). False Data Detection and Secure Aggregation in Wireless Sensor Networks. *Security in Distributed Grid Mobile and Pervasive Computing*, Yang Xiao (ed.), Auerbach Publications, CRC Press, April 2007.

Cam, H.; Ozdemir, S.; Nair, P.; Muthuavinashiappan, D. & Sanli, H. O. (2006a). Energy-Efficient Secure Pattern Based Data Aggregation for Wireless Sensor Networks. *Computer Communications*, Vol 29, No 4, pp. 446-455, February 2006.

Cam, H.; Ozdemir, S.; Sanli, H. O. & Nair, P. (2006b). Secure Differential Data Aggregation for Wireless Sensor Networks. *Sensor Network Operations*, Phoha et al. (eds.), pp. 422-441, Wiley-IEEE Press, May 2006.

Castelluccia, C.; Chan, A. C-F.; Mykletun, E. & Tsudik, G. (2009). Efficient and Provably Secure Aggregation of Encrypted Data in Wireless Sensor Networks. *ACM Transactions on Sensor Networks*, Vol 5, No 3, May 2009.

Castelluccia, C. Mykletun, E. & Tsudik, G. (2005). Efficient Aggregation of Encrypted Data in Wireless Sensor Networks. *Proceedings of the 2nd Annual International Conference on Mobile and Ubiquitous Systems: Networking and Services (MobiQuitous'05)*, pp. 109-117, San Diego, California, USA, July 2005.

Chan, H.; Perrig, A.; Przydatek, B. & Song, D. (2007). SIA: Secure Information Aggregation in Sensor Networks. *Journal of Computer Security – Special Issue on Security of Ad Hoc and Sensor Networks*, Vol 15, No 1, pp. 69-102, January 2007.

Chaum, D. (1988). The Dining Cryptographers Problem: Unconditional Sender and Recipient Untraceability. *Journal of Cryptology*, Vol 1, No 1, pp. 65–75, 1988.

Deng, J.; Han, R. & Mishra, S. (2003). Security Support for In-network Processing in Wireless Sensor Networks. *Proceedings of the 1st ACM Workshop on Security of Ad Hoc and Sensor Networks (SASN'03)*, pp. 83-93, Fairfax, Virginia, USA, October 2003.

Du, W.; Deng, J.; Han, Y. S. & Varshney, P. K. (2003). A Witness-Based Approach for Data Fusion Assurance in Wireless Sensor Networks. *Proceedings of IEEE Global Telecommunications Conference (GLOBECOM'03)*, Vol 3, pp. 1435-1439, San Fransisco, USA, December 2003.

Eschenauer, L. & Gligor, V. D. (2002). A Key-Management Scheme for Distributed Sensor Networks. *Proceedings of the 9th ACM Conference on Computing and Communications Security (CCS'02)*, pp. 41- 47, Washington, DC, USA, November 2002.

Estrin, D.; Govindan, R.; Heidemann, J. S. & Kumar, S. (1999). Next Century Challenges: Scalable Coordination in Sensor Networks. *Proceedings of the 5th ACM/IEEE International Conference on Mobile Computing and Networking (MobiCom'99)*, pp. 263-270, Seattle, Washington, USA, August 1999.

Fontaine, C. & Galand, F. (2007). A Survey of Homomorphic Encryption for Nonspecialists. *EURASIP Journal on Information Security*, Vol 2007, Article ID 13801, January 2007.

Gentry, C. (2009). *A Fully Homomorphic Encryption Scheme*. Doctoral Dissertation, Department of Computer Science, Stanford University, USA, September 2009.

Girao, J.; Westhoff, D. & Schneider, M. (2005) CDA: Concealed Data Aggregation for Reverse Multicast Traffic in Wireless Sensor Networks. *Proceedings of the 40th IEEE Conference on Communications (IEEE ICC'05)*, Vol. 5, pp. 3044–3049, Seoul, Korea, May 2005.

Goel, S. & Imielinski. (2001). Prediction-Based Monitoring in Sensor Networks: Taking Lessons from MPEG. *ACM SIGCOMM Computing and Communication Review-Special Issue on Wireless Extensions to the Internet*, Vol 31, No 5, pp. 82-98, ACM Press, New York, October 2001.

He, W.; Liu, X.; Nguyen, H.; Nahrstedt, K. & Abdelzaher, T. (2007). PDA: Privacy-Preserving Data Aggregation in Wireless Sensor Networks. *Proceedings of the 26th IEEE International Conference on Computer Communications (INFOCOM'07)*, pp. 2045-2053, Anchorage, Alaska, USA, May 2007.

Heidemann, J.; Silva, F.; Intanagonwiwat, C.; Govindan, R.; Estrin, D. & Ganesan, D. (2001). Building Efficient Wireless Sensor Networks with Low-Level Naming. *Proceedings the 18th ACM Symposium of Operating Systems Principles (SOS'01)*, Banff, Canada, October 2001.

Hu, L. & Evans, D. (2003). Secure Aggregation for Wireless Networks. *Proceedings of the Symposium on Applications and the Internet Workshops (SAINT'03)*, pp. 384-391, Orlando, Florida, USA, January 2003.

Jaikaeo, C.; Srisathapomphat, C. & Shen, C. (2000). Querying and Tasking of Sensor Networks. *Proceedings of SPIE's 14th Annual International Symposium on Aerospace/Defence Sensing, Simulation and Control (Digitization of the Battlespace V)*, pp. 26-27, Orlando, Florida, USA, April 2000.

Karlof, C. & Wagner, D. (2003). Secure Routing in Sensor Networks: Attacks and Countermeasures. *AD Hoc Networks*, Vol 1, pp, 293-315, May, 2003.

Madden, S. R.; Franklin, M. J.; Hellerstein, J. M. & Hong, W. (2002). TAG: A Tiny Aggregation Service for Ad-Hoc Sensor Networks. *Proceedings of the 5th Symposium on Operating Systems Design and Implementation (OSDI'02)*, pp. 131-146, Boston, Massachusetts, USA, December 2002.

Madden, S. R.; Franklin, M. J.; Hellerstein, J. M & Hong, W. (2005). TinyDB: An Acquisitional Query Processing System for Sensor Networks. *ACM Transactions on Database Systems*, Vol 30, No 1, pp. 122-173, March 2005.

Mahimkar, A. & Rappaport, T. S. (2004). SecureDAV: A Secure Data Aggregation and Verification Protocol for Wireless Sensor Networks. *Proceedings of the 47th IEEE Global Telecommunications Conference (GLOBECOM)*, Vol 4, pp. 2175-2179, Dallas, Texas, USA, November- December, 2004.

Mannasim. (2002). Mannasim *Wireless Network Simulation Environment*. URL: http://www.mannasim.dcc.ufmg.br.

McGlynn, M. J. & Borbash, S. A. (2001). Birthday Protocols for Low-Energy Deployment and Flexible Neighbour Discovery in Ad Hoc Wireless Networks. *Proceedings of the 2nd ACM International Symposium on Mobile Ad Hoc Networking and Computing (MobiHoc'01)*, pp. 137-145, Long beach, California, USA, October 2001.

Merkle, R. C. (1980). Protocols for Public Key Cryptosystems. *Proceedings of the IEEE Symposium on Security and Privacy*, pp. 122-134, Oakland, California, USA, April 1980.

Ozdemir, S. (2007). Secure and Reliable Data Aggregation for Wireless Sensor Networks. *Proceedings of the 4th International Conference on Ubiquitous Computing Systems (UCS'07). Lecture Notes in Computer Science (LNCS)*, Ichikawa et al. (eds.), Vol 4836, pp. 102-109, Springer-Verlag Berlin, Heidelberg, Germany2007.

Ozdemir, S. (2008). Secure Data Aggregation in Wireless Sensor Networks via Homomorphic Encryption. *Journal of The Faculty of Engineering and Architecture of Gazi University*, Ankara, Turkey, Vol 23, No 2, pp. 365-373, September 2008.

Parekh, B. & Cam, H. (2007). Minimizing False Alarms on Intrusion Detection for Wireless Sensor Networks in Realistic Environments. *Proceedings of the IEEE Military Communications Conference (MILCOM'07)*, pp. 1-7, Orlando, Florida, USA, October 2007.

Peter, S.; Westhoff, D. & Castelluccia, C. (2010). A Survey on the Encryption of Convergecast Traffic with In-Network Processing. *IEEE Transactions on Dependable and Secure Computing*, Vol 7, No 1, pp. 20–34, February 2010.

Przydatek, B.; Song, D. & Perrig, A. (2003). SIA: Secure Information Aggregation in Sensor Networks. *Proceedings of the 1st International Conference on Embedded Networked Systems (SenSys'03)*, pp. 255-265, Los Angeles, California, USA, November 2003.

Sanli, H. O.; Ozdemir, S. & Cam, H. (2004). SRDA: Secure Reference-Based Data Aggregation Protocol for Wireless Sensor Networks. *Proceedings of the 60th IEEE Vehicular Technology Conference (VTC'04 Fall)*, Vol 7, pp. 4650-4654, Los Angeles, California, USA, September 2004.

Sen, J. (2009). A Survey on Wireless Sensor Network Security. *International Journal of Communication Networks and Information Security (IJCNIS)*, Vol 1, No 2, pp. 59-82, August 2009.

Sen, J. (2010a). Privacy Preservation Technologies for Internet of Things. *Proceedings of the International Conference on Emerging Trends in Mathematics, Technology and Management*, pp. 496-504, Shantiniketan, West Bengal, India, January 2010.

Sen, J. (2010b). A Distributed Trust and reputation Framework for Mobile Ad Hoc Networks. *Proceedings of the 1st International Conference on Network Security and its Applications (CNSA'10)*, Chennai, India, July 2010. *Recent Trends in Network Security and its Applications*, Meghanathan et al. (eds.), pp. 528–537, *Communications in Computer and Information Science (CCIS)*, Springer-Verlag, Heidelberg, Germany, July 2010.

Sen, J. (2010c). A Trust-Based Detection Algorithm of Selfish Packet Dropping Nodes in a Peer-to-Peer Wireless Mesh Networks. *Proceedings of the 1st International Conference* on *Network Security and its Applications (CNSA'10)*, Chennai, India, July 2010. *Recent Trends in Network Security and its Applications*, Meghanathan et al. (eds.), pp. 538–547, *Communications in Computer and Information Science (CCIS)*, Springer-Verlag, Heidelberg, Germany, July 2010.

Sen, J. (2010d). Reputation- and Trust-Based Systems for Wireless Self-Organizing Networks, pp. 91-122. *Security of Self-Organizing Networks: MANET, WSN, WMN, VANET*, A-S. K. Pathan (ed.), Aurbach Publications, CRC Press, USA, December 2010.

Sen, J. (2011). A Robust and Secure Aggregation Protocol for Wireless Sensor Networks. *Proceedings of the 6th International Symposium on Electronic Design, Test and Applications (DELTA'11)*, pp. 222-227, Queenstown, New Zealand, January, 2011.

Sen, J. & Maitra, S. (2011). An Attack on Privacy-Preserving Data Aggregation Protocol for Wireless Sensor Networks. *Proceedings of the 16th Nordic Conference in Secure IT Systems (NordSec'11)*, Tallin, Estonia, October, 2011. *Lecture Notes in Computer Science (LNCS)*, Laud, P. (ed.), Vol 7161, pp. 205-222, Springer, Heidelberg, Germany.

Shrivastava, N; Buragohain, C.; Agrawal, D. & Suri. (2004). Medians and Beyond: New Aggregation Configuration techniques for Sensor Networks. *Proceedings of the 2nd International Conference on Embedded Networked Sensor Systems*, pp. 239-249, ACM Press, New York, November 2004.

Wagner, D. (2004). Resilient Aggregation in Sensor Networks. *Proceedings of the 2nd ACM Workshop on Security of Ad Hoc and Sensor Networks (SASN'04)*, pp. 78-87, ACM Press, New York, USA, October 2004.

Westhoff, D.; Girao, J. & Acharya, M. (2006). Concealed Data Aggregation for Reverse Multicast Traffic in Sensor Networks: Encryption, Key Distribution, and Routing Adaptation. *IEEE Transactions on Mobile Computing*, Vol 5, No 10, pp. 1417-1431, October 2006.

Wu, K.; Dreef, D.; Sun, B. & Xiao, Y. (2007). Secure Data Aggregation without Persistent Cryptographic Operations in Wireless Sensor Networks. *Ad Hoc Networks*, Vol 5, No 1, pp. 100–111, January 2007.

Yang, Y.; Wang, X.; Zhu, S. & Cao, G. (2006). SDAP: A Secure Hop-by-Hop Data Aggregation Protocol for Sensor Networks. *ACM Transactions on Information and System Security (TISSEC)*, Vol 11, No 4, July 2008. *Proceedings of the 7th ACM International Symposium on Mobile Ad Hoc Networking and Computing (MOBIHOC'06)*, Florence, Italy, May 2006.

Ye, F.; Luo, H. & Lu, S. & Zhang, L. (2004). Statistical En-Route Filtering of Injected False Data in Sensor Networks. *Proceedings of the 23rd IEEE Annual International Computer and Communications (INFOCOM'04)*, Vol 4, pp. 2446-2457, Hong Kong, March 2004.

Ye, F.; Luo, H.; Lu, S. & Zhang, L. (2005). Statistical En-route Filtering of Injected False Data in Sensor Networks. *IEEE Journal on Selected Areas in Communications*, Vol 23, No 4, pp. 839-850, April 2005.

Zhang, W.; Liu, Y.; Das, S. K. & De, P. (2008). Secure Data Aggregation in Wireless Sensor Networks: A Watermark Based Authentication Supportive Approach. *Pervasive Mobile Computing*, Vol 4, No 5, pp. 658-680, Elsevier Press, October 2008.

Zhao, Y. J.; Govindan, R. & Estrin, D. (2002). Residual Energy Scan for Monitoring Sensor Networks. *Proceedings of IEEE Wireless Communications and Networking Conference (WCNC'02)*, Vol 1, pp. 356-362, March 2002.

10

Potential Applications of IPsec in Next Generation Networks

Cristina-Elena Vintilă
Military Technical Academy, Bucharest,
Romania

1. Introduction

IPsec is one of the most secure technologies nowadays. It is used in almost all institutions that are concerned with protecting their communications. Although IPsec is not a very hard set of protocols to understand and use, once you get into its details and try to understand how it works, what is its applicability and what are its limitations, you will find yourself surrounded by mathematics, cryptography and network protocol design challenges. Because IPsec is not just another "encryption" protocol. It is actually an entire stack of protocols, ranging from negotiation protocols, to authentication protocols, to access network technologies, tunnelling protocols, PKI availability, routing and last, but not least, a good deal of cryptography. Companies use IPsec to securely connect their branches to the headquarters or between each other, over the Internet. Just the same, the remote workers have the possibility to securely access their data located at their work place premises no matter where they are. One of the most important aspects of this technology is its authentication role. By itself, IPsec does not provide network authentication. The authentication role of this stack of protocols is reserved for the IKE procedures. Currently at version 2, IKE has managed to simplify the authentication process of a peer and at the same time has managed to increase the security of this process. One of the latest additions to these authentication procedures is the support for mobile subscriber authentication. This functionality is achieved by incorporating the UMTS-SIM and UMTS-AKA key exchange protocols, useful in the NGN world.

Authentication functionality is closely related to identity protection and identification. In a world of mobile devices and wireless communication, the identity theft and impersonation are a continuously raising concern. The NGN technologies require the provisioning of services at an end-to-end guaranteed quality of experience, provided through high data rates and aggressive SLAs. The aim of the future technologies is to provide multimedia services no matter the location of the subscribers, which assumes inter-operator agreements all over the Globe, location and presence services. In order to maintain a high level of quality and availability, proper authentication, correct authorization and detailed and rigorous accounting are essential. Examples of NGN networks range from 4G access networks, like WiMAX and SAE to the converged services core, as it is IMS. These technologies are still under development. Even though there are already a number of production implementations, the technologies are still perfecting; one aspect of this process is security. IPsec is an important part of the design of any NGN system, for its proved security in the wireline industry (Liu, 2010). It supports IPv4 a set of protocols on top of layer 3 design and it is natively integrated into IPv6. The development of IPv6 considered this technology as a native part of the layer 3 design, in order to provide for security mechanism of the future networks. IMS design (TS 24.229) was originally described as running only over IPv6.

This paper does a brief analysis of the security issues faced by the NGN mobile equipment users, as well as the ones faced by the NGN operators. As it describes the security challenges the NGN is going to face, it explores the areas where IPsec has been described as the answer to the question for a secure communication environment in the near future. The paper goes over the IPsec applications in a near future access network as WiMAX and SAE are, as well as the usage of this technology in the IMS world. IPsec integrates technologies like key agreement and management via the EAP and PKI frameworks. One goal of this paper is to identify use cases and scenarios where the IPsec of the future is going to take effect. Even though the NGN mobile terminals are already powerful enough to support the cryptographic computations necessary to function as an IPsec peer, these terminals may make use of the ECC technology to improve their performances. While encrypting the traffic with IPsec is a good security practice, applying this practice to VoIP or Video traffic, sensitive to delays and latencies, poses a number of efficiency challenges. This is when the IKE capabilities come into play; IPsec provides key exchange functionality for SIP negotiation, so that the IMS voice and video traffic is to be protected (RFC4475, 2006; Vrakas, 2010; Wang, 2009). While reviewing the role and capabilities of the IPsec, as well as its possible applications in the next generation architectures, this paper also identifies some of the challenges and limitations this framework faces in the NGN context: mobile IP and mobility management, resistance to denial of service attacks, multimedia protocols, IPv6 control protocols and so on. Though a classic security solution for wireline technologies, IPsec diversifies and evolves, acquires new features and capabilities, while at the same time getting lighter to accommodate the requirements of the mobile subscribers. This paper proposes a journey of understanding how the technology that secures our communications works and how it can be applied in the near-future applications and network design.

2. IPsec technologies

IPsec (Internet Protocol Security) can be defined as a complex set of protocols on top of IP, supported on both IPv4 and IPv6. By itself, IPsec refers to the technology employed in order to secure the transmission of information over an unprotected medium. The security of the transmission may be achieved by using two sets of protocols: ESP (Encapsulated Security Payload) and AH (Authentication Header). In order to be able to use one of these two protocols, or both of them at the same time, security information in the form of encryption and/or authentication keys must be available. This information may be statically pre-configured by a security administrator or it may be dynamically negotiated between the IPsec entities/peer. The first case is referred to as *manual keying*. In this case, the security administrator has already configured security information on both end of the IPsec communication channel; the traffic passing through the IPsec equipment and matching several conditions is to be protected using this information. The second way of achieving the security agreement between the IPsec aware devices is to dynamically negotiate the session information between the IPsec peers. This method has the advantage of dynamic keying, but it may also be susceptible to man-in-the-middle attacks in the first phases of the negotiation. The generic protocol employed to do the negotiation is called ISAKMP (Internet Security Association and Key Management Protocol), represented most commonly by the IKE (Internet Key Exchange) protocol, which has reached its second version. When discussion the use-cases that can take place in an IPsec environment, the IPsec peers may find themselves in one of these two scenarios: one is called *site-to-site* and the other one is called *remote-access*. These two scenarios both refer to the situation where the IPsec computation takes place either between two security gateways or between a security gateway and a stand-alone unit (laptop, pda, smartphone...) called *roadwarrior*; this scenario is also called *dial-up vpn* by some security vendors. There is a separate case where the IPsec peers want to transmit information between each-other in a secure manner, but without the use of an external service provider (as it is a security gateway). This case is called *transport mode*.

2.1 IPsec architecture and traffic logic

The main components of the IPsec architecture are the following:

a.   the Policy Agent: this component has the responsibility of negotiating the IPsec cryptographic parameters; these parameters refer to traffic identifiers (also called traffic selectors) that are input as a tuple in the Security Policy Database
b.   the Security Policy Database(SPD): this component is a database (considering it as a stand-alone database implementation or part of an operating system kernel); it consists of tuples that represent the traffic selectors of an IPsec agreement: the IP addresses or the subnet which the traffic to be secured belongs to, or, for some of the IPsec equipment on the market, it may also contain port numbers in order to identify the traffic
c.   the Security Association Database(SAD): this component is a database as well (stand-alone or part of a kernel implementation); it contains the IKE and IPsec security parameters that are negotiated: cryptographic algorithms, authentication information and identification information

Tuples in both databases are indexed and retrieved at run-time via their index, called SPI (Security Parameter Index), a value transmitted at run-time in each IPsec packet, in order for the receiver to select the proper tuple for decryption of the packet. The traffic logic flow of an IPsec use-case is the following: the Policy Agent is the one to start the IKE negotiation process, which consists of two phases (for each IKEv1 and IKEv2 protocols). The output of the Phase 1 is called ISAKMP SA(Security Association). The output of the Phase 2 is called IPsec SA. The IPsec processing engine adds a new layer of transformation for the actual network traffic; the engine is integrated to the TCP/IP stack of the system and it is called when a particular IP or a layer 4 segment matches the conditions for IPsec. Depending on each implementation, there may be available the configuration of different keys per traffic direction or a single set of keys for each IPsec tunnel. Also, there are ways to configure the Policy Agent to function based on the policy configured for that equipment (*policy-based tunnelling*), or to be triggered by a route utilization (*route-based tunnelling*).

2.2 Secure tunnel negotiation

In order to securely establish a dynamic IPsec tunnel, the ISAKMP – IKE protocol is used, whether its version 1 or version 2. Version 1 is considered less safe than version 2, where multiple security vulnerabilities where covered by safer implementation. IKEv1 is considered more difficult to implement. IKEv1 is described in RFC 2409 and it is currently implemented by all the major security equipment providers. Both IKEv1 and IKEv2 negotiate the IPsec SA in two phases. Phase 1 in IKEv1 can be accomplished in two separate and incompatible flows. One of them is referred to as *Main Mode* and it has 6 messages (or 3 exchanges), and the second one is called *Aggressive Mode* and it consists of 3 messages. Phase 2 of IKEv1 is referred to as *Quick Mode* and it has 3 messages.

The Main Mode messages are the following:

-   HDR ISAKMP SAi Proposal – request sent by the Initiator of the tunnel to the Responder, containing the encryption and authentication algorithms
-   HDR ISAKMP SAr Response – response sent by the Responder, containing its available encryption and authentication methods
-   HDR DH KEi, Ni – message identifying the Diffie-Hellman group and keying material, as well as the Initiator nonce
-   HDR DH KEr, Nr – same as the previous message, but identifying the Responder's capabilities
-   HDR IDi, Hashi – authenticates the Initiator's Identity
-   HDR IDr, Hashr – authenticates the Responder's Identity

Because the 5th and 6th messages are preceded by the exchange of cryptographic information and DH groups, the identities exchanged by them are already encrypted; this makes Main Mode exchange referred to as providing Identity Protection. This protection if identity does not happen for Aggressive Mode, where the phase 1 of IKEv1 has only 3 messages:

-   ISAKMP SAi Proposal, DH KEi, Ni, IDi – request sent by the Initiator, containing cryptographic information, Diffie-Hellman material, a nonce and the Identity of the Initiator – in clear
-   ISAKMP SAi Response, DH KEr, Nr, IDr, Hashr – same as the proposal, but with the Responder's information
-   HDR Hashi2 – the Initiator's hash

In the notations above, the "i" refers to the initiator of the IPsec negotiation, while the "r" refers to the responder of the IPsec negotiation offer.

Phase 1 is followed by Phase 2, also called *Quick Mode*. The purpose of this exchange is to negotiate the traffic selectors and the cryptographic information for the actual data-plane encapsulation. This traffic is referred to as *non-ISAKMP* by RFC 2409. Quick Mode is composed of three messages:

-   HDR, Hashi, SA, Ni, [KEi, IDi, IDr] – this message contains the IKE header, hash, SA, nonce and optionally the new DH key, and identities of the parties and it is send by the Initiator
-   HDR, Hashr, SA, Nr, [KEr, IDi, IDr] – same as above, but on the Responder side
-   HDR, Hashi2 – last message of the Initiator before sending traffic

The second version of IKE, IKEv2 is not fully supported by all equipments on the market, but it is starting to get more and more attention, due to its capabilities: faster tunnel setup, more secure negotiations, more consistent authentication and identification rules, simpler implementation etc. There is only one type of so-called Phase 1 and Phase 2 in IKEv2. The IKEv2 exchange is the following:

- HDR (IKE_SA_INIT), SAi1, KEi, Ni – the initial request coming from the Initiator and containing the cryptographic parameters, DH keys and a nonce
- HDR (IKE_SA_INIT), SAir, KEr, Nr, [CERTREQ] – same as above, the Responder having the possibility to ask for a digital certificate at this point
- HDR (IKE_AUTH), SK {IDi, [CERT,] [CERTREQ,] [IDr], AUTH, SAi2, TSi, TSr} – authentication message, encrypted and authenticated (as in the first exchange there was already sent the DH information), containing the authentication information, ID of the other party, SA and traffic selectors of the Initiator as well as the Responder
- HDR (IKE_AUTH) SK {IDr, [CERT,] AUTH, SAr2, TSi, TSr} – same as above, but from the Responder's side
- HDR (CREATE_CHILD_SA), SK {[N], SA, Ni, [KEi], [TSi, TSr]} – request for creating an SA (IPsec SA) with the nonces, DH keys and traffic selectors indicated
- HDR (CREATE_CHILD_SA) SK {SA, Nr, [KEr], [TSi, TSr]} – same as above, from Responder's side

The first four messages can be assimilated as Phase 1 of the IKEv2, and the last two messages as Phase 2 of the IKEv2. Nevertheless, at tunnel establishment time, only the first four messages appear in the negotiation, as usually the information provided by the last two messages is comprised in messages 3 and 4. The last 2 messages are used for the re-keying process.

2.3 Secure data transmission

After having established the secure parameters to be employed in order to protect the transmission of the data, two protocols can be used to achieved this security, either separate or both at the same time. These protocols are AH (RFC 4302) and ESP (RFC 4303). AH protocol number is 51 and the purpose of this protocol is to ensure protection against replay attacks, due to the integrity check and sequencing it employs. AH method makes a hash of the entire IP packet (both headers and data payload) and adds this has value to the packet sent over the wire. The only fields not taken into consideration when computing the hash value are the ones that are expected to change when routing occurs in a normal network: TTL, TOS, CRC etc. The ESP protocol number is 50 and this method encrypts the data using the material and algorithms negotiated earlier. ESP only encapsulates the payload.

2.4 Authentication and Identification

Two of the most important aspects of the IPsec negotiation are the authentication and identification. Not only do they perform two important functions (authenticating the IPsec peers to each other and identifying the peers to each other), but they are a crucial point for interoperability between different IPsec implementations. Not all networks worldwide happen to use exactly the same equipment as IPsec peers, so interoperability issues arise in many situations. RFC 2409 defines only two types of authentication available for IKEv1: PSK (pre-shared key) and digital certificates/RSA, while RFC 4306 for IKEv2 defines four authentication types: PSK, RSA, DSS and EAP (Extensible Authentication Protocol). The way these options are combined it is a totally different discussion. Most of the site-to-site implementations use a symmetrical authentication scheme (both peers use the same type of authentication for the tunnel being established). On the other hand, the remote-access scenarios many times use a hybrid authentication scheme, where the security gateway authenticates to the road-warriors via a digital certificate, while the clients are authenticated via a password. At the same time, if we are discussing IKEv2, where the EAP method is available, there are many more ways of authentication of the road-warriors.

Configuring PSK on devices is many time straight forward. The RSA configuration tends to be more difficult, as it assume the existence of a PKI infrastructure. As an example, on Strongswan, by default, there is a dedicated directory where the root certificates should reside (*/etc/ipsec.d/cacerts*). In */etc/ipsec.d/certs* the administrator should copy the IPsec certificates for the local machine. All these files paths may be changed from a configuration file (*/etc/ipsec.conf*). The certificates are usually supplied in *pem* format, but they can also be parsed in *der* format (this option is default for Windows CA servers) and the administrator can convert a certificate from one format to another using a tool like *openssl*. When exporting a certificate generated on the CA, both the public and the private keys are downloaded (because the *csr* file has been directly generated on the CA). In this case, the format presented is PKCS12. From PKCS12, the administrator is able to extract both the public key (in a digital certificate) and the private key, in separate files.

- from DER to PEM format:
openssl x509 -inform DER -in local.cer -outform PEM -out local.pem
- from PKCS12 to PEM format:
openssl pkcs12 -in myFile.p12 -out cert.pem -clcerts –nokeys

IOS, JunOS or StokeOS network operating systems usually keep the certificate information in their non-volatile memory.

The next step after achieve peer authentication is the proper identification of the peers to each other. This step is very important and it is also very important that the identities of the peers are not disclosed to unauthorized parties. This is one reason why Aggressive Mode method, which does not provide Identity Protection, is no longer included in IKEv2. RFC 2407 identifies the syntax for the identification variables in IKEv1, and RFC 4306 describes this syntax for IKEv2. The identification payload types for IKEv1 are the following: ID_IPv4_ADDR, ID_FQDN, ID_USER_FQDN, ID_IPV4_ADDR_SUBNET, ID_IPV6_ADDR, ID_IPV6_ADDR_SUBNET, ID_IPV4_ADDR_RANGE, IP_IPV6_ADDR_RANGE, ID_DER_ASN1_DN, ID_DER_ASN1_GN, ID_KEY_ID, and the ones for IKEv2 are the following: ID_IPV4_ADDR, ID_IPV6_ADDR, ID_FQDN, ID_RFC822_ADDR, ID_DER_ASN1_DN, ID_DER_ASN1_GN, ID_KEY_ID.

Identification is one of the major aspects when it comes to interoperability issues, especially when the administrator has to configure a particular type of identification mechanism which is not supported on the peer equipment. Strongswan for instance accepts ID_IP_ADDR (and ID_IP_ADDR_SUBNET for IKEv1), both v4 and v6, ID_FQDN, as in the certificate. The file also permits the configuration of an ID_ASN1_DER_CN, where the administrator can enter the entire subject of the certificate or only certain fields.

```
conn connection1
    left=192.168.0.1
    right=192.168.0.2
    leftid="C=RO,     ST=Romania,     L=Bucharest,     O=Company,     OU=Department,
    CN=DebianTest/emailAddress=debian@test.com"
    rightid="C=US,    ST=California,    L=Calabasas,    O=Company,    OU=Department,
    CN=Test1"
```

Other equipment has a more or less similar way of defining this set of parameters.

A particular case is IEKv2-EAP. This protocol is described by RFC 3748 and it supports the following internal EAP methods: MD5, TLS, SIM, AKA etc. While MD5 is a simple protocol that can be implemented locally on the IPsec peer, TLS, SIM or AKA usually require an external Radius server, like ACS, FreeRadius or NPS. This is not a mandatory condition, but it is a good practice to have the authentication server separated from the IPsec peer. TLS can be used for almost any type of connection and it may also only authentication the server to the client, as per the TLS specifications. SIM protocol was defined for authentication in 2G networks, used for proving the GSM Subscriber Identity of the client to the 3G access network; this protocol is described in RFC 4186. EAP-AKA (Authentication and Key Agreement) has been defined for authentication of the 3G subscribers to the 3G networks which have a Radius server. Further on, the EAP-AKA is the preferred method of the 4G network authentication procedures, when the mobile equipment to be authenticated is a non-native 4G equipment. LTE uses the native AKA procedure for authenticating the native 4G handset, using the AAA proxy for mobile devices connecting from WiFi or WLAN areas.

An example of an EAP-SIM and EAP-AKA users as they are defined in a FreeRadius implementation is described below.

```
user1 Auth-Type := EAP, EAP-Type := EAP-TLS, Password == "p@ssw0rd"
eapsim1 Auth-Type := EAP, EAP-Type := SIM
EAP-Sim-RAND1 = 0x201112131415161718191a1b1c1d1e1f,
EAP-Sim-SRES1 = 0xd2d2d3d4,
EAP-Sim-KC1 = 0xa0a2a2a3a4a5a6a7,
eapaka1 Auth-Type := EAP, EAP-Type := AKA
EAP-Sim-AUTN = 0xa0a0a0a0a0a0a0a0a0a0a0a0a0a0a0a0,
EAP-Aka-IK = 0xb0b0b0b0b0b0b0b0b0b0b0b0b0b0b0b0,
EAP-Aka-CK = 0xc0c0c0c0c0c0c0c0c0c0c0c0c0c0c0c0,
EAP-Sim-RES = 0xd0d0d0d0d0d0d0d0d0d0d0d0d0d0d0d0,
EAP-Sim-RAND = 0xe0e0e0e0e0e0e0e0e0e0e0e0e0e0e0e0,
```

As for the moment, the IPsec technology is mature enough and considered stable. Improvements have been made to IKEv2 to support a large range of scenarios. What is of interest in this paper is how much of IPsec can actually be used in the Next Generation Networks, with emphasis on 4G-SAE, the mobile technology that has the greatest area of attention at the moment. We can use IPsec in a peer-to-peer manner for providing hop-by-hop security between core network elements, but we should be able to learn a lot from its authentication and negotiation stages in order to secure the 4G access level, which is of bigger interest due to the large number of devices that will try to connect, as well as due to the large number of connectivity and mobility scenarios employed (Wang, 2008).

There are multiple studies regarding the security of the IPsec, and specially the IKE protocols. One of them (Cremers, 2011) identifies the following vulnerabilities: Reflection attack on IKEv1 Main Mode with digital signatures or pre-shared keys, Reflection attack on IKEv1 Quick Mode, Reflection attack on IKEv1 Main Mode with public key encryption, Authentication failure on IKEv1 Aggressive Mode with digital signatures, Authentication failure on IKEv1 Main Mode with digital signatures that does not require self-communication, Reflection attack on IKEv2 phase 2 exchange. Another important aspect of the IPsec protocol is the computational overhead, described in detail in (Xenakis, 2006). The factors taken into account are the encryption type and the authentication mechanism, and the resultants reflect in the system throughput, total delay and rate increase of the protected data. (Shue, 2007) Overall, the throughput overhead is larger than the overhead brought in by upper layer security protocols, like SSL or TLS, but the security offered by IPsec is also higher and the protocol can tunnel and secure a larger variety of traffic protocols than SSL or TLS can.

3. 4G and services networks technologies

4G is the next generation network technology at the moment. 4G is a generic term that defines a set of features and capabilities for a radio network, as well as for quality of service, mobility and services provided to the customer. It is not strictly related to a particular technology. It has been declared that both WiMAX and LTE are considered 4G technologies. WiMAX is being standardized by the WiMAX forum, being developed from the 802.16 family of wireless standards. The 802.16 is also being called *fixed* WiMAX and was published in 2001. In 2005, the 802.16e family was deployed, called *mobile* WiMAX. In 2011, there have begun to appear implementations of 802.16m. At the same time, the 3GPP forum also worked on improving the UMTS technology, which is considered a 3G generation. This is how the LTE (Long Term Evolution) technology came into existence. LTE is considered a 4G technology and it proposes an all-IP network, simplifying the access level of the network, as well as providing support for higher transmission rates due to improvements on the radio side and dynamic or seamless handover to both 3G networks, as well as to non-3GPP networks, like WiMAX or WLAN. Both 4G technologies are aiming at providing a simple and transparent access to the services network, for their subscribers. One example of services network is the IMS (IP Multimedia Subsystem), developed by 3GPP. IMS supports a large area of services, from simple data, voice and video to sms, mms, push-to-talk, conferencing and presence. A different approach to connecting to an IMS network is the direct access to Internet, where the services accessed may be the same ones as accessed from a wireless connection, without being provided in a unified manner, as in IMS. There is also possible an intermediary solution, where the services network is only referring to the Application Servers (AS) part of the IMS, overlooking the call session functions (Plewes, 2007; Sayyad, 2011).

From now on, the paper will provide a short introduction into the 3GPP LTE technology and discuss the security issues that appear at the access layer of this architecture (Kowtarapu, 2009). We will see what decisions the 3GPP forum has made in terms of protocols to use, their advantages and vulnerabilities and investigate how we can use the lessons learnt from our experience with IPsec.

3.1 3GPP LTE architecture and services network

The 4G-LTE architectures comprises two main components: the radio access network and the EPC (Evolved Packet Core). The radio access network is the eNodeB(the antenna) and the radio medium. The core network contains multiple devices, with roles in signaling, authentication, routing, providing quality of service and so on. The following elements are the most common devices located in the LTE core network (TS 23.203, TS 23.401, TS 29.274, TS 33.401):

a.   MME (Mobility Management Entity): it deals with user registration to the network, signalling and mobility management; it can be partially assimilated with the SGSN (Serving GPRS Support Node) from the UMTS architecture, with two major differences: the MME, unlike the SGSN, only does signalling, and, unlike SGSN, additionally has a management position towards the antennas; the MME connects to the database that holds the subscriber authentication information, having a very important role in the user authentication; in 3G, the RNC (Radio Network Controller) had the dedicated function of antenna management;

b.   SGW (Serving Gateway): unlike the MME, this entity does both signalling and traffic plane and it is responsible for routing data traffic to a particular set of radio cells (called Tracking Areas);

c.   PGW (Packet Data Network Gateway): this component is the one connecting the access network (LTE network) to the services network (IMS, Internet, Intranet etc); it is also one of the QoS enforcement points, together with the antenna; the PGW is connected to the database that holds the subscriber information; this entity may be assimilated to the 3G GGSN (Gateway GPRS Support Node) (Good, 2007);

d.   PCRF (Policy Charging and Rules Function): the policy database holding the subscription information material (Yang, 2011);

e.   HSS (Home Subscriber Server): the database holding information about the mobile equipment identity and credentials;

The picture below is a schematic representation of a typical 4G network (TS 29.061), where the access side is done via native 4G environment, as well as via 3G and non-3GPP media.

The antenna is the first point of contact of the user to the LTE network. The mobile equipment connects to the network, identifies this network and upon the user signalling to the network, the LTE starts the authentication process. The entities involved in this process are the mobile equipment, as one of the authentication peers (the client), the HSS, as the second authentication peer (the server), the MME as the authenticator and the eNB, as a sort of authentication relay. The MME is the one requesting the UE (User Equipment) its identity information, when downloading credentials from the HSS, in order to start the authentication process and secure key establishment with the mobile. The protocol used for this process is AKA (in native 4G and 3G) and EAP-AKA for the non-3GPP access. Once the authentication is complete, there take place several keys determination, based on mathematical functions defined by 3GPP. The key hierarchy is different for each case: 3G. 4G and non-3GPP. In the 4G case, there are keys for securing and/or authenticating both signalling and data-plane traffic flows, unlike 3G, where only the data-plane was secured. Also, there are specific requirements on how to assure a safe interoperability function between these types of access levels. For instance, the handover from a 4G network to a 3G network is simpler and does not require additional cryptographic computation, while the handover from a 3G network to a 4G network is more cumbersome. In order to achieve authentication for the non-3GPP devices, one or more 3GPP-AAA servers are needed and a ePDG (Evolved Packet Data Gateway). This ePDG entity is the other end of the authentication scenario, the peer the mobile connects to for authentication (Guo, 2010).

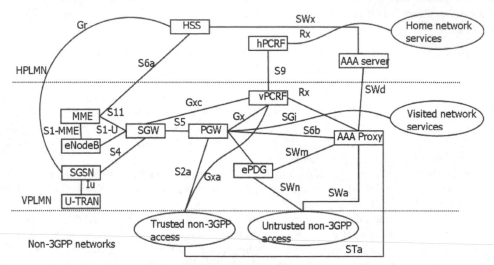

Fig. 1. NGN architecture; local breakout with home & visited network operator's functions

Roaming is an aspect with importance when it comes to security (authentication, authorization as well as accounting and charging). Generically, there are three types of roaming: home routed traffic (the PGW is located in the home network), local breakout with home operator's application functions only (the PGW is located in the visited network, but the services the user accesses are provided by its home network, as it is the example of using an e-mail service) and local breakout with visited operator's application functions only (the PGW is in the visited network as well, but the visited network also provides the services in this case, having a roaming agreement with the home network, in order for that; the home network only serves at assuring the authentication of the user and the policy verification).

Independent of the details of implementation of the access network, the PGW ultimately connects the UE to an APN (Access Point Name) via the SGi interface, an IP-based logical interface. The APN is the services network, no matter the actual format of this network: Internet, Intranet, IMS etc. The typical case considered in this paper is the IMS network. In this case, the PGW connects to the P-CSCF equipment of the IMS core.

The centre of the IMS functionality is the CSCF (Call Session Control Function), provided via three different logical entities: a Proxy (P-CSCF), an Interrogating unit (I-CSCF) and a Serving unit (S-CSCF). The P-CSCF is the first point of contact in the IMS network, staying always in the SIP signalling path and being able to do traffic inspection, SIP header compression (SigComp) and secure tunnelling to the UE: this is the entity the mobile IMS-aware handset establishes and IPsec session with. The P-CSCF can also do media-plane QoS enforcement. The S-CSCF is responsible for registration, message inspection and for selecting the AS (Application Server) that is to serve the subscriber. Assigning a particular S-CSCF to a certain subscriber is the task of the HSS, which is interrogated by the I-CSCF to provide this information. Just as for the 4G network, the IMS relies on the existence of HSS and PCRF databases. The standards move towards a more intimate and efficient integration of the 4G and IMS networks.

3.2 Security aspects

The security aspects in such a complex environment are many and complex. 3GPP has defined five security levels in order to separate the areas that are somehow independent of each other (TS 33.203).

a.   Network Access Security: this area deals with granting access to the (core) network only to those users that prove their identity, that identity matching a network's registered user, with valid authentication credentials and with a subscription that allows services to be delivered to this user;
b.   Network Domain Security: this area deals with the secure interoperation between the Evolved Packet Core (EPC) network entities; this security is described by the protocols involved in securing the communications between EPC nodes: IPsec (recommended by Specs to take place within an operator's premises) and TLS (usually for inter-operator secure communications);
c.   User Domain Security: this area deals with the secure access to the mobile stations;
d.   d. Application Domain Security: this area is concerned with how to secure the communication between the applications that reside on the user's mobile device and the core network application servers; as a layer 7 application, this area may implement a large variety of security structures;
e.   Visibility and Configurability of Security: this is an informational area, for the user; the subscriber must have constant access to the information concerning the security features available on his device, whether or not they are functioning properly and whether or not they are required for the secure operation of a certain service

When it comes to access to the 4G network, there are two aspects that threaten the security of the model. These aspects are related to the EPS-AKA procedures and there are the lack of identity protection at the first Initial Attach to the network (where the user must send its IMSI over the air, unencrypted) and the lack of the PFS (Perfect Forward Secrecy) property of the AKA algorithm. Sending the IMSI over the air is a problem only for the very first Attach Request, because the subsequent requests are done using a temporary global identity (GUTI).

This attach request message is sent by the UE to the MME; this request may be a TAU (Tracking Area Update), procedure mandatory when moving between areas of radio cells. When the new MME receives this message, it retrieves the identity of the previous MME from the message, and contacts this previous MME. In the message, the new MME requests the IMSI for the GUTI it provides. This way, under the fair assumption that the connection between MMEs is secured (via IPsec for instance), the IMSI identity of the UE is protected.

With regards to the services network, there are a lot of vulnerabilities, some related directly to the security capabilities of the SIP and RTP protocols, while some other to the network design, authentication, authorization and user profile. ETSI has developed the TVRA model in order to organize a table of security vulnerabilities description. The table below proposes a summary of the VoIP networks vulnerabilities, organized on the TVRA model (Edwards 2007; Karopoulos, 2010; VoIPSA, 2011).

No.	Asset	Weakness	Threat	Location	Incident	Objective
1	SIP Session	Signal w/o confidentiality	SIP sniffer	Gm	Loss of privacy	Confidentiality
2	Network topology	Weak authentication and control mechanism	Scan	Gm/Mw	Loss or privacy	Confidentiality
3	SIP Session	Signal w/o confidentiality	SIP Bye attack	Gm	Session damage	Integrity
4	SIP Register	UE configuration	configuration tampering	UE	DoS	Availability
5	SIP Register	DNS reliability	DNS cache attacks	Gm	DoS	Availability
6	SIP Register	Weak authentication and control mechanism	P-CSCF-in-the-middle attack	Gm	Impersonation attack (P-CSCF)	Authentication
7	SIP	Lack of DoS/DDoS prevention	SIP Register flooding	Gm	DoS	Availability
8	SIP Session	Weak authentication and control mechanism	Message Spoofing	Gm	Impersonation attack (user)	Authentication
9	RTP Session	No integrity protection	RTP insert attack	Gm	Session damage	Integrity
10	RTP Session	Weak control of streams	Media theft	UE-UE	Service theft	Accountability
11	RTP Session	Weak authentication and control mechanism	SPIT	UE-UE	User exhaust	Controllability
12	User profile	Weak authentication and control mechanism	SIP SQL injection	HSS	DoS	Availability

Table 1. VoIP TVRA model example

Along with the list of vulnerabilities, there are organizations that discuss these security issues in more details and also present the current status of the security tools available for assessing the level of security of this type of networks (Plewes, 2007).

4. Security solutions and alternative models

4.1 4G GAA security solution

The 3GPP forum defines a generic authentication scheme, named GAA (Generic Authentication Architecture), which as two main components: the component responsible for authentication via shared secrets, GBA (Generic Bootstrapping Authentication) and the component responsible for authentication via digital certificates, SSC (Support for Subscriber Certificates). There are six entities as defined by the GAA: HSS, BSF, NAF, ZnProxy, SLF and UE. The figure below describes an authentication scenario where the UE is located in roaming, and there is a third, untrusted, network between the visited and the home network.

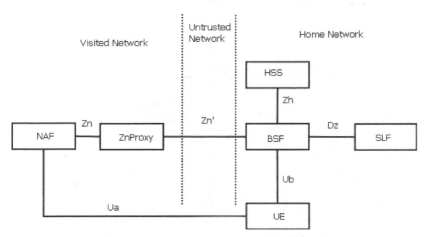

Fig. 2. GBA simplified architecture

The HSS is the database holding the USS (User Security Settings). It has the purpose of mapping the USS to one or more private user identities, which in IMS is called IMPI (IP Multimedia Private Identity). An example of USS is the GUSS (GBA User Security Settings), which may contain the following parameters: type of UICC, lifetime of the subscriber's key, timestamp etc. The BSF (Bootstrapping Server Function) has the role to authenticate the UE, via the AKA method. Before that, it communicates to the HSS in order to download AV (Authentication Vector) parameters used to derive the keying material for AKA. A native 4G handset should support discussion EPS-AKA with the BSF. The NAF (Network Application Function) is a generic server that the UE tries to connect to. The BSF derives the Ks_NAF key and sends it to the NAF. The UE also generates also a Ks_NAF key. For this procedure to function properly, the BSF should have connectivity to the NAF the user connects to. The BSF should keep a list of NAFs and a list of groups of NAFs, in order to be able to identify at any given moment which NAF should be chosen if an application-specific USS appears. (Aiash, 2010; Keromytis, 2010) The ZnProxy appears in the roaming cases, and it may be a stand-alone device or part of the functionality of an existing device, like the visited NAF, visited AAA server or an application server. This entity has the role of locating the user's home BSF device. In cases where there are multiple HSS databases, the SLF (Subscriber Location Function) is the entity queried by the BSF in order to locate the HSS containing the authentication information. The following steps describe the bootstrapping procedure:

1.   UE sends the HTTP request to the BSF, inserting an user identity, either its IMPI or its TMPI, if it has a temporary ID available;
2.   The BSF identifies whether it received a TMPI or an IMPI; if it was a TMPI, it looks for the corresponding IMPI in its cache, and if it's not found, it gives an error to the UE, requesting the IMPI, otherwise it continues authenticating the UE to the HSS.

Then the BSF tries to locate the HSS and retrieve the GUSS and the AV from it, where AV=(RAND||AUTN||XRES||CK||IK), over Zh;

3.   BSF forwards the RAND and AUTN to the UE, in order to authenticate it;
4.   The UE uses AUTN to authenticate the network, then computes the XRES, CK and IK and
5.   sends the XRES to the BSF, in order to be authenticated by this entity and

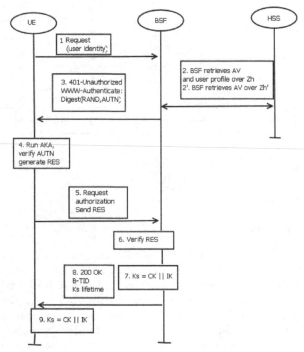

Fig. 3. GBA procedure

1.   the BSF verifies the XRES against its already computed RES; if they match, the UE is authenticated;
2.   The BSF obtains the Ks by concatenating CK and IK, same as the UE and
3.   replies to the UE with a B-TID in the 200 OK message;
4.   The UE also obtains the Ks by concatenating its CK and IK

At this point, both the UE and the BSF derive the Ks_NAF key, the actual key that will be used to secure the communication between the UE and the NAF.

Ks_NAF = KDF (Ks, "gba-me", RAND, IMPI, NAF_Id), where KDF is the key derivation function and the NAF_Id looks like this: NAF_Id = FQDN of the NAF || Ua security protocol identifier. All the values possible and structure of these components are defined in references.

4.2 IMS AKA procedure

The IMS network is the NAF server from the above topology (more exactly, the P-CSCF plays the role of the NAF server). Another method to do subscriber authentication is the SIP-AKA procedure. The purpose of this procedure is to authenticate the user and exchange keying material for IPsec (Chen, 2008; MSF, 2011; Nasser, 2009; TR 33.978).

I have executed several tests, using an IMS client and an IMS CSCF solution. The figure below describes the theoretical exchange, while some of the traffic captures are included following the theoretical description.

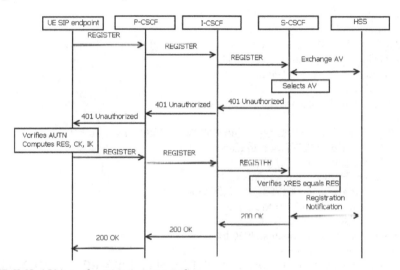

Fig. 4. SIP-IMS-AKA authentication procedure

The first packet of the conversation is the SIP REGISTER, which at first does not contain any authentication methods, nor information.
Request-Line: REGISTER sip:open-ims.test SIP/2.0
Method: REGISTER
Request-URI: sip:open-ims.test
[Resent Packet: False]
Message Header
Via: SIP/2.0/UDP 172.20.1.1:1143;rport;branch=z9hG4bK1275411663890
From: <sip:11111@open-ims.test>;tag=6334
    To: <sip:11111@open-ims.test>
Call-ID: M-50a5456166f246b78f081ac2453ee4ea
    CSeq: 901 REGISTER
Max-Forwards: 70
Allow: INVITE, ACK, CANCEL, BYE, MESSAGE, OPTIONS, NOTIFY, PRACK, UPDATE, REFER

Contact: <sip:11111@172.20.1.1:1143;transport=udp>;expires=600000;+deviceID="3ca50bcb-7a67-44f1-afd0-994a55f930f4";mobility="fixed"
User-Agent: IM-client/OMA1.0 Mercuro-Bronze/v4.0.1624.0
P-Preferred-Identity: <sip:11111@open-ims.test>
Supported: path
P-Access-Network-Info: ADSL;eutran-cell-id-3gpp=00000000
Privacy: none
Content-Length: 0

The P-CSCF locates the S-CSCF assigned by the HSS and collects the AKA information from there, one or more AVs, containing the following parameters: RAND, AUTN, XRES, IK, CK. The RAND and AUTN are passed on to the UE, via the 401 Unauthorized SIP message, while the XRES is kept for comparison.

Status-Line: SIP/2.0 401 Unauthorized - Challenging the UE
Message Header
Via: SIP/2.0/UDP 172.20.1.1:1143;rport=1143;branch=z9hG4bK1275411663890
From: <sip:11111@open-ims.test>;tag=6334
    SIP from address: sip:11111@open-ims.test
    SIP from address User Part: 11111
    SIP from address Host Part: open-ims.test
    SIP tag: 6334
To: <sip:11111@open-ims.test>;tag=925746a962736b96138042b427df6549-2212
    SIP to address: sip:11111@open-ims.test
    SIP to address User Part: 11111
    SIP to address Host Part: open-ims.test
    SIP tag: 925746a962736b96138042b427df6549-2212
Call-ID: M-50a5456166f246b78f081ac2453ee4ea
CSeq: 901 REGISTER
Path: <sip:term@pcscf.open-ims.test:4060;lr>
Service-Route: <sip:orig@scscf.open-ims.test:6060;lr>
Allow: INVITE, ACK, CANCEL, OPTIONS, BYE, REFER, SUBSCRIBE, NOTIFY, PUBLISH, MESSAGE, INFO
Server: Sip EXpress router (2.1.0-dev1 OpenIMSCore (i386/linux))
Content-Length: 0
Warning: 392 172.21.119.1:6060 "Noisy feedback tells: pid=2028 req_src_ip=172.21.118.1 req_src_port=5060 in_uri=sip:scscf.open-ims.test:6060 out_uri=sip:scscf.open-ims.test:6060 via_cnt==3"
WWW-Authenticate: Digest realm="open-ims.test", nonce = "qxZ3KUqjXlvgogK8aNtyH L4yoDzYBwAAFNpK0YllC1w=", algorithm = AKAv1-MD5, qop="auth,auth-int"
Authentication Scheme: Digest
realm="open-ims.test"
nonce="qxZ3KUqjXlvgogK8aNtyHL4yoDzYBwAAFNpK0YllC1w="
algorithm=AKAv1-MD5
qop="auth

SIP-AKA provides mutual authentication. The UE uses the AUTN to authenticate the network and if this authentication is successful, it then computes the RES (response) and sends it to the P-CSCF. It also derives the CK and IK keys.

Request-Line: REGISTER sip:open-ims.test SIP/2.0
Message Header
Via: SIP/2.0/UDP 172.20.1.1:1143;rport;branch=z9hG4bK1275411663891
From: <sip:11111@open-ims.test>;tag=6334
To: <sip:11111@open-ims.test>
Call-ID: M-50a5456166f246b78f081ac2453ee4ea
CSeq: 902 REGISTER
Max-Forwards: 70
Allow: INVITE, ACK, CANCEL, BYE, MESSAGE, OPTIONS, NOTIFY, PRACK, UPDATE, REFER
Contact: <sip:11111@172.20.1.1:1143;transport=udp>;expires=600000;+deviceID="3ca50bcb-7a67-44f1-afd0-994a55f930f4";mobility="fixed"
User-Agent: IM-client/OMA1.0 Mercuro-Bronze/v4.0.1624.0
Authorization: Digest algorithm=AKAv1-MD5,username="11111@open-ims.test", realm= "open-ims.test",nonce="qxZ3KUqjXlvgogK8aNtyHL4yoDzYBwAAFNpK0YllC1w=",uri="sip:open-ims.test",response="974679fa1f988670b52ebd3b058cf42a",qop=auth-in
    P-Preferred-Identity: <sip:11111@open-ims.test>
    Supported: path
    P-Access-Network-Info: ADSL;eutran-cell-id-3gpp=00000000
    Privacy: none
    Content-Length: 0

Upon the receipt of this message, the P-CSCF authenticates the user by comparing the RES and XRES values, and sends a reply back to acknowledge this fact.

Status-Line: SIP/2.0 200 OK - SAR successful and registrar saved
Message Header
Via: SIP/2.0/UDP 172.20.1.1:1143;rport=1143;branch=z9hG4bK1275411663891
From: <sip:11111@open-ims.test>;tag=6334
To: <sip:11111@open-ims.test>;tag=925746a962736b96138042b427df6549-5b6b
Call-ID: M-50a5456166f246b78f081ac2453ee4ea
CSeq: 902 REGISTER
P-Associated-URI: <sip:11111@open-ims.test>
Contact: <sip:11111@172.20.1.1:1143;transport=udp>;expires=600000
Path: <sip:term@pcscf.open-ims.est:4060;lr>
Service-Route: <sip:orig@scscf.open-ims.test:6060;lr>
Allow: INVITE, ACK, CANCEL, OPTIONS, BYE, REFER, SUBSCRIBE, NOTIFY, PUBLISH, MESSAGE, INFO
Server: Sip EXpress router (2.1.0-dev1 OpenIMSCore (i386/linux))
Content-Length: 0
Warning: 392 172.21.119.1:6060 "Noisy feedback tells: pid=2027 req_src_ip=172.21.118.1 req_src_port=5060 in_uri=sip:scscf.open-ims.test:6060 out_uri=sip:scscf.open-ims.test:6060 via_cnt==3"

The two parties (the UE and the P-CSCF) may use the CK and IK keys to establish an IPsec tunnel.

4.3 IPsec in end-to-end security

The most common case of the IPsec usage in a 4G network is the simple end-to-end implementation of the protocol between the mobile device and the services network peer (a security gateway, server or another peer) (Vintilă, 2010). A representation of this scenario is pictured in the figure below.

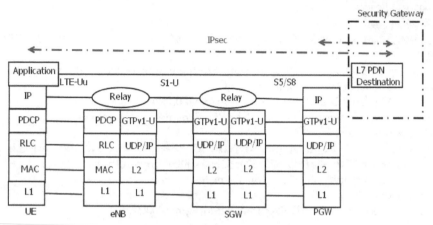

Fig. 5. IPsec scheme in LTE topology

The ends of the IPsec tunnels are the UE and the P-CSCF. The IMS negotiation messages would look the following. The first REGISTER message contains the IPsec declaration. Some of the headers have been excluded to save editing space.

Request-Line: REGISTER sip:open-ims.test SIP/2.0
Security-Client: ipsec-3gpp; alg=hmac-sha-1-96; spi-c=666; spi-s=777; port-c=1234; port-s=5678
Require: sec-agree
Proxy-Require: sec-agree
The reply from the P-CSCF is initially a 401 Unauthorized.
Status-Line: SIP/2.0 401 Unauthorized - Challenging the UE
Message Header
Security-Server: ipsec-3gpp; q=0.1; alg=hmac-sha-1-96;spi-c=222;spe-s=333;port-c=2345;port-s=3456

The second REGISTER message looks like this:

Request-Line: REGISTER sip:open-ims.test SIP/2.0
Security-Client: ipsec-3gpp; alg=hmac-sha-1-96; spi-c=666; spi-s=777; port-c=1234; port-s=5678
Security-Verify: ipsec-3gpp; q=0.1; alg=hmac-sha-1-96;spi-c=222;spe-s=333;port-c=2345;port-s=3456
Require: sec-agree
Proxy-Require: sec-agree

The IPsec tunnel is thus negotiated.

For the VoIP networks, there can be used up to five different security mechanisms: digest, TLS, IPsec-IKE, IPsec-man and IPsec-3gpp, the latter being specified by 3GPP. This end-to-end security mechanism should not be influenced by the handover scenarios. This is because the local security association between the UE, the MME and eNB are refreshed during handover and/or TAU procedures, while the "application" security associations are maintained. This assumption holds as long as the UE is attached to a particular PGW. If the UE detaches, there is no guarantee it will get the same IP the next time it attaches and even in that case, the IPsec tunnel is torn down.

In the NAT scenarios, the issues that impact the wireline IPsec are the same in the NGN case.

The mobile device has to follow specific steps to get authenticated in the 4G network. Similar or totally different steps must be taken to authenticate to each services network. The process for 4G is EPS-AKA or EAP-AKA. In the IMS network it can authenticate via IMS-AKA and secure the traffic via TLS or IPsec. But, because IMS is a special kind of services network, being closely described by 3GPP in conjunction with the access network, some part of the security weight already established can be used to secure the access to the services network. The following scheme tries to lessen the cryptographic and message exchange burden of the UE to IMS authentication process, by using the PGW as an authentication proxy. This happens because the PGW is the closest 4G entity to the IMS network. It should be in direct connection to the P-CSCF. The PGW unpacks both the signaling GTPv2-c packets as well as the GTPv1-u data-plane packets that arrive on the S5/S8 interface. Being at the edge of the 4G network, it is also able to inspect the content of these message or forward packets that match some particular criteria (port number, protocol number, ToS value etc) to a separate, dedicated, inspection entity. It is fairly simple to identity the IMS SIP packets (for instance by the port number, usually 5060). In the classic model, the SIP packets would simply be forwarded to the P-CSCF, as the PGW (GGSN) has no specific IMS-aware functionality (Vintilă, 2011).

In the proposed scheme, before the Initial Attach procedure, the UE selects 'p' and 'g' primes non-null and a secret 'a', then uses these values to derive value A from the Diffie-Hellman procedure: $A=g^{\wedge}a \bmod p$. Then the UE inserts value A, p and g (or only A if p and g are somehow agreed upon from a pre-configured setting), then adds them to the PCO (Protocol Configuration Options) IE in the Attach Request message to the MME, PCO IE that propagates to the PGW in the Create Session Request message. This entity looks at the values received and computes value $B=g^{\wedge}b \bmod p$, where b is its key. After it verifies that the UE is valid and sends it an IP (or an empty IP, if it is to be configured later dynamically), and includes also the B value in the PCO from the Create Session Response. The response gets back to the UE in the Attach Accept message. At this moment, the UE and the PGW derive a common Diffie-Hellman key K, which they can use as a symmetrical encryption key or as a master key to derive further key for securing traffic between them. The UE sends the SIP Register message and includes its secret key SIP-K, encrypted with K. This message arrives at the PGW.

The P-CSCF discovery procedure follows next, while the PGW acts on behalf of the UE during the IMS authentication. If the authentication is successful, the PGW will announce the UE (via a 200 OK message) that the UE is connected to the IMS core.

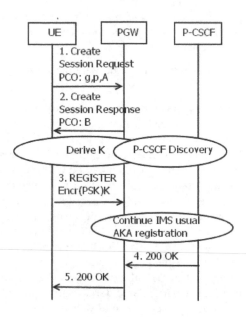

Fig. 6. Proposed scheme

Although it saves only a few messages, this scheme has the main advantage of decreasing both the network load, as well as the cryptographic computation on the UE. One of the disadvantages of this scheme is that the cryptographic computation actually increases in the beginning, due to the DH procedure. The advantage is that the DH key can be used as a master key for further exchanges and this key remains valid for duration of the attach. Another disadvantage is that the model produces small functionality changes in the UE functionality. The SIP implementation will need to store the secret key in a dedicated header. This should not be a great impediment in the implementation of this feature, as the SIP protocol is highly flexible and there is no 100% agreed implementation in the industry, at this moment. Another advantage is that the IMS model, being relatively mature and stable, is not needed to implement this mode. The internal IMS-AKA procedure remains unchanged. The PGW replies to the 401 Unauthorized message; it verifies the AUTN, computes the RES and replies to P-CSCF. A secondary benefit is the generation of a secret key which can be used as a master key to derive cryptographically resistant session keys for later use.

5. Conclusion

IPsec is considered one of the most secure protocols in the Internet. It is being successfully used in securing traffic all over the Internet, in the wireline technologies. Whether the use case involves companies trying to secure traffic between their branches or trying to assure a secure remote connection for its mobile workers, the IPsec is one of the preferred protocols. IPsec is a complex set of protocols, and none of the solutions right now on the market actually implement all of it. This situation leads to many incompatibility cases between different IPsec implementations. Nonetheless, IPsec is widely implemented and the differences in implementation many times constitute market differentiators.

As it is so popular in wireline technologies, industry and researchers investigate ways to implement IPsec or parts of it in the wireless technologies, as well, in order to export its benefits to the telecommunications world. Protocols used in IPsec are already implemented in technologies like WiMAX and UMTS: AKA, used as an EAP method in IPsec – IKEv2 authentication procedures. In 4G, the 3GPP forum looks into the EAP-AKA procedure for authenticating mobile handsets that attach to the 4G network from non-3GPP access radio networks. 3GPP also makes use of the IPsec in the IMS security: IPsec-3GPP, negotiated not via IKE, but via SIP signaling. Other IPsec alternatives appear as IPsec-man and IPsec-IKE in the SIP negotiation, along with digest and TLS.

The examples provided using open-source implementations in tools like OpenIMSCore, Strongswan or FreeRadius demonstrate how the IPsec protocols can be configured. Although different security equipment producers provide alternative configuration methods, the overall input aspect is similar, according to the purpose served. Adapting IPsec onto mobile devices would mean a significant work on improving its computational overhead and also some of the security aspects. One idea would be to use elliptic curve cryptography, used already in IPsec, but not implemented extensively in the industry so far.

The model proposed in this paper does a very short incursion in a scenario where the PGW, a very powerful device of the LTE core network, takes up part of the cryptographic burden of the authentication process of a mobile device to an IMS network. There is no doubt IPsec has gained a powerful sit in the NGN world and there are to be expected many improvements that address the shortcomings of its implementation in the mobile world.

6. References

Mahdi Aiash, Glenford Mapp, Aboubaker Lasebae, Raphael Phan, Providing Security in 4G Systems: Unveiling the Challenges, *AICT '10 Proceedings of the 2010 Sixth Advanced International Conference on Telecommunications*, ISBN: 978-0-7695-4021-4 [last access: June 2011]

Chi-Yuan Chen, Tin-Yu Wu, Yueh-Min Huang, Han-Chieh Chao, An efficient end-to-end security mechanism for IP multimedia subsystem, *Computer Communications*, Volume 31 Issue 18, December, 2008 [last access: June 2011]

Cas Cremers, Key Exchange in IPsec revisited: Formal Analysis of IKEv1 and IKEv2, ETH Zurich, Switzerland, *ESORICS 2011, Leuven, September 2011*

John Edwards, A Guide to Understanding the VoIP Security Threat, February 2007,
        http://www.voip-news.com/feature/voip-security-threat-021407/ [last access: June
        2011]

Richard Good, Fabricio Carvalho Gouveia, Shengyao Chen,Neco Ventura, Thomas
        Magedanz, Critical Issues for QoS Management and Provisioning in the IP
        Multimedia Subsystem, *Journal of Network and Systems Management*, Volume 16
        Issue 2, June 2008 [last access: June 2011]

Xiaogang Guo, Hao Xue, Shuguang Chen, The optimized data network security system
        based on 4G system for power grid system, *GMC '10 Proceedings of the 2010 Global
        Mobile Congress*, ISBN: 978-1-4244-9001-1 [last access: June 2011]

Giorgos Karopoulos, Georgios Kambourakis, Stefanos Gritzalis, Elisavet Konstantinou, A
        framework for identity privacy in SIP, *Journal of Network and Computer Applications*,
        Volume 33 Issue 1, January, 2010 [last access: June 2011]

Angelos D. Keromytis, Voice over IP: Risks, Threats and Vulnerabilities, *5th Ph.D. School on
        Security in Wireless Networking (SWING)*, Bertinoro, Italy, June/July 2010 [last
        access: June 2011]

Chakravarthy Kowtarapu, Chetan Anand, Guruprasad K.G., Shishir Sharma, Network
        separation and IPsec CA certificates-based security management for 4G networks,
        Bell Labs Technical Journal - 4G Wireless Technologies, Volume 13 Issue 4, February
        2009 [last access: June 2011]

Yang Liu, Zhikui Chen, Feng Xia, Xiaoning Lv, Fanyu BuA, Trust Model Based on Service
        Classification in Mobile Services, *GREENCOM-CPSCOM '10 Proceedings of the 2010
        IEEE/ACM Int'l Conference on Green Computing and Communications & Int'l
        Conference on Cyber, Physical and Social Computing*, ISBN: 978-0-7695-4331-4 [last
        access: June 2011]

MSF forum - VoLTE seminar
        http://www.msforum.org/interoperability/MSF-VoLTE-SCN-001-FINAL.pdf
        [last access: June 2011]

Nidal Nasser, Ming Shang, Policy control framework for IP Multimedia Subsystem, *ISTA
        '09 Proceedings of the 2009 conference on Information Science, Technology and
        Applications*, ISBN: 978-1-60558-478-2 [last access: June 2011]

Anthony Plewes, The biggest VoIP security threats - and how to stop them, March 2007,
        http://www.silicon.com/legacy/research/specialreports/voipsecurity/0,3800013
        656,39166479,00.htm [last access: June 2011]

Anthony Plewes, VoIP threats to watch out for, March 2007,
        http://www.silicon.com/special-features/voip-security/2007/03/09/voip-
        threats-to-watch-out-for-39166244/ [last access: June 2011]

M. Sayyad, N. Ansari, S. Burli, H. Shah   Thakur, A. Khatanhar, Review of IP multimedia
        subsystem, *ICWET '11 Proceedings of the International Conference & Workshop on
        Emerging Trends in Technology*, ISBN: 978-1-4503-0449-8 [last access: June 2011]

Craig A. Shue, Minaxi Gupta, Stefan A. Myers, IPSec: Performance Analysis and
        Enhancements, CiteSeer,
        http://www.cs.indiana.edu/cgi-pub/cshue/research/icc07.pdf   [last   access:
        September 2011]

SIP Torture Test Messages
    http://www.ietf.org/rfc/rfc4475.txt [last access: June 2011]
TS 23.203, Policy and Charging control architecture,
    http://www.3gpp.org/ftp/specs/archive/23_series/23.203/ [last access: June 2011]
TS 23.401, GPRS enhancements for E-UTRAN access,
    http://www.3gpp.org/ftp/specs/archive/23_series/23.401/ [last access: June 2011]
TS 24.229, IMS Call Control based on SIP and SDP,
    http://www.3gpp.org/ftp/specs/archive/24_series/24.229/ [last access: June 2011]
TS 29.061, Interworking between PLMN supporting packet-based services and PDN,
    http://www.3gpp.org/ftp/specs/archive/29_series/29.061/ [last access: June 2011]
TS 29.274, EPS – GTPv2-C
    http://www.3gpp.org/ftp/specs/archive/29_series/29.274 [last access: June 2011]
TS 33.203, 3G security,
    http://www.3gpp.org/ftp/specs/archive/33_series/33.203/ [last access: June 2011]
TS 33.401, SAE – Security Architecture,
    http://www.3gpp.org/ftp/Specs/archive/33_series/33.401/ [last access: June 2011]
TR 33.978, Security Aspects of Early IMS,
    http://www.3gpp.org/ftp/specs/archive/33_series/33.978/ [last access: June 2011]
Cristina-Elena Vintilă, A solution for secure SIP conferencing over IMS and SAE, *WSEAS TRANSACTIONS on COMMUNICATIONS*, Volume 9 Issue 7, July 2010 [last access: June 2011]
Cristina-Elena Vintilă, Victor-Valeriu Patriciu, Ion Bica, A J-PAKE based solution for secure authentication in a 4G network, *NEHIPISIC'11 Proceeding of 10th WSEAS international conference on electronics, hardware, wireless and optical communications, and 10th WSEAS international conference on signal processing, robotics and automation, and 3rd WSEAS international conference on nanotechnology, and 2nd WSEAS international conference on Plasma-fusion-nuclear physics*, 2011 ISBN: 978-960-474-276-9 [last access: June 2011]
VoIPSA – Voice over IP Security Alliance
    http://www.voipsa.org/ [last access: June 2011]
N. Vrakas, D. Geneiatakis, C. Lambrinoudakis, A Call Conference Room Interception Attack and Detection, *Proceedings of the 7th International Conference on Trust, Privacy & Security in Digital Business* (TrustBus 2010), Bilbao, Spain, 2010, Lecture Notes in Computer Science LNCS, Springer
Dong Wang, Chen Liu, Model-based Vulnerability Analysis of IMS Network, *Journal of Networks*, Vol. 4, No. 4, June 2009 [last access: June 2011]
TS 23.228, IMS Release 8,
    http://www.3gpp.org/ftp/specs/archive/23_series/23.228/ [last access: June 2011]
Christos Xenakis, Nikolaos Laoutaris, Lazaros Merakos, Ioannis Stavrakakis, A generic characterization of the overheads imposed by IPsec and associated cryptographic algorithms, *Computer Networks*, Volume 50, Issue 17, 5 December 2006, Pages 3225-3241 [last access: September 2011]
Yong Yang, Fernandez Alonso, Charging correlation for dedicated bearers, WIPO Patent Application WO/2011/039348 [last access: June 2011]

Yu-mei Wang, Jian Qin, Rong-jun Li,Jia-Jia Wen, Managing feature interaction based on service broker in IP multimedia subsystem, *Proceeding Mobility '08 Proceedings of the International Conference on Mobile Technology, Applications, and Systems*, ISBN: 978-1-60558-089-0 [last access: June 2011]

11

Comparative Analysis of Master-Key and Interpretative Key Management (IKM) Frameworks

Saman Shojae Chaeikar, Azizah Bt Abdul Manaf and Mazdak Zamani
Universiti Teknologi Malaysia
Malaysia

1. Introduction

The process of generating, distributing and revoking a cryptographic key is called key management (Piper & Murphy, 2002; Fumy & Landrock, 1993). Key management is a very challenging area between cryptographers and attackers, and since finding keys of approved cryptographic techniques computationally is impossible, attackers prefer to somehow breach the key management process instead of trying to crack keys (Techateerawat & Jennings, 2007).

Today many techniques like DES, 3DES, RSA etc. have emerged for protecting data secrecy. One internationally approved and widely used key management method is master-key which empowers a computer to generate keys from a Key Derivation Key (KDK), the parties' identity, labels and some other information (Chen, 2009). By utilizing master-key a computer can generate new keys and distribute them among its nodes, sometimes even establishing a hierarchy among them (Onmez, 2009).

IKM has developed from performing some changes on workflow and key generation algorithms of master-key to achieving more dynamism and some advanced features like intelligent attack resiliency (Chaeikar et al., 2010b, 2010a).

Master-key and IKM have many features in common. In both there are algorithms of key generation, both use environmental parameters as key generation parameters, both generate symmetric keys, both generate keys of variable length and so on. Therefore it was felt that there was a need for guidelines on both schemes to facilitate making a choice regarding requirements. The purpose of this article is to provide a guideline for helping researchers and developers to choose the proper cryptographic scheme between master-key and IKM regarding their goal of application and working criteria. To do so, master-key and IKM are compared according their security features and amount of imposed traffic load on the server and network.

The second section of this chapter explains the process of master-key key generation in three modes. The third part discusses IKM key generation workflow and algorithms concisely. The fourth part compares these two methods in terms of security and performance to help researchers and developers to choose the most convenient technique between master-key and IKM with regard to their required features and criteria. The last section summarizes the results of this analysis in a few paragraphs for fast review of this article.

2. Master-key

A key derivation function is a function that uses an input key and some other input data to produce keying material which will be employed by a cryptographic algorithm. A key that is input of key derivation function is called a Key Derivation Key (KDK). This key either can be generated by an automated key generation process (Piper & Murphy, 2002; Fumy & Landrock, 1993) or by an approved random bit generator function (Onmez, 2009). If a KDK is generated through an automated key generation process then it will be considered as part of secret keying material of that process.

Any chosen part of derived keying material which meets the needed key length can be used as input of cryptographic algorithm. To ensure that all parties using the same Key Derivation Function (KDF) are synchronized they must agree on the way that the keying material will convert into a cryptographic key. For instance, if derived keying material length is 256 bits then the first segment (first 128 bits) can be used as an authentication key and the second segment (second 128 bits) as an encryption key.

If KDF uses Pseudo Random Function (PRF) then based on desired length of keying material the KDF might require calling PRF several times to achieve the desired length. This article explains three types of master-key key generation modes. The following notations are described concisely for a better understanding of algorithms.

K_I: a key which will be fed into a KDF for deriving the keying material.

K_O: binary string output of KDF.

Label: a binary string that explains the goal of key derivation.

Context: a binary string including information such as identities of parties which are deriving/using derived keying material and sometimes a nonce which is known by those parties who derived the keys.

IV: initial binary string value of first iteration of feedback mode which either can be kept public or secret. IV also might be an empty string.

L: an integer which shows length of derived keying material K_O in bits. Length of binary string varies based on the encoding method of input data.

h: an integer which shows length of PRF output in bits.

n: an integer which shows the number of needed PRF iterations to achieve L bits of keying materials.

i: binary string input of PRF in each iteration.

r: an integer smaller or equal to 32 which shows binary length of counter i.

{X}: shows that the value of X is an optional value for KDF.

0x00: separator of different parts of variable length data fields.

A PRF type KDF concatenates n times output of PRF until it achieves the L bits of desired length where $n=\lceil L/h \rceil$. In counter mode n should not exceed $2^r - 1$ while $r \leq 32$. For double-pipeline iteration and feedback mode maximum value of n is $2^{32} - 1$. In every iteration of PRF the KDK K_I will be used as key and the input data includes both fixed input data and an iteration variable. Iteration value depending on iteration mode can be a counter, the result of last iteration of PRF, a mix of both or the result of first iteration if the mode is double pipeline.

2.1 Counter mode key derivation function (KDF)

Counter mode result of PRF will use a counter as iteration value. Counter mode is structured as follows:

h: PRF result length in bits.
r: length of binary format of counter i.

Input data: K_I, L, Context, and Label   *Output*: K_O

Counter mode KDF algorithm:

1.   n=⌈L/h⌉
2.   if n > 2^r − 1 then error
3.   result(0):= ∅
4.   for i=1 to n do
       4.1. K(i):= PRF(K_I,[i]$_2$ | | Label| | 0x00| | Context| | [L]$_2$)
       4.2. Result(i):= result(i-1)| | K(i)
5.   Return: K_O:= first L bits of result(n)

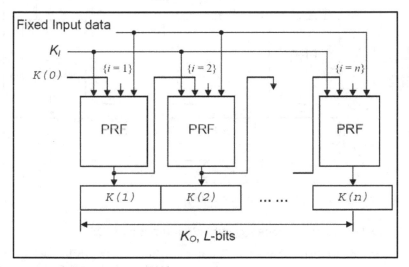

Fig. 1. Counter mode KDF structure (Chen, 2009)

In every round of iteration constant input values are Label| |0x00| |Context| |[L]$_2$ and iteration variables are K(i-1){| | [i]$_2$}. The structure of counter mode is illustrated in Fig. 1.

2.2 Feedback mode key derivation function (KDF)

In feedback mode the result of the PRF is generated according the results of last iteration and counter of number of iterations. Feedback mode is structured as follows:

h: PRF result length in bits.
r: length of binary format of counter i.

Input data: K_I, L, IV, Context, and Label.   *Output*: K_O.

Feedback mode KDF algorithm:

1. $n=\lceil L/h \rceil$
2. If $n > 2^{32} - 1$ then error
3. Result(0):= $\emptyset$ and K(0):= IV
4. For i = 1 to n, do
   4.1 $K(i):= PRF (K_I, K(i-1)\{||[i]_2\}||Label||0x00||Context||(L)_2)$
   4.2 Result(i):=result(i-1)||K(i)
5. Return: K_O:= first L bits of result(n)

In every round of iteration constant input values are Label$||0x00||$Context$||[L]_2$ and iteration variables are $K(i-1)\{||[i]_2\}$. The structure of feedback mode is illustrated in Fig. 2.

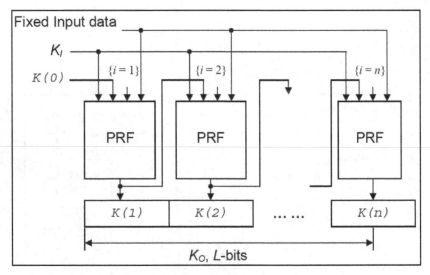

Fig. 2. Feedback mode KDF structure (Chen, 2009)

2.3 Double pipeline iteration mode key derivation function (KDF)

In counter mode or feedback mode the PRF iterates in a single pipeline while in double pipeline iteration mode there are two pipelines. In the first pipeline series of secret values A(i) will be generated which then will be fed into respective PRF iteration of the second pipeline. Double pipeline iteration mode is structured as follows:

h: PRF result length in bits.
r: length of binary format of counter i.

Input data: K_I, L, Context, and Label   *output*: K_O.

Double pipeline mode KDF algorithm:

1. $n= \lceil L/h \rceil$

2. if $n \leq 2^{32}$ then error
3. result(0):= $\emptyset$

4. $A(0):=IV=Label||0x00||Context||[L]_2$
5.   For i=1 to n do
5.1 $A(i) := PRF (K_I, A(i-1))$
5.2 $K(i) := PRF (KI, A(i)\{||[i]_2\}||Label||0x00||Context||[L]_2)$
5.3 Result (i) := result(i-1) $||K(i)$
6.   Return:K_0, i.e., first L bits of result(n)

The first iteration pipeline uses the result of feedback mode with the initial value of $A(0)=IV=Label||0x00||Context||(L)_2$. $K(i)$ by using $A(i)$, and as an optional choice, counter $(i)_2$ are iteration variables in every iteration of the second pipeline. The following figure illustrates double pipeline KDF.

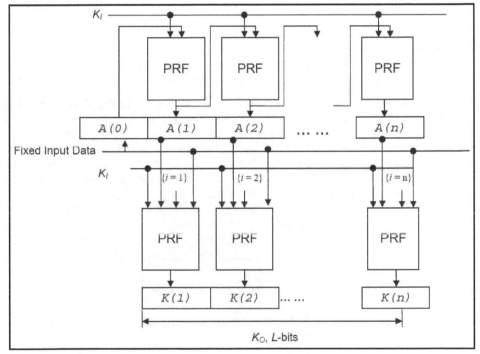

Fig. 3. Double pipeline mode KDF structure (Chen, 2009)

2.4 Key derivation key (KDK) length

In some of KDFs length of KDK depends on PRF. For instance, if Cipher-based Message Authentication Code (CMAC) was being used as PRF then key length directly depends on length of the respective block cipher. Therefore, at application time, consistency of PRF and KDK must be checked.

In contrast to CMAC if Keyed-hash Message Authentication Code (HMAC) was being used as PRF then the KDK can be almost any length. To provide consistency of PRF output and block length, if the key is longer than hash function block length then the key will be hashed into the length of the hash function output.

2.5 Conversion of keying material into cryptographic keys

The derived keying material length depends on the chosen cryptographic algorithm. The algorithm that will apply generated cryptographic key, like message authentication code, will determine its length. If no limitation is defined by the application then any portion of derived keying material, which has needed length, can be employed as a cryptographic key only if there is no overlapping among derived keys from KDF output. Therefore, length of derived keying material must be more or equal with the sum of keys.

3. Interpretative key management (IKM)

Core of Interpretative Key Management (IKM) workflow is a key server which is responsible for:

Producing the interpreter
Distributing the produced interpreter among nodes
Supervising nodes' activities for higher security
Declaration of revocation of the interpreter to nodes when it expires

The first responsibility of the server is generating the interpreter to be distributed among the nodes. The interpreter includes a time zone, a calendar, a bit-stream source address, a 24 digit number, a key generation algorithm and a revocation code. Once the interpreter has been created then it must be distributed among authorized nodes through a secure channel. When the interpreter is installed on nodes then the first 512 bits of the defined file from the given address will be downloaded. Since keys are time-dependent and key generation components which are bit-stream source, defined time zone and calendar, 24 digits and key generation algorithm are the same among all computers and they will be able to generate identical time-dependent keys in future without any coordination or key distribution. Also because keys have a predefined lifetime then without a key revocation call they will expire.

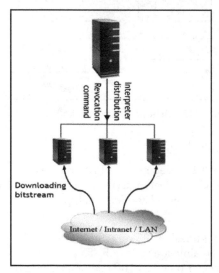

Fig. 4. Interpretative key management (IKM) workflow

One of the main key management issues is the existence of key storage, but in IKM because keys will be generated when they are needed and keys are constantly changing then no key storage is required. IKM keys expire automatically after the lifetime expires and a new one will replace automatically. But once the server issues a revocation call this means that the interpreter is expired and generated keys will no longer be valid. The following sections explain the detailed responsibilities of IKM components.

3.1 Server

The server role starts with generating the interpreter. To generate it a time zone, a calendar, a bit-stream source, a revocation code, a key generation algorithm and 24 digits must be selected and embedded into it. Once it has been generated then through an established secure channel, like Diffie-Hellman, it must be distributed among authorized parties.

Every generated key will be expired when its lifetime expires, but the interpreter will continue working until it receives a revocation call which means one of the interpreters is either compromised or is suspected to be compromised. In such a case all nodes will stop using the current interpreter and will wait until they receive a new version.

Once the interpreter has been generated and distributed then the server will supervise the security status of nodes. Because the interpreter is in charge of encryption and decryption, and keys are time-dependent then it can distinguish genuine packets from attack packets and report the number and type of attacks to the server. The server, based on received security reports, will decide whether the node can continue working, temporarily must stop working or must shut down completely.

3.2 Interpreter

The interpreter's task is to generate fresh synchronized keys and to send security status reports to the server. The interpreter's components and important points are as follows.

3.2.1 Bit-stream source

The bit-stream source is the address of a file on the network, the first 512 bits of which will be downloaded to construct a bit matrix to be fed into the key generation algorithm. The first 512 bits of the file, regardless of file type, will be downloaded and arranged into a 22*23 matrix. One of the most important criteria for choosing a bit-stream source is its updating intervals which, if not long enough, will result in inconsistency of keys among different interpreters because they may download different bit-streams at different times and eventually generate different keys. If the IKM being deployed is on a WAN then a shared file via FTP service can be utilized as a bit-stream source.

The bit-stream source can either be placed on the network or can be a file with its update intervals known by the administrator of the established encrypted sessions. For instance, if the administrator decides to use the available sources then an online PDF version of a newspaper which updates at particular times would be the proper choice. In this case the chosen source will be changed every day at a particular time and all nodes must update their bit-stream every time it changes. But if the updating interval of the chosen source is longer than our needed time or the source is located on the server, then renewing the bit-stream is not necessary.

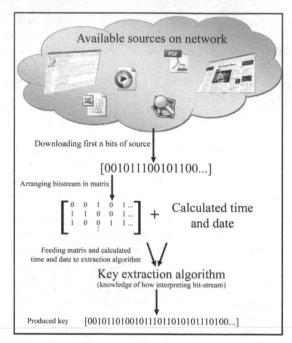

Fig. 5. IKM key generation process

3.2.2 Time, date and 24 digits

Date and time are two parameters used in the process of synchronized key generation, but because nodes might be distributed around the world then they will use different regions' time and calendar. So to unify the time and date of all nodes they must agree to the same time zone and calendar. For instance, the UTC time and Gregorian calendar can be chosen so that computers have the same parameters. Then each computer will compute the difference of time and date to be used at the key generation process.

Time and date unification is a very important process because firstly using time and date will lead to having time-dependent keys that can resist against attacks like replay attack. Secondly if there are any problems for a node in synchronizing itself then it will not be able to communicate with other nodes. The IKM server, designated web site or any publicly available time server can be utilized for synchronizing nodes.

From the viewpoint of attackers, guessing date and time is a very easy step to achieving two important key generation factors. Therefore, for tightening IKM key generation security, full format time and date will be repeated twice to achieve 24 digits. Then the 24 embedded digits will be added to the time and date 24 digits to make it unbreakable for attackers. For example, if the current date and time is 27/7/2010, 5:44 then its twice repeated full format will be 270720100544270720100544. Then the 24 randomly generated and embedded digits will produce 24 new digits that are not guessable by attackers and will change every minute. Fig. 6 illustrates process of converting date, time and 24 digits into new 24 digits.

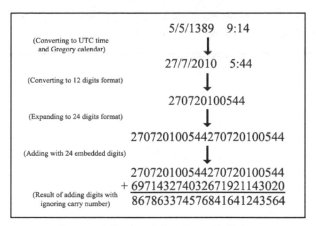

Fig. 6. Conversion process of current time and date into 24 digits

3.2.3 Revocation code

The revocation code is an embedded secret code in the interpreter that once received from the server means that the current version of the interpreter either is compromised or, according to the decision of the IKM server administrator for security reasons, is no longer valid and must stop working. All nodes will send their security reports to the IKM server for monitoring purposes and regarding received reports it can decide whether the current version is compromised, is suspected of being compromised or can continue working. Also for enhancing security it is better to renew interpreter periodically.

3.2.4 IKM key lifetime

Regarding the IKM structure and level of desired secrecy, three types of key lifetime are introduced in IKM. Because of utilizing time and date in key generation process, period of updating keys can be every minute, hour, or day.

A new key will be produced and employed every minute, hour or day. If a new key every minute is chosen then a new key will be generated and employed every minute. If the hourly key is selected then a specific minute of every hour will be considered as the parameter of key generation regardless of whether the nodes are going to join before or after it. For a daily key, a specific hour and minute will be considered as the time parameter of the key generation process.

Early seconds of changing key, both new and previous keys will be valid for decryption. Those packets which are encrypted and sent at the last moments of the changing minute will most likely be received in the early seconds of the following minute. Therefore, those packets are encrypted with the last key and cannot be decrypted with the new key. The maximum time needed for sending a packet between two distant nodes will be the time of double key checking. Once a packet is received in the first seconds of the changing key firstly an attempt will be made at being decrypted with the new key, but if this process fails then it will be decrypted with the last key. If neither new key nor the last key could decrypt it then this packet runs the likelihood of being a running replay attack against the node and if it is repeated many times then it will be reported as an attack to the IKM server. Fig. 7 shows the process of decryption of received packets.

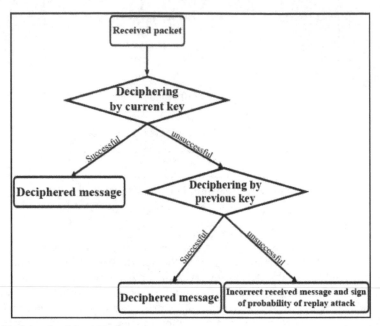

Fig. 7. Double key checking diagram

3.2.5 Key generation algorithm

IKM utilizes many key generation schemes and one of them is the matrix technique. The matrix technique is downloading a bit-stream, arranging it in a matrix and surveying the matrix according to 24 generated digits. The 24 digits explain how the matrix must be surveyed from the start point of (0,0). If the digit is even then it means that the matrix must be surveyed vertically and for odd numbers surveyed horizontally. This process will continue until the desired key length is being produced. For odd numbers if while key generation algorithm is picking up bits from the matrix reaches to the end of row, then the algorithm will pick up bits from beginning of next row. For even numbers if it reaches to end of column then will continue form beginning of next column. In the case of finishing 24 digits before producing the desired key length then the 24 digits will be used again and if it obtains the desired length before finishing the numbers then the remaining digits will be ignored. Fig. 8 illustrates the survey of a matrix with the first 12 digits if the digits are 493148769486.

In addition to different key generation intervals, the interpreter can produce keys of different lengths. A combination of different key lengths and three key lifetime types produces a variety of key types which vary from long minute keys to short daily keys that are convenient for different purposes. The strongest type is the long minute key which can guaranty security of top secret data encryption and the weakest type is the short daily key which is suitable for providing the lowest level of security.

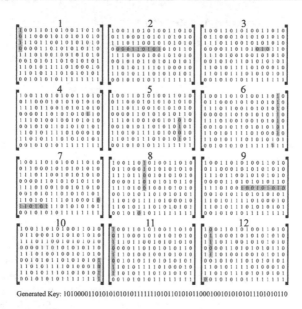

Generated Key: 101000011010101010101011111110101101010110001001010101011101010110

Fig. 8. Matrix technique bit-extraction illustration

3.2.6 Nodes' joining and disjoining process

For a new node joining it must send its request to the IKM server and if it passes the authentication process then it will be eligible to download the interpreter to start communicating securely with other parties. Those nodes which have already downloaded the interpreter, but for a while were inactive, must send a test packet to a neighbour node. If the test packet replied then it shows the current interpreter is still valid, but if no response is received then the process of downloading a new version is the same as joining a new node.

If a node is going to leave sessions permanently then the installed interpreter must be removed to reduce the likelihood of compromising the interpreter. If the disjoined node is trustworthy and the interpreter is removed successfully then other nodes can continue utilizing the current version, or else revoking the current version and installing the new version is a compulsory process. To renew the interpreter version, only replacing the old 24 digits with new 24 digits is enough. For example, if three counterpart companies are going to establish secure sessions then they can utilize IKM for providing security. Therefore, all computers must install the same interpreter to enable them to communicate securely. While they are working together, nodes can join and disjoin sessions, but if one of companies decides to disjoin permanently then the current interpreter must be revoked and a new version must be distributed among authorized parties.

4. Security and performance comparison between IKM and master-key

To compare two methods, their features and capabilities must be compared to help readers choose more convenient choice regarding their requirements. To do so, in this section we compare IKM and Master-Key methods in term of security and performance.

4.1 Security comparison between master-key and IKM

To compare security between master-key and IKM, five important features are analyzed and compared.

4.1.1 Key storage

One issue in key management is storing keys for future use which means encrypting the key and restoring it after going through a password check. This process increases the probability of compromising keys, but IKM only produces the key when needed and never saves it as the keys are changing continuously. Even at double valid key time after a few seconds the interpreter eliminates the old key from the memory.

4.1.2 Replacing multiple key distribution with one time interpreter distribution

Some attacks like man in the middle attack, known plain text attack, replay attack and brute force attack endanger the safety of the key distribution process (Techateerawat & Jennings, 2007). By increasing key distribution times, the likelihood of attacks happening will also increase. IKM only needs interpreter distribution to be done once and afterwards will deploy unlimited fresh keys without any necessity for key distribution. In current practices to have unique key per session for n sessions, n times key distribution is needed which n times increases the likelihood of compromising. But for IKM this process will only be run once and there is less likelihood of compromising. By reducing n times to once, compromising likelihood reduces to $1/n$ as well. Since IKM only once goes through key distribution process and establishes more complicated secure channels then it can provide higher level of security.

4.1.3 Utilizing unique or multiple key per session

Ideally in cryptography every transaction must be encrypted with a unique key, but in light of cost and difficulties in implementation it is not practiced widely yet. IKM nodes produce keys instead of receiving them and generating key makes less traffic than distributing it over the network. Since generating keys does not impose traffic on the network and has less cost, therefore node-side key production is cheaper and easier, and converts the ideal of cryptography into reality. For example, if every ATM user took 90 seconds to do a transaction and the ATM uses a per minute IKM key, then every ATM transaction would be encrypted with a unique key meaning the ideal encryption becomes reality.

4.1.4 Attack resistance capability

During the running time the interpreter records the amount and type of incorrect packets received and sends this to the IKM server. Depending on the received statistics the IKM server will decide whether that specific interpreter must continue working, stop temporarily or stop working completely. Also regarding received statistics the IKM server will decide whether is better to renew the current interpreter or whether it is still safe to produce a key.

The IKM structure enables resistance to some attacks that endanger the safety of key production and distribution, and reacts intelligently against attacks while there is no same feature in master-key.

4.1.5 No key revocation

Since IKM keys have a predefined validity term, they will expire automatically and there is no need for a revocation call unless for revoking the interpreter. But each key of the master-key technique must be expired by issuing a revocation call from the server. Therefore, no necessity for a key revocation is counted as an advantage of IKM versus master-key.

4.2 Performance comparison between IKM and master-key

To compare performance between IKM and master-key, imposed traffic load on network for specific duration and imposed traffic load on network per generated key are calculated and compared.

4.2.1 Key management imposed traffic load

To make an analogy about imposed key management traffic between IKM and master-key we can assume each key will last for one day and bit-stream reloading happens once a week. The contents of table 1 represent load of activities in the real world and the following formulas are used to calculate table 2 and table 3, and Fig. 9 values are used to make an analogy between these two methods. Table 3 and table 4 show differences of running master-key and IKM for minutely, hourly and daily keys.

$$\text{Master-key load for } n_w = (k_{dl} + k_{rl}) * 7 * n_w \qquad (1)$$

$$\text{IKM load for } n_w = (i_{dl} + i_{rl}) + (n_w * b_{dl}) \qquad (2)$$

Item explanation	Metric	Symbol
Key distribution load (master-key)	1KB	k_{dl}
Key revocation load (master-key)	0.5KB	k_{rl}
Interpreter distribution load (IKM)	50KB	i_{dl}
Interpreter revocation load (IKM)	0.5KB	i_{rl}
Bit-stream downloading load	0.5KB	b_{dl}
Number of weeks	-	n_w

Table 1. Traffic load and symbol of activities

Number of weeks	Master-key	IKM
1	10.5	51
4	42	52.5
13	136.5	57
26	273	63.5
52	546	76.5

Table 2. Daily key imposed load on server and network per node

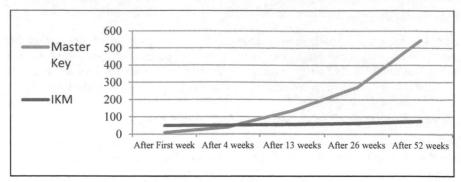

Fig. 9. Analogy of IKM and master-key traffic load on key management server for daily key

As is visible in the results of table 3 and table 4 after one year IKM's imposed traffic for the daily key is $\frac{1}{7}$, for the hourly key is $\frac{1}{171}$, and for the minutely key is $\frac{1}{10345}$ of master-key imposed traffic.

Key per session	
No. of keys	Load per key
364	1.5KB

Table 3. Number and imposed traffic load of key per session after 52 weeks

IKM					
Minutely key		Hourly key		Daily key	
No. of keys	Load per key	No. of keys	Load per key	No. of keys	Load per key
524160	0.000145KB	8736	0.00875 KB	364	0.208 KB

Table 4. Number and imposed traffic load of IKM keys after 52 weeks for minutely, hourly and daily keys

Feature	IKM	Master-key
Replay attack resistance	√	
Man in the middle resistance		√
Brute force attack resistance	√	
Less key management traffic	√	
Intelligent reaction against attackers	√	
Easy key distribution	√	
Easy key revocation	√	
Dynamism	√	
Less traffic per key	√	

Table 5. IKM and master-key features comparison

4.2.2 Analysis of comparison results

Figure 9 is drawn based on table 1 and table 2 values. It shows that employing IKM would be more beneficial if the number of needed fresh keys is over 34. When the number of fresh keys for sessions is less than 34, utilizing master-key is easier and more cost effective, but when it exceeds this threshold then IKM would be more secure and economic. As the number of needed keys increases, IKM imposes less traffic and even after one year for IKM's minutely key it would be less than one bit per generated key.

The second important point is the level of desired security. IKM reacts more intelligently than master-key against attacks. Because of IKM's structure, running brute force and replay attacks against IKM is impossible, but for man in the middle master-key is safer.

Altogether, if terms of running encrypted sessions longer than 34 keys (34 days for daily key, 34 hours for hourly key or 34 minutes for minutely key) and if a safer technique is needed then IKM is the more convenient choice, but for short-term sessions the master-key is more reasonable.

5. Conclusion

Cryptography is the technique of making information unintelligible for unauthorized parties. To do so many techniques have been developed which guaranty secrecy of encrypted information. Master-key is one internationally approved technique that can generate cryptographic keys using some environmental parameters like parties' information. Interpretative key management (IKM) framework is a newly devised method that has many similarities with master-key such as the power of key generation and using environmental parameters in key generation.

Since both techniques have some features in common, this article gives a comparative analysis to help researchers or developers who are going to utilize one of them and gives a guide for choosing between these two regarding their requirements and criteria.

A comparison of the results shows that for short-term or temporary secured sessions utilizing master-key is easier and more cost effective. But in the long run, utilizing IKM is not only more beneficial but also, because of its intelligent attack resiliency features, is more secure. Regarding imposed traffic load on the network, threshold of moving from master key to IKM is using 34 keys which depend on chosen IKM key generation method would vary from 34 minutes to 34 days. From the point of view of equipment needed both schemes need to have a server. For master-key the server is responsible of generating and distributing fresh keys and with regard to providing a key per session it is almost steadily in the process of generating and distributing fresh keys. While for IKM the server generates and distributes the interpreter once and then afterwards only supervises the security status of nodes.

To sum up the main criteria for choosing either master-key or IKM is the period of running secured sessions and the necessity for intelligent security features.

6. References

Chen, L. 2009. *Recommendation for Key Derivation Using Pseudorandom Functions*, National Institute of Standards and Technology (NIST), Retrieved from http://csrc.nist.gov/publications/nistpubs/800-108/sp800-108.pdf

Fumy, W.z & Landrock, P. (1993). Principles of Key Management. *IEEE JOURNAL ON SELECTED AREAS IN COMMUNICATIONS*, Vol. 11, No. 5, pp. 785-793

Onmez, O. 2009. *Symmetric Key Management: Key Derivation and Key Wrap*, Ruhr-Universit"at Bochum, Retrieved from
http://www.emsec.rub.de/media/crypto/attachments/files/2011/03/soenmez.pdf

Piper, F. 2002 , Murphy, S. *Cryptography: A Very Short Introduction*, Oxford University Press

Chaeikar, S. S. 2010. Interpretative Key Management (IKM), A Novel Framework, Proceedings of 2010 Second International Conference on Computer Research and Development, Kuala Lumpur, Malaysia, 2010

Chaeikar, S. S. 2010. Node Based Interpretative Key Management Framework, Proceedings of The 2010 Congress in Computer science, Computer engineering, and Applied Computing (The 2010 International Conference on Security and Management SAM'10), WORLDCOMP'2010, Las Vegas, USA, July 2010

Techateerawat, P. 2007, Analyzing the Key Distribution from Security Attacks in Wireless Sensor. Proceedings of Springer Innovative Algorithms and Techniques in Automation 2007, pp 353-357

Permissions

The contributors of this book come from diverse backgrounds, making this book a truly international effort. This book will bring forth new frontiers with its revolutionizing research information and detailed analysis of the nascent developments around the world.

We would like to thank Jaydip Sen, for lending his expertise to make the book truly unique. He has played a crucial role in the development of this book. Without his invaluable contribution this book wouldn't have been possible. He has made vital efforts to compile up to date information on the varied aspects of this subject to make this book a valuable addition to the collection of many professionals and students.

This book was conceptualized with the vision of imparting up-to-date information and advanced data in this field. To ensure the same, a matchless editorial board was set up. Every individual on the board went through rigorous rounds of assessment to prove their worth. After which they invested a large part of their time researching and compiling the most relevant data for our readers. Conferences and sessions were held from time to time between the editorial board and the contributing authors to present the data in the most comprehensible form. The editorial team has worked tirelessly to provide valuable and valid information to help people across the globe.

Every chapter published in this book has been scrutinized by our experts. Their significance has been extensively debated. The topics covered herein carry significant findings which will fuel the growth of the discipline. They may even be implemented as practical applications or may be referred to as a beginning point for another development. Chapters in this book were first published by InTech; hereby published with permission under the Creative Commons Attribution License or equivalent.

The editorial board has been involved in producing this book since its inception. They have spent rigorous hours researching and exploring the diverse topics which have resulted in the successful publishing of this book. They have passed on their knowledge of decades through this book. To expedite this challenging task, the publisher supported the team at every step. A small team of assistant editors was also appointed to further simplify the editing procedure and attain best results for the readers.

Our editorial team has been hand-picked from every corner of the world. Their multi-ethnicity adds dynamic inputs to the discussions which result in innovative outcomes. These outcomes are then further discussed with the researchers and contributors who give their valuable feedback and opinion regarding the same. The feedback is then collaborated with the researches and they are edited in a comprehensive manner to aid the understanding of the subject.

Apart from the editorial board, the designing team has also invested a significant amount of their time in understanding the subject and creating the most relevant covers. They scrutinized every image to scout for the most suitable representation of the subject and create an appropriate cover for the book.

The publishing team has been involved in this book since its early stages. They were actively engaged in every process, be it collecting the data, connecting with the contributors or procuring relevant information. The team has been an ardent support to the editorial, designing and production team. Their endless efforts to recruit the best for this project, has resulted in the accomplishment of this book. They are a veteran in the field of academics and their pool of knowledge is as vast as their experience in printing. Their expertise and guidance has proved useful at every step. Their uncompromising quality standards have made this book an exceptional effort. Their encouragement from time to time has been an inspiration for everyone.

The publisher and the editorial board hope that this book will prove to be a valuable piece of knowledge for researchers, students, practitioners and scholars across the globe.

List of Contributors

Sergey I. Nikolenko
Steklov Mathematical Institute, St. Petersburg, Russia

José Antonio Álvarez-Cubero and Pedro J. Zufiria
Universidad Politécnica de Madrid (UPM), Spain

Jose Torres-Jimenez and Loreto Gonzalez-Hernandez
CINVESTAV-Tamaulipas, Information Technology Laboratory, Mexico

Himer Avila-George
Instituto de Instrumentación para Imagen Molecular (I3M), Centro mixto CSIC - Universitat
Politécnica de Valéncia - CIEMAT, Valencia, Spain

Nelson Rangel-Valdez
Universidad Politécnica de Victoria, México

Eric Filiol
Laboratoire de Cryptologie et De Virologie Opérationnelles ESIEA, France

Hailiza Kamarulhaili and Liew Khang Jie
School of Mathematical Sciences, Universiti Sains Malaysia, Minden, Penang Malaysia

Abdulah Abdulah Zadeh
Memorial University of Newfoundland, Canada

Ryuta Nara, Masao Yanagisawa and Nozomu Togawa
Waseda University, Japan

Hilal M. Yousif Al-Bayatti
Applied Science University, Kingdom of Bahrain, Iraq

Abdul Monem S. Rahma and Hala Bhjat Abdul Wahab
Computer Science Depart, University of Technology, Baghdad, Iraq

Jaydip Sen
Innovation Lab, Tata Consultancy Services Ltd., India

Cristina-Elena Vintilă
Military Technical Academy, Bucharest, Romania

Saman Shojae Chaeikar, Azizah Bt Abdul Manaf and Mazdak Zamani
Universiti Teknologi Malaysia, Malaysia

Printed in the USA
CPSIA information can be obtained
at www.ICGtesting.com
JSHW011432221024
72173JS00004B/778